Contending Persp
Global Governanc

The end of the Cold War and the birth of the twenty-first century, with their attendant changes in world politics, have spurred intense interest in "new" approaches to understanding world politics. Concurrent and related to this interest, the term "global governance" has experienced growing usage. For many scholars and policymakers, global governance seems to capture important, if ambiguous, changes in world politics. This volume represents an important step towards clarifying the concept of global governance, and the ideas and dynamics associated with its emergence.

Contending Perspectives on Global Governance is an exploration of global governance from multiple perspectives. This volume provides:

- conceptual tools and a common vocabulary for navigating the maze that is the global-governance literature;
- chapters that individually provide fascinating theoretical and empirical examinations of global governance;
- insight on key points of debate and agreement between contending perspectives about the structure and process of global governance, and the nature of change in world politics;
- a window into how traditional international relations theory is responding to the "new" dynamic of global governance as well as how the phenomenon of global governance is inspiring theoretical innovations in international relation theory.

This book is essential reading for professionals, academics and students with interests in global governance and international politics.

Alice D. Ba and **Matthew J. Hoffmann** are Assistant Professors in the Department of Political Science and International Relations at the University of Delaware. Alice Ba's areas of research and publication include regionalism in East and Southeast Asia, China–Southeast Asia relations, international organizations and social constructivism. Matthew Hoffmann specializes in global environmental politics, social constructivism, and complexity theory. He is author of a volume on global environmental governance: *Ozone Depletion and Climate Change: Constructing a Global Response* (2005).

Contending Perspectives on Global Governance

Coherence, contestation and world order

Edited by Alice D. Ba and Matthew J. Hoffmann

Routledge
Taylor & Francis Group

LONDON AND NEW YORK

First published 2005
by Routledge
2 Park Square, Milton Park, Abingdon, Oxon OX14 4RN

Simultaneously published in the USA and Canada
by Routledge
270 Madison Ave, New York, NY 10016

Routledge is an imprint of the Taylor & Francis Group

© 2005 Alice D. Ba and Matthew J. Hoffmann

Typeset in Baskerville by
Taylor & Francis Books

Printed and bound in Great Britain by
MPG Books Ltd, Bodmin

British Library Cataloguing in Publication Data
A catalogue record for this book is available from the British Library

Library of Congress Cataloging in Publication Data
A catalog record for this book has been requested.

ISBN 0–415–35674–1 (hbk)
ISBN 0–415–35675–X (pbk)

Taylor & Francis Group is the Academic Division of T&F Informa plc.

Contents

Contributors

Giovanni Arrighi is Professor of Sociology at Johns Hopkins University. His main interests are in the fields of comparative and historical sociology, world-systems analysis and economic sociology. He has done research on the origins and transformations of the world capitalist system and on the stratification of the global economy. He is author of *The Long Twentieth Century: Money, Power, and the Origins of Our Time* (1994) and co-author of *Chaos and Governance in the Modern World System* (1999).

Alice D. Ba is Assistant Professor in the Department of Political Science and International Relations at the University of Delaware. Her areas of research and publication include regionalism in East and Southeast Asia, China–Southeast Asia relations, international organizations, and social constructivism.

Cornel Ban is a Ph.D. student in the Department of Political Science at the University of Maryland.

Tim Dunne is Reader in International Relations and Head of the Department of Politics, University of Exeter, UK. He is author and editor of seven books, including *Human Rights in Global Politics* (with Nicholas J. Wheeler, 1998) and *Worlds in Collision: Terror and the Future of Global Order* (with Ken Booth, 2002).

Leslie Friedman Goldstein is the Judge Hugh M. Morris Professor of Political Science and International Relations, University of Delaware, and has written on public law, gender and law, and political theory. Recent work includes *Constituting Federal Sovereignty: the European Union in Comparative Context* (2001).

Daniel Green is Associate Professor in the Department of Political Science and International Relations at the University of Delaware. His research interests are in global governance, global-order-building episodes, and constructivist methods of analysis. He recently edited *Constructivism and Comparative Politics* (2002).

Matthew J. Hoffmann is Assistant Professor in the Department of Political Science and International Relations at the University of Delaware. He is author of a volume on global environmental governance: *Ozone Depletion and Climate Change: Constructing a Global Response* (2005).

Robert O'Brien is LIUNA/Mancinelli Professor of Global Labour Issues and Associate Director of the Institute on Globalization and the Human Condition at McMaster University in Canada. His most recent book is an introductory IPE text with Marc Williams titled *Global Political Economy: Evolution and Dynamics* (2004).

Henk Overbeek is Professor of International Relations in the Department of Political Science of the Vrije Universiteit Amsterdam. His research interests are in international political economy. He is the author of *Global Capitalism and National Decline* (1990) and the editor of *Restructuring Hegemony in the Global Political Economy* (1993). His most recent book is *The Political Economy of European Employment: European Integration and the Transnationalization of the (Un)Employment Question* (editor, 2003).

James N. Rosenau is University Professor of International Affairs at the George Washington University. A Guggenheim Fellow and former President of the International Studies Association, his most recent books include *Distant Proximities* (2003), *Along the Domestic–Foreign Frontier* (1997), and *Turbulence in World Politics* (1990).

Timothy J. Sinclair is a political scientist at the University of Warwick in England. A former New Zealand Treasury official, Dr Sinclair spent 2001/2002 as a visiting scholar at Harvard University. His book *The New Masters of Capital: American Bond Rating Agencies and the Politics of Creditworthiness* was published in 2005.

Jennifer Sterling-Folker is an Associate Professor of Political Science at the University of Connecticut. She is the author of *Theories of International Cooperation and the Primacy of Anarchy: Explaining U.S. International Monetary Policy-making After Bretton Woods* (2002) and editor of *Making Sense of International Relations Theory* (2005).

Oran R. Young is a Professor in the Donald Bren School of Environmental Science and Management, University of California, Santa Barbara. He is the author and editor of several books, including *International Governance: Protecting the Environment in a Stateless Society* (1994), *Global Governance: Drawing Insight from the Environmental Experience* (1997), and *Governance in World Affairs* (1999).

Preface and acknowledgements

The project that produced this volume began as part of a series of discussions aimed at implementing a new graduate program in Global Governance at the University of Delaware in the spring and summer of 2001. The discussions grew into an International Studies Association workshop grant application and a speaker series the following year. The project culminated in a workshop at the University of Delaware in October of 2002 and a follow-up meeting at the annual meeting of the ISA in spring 2003. Throughout this period, the goal has remained the same—to elucidate the concept of global governance (GG). The goal is lofty, and any attempt to arrive at a definitive understanding of GG may be a chimera. Indeed, GG entails multiple perspectives on world politics and social life in an era of globalization. Thus rather than offer a false synthesis, we have aimed to highlight areas of agreement and contestation between diverse and distinct perspectives. Taken as a whole, this volume moves the GG debate forward and offers a common vocabulary to describe changes in our world, our politics, and our thinking.

Numerous people have contributed in myriad ways to bringing this project to fruition. We would like to acknowledge the International Studies Association Workshop Grant program for the initial funding to bring together our contributors for lively discussion and debate. The Department of Political Science and International Relations and the College of Arts and Sciences at the University of Delaware also provided significant resources without which this volume would not have been possible. In addition to financial resources we drew upon the intellectual and organizational skills of many people at the University of Delaware. We would like especially to thank: Joseph Pika, Cindy Waksmonski, Julie Demgen, Jarret Brachman, and Pooja Rishi. For their contributions as discussants and commentators at the Delaware Workshop we would like to extend our appreciation to James K. Oliver, Robert Denemark, Rick Sylves, Kenneth Campbell, William Meyer, Craig Murphy, and Rorden Wilkinson. Our contributors were models of patience and professionalism in their preparation for the workshops and this volume—making our jobs as editors a pleasure. We would also like to thank the anonymous reviewer from Routledge for insightful commentary. Finally, we extend our appreciation to Craig Fowlie and Laura Sacha, who have been most supportive in moving this project forward.

Alice D. Ba and Matthew J. Hoffmann

1 Introduction

Coherence and contestation

Matthew J. Hoffmann and Alice D. Ba

Introduction

The end of the Cold War and the birth of the twenty-first century, with their attendant changes in world politics, have spurred intense interest in "new" approaches to understanding world politics. Concurrent and related to this interest, the term "global governance" (GG) has experienced growing usage. For many scholars and policymakers, GG seems to capture important (if ambiguous) aspects of world politics. It is a way to signal something new empirically and analytically, as much as a response to what many see to be the limitations of more traditional approaches to world politics. Reminiscent of globalization before it, GG appears poised to become the next concept to envelop the discipline of international relations.

As with globalization, however, GG can also be an entirely frustrating term and area of inquiry. Though it seems increasingly ubiquitous, GG also remains an indefinite term (analytically or in policy terms). Thus, the danger is that it will become a trendy catchall phrase, rendered useless by multiple, overlapping or mutually exclusive applications. If GG is not to be a "full of sound and fury signifying nothing" term, we need to be more specific about what the term means and what has actually changed (and not changed). Absent more focused reflection, it seems very possible that GG will remain, in the words of Craig Murphy (2000), "poorly done and poorly understood." This volume attempts to answer Murphy's challenge.

Leaving aside, for the moment, the normative question of whether GG is poorly done, one reason that GG is poorly understood is the cacophony of voices and perspectives that use the label "GG." The lack of solid consensus as to what GG is leads to the confusion that, in part, impedes our understanding of GG. Even a brief survey of the literature provides no fewer than nine separate uses of the label GG (with some obviously overlapping): 1. international regimes (Young 1997, 1999); 2. international society (Bull 1977); 3. hegemonic stability (Gilpin 1981); 4. dynamics of globalization (Mittleman 1997; Väyrynen 1999); 5. the pursuit of IMF/World Bank/UN goals (Commission on Global Governance 1995; Smouts 1998; O'Brien, Goetz, Scholte and Williams 2000); 6. global change/global order (Rosenau 1997; Rosenau and Czempiel 1992); 7. a restructuring of the global political economy (Hewson and Sinclair 1999; Cox 1987); 8. world government (Harris and Yunker 1999); and 9. global civil society (Lipshutz 1996; Wapner 1996).

Further adding to the confusion is a growing cottage industry dedicated to defining global governance or critiquing the entire global-governance enterprise.[1] These global-governance studies begin with a standard apology or criticism akin to these:

> The rubric of "global governance" is akin to "post-cold war," which signifies that one period has ended but that we do not as yet have an accurate shorthand to depict the essential dynamics of the new epoch.
>
> (Weiss 2000: 806)

> Far from becoming clearer with use, it [governance] currently serves as a catchall term sometimes associated with the notion of "regime," sometimes with the concept of "global order"...
>
> (Smouts 1998: 81)

This volume takes a different approach. In our view, a diversity of voices need not equal chaos. What is necessary is not an artificial consensus on the definition and nature of GG. As astute readers will no doubt notice, we neglect to define GG in this introductory chapter. Beyond the broad notion that GG is some sort of order (rules, patterns, institutions, norms, etc.) in anarchic spaces, we leave the defining to the individual perspectives represented in the following chapters.[2] Instead, this volume is designed to be an exploration of GG from multiple perspectives. We hope that careful delineation of the cacophony of voices and deliberation among them will facilitate greater understanding of GG—or at least clarity on the multiple expressions of GG. Such an endeavor is designed to accomplish three broad goals. First, we provide conceptual tools for navigating the maze that is the GG literature in order to bring a sense of order and to facilitate comparisons across perspectives. Second, the chapters individually provide fascinating theoretical and empirical examinations of GG, taking stock of the state of the art across international-relations theory. Finally, taken as a whole, the volume provides insight into both how traditional international-relations theory has responded to the "new" dynamics of GG as well as how the phenomenon of GG has inspired theoretical innovations in international-relations theory.

In this introductory chapter we first briefly explore the concept of GG, categorizing the multiple instantiations in the literature. We then turn to the specifics of this volume, discussing the coherence and contestation to be found in multiple perspectives on GG and introducing the contributors and chapters. Finally we discuss the organizing principle of the volume.

Global governance: the old and the new

Depending on one's perspective, GG has arguably always been the focus of study for the international relations discipline. Whether or not scholars explicitly discuss *global* governance, *governance* has always been at the center of the study of world politics—"Governance is now fashionable, but the concept is as old as human history" (Weiss 2000: 795). All of the studies of cooperation under anarchy, all of the various (neo)realist treatises on balance of power, all of the analyses of regimes, and all of the English School's work with international society are at heart concerned with discerning the order that actors in world politics create and follow in an anarchical world.

Thus the broadest category of studies that are or could be labeled global governance is merely traditional international-relations theory and in this sense GG is nothing new. Traditional perspectives focus on trends, events, processes, or outcomes evident in world politics; defining and/or identifying instances of governance (or regimes, order, institutions, cooperation) and explaining when and why governance is achieved or not. In this sense we could be discussing contending perspectives on world politics as much as contending perspectives on GG.

Of course, the label GG does not sit comfortably with many international-relations theorists—precisely, as we argue below, because GG has come to mean something new and different. Robert Gilpin claims that global or international governance, "as many scholars employ the term...in contemporary discourse," is antithetical to at least one traditional perspective—political realism (Gilpin 2002: 237). However, even Gilpin dedicates significant effort exploring international governance in his classic *War and Change* (1981). He identifies governance as control over the international system or influence over state interactions and he explains how it is achieved—through the actions of a hegemon (Gilpin 1981: 28–35). The critique of widespread usage and growth of the GG label extends beyond theorists of mainstream international relations. Other approaches also balk at the notion that traditional, state-centric approaches to world politics are truly discussing GG.[3] Hewson and Sinclair articulate this view when they argue that "The pattern of global governance [during the Cold War] appeared to be essentially unchanging, and its organization around the territorial principle could therefore be safely left out of the study of world politics" (1999: 3–4).

Thus, while governance is and always has been at the heart of the study of international relations, GG is not merely a new moniker for the discipline. There are significant literatures (both traditional and more recent) that consider GG to be something qualitatively different. By this view, the label GG now signals a new state of affairs in world politics (a new set of phenomena to be studied) and/or a new way to approach world politics (a new analytic framework). It is possible to discern at least three ways that GG is conceived of—three categories of GG studies or worldviews currently in the literature and in academia.

Global governance as phenomenon: managing global problems

A significant portion of the GG literature conceives of GG as being the self-conscious activities of specific organizations/institutions. GG is new because of the "global" modifier for governance. This vision looks upon world politics and perceives a series of new or expanded issues (environmental destruction, refugees, poverty, AIDS, economic development, furthering of the global capitalist system, etc.) that need to be dealt with or managed on a more global scale, and global governance is the set of tools or activities that exist or need to be designed. In other words: "*Global governance* refers to collective actions to establish international institutions and norms to cope with the causes and consequences of adverse supranational, transnational, or national problems" (Väyrynen 1999: 25).

Not all observers who conceive of GG as a conscious activity agree as to what kind of activity it entails. At least three categories are apparent even within this literature. First global governance can be seen as the activities of international organizations like the UN and/or international financial institutions (Commission on Global Governance 1995; O'Brien *et al.* 2000). Second, there is a take on global governance that is looking forward to global *government* (Harris and Yunker 1999). Third, there is a strain of thinking that is explicitly concerned with institutional design for managing globalization (Keohane 2001).

Global governance as project: the growth of (liberal) world order

Some observers see the management of specific global problems in a larger context of world order (Boli and Thomas 1999). GG becomes the emergence and spread of a liberal order or society—with its concurrent rules and norms. Some scholars welcome this development—Cosmopolitans and World Polity school. This view became particularly prominent during the "new world order" years immediately following the end of the Cold War. Others see a less than benign world order (Murphy 2000). Indeed, there is a large and growing tradition that takes a critical stance on the global-governance project. These studies are concerned that the global-governance activities of global institutions are potentially (or actually) oppressive and act to continue an oppressive political/economic world order (Mittleman 1997; Alcantara 1998; Senarclens 1998; Smouts 1998; Murphy 2000; Wilkinson and Hughes 2002). Murphy identifies an example of this line of thought as a class-based approach to global governance and notes that: "Global governance is more a site, one of many sites, in which struggles over wealth, power, and knowledge are taking place…contemporary global governance remains a predictable institutional response…to the overall logic of industrial capitalism" (2000: 799).

Global governance as worldview: new analytic approach

A third umbrella approach to GG sees global governance as the focal point for transforming our understanding of world politics and the international-relations discipline altogether. As such, global governance is a useful analytic and conceptual tool, a way to indicate that the world has changed and continues to change. These studies, centers, and journals look upon world politics today as fundamentally different from the past (usually since the end of the Cold War)—less state-centric, more dynamic and they use the label "GG" to signify this new thinking. As Smouts argues: "First and foremost, governance places emphasis on the multiplicity and diversity of the actors. It makes it possible to consider management of international affairs" not as an interstate activity, but as a negotiation/interaction process among heterogeneous participants (1998: 84). This trend toward transformation is seen in the new global governance literature. Hewson and Sinclair challenge us to look upon global governance as a "perspective on global life, a vantage point designed to foster a regard for the immense complexity and diversity of global life" (1999: 7). Weiss concurs and argues that we should use global governance "as a heuristic device to capture and describe the confusing and seemingly ever-accelerating transformation of the international system" (2000: 808).

Some transformation is also evident in the structure of academia itself with the establishment of global governance centers, programs, journals, and conferences.[4] The London School of Economics has established a global-governance center that focusses on "globalisation from below" and global civil society.[5] Victoria University in Canada focusses on global governance at their Global Studies Center,[6] while in Germany the University of Bremen, in conjunction with International University Bremen, offers a master's degree in global governance and social theory.[7] The University of Connecticut offers a graduate certificate in Global Governance Studies. Rutgers University has recently established a Center for Global Change and Governance.[8] Similarly, at the University of Delaware, the entire graduate program is now focused on global governance: "An approach to politics, law, and administration that transcends the nation-state and its formal institutions of government."[9] Included in this trend and as further illustration of its growing significance are also the growing number of courses that revolve around, or at least must respond to, the concept or theme of global governance.

This last perspective, the self-labeled GG literature (Rosenau and Czempiel 1992; Hewson and Sinclair 1999; Held and McGrew 2002; Cooper *et al.* 2002; Wilkinson and Hughes 2002), is particularly important in that it makes a conscious effort to break with traditional approaches to world politics and it uses the GG label to signal this separation. GG studies and scholars in this vein use the global-governance label or concept to signal new thinking about global politics. They separate themselves from plain old international-relations theory in three ways. First, they have broadened the scope of analysis to include a variety of actors on the world stage as well as a variety of new issues. GG scholars examine the roles that nongovernmental organizations (NGOs), multinational corporations (MNCs), civil society, transnational organizations, ethnic groups, citizen groups, information technology, and more play in the construction and evolution of governance structures. In addition, these scholars have moved beyond "high" politics and focus on issues such as the environment, human rights, labor, and intellectual property, in addition to traditional security and political-economy issues.

Second, GG theorists tend to focus on rules and rule systems that constrain or influence the behavior of actors in world politics as opposed to a more traditional focus on power and uninhibited state interactions. Though the scholars lumped under the GG label often have vastly different viewpoints and concerns (even within perspectives, there are significant differences from scholar to scholar over what GG actually is and/or means), most are united in the idea that GG studies surround the exploration of rules. Finally, most GG scholars and studies are conceiving world politics to be more complex and dynamic than the static conceptions of traditional approaches. GG scholarship is drawn from work on globalization, global civil society, social movements, and other areas that flowered with the demise of the Cold War. These approaches see world politics in a very different light: they see change; they see evolution. GG studies thus tend to concentrate on the dynamics of world politics.

Where does GG go from here?

With all of these potential (and actual) uses of the label GG, it is easy to see why GG is such a frustrating concept. Adding to the frustration is how "debates" reduce various perspectives into extreme caricatures of themselves. Traditional/established international-relations theory, in its readiness to adopt a "politics as usual" view of world developments, has a tendency to dismiss global governance/challenger approaches as something akin to "peace studies"—naïve, misguided, or at least an example of wishful thinking. By the same token, perspectives attempting to break with traditional approaches to GG are too ready to reject the insights offered by traditional approaches as having little relevance for a changed world. All too often, what is clearly missing is meaningful debate. In the next section we lay out a means for approaching any GG study and for comparing GG studies drawn from contending perspectives.

Navigating the contending perspectives on GG

Categorizing the extant uses of the GG label is potentially useful, but does not go very far toward making GG well understood. In addition, it is clear that the categories are not mutually exclusive. Indeed, one source of confusion for students and scholars alike is the use of the term GG to reference all three of those potential categories—sometimes in the same work. The confusion in the literature stems from the overuse of the label GG without a concurrent understanding of diverse perspectives on GG. Too often current scholarship on GG tends either to assume a single perspective (i.e. GG is the work of multilateral organizations) or to claim a synthesis of a single definition of GG (a very specific worldview). Unfortunately such activities have the potential to downplay, ignore, or confuse the variety and diversity of approaches to, conceptions of, and definitions for GG.

In contrast, this volume looks for coherence by specifically delineating how varying theoretical perspectives approach the concept of GG. Instead of beginning with synthesis, our contributors begin with diversity, exploring the multiple, and often contradictory, ways that different theoretical perspectives conceive of GG in the interest of catalyzing debate and discussion amongst varying perspectives. This volume offers a guide to GG thinking across international relations and social science in general through the lens of multiple viewpoints and by identifying commonalities and differences in existing understandings of GG.

We began this project *tabula rasa* and invited scholars of different perspectives and theoretical worldviews to take part in a discussion on GG. Our authors represent both traditional international-relations theories as well as alternative theoretical approaches that have emerged (at least in part) in response to patterns and dynamics identified as GG:

Realism
Historical materialism
World system
English school
Regime theory
Social constructivism
Post-international theory
Public law
Private authority
Regionalism
Global civil society
Liberal imperialism

We asked each scholar to address a series of questions designed to elicit his or her understanding of global governance from a specific theoretical perspective.

1 Is there GG?
2 If yes, is it new, what is it, and how should we study it?
3 If no, why not? And will there ever be GG?
4 How much GG or order is extant in world politics?
5 Who makes the rules of GG and how are they made?
6 Is there a logical end or trend for governance processes?
7 Are there common themes across perspectives?
8 What can different perspectives learn from one another?
9 Is there enough common ground and analytic leverage to make governance a useful term?
10 What tools of its own can a GG perspective employ to contribute to political studies?

These questions provided points of departure for debate and the foundation for interesting and intense discussions at two workshop meetings at the University of Delaware in October 2002 and at the International Studies Association meeting in March 2003. Though the authors were all in agreement that GG does exist in some form, perhaps inevitably, and certainly most interestingly, we failed to reach consensus on the answers to the other questions. Instead what emerged through the discussions was both coherence and contestation. Rather than reaching consensus on what GG is or how it works or how important it is (or is not), our authors came to agreement as to the terms and scope of the debate. It is in this agreement that we find the possibility of comparison, focal points for understanding (and classifying) the different perspectives on GG, and, perhaps most important, a common vocabulary that allows for a real exchange on our world politics.

Structure and process

At the risk of oversimplification, we found that all definitions and indeed all potential definitions of GG contained understandings of both structure and process. Structure is the form of GG, that is, GG as noun—something to be achieved: control, government, management, solutions to a problem, or norms and social arrangements. Process is how GG (however conceived) proceeds or comes about, that is GG as verb. These broad concepts are the thread that runs through each of the chapters, providing a baseline for comparing contending perspectives. A baseline or common vocabulary is crucial because beyond agreement about the existence of world order, there remained significant contestation among our authors about its form and content. We disagreed not only about the structure of world order, but also its process(es).

On the structure of GG, discussions revealed a prominent fault line between those who saw world order as a *single, coherent system of rule*, and those who saw world order as composed of *multiple, disaggregated rule systems*. Even within each categorization there were still many areas of contestation between authors. In particular, there is contestation within categories over the form of world order. In other words, what does the single, coherent system of rule look like? What do the multiple, disaggregated rule systems look like? Different perspectives obviously have different answers to these questions. On the process of GG, our contributors did not fall nicely into two camps. In examining the unfolding of GG by perspective, we find incredible (and not unexpected) diversity. Processes of hegemony, rational calculation, social construction, liberal projects, contestation, and deliberation/negotiation are all seen as the dynamics through which GG unfolds.

The structure/process heuristic facilitates comparing and contrasting our contending perspectives by providing a single vocabulary. In this volume, Henk Overbeek, Giovanni Arrighi, Tim Dunne, Daniel Green, and Jennifer Sterling-Folker see the "stuff" of GG being a more overarching rule or set of ideas or structures that fundamentally shape political, social, and economic life throughout the global system. However, despite their common characterization of the structure of GG as a single, coherent system of rule, they nevertheless found much to debate about world order's form and driving processes.

For example, both Overbeek and Arrighi take a macrohistorical view of global governance and conceive the structure of GG in similar terms (as global capitalist system), but diverge in significant ways on the process of GG. With a historical-materialism approach, Overbeek lays bare the structures of domination that Marxists associate with GG. Arrighi, a sociologist representing the World System perspective, describes the cyclical rise and fall of hegemony as ever present and the processes of accumulation as historically transcendent, reaching well before world capitalism became the dominant mode of production.

Dunne's English School approach and Sterling-Folker's neoclassical-realist account provide different contrasts. Both stress the ways that powerful actors (states in the modern era) define the rules of world order. Both also emphasize important relational dynamics of global governance; however, where Dunne's conception of global governance places greatest stress on international society— the practices, rules, and institutions that constrain state action—as a function of common interests and minimum degree of interaction capacity, Sterling-Folker's very skeptical account of GG sees it as a function of human beings' biological imperative to be social.

Finally, Green's perspective of liberal imperialism in which GG is a liberal project carried out in recent years by an Anglo-American alliance shares with the authors above an interest in power and hegemony as part of the structure of global governance but combines it with an explicitly liberal argument about liberal order.

In contrast, this volume's remaining authors consider the structure of GG to consist of multiple rule systems. Compared with the first set of perspectives, their rule systems are more constrained and bound by a particular time, space, and set of actors. These authors do not ignore larger, global-order questions; rather they tend to see global or world order as more of a patchwork. For them, world order is characterized by a series of diverse rule systems—sometimes distinct, other times crosscutting and overlapping. In short, the key difference between the two groups is that the first tends to see GG in terms of an all-encompassing, over-arching, and more truly global configuration of arrangements, while the other views GG in terms of more varied, circumscribed, and limited rule systems that do not necessarily make up a coherent whole.

Like the first set of authors, however, these authors also found themselves divided on critical questions regarding what multiple-rule systems look like and how they come about. In his discussion of international regimes as a major precursor to the GG literature, Oran Young describes how GG can be conceived of as an amalgamation of specific, functional regimes. By contrast, Alice Ba's and Robert O'Brien's discussions on GG emphasize important processes of contestation as the driving processes of GG. Their chapters also stand out for seeing both coherence/singularity and disaggregation/multiplicity in the structure of GG, and for seeing the institutions of GG as co-evolving systems. At the same time, Ba and O'Brien also diverge in important ways. Ba's discussion of regionalism as varied in its relationship to GG gives greatest emphasis to inter-state relations, whereas O'Brien's discussion on global civil society and the emergence of private networks challenges the state-centrism that has become part of the structure of GG.

In a similar vein, Timothy Sinclair addresses private authority head on, describing the ways in which bond-rating agencies have come to significantly influence the GG of international political economy. Matthew Hoffmann's social-constructivist account of global governance and discussion on the evolution of participation norms in the global environmental treaty negotiation—that is, what is "global" about global environmental governance—also has much to say about the state-centric character of GG and our understandings of GG. Hoffmann characterizes social constructivism as agnostic on the structure of GG, but also highlights how social constructivism can explain the emergence and evolution of multiple normative systems that are the foundation of GG.

James N. Rosenau's post-international perspective on global governance is perhaps most representative of the growing attention to non-state actors and significant break from the state-centrism of many of the previous discussions. Rosenau's discussion on GG as characterized by both fragmenting and integrative processes—a "fragmegrative" world—and as a "crazy quilt" of multiple, overlapping spheres of authority seems to capture especially well the kind of mixed system of state and non-state actors we find in world politics today.

Finally, Leslie Goldstein and Cornel Ban continue the discussion of specific regions by highlighting the growth and influence of legal regimes in Europe as a form of GG. Similar to both Young and Ba, Goldstein and Ban examine the interaction of domestic factors and overarching principles in the development of the functional, legal regimes that are key components of GG.

In that each perspective contains an understanding of structure and process, it is possible to make more focussed comparisons and contrasts. Indeed, it became clear in some of our early discussions that structure and process can offer a ready heuristic device to facilitate communication and debate between and across perspectives. Organizing each chapter around the common thread of structure and process allows us to avoid imposing a false synthesis but at the same time bring these contending perspectives into a single conversation.

The challenge to international-relations theory

In addition to structure and process, the conversation(s) in this volume are also about international relations as a discipline—what we study and how we study it. The 12 perspectives above do not exhaust the realm of international-relations theory and, certainly, they are not fully representative of the many perspectives that exist in international relations. However, in their common effort to address the significance of GG and to identify both what is constant and what is not in world politics, these twelve discussions contribute to ongoing debates in international-relations theory more generally. In this sense, "global governance"—by offering new perspectives and challenging more established theories to respond to them—is pushing the bounds of established international-relations theories and at the same time catalyzing new directions and areas of theoretical inquiry. The volume as a whole thus provides a window onto the cutting edge of theoretical and empirical approaches to international relations.

If structure and process provide the running thread through this volume's various chapters, the tension between established and newer/alternative approaches to world politics provides the organization of this book. Specifically, the volume is organized into two parts. Part I is made up of chapters representing more established perspectives and theoretical approaches (Neoclassical)

Realism, Transhistorical Materialism, World System, English School, Regime Theory, Social Constructivism). Part II is made up of alternative approaches or emerging challengers to established approaches in terms of the key actors and processes of world order and world politics (Post-international Theory, Transnational Public Law, Private Authority, Regionalism, Global Civil Society, Liberal Empire).

Our decision to organize the volume in terms of established and alternative approaches allows us to highlight evolving debates and the particular challenge posed by "global governance" to our study of international relations. In addition, it was important to us that this volume considers not only the dynamism that exists in world politics but also the dynamism that exists in the study of world politics.

As in the debates on structure and process, we find that a similar combination of coherence and contestation characterizes debates between (and within) established and newer approaches to world politics. For this reason too, not all chapters were easily categorized, and our decisions to place certain chapters in one category or the other mostly serve to draw attention to certain arguments of authors. Authors in Part I, for example, are distinguished by their view that global governance does not warrant a fundamental change in thinking about the way world politics works. For these authors, there is a shared view of GG and its processes as being transhistorical.

With the exception of Hoffmann's chapter on social constructivism, authors in Part I also tend to share an emphasis on the material foundations of world order, including GG. Though many of these authors also see an important dynamism in GG's content (depending on functional imperatives or historical epoch, for example), they also tend to see the most fundamental processes of world politics as unchanging. Both Arrighi and Overbeek see deep historical patterns unfolding and now being called GG. Young sees important connections between state-centric functional regimes and the dynamics now discussed as GG. Dunne's English School approach recognizes international society in GG and Sterling-Folker sees GG as a surface manifestation of larger (genetic/biological) forces in combination with historical contingency. As for Hoffmann, the emphasis/primacy that social constructivism places on the ideational foundations of global governance contrasts with the mostly materialist accounts of other authors in Part I. And though there is a case to be made that social constructivism belongs best among Part II's "newer" approaches, we include his chapter in Part I because constructivism's development as an approach to world politics was not tied to the emergence of GG phenomena.

As for the authors in Part II, their approaches are distinguished by the fact that most, if not all, are in some way responding to the emergence of GG (however they define it). They can be considered "newer" in the sense that each, in its own way, draws attention to something novel or changing about GG and world politics. Some highlight new actors; others draw attention to different ways of thinking about change in world politics. Still others draw attention to the process of change itself. Some do all three. Rosenau presents the most sweeping critique and challenge to traditional approaches, claiming that the fragmegrative dynamics of GG are fundamentally altering world politics across the board. Sinclair and O'Brien challenge established theories to consider the role of societal actors and transnational networks and the ways that new actors may be destabilizing the state-based norms, values, and practices of world politics. In a similar but also different vein, Goldstein and Ban examine the emergence of the European Court of Human Rights, a unique actor that was created by states but is also state-transcendent. They also examine how law itself (who is a party to law, jurisdictions) is changing in response to GG.

Ba challenges the notion that regional governance and GG form a seamless web and instead posits that regional processes may in fact contest global processes. Part II concludes with the chapter by Daniel Green, who sees the content of GG as being steeped in a particular ideology—liberalism—that is now approaching the apogee of its influence as a result of the particularly activist and "agentic" efforts of the Anglo-American partnership.

Together these chapters and their diverse perspectives provide a fuller picture of GG. They are far from providing the definitive or complete answer on the question of GG, but the dialogue between them hopefully will generate new focal points for future discussions and debates. In the end, both coherence and contestation are necessary ingredients if there is to be a meaningful cross-perspective discussion on the nature of GG and if GG will ever be well understood or well done.

Notes

1 See the recent symposium in the *International Social Science Journal* (1998); Murphy (2000); and Weiss (2000).
2 Indeed, some of our authors would dispute even this baseline.
3 See, e.g., Lipshutz (1996); Wapner (1996); Hewson and Sinclair (1999); O'Brien *et al.* (2000).
4 The journals *Global Governance* and *Governance* are relevant. A number of conferences on GG are also illustrative. In addition to the workshop at the University of Delaware (October 2002), other conferences include those held at the University of Toronto (2002), University of Hull (2002), George Washington University (2003), London School of Economics (2004), and Monash University (2004).
5 http://www.lse.ac.uk/Depts/global/AboutCsglobalgovernance.html
6 http://www.globalcentres.org/html/governance.html
7 http://www.iu-bremen.de/globalgov/
8 http://cgcg.rutgers.edu/
9 http://www.udel.edu/poscir/gradhome.html

References

Alcantara, C.H. de. (1998) "Uses and Abuses of the Concept of Governance," *International Social Science Journal* 155 (March): 105–113.

Boli, J. and Thomas, G. (eds) (1999) *Constructing World Culture*, Stanford: Stanford University Press.

Bull, H. (1977) *The Anarchical Society*, New York: Columbia University Press.

Commission on Global Governance (1995) *Our Global Neighborhood*, Oxford: Oxford University Press.

Cooper, A., English, J. and Thakur, R. (eds) (2002) *Enhancing Global Governance: Towards a New Diplomacy*, Tokyo: United Nations University Press.

Cox, R. (1987) *Production, Power, and World Order: Social Forces in the Making of History*, New York: Columbia University Press.

Gilpin, R. (1981) *War and Change in World Politics*, Cambridge: Cambridge University Press.

Gilpin, R. (2002) "A Realist Perspective on International Governance," in D. Held and A. McGrew (eds) *Governing Globalization: Power, Authority, and Global Governance*, Cambridge: Polity Press.

Harris, E. and Yunker, J. (eds) (1999) *Toward Genuine Global Governance: Critical Reactions to "Our Global Neighborhood,"* Westport: Praeger.

Hewson, M. and Sinclair, T. (eds) (1999) *Approaches to Global Governance Theory*, Albany: SUNY Press.

Keohane, R. (2001) "Governance in a Partially Globalized World," *American Political Science Association* 95(1): 1–14.

Lipshutz, R. (1996) *Global Civil Society and Global Environmental Governance*, Albany: SUNY Press.

Mittleman, J. (ed.) (1997) *Globalization: Critical Reflections*, Boulder: Lynne Reinner.

Murphy, C. (2000) "Global Governance: Poorly Done and Poorly Understood," *International Affairs* 76(4): 789–803.

O'Brien, R., Goetz, A.M., Scholte, J.A. and Williams, M. (2000) *Contesting Global Governance*, Cambridge: Cambridge University Press.

Rosenau, J.N. (1997) *Along the Domestic–Foreign Frontier*, Cambridge: Cambridge University Press.

Rosenau, J.N. and Czempiel, O. (eds) (1992) *Governance without Government: Order and Change in World Politics*, Cambridge: Cambridge University Press.

Senarclens, P. de. (1998) "Governance and the Crisis in the International Mechanisms of Regulation," *International Social Science Journal* 155 (March): 91–104.

Smouts, Marie Claude (1998) "The Proper Use of Governance in International Relations" *International Social Science Journal* 155(March): 81–89.

Väyrynen, R. (ed.) (1999) *Globalization and Global Governance*, New York: Rowman and Littlefield.

Wapner, P. (1996) *Environmental Activism and World Civic Politics*, Albany: SUNY Press.

Weiss, T. (2000) "Governance, Good Governance, and Global Governance: Conceptual and Actual Challenges," *Third World Quarterly* 21(5): 795–814.

Wilkinson, R. and Hughes, S. (eds) (2002) *Global Governance: Critical Perspectives*, London: Routledge.

Young, O. (ed.) (1997) *Global Governance: Drawing Insights from the Environmental Experience*, Cambridge: The MIT Press.

Young, O. (1999) *Governance in World Affairs*, Ithaca: Cornell University Press.

Part I

Confronting global governance with established perspectives

2 Realist global governance

Revisiting *cave! hic dragones* and beyond

Jennifer Sterling-Folker

Introduction

In her contribution to the 1983 volume *International Regimes*, Susan Strange provided a scathing commentary on the concept of international regimes and the enthusiastic endorsement it was receiving by the international relations (IR) theoretical community at the time. The title of her essay, translated from pre-Columbian maps of the world beyond Europe, was "beware! here be dragons!" and it indicated her belief that there were a number of "dragons" that IR scholars would encounter if they insisted upon utilizing the concept of regimes as it had been formulated for the volume (Strange 1983: 337). Many of us know that essay well and, although its warnings went unheeded, many of the dragons Strange identified remain topical to the study of international regimes and other approaches in IR. As with Strange's contribution to the regimes volume, this essay finds much to be skeptical about the promotion of GG as a new approach to the study of IR. The editors of this collection have correctly identified the essential fault-lines embedded in our discussions of GG. In doing so they have underscored the fact that while there are multiple definitions and eclectic approaches to GG, there are also lurking dragons embedded in and common to many of them.

One of the more significant of these dragons is how to examine GG as a phenomenon that is simultaneously about structure and process. If the rallying cry for co-determination is going to mean anything, we need to think in terms of theoretical frameworks that allow for the combination of structure and history or, as Walker has argued, that "recognize that the claims of identity and those of difference are not mutually exclusive" (1987: 83). Realism has traditionally been harangued for having placed, as Lapid puts it, an "exclusive bet on stability and continuity" (1996a: 6), and for, according to Ferguson and Mansbach, having paid "inadequate attention to the dynamic side of world politics—the sources and consequences of change" (1996: 16).[1] Alternatively, many approaches to and discussions of GG have chosen instead to bet on the dynamic aspects of world politics, insisting that GG is primarily a verb and can only be understood as such.[2] The problem with any exclusive bet, however, whether it is on structural stability or process dynamics, is that it entails value judgments about what is worthy of study and how to do so. It reflects an academic practice that Strange characterized as "a kind of analytical *chiaroscuro*" (1983: 349), which leaves in the shadow those aspects of world politics that do not fit a particular analytical perspective, while highlighting those aspects that do.

The application of a term such as "governance" to the global level unwittingly assists in this obfuscation, by suggesting that regulation, restraint, and control do not depend on or require the existence of sovereign political units. In so doing, the standard notion of GG indirectly reifies the very things that so many well-intentioned transnational activists would seek to change. It gives the erroneous impression that governance, as with regimes, is "indeed slowly advancing against the forces of disorder and anarchy" (Strange 1983: 349), and it directs attention away from the underlying structures of sovereignty and the sites of political and economic power in the global system. Thus as with Strange's response to international regimes, I am concerned not simply with whether a GG approach to global politics will prove helpful to students and scholars seeking to understand it, but "whether it may not even be actually negative in its influence, obfuscating and confusing instead of clarifying and illuminating, and distorting by concealing bias instead of revealing and removing it" (Strange 1983: 337).

My own realist alternative perspective to process-based definitions of and approaches to GG would be more accurately characterized as a description of the transhistorical power project that makes particular, historical regional/world orders and rule systems possible. As such, it is a realist explanation for co-determination in global politics in that it strives to theoretically combine structure/noun and process/verb in a deductively satisfying manner. It is but one version of co-determination, as other chapters in this volume indicate, and I am not the only author in this collection concerned with the fire-breathing dragons that attend most discussions of GG.[3] But perhaps it is always the job of the realist to ferret such dragons out, since some level of cynicism is embedded in the realist approach itself. As Guzzini observes, "the bottom-line of realism is a particular form of skepticism," (1998: 203) or Buzan that, "much of realism can be read as a sophisticated form of fatalism" (1996: 61). One suspects that the role of skeptic and that of realist are considered to be one and the same within the discipline, and in that regard I will not disappoint. I do insist, however, that such skepticism does not contradict a position of ethics and that, as Spegele (2001) has argued, it may even be the necessary foundation for it.

Structure, history, and realism

How can a commitment to atemporal structuralism be consistent with the political-cultural dynamism that swirls around us on a daily global basis? Clearly no explanatory resolutions are achieved or knowledge gained by simply trading in structure for history. I gather this is the point when Ferguson and Mansbach note that a complete rejection of realism would be to "throw the baby out with the bath water" (1996: 6) or when Beer and Hariman observe that one "can never wholly do without realism" (1996: 25). Yet how can a structural realist commitment provide an understanding of GG as a co-determined phenomenon? It is perhaps simplest to start with the end point, a basic definition of GG, and then explain how it is possible to arrive at such a definition with realism.

GG can be defined as the existence of some semblance of order and organization in the affairs of interacting human groupings, these in turn having internal structures which allocate resources essential to their members. As an inter-group phenomenon, GG is a structural regularity born out of species sociability and the dynamics of inter-group interaction, which include the need to order interaction in some way (for practical, moral, and psychological reasons) and relative, allocative power as a primary means to do so. There has always been inter-group governance in this sense and there always will be, although until recently its scope was historically more regional than global and its specific content has and always will vary from epoch to epoch.[4] In other words, GG is simultaneously a structural and historical phenomenon. It is structural in that its reoccurrence as a general phenomenon is due to the social nature of human beings as a species. But it is also historical in that its content varies according to the vagaries of the powerful actors who are responsible for creating any particular rule system.

Realism's capacity to provide such a perspective on GG, and thereby treat structure and history as co-determining, derives from its conception of anarchy as an environment separate from what human beings do in it. Despite that separation, or actually because of it, realist explanations have always needed real human beings of flesh and blood to make choices in response to and as a reflection of their environment. It is only through individuals and the collective social practices they create that structure is manifest and the universal both realized and recognized. In this regard, human beings are not empty vessels into which structure pours its deterministic effects. Rather human beings, as a species, bring something with them to the historical table that produces human structural effects that no single individual or collective of human beings in history can control or prevent.

Such a statement clearly marks my structuralist perspective as neoclassical rather than neo-realist, since it intentionally throws human nature back into the explanatory mix.[5] But it is not the qualities of power or aggression that are relevant here; it is instead the tendency to form groups itself, the predisposition *to be* social as a species, that human beings are bringing with them to the table. That predisposition leads to the formation of collectives with social practices which bind and differentiate them from other collectives. It thereby provides a boundary within which all human beings exist and interact, and that boundary produces dynamics of its own that human beings have replicated throughout history, even as they have found infinite ways to socially differentiate themselves and their collectives.

It is interesting to consider how common it has become in IR theory circles to state, in opposition to a structural realist perspective, that human beings are social creatures, as if being social were incompatible with realist theorizing or meant that we have a better chance of creating nicer polities with nicer people in them that produce nicer outcomes. In fact, however, most scholars who hail socialization as a vindication of non-realist assumptions have failed to consider *why* it is that we are social and how these ultimate causes have already been anticipated by realists.[6] The *why* only makes sense from a Darwinian evolutionary perspective, of which realism is an explanatory replication in the realm of politics. Being social evolved as an adaptive mechanism for species survival and came about due to the competitive selection pressures of the natural environment. The length and particulars of the human infant's gestation were undoubtedly contributing factors; so too was the extent to which individual humans survived longer and in better health when they stayed together, thereby providing a better chance to reproduce. The result of these selection pressures was and still is a natural predisposition to sociability on the part of the species.

This predisposition does not derive from a single gene, nor is it a single characteristic. It is entwined with intelligence, consciousness, emotions, and language, and it resides in the entire human body and mind, which have been "hardwired" to be social, to seek identification with other human beings, and to form collectives with other human beings. This is a result of biological evolutionary processes for the species itself. That humans, society, and reasoning go together at all is rooted in natural-selection processes and species survival, which is ultimately and decidedly a realist answer in quality, even if Onuf is correct that the proximate causes for social practice and reason are not biological (1989: 46, 100). Put another way, realists assume that a human being is, as Crawford notes, "an animal capable of reason" (2000: 73–4), because it is only by virtue of having been quite literally animals that reasoning became a possibility for the human species.

It is also important to underscore that to be social is not to be nice, however much our popular usage of the term in English might suggest. A quick check of the thesaurus reveals that in English not only does it mean friendly, affable, and pleasant, but also human, worldly, cultural, political, public, racial, secular, and common. These are not words we usually associate with the friends we interact with at dinner parties, but then again it is precisely because people *are* social that they can organize quite effectively for war and kill large numbers of their own species in relatively short order. No wonder then, that Lapid accurately describes realism as "a tradition that subscribes to an ontology of conflictual group fragmentation," and that there is a "realist consensus concerning ontology (conflictual group fragmentation) and problematique (survival/war)" (1996b: 239, 240). Realists have always put groups at the center of their analysis, and groups exist because human beings are a fundamentally social species. Obviously human beings are made up of myriad biological, physiological, and psychological attributes and processes that make their sociability distinct from other social species. The point is, however, that to be social does not mean we get along well with others or that we can control our own destinies through our social practices.

What it does mean is that we form collectives which differentiate themselves from other collectives by a variety of means, but primarily (and distinctively, relative to other species) by developing and adopting differing social practices. These social practices bind us together, give meaning to our identities and actions, provide us with a means of acquiring and allocating resources, and direct us toward distinguishing difference with other individuals and collectives. It is in the development of these collectives that we produce a structural pattern of in-group/out-group bias which is and will remain basic to human interaction. As Kowert and Legro put it, "people's *need* for identity in social relations" is "so strong that they will invent in-group and out-group identities and differences even when there is no rational basis for doing so" (1996: 204, emphasis original; see also Mercer 1995). Why people have this need and the transhistorical patterns it produces are the stuff of realist theory.

Yet being social is merely the ultimate cause for these patterns; it can tell us nothing of the content of being social or the proximate causes for social practices. In other words, as humans form groups and interact across groups, they unintentionally create recognizable patterns, but these patterns do not determine the content of groups or their social practices. These patterns are instead the structural boundaries which devolve from the need on the part of human beings to form groups in the first place. They serve as boundaries for human interaction itself and within which the social practices they create will develop and evolve. Patterns such as in-group/out-group favoritism and discrimination, cooperative social practices within groups and competitive social practices without, a fixation on relative power between groups, the imitation of alternative social practice, and the institutional layering of imitated practices can all be derived from the very act of group formation. Thus structure is born from what human beings are and is the dynamic that arises when what they are *naturally* promotes their interaction with one another.

However, because Onuf is correct that we are not actualized as human beings until we are socialized as human beings, our biological "stuff" does not and cannot determine our lives, our becoming-in-the-world, and even our being.[7] *We* do that in the sense that we develop the "ties that bind," the intersubjective meanings to communicate thoughts and emotions and purposes, and the practices and institutions that give meaning to our activities and guide our activities and meanings in turn. These can only have been licensed by a biological predisposition to be social, but there is no primordial "right way," no handbook given out to every species at the dawn of evolutionary time for how to guarantee survival in an environment of resource competition and natural selection. Because we also have minds, consciousness, feelings, and above all language, our individual and species survival is as tied to the social practices we create as those practices are in turn a result of our need to survive. They are both a means to an end and an end in themselves, which is why human beings experiment almost endlessly with social practices and yet simultaneously cling dearly to them. The *why* we form groups is clear and beyond our grasp, the *how* we form groups is not clear but within our grasp.

The creation of social practice and intersubjective meanings is also an imaginative act and our imaginations are vast and amazing indeed. But it is not imagination without limits, because it is bounded by why we needed to be social in the first place, and so imagination conforms to the boundaries of group inter-action in their broadest outline, even as its content is varied and unique. And because we can never be sure that what we create really will obtain our survival, we are predisposed to experiment with and imitate social practice, even as we seek to demarcate and reify social practice because it is so essential to our survival. The dual tendency to experiment and reify derives from the same source, the *how*, and leads to ever more unique and particular practices, them-selves often the unintended consequences of their creators and imitators. All of which remains bounded by the dynamics of group interaction, the *why*, which the particularisms of social practice can never surmount. Indeed human particu-larisms can only exist because there is a specific structure to human existence, yet simultaneously the specific structure of human existence can only occur because there are human particularisms in social practice. Structure and history are indi-visible, not alternative, with atemporal forms of social interaction deriving from structure, particular contents of social interaction deriving from history, and with being and becoming both deriving concurrently from the same source—the human imperative to be social.

What this means for explanation is that while the broad-brush strokes of structure may be predictable, what is not predictable are the colors and precise positioning of the strokes. The former are atemporal, while the latter are histor-ically contingent. To understand the first we must examine the patterns of group formation and interaction throughout recorded human history; to under-stand the second we must study the particular agents and unique institutions of the historical moment. Put another way, structure involves broad themes such as balance of power, and we may observe instances of it in much the same way that a biologist observes that a species has wings or an art historian that a painting is of the Madonna and Child. The form tells us nothing of the specifics. It cannot tell us what the relative size or shape of the wing will be in different species, nor can it predict that there will be stark differences between an early Gothic British or Byzantine rendering of the same religious subject.[8] Similarly form cannot tell us specifically who will balance, against whom and what the immediate causes for this will be, how the effort will exactly unfold, what the outcome will look like precisely, and any specific effects on the actors involved or on global politics in general and into the future. This is the content of history and to understand it one must study history, not structure. Alternatively it is the latter that explains why balances-of-power form at all. The general form of balance-of-power is repeated, patterned, and knowable. The specific content of balances-of-power is not.

What this means for explanation is that there are limitations on what either structure or history alone can explain, and these limitations need to be recog-nized before one plunges into the empirical morass of daily life in order to draw conclusions about what is happening, why it is happening, and what will happen in global politics in the future. Too often theoretical IR analyses, both of the realist and non-realist kind, either confuse structural and historical effects, thereby reifying historical effects as if they were structural and vice versa, or choose between the two, thereby falling victim to pure forms of universalism or particularism that are neither satisfying as explanation nor relevant to the way in which we live our lives now and in the future. It is only by examining how structure and history come together in any particular moment in time that we confront the most pertinent political questions of our times and have something relevant to say to agents beyond the academy. Realism's unswerving commitment to structuralism actually allows it to incorporate both history and structure under the same rubric and in a way that theoretical approaches which only see change and history cannot. As Walker has noted, "the problematic of change, time, and becoming is in fact constitutive of the realist position itself" (1987: 72), and I would add that approaches which reject or jettison structuralism will fail to confront this essential problematic in any meaningful way, if at all.

Global governance as a transhistorical power project

How, then, does this discussion help us understand GG as a co-determined phenomenon? First, it indicates that what accounts for the regular production of GG systems throughout history is species sociability itself. That is, humans will form groups and, for a variety of reasons (practical, moral, psychological, etc.), human groupings create some degree of order and organization in their interactions with one another. Second, it indicates that GG will always be produced by the choices and actions of the relatively powerful groups, and so the primary means by which inter-group order is established is relative, allocative power. These are the structural parameters of GG, in that the human propensity to form groups promotes inter-group competition for resource allocation and, by necessity, elevates power as a primary means to achieve this end. Yet such inter-group competition also promotes an historical process that makes GG a time-bound phenomenon that could just as easily be analyzed as a verb.

This is because the relatively powerful groups will shape the content of GG systems based on their own internal particulars. Hence the content of GG varies according to the interests and social practices of the powerful human groupings of the particular epoch, be they clans, tribes, kingships, city-states, empires, nation-states, or principalities. While Ferguson and Mansbach (1996) have documented the multiple, varied identities and loyalties which create simultaneous and overlapping polities in any given time period, it is still possible to identify the relatively powerful polities of a period and in a region. One can do so by comparing both the allocative capacities of alternative institutional forms among existing polities (along the lines of Spruyt 1994), and the relative power among polities that share similarly effective allocative capacities and institutional forms (along the lines of Waltz 1979).[9] These polities will promote and propagate a form of collective inter-group order that will be specific to them, and they will do so because they believe (rightfully so) that it will allow them to obtain what is of socially constructed importance to them.

Hence the basis for any system of GG will be the social practices to which the powerful groups themselves subscribe. To put this another way, in order to exist at all, according to Reus-Smit, a group must develop a set of "hegemonic beliefs about the moral purpose" of its own existence. This serves as a core from which a normative complex derives involving "the justificatory foundations for the organizing principle of sovereignty" (thereby helping to differentiate this collective from that one), and "the norm of procedural justice" necessary to the effective function of allocative institutions and decisions within the collective (thereby determining who gets what within the group) (1999: 6). Reus-Smit refers to this normative complex as a "meta-value ensemble," and they determine what he calls the "licensing mentalities" or the mental horizons of systemic institutional builders. It is from this internal normative complex that the specific institutions and procedures of governance arise within a given collective. And, he argues, these same ensembles are the basis for ordering collective interactions on a regional or global scale.[10]

While Reus-Smit acknowledges that power plays a role in determining *whose* normative complexes become the basis for inter-group governance, he leaves unanalyzed the extent to which any particular GG system is but one example of a transhistorical power project. The form that GG takes in any given period of time always derives from the meta-value ensembles of the relatively powerful polities. Such polities propagate some form of GG because it allows them to obtain what is of socially constructed importance to them in both a material and ideational sense. It is not simply that the powerful determine how to "do business" with one another in a utilitarian, rule-system sense. It is, in addition and more importantly, that the powerful determine who counts as an appropriate entity, what counts as an appropriate activity, and what counts as existence itself for any given period of time.[11] Although at first glance GG may simply appear to be a collective good that allows groups to mutually obtain their self-interests, in fact a system of GG is one of the ultimate expressions of power and its structural centrality to global politics.

Because any given system of GG will always be licensed and bounded by the social practices of the powerful, both its existence (noun) and practice (verb) are a form of embedded power. In fact, the creation of any particular GG system should be ranked on a par with waging and winning world wars, which is something that classical realists certainly recognized and some of the more contemporary realist scholarship has come to acknowledge as well.[12] All other individuals and entities on the planet who will be subjected to a particular system of GG have one basic choice: either participate in the system or try to get out of its way.[13] Even direct challengers who wish to reconfigure a particular GG system will, as Gilpin (1981) and Waltz (1979) have both observed, engage with it and frequently participate competitively as a means to amass the power necessary to try to change it. However participation by those who do not share the same meta-value ensembles does not necessarily require coercion. As Ikenberry and Kupchan have noted, "although socialization is triggered by coercion and material inducements, the process of socialization can lead to outcomes that are not explicable simply in terms of the exercise of coercive power" (1990: 315). This is because groups with dissimilar social practices often voluntarily adopt the alternative ordering parameters of the powerful. Social practices are the means to the end of survival within anarchy, and the ensembles of the relatively powerful are particularly attractive means, thereby being the subject of considerable imitation by others.

Yet because identity is always formed and given meaning within group social practices, there is a simultaneous structural incentive for groups to reify preexisting social practices. Imitators will layer and meld alternative mental horizons and institutions onto existing ensembles, thereby unintentionally creating new institutional and meta-value ensemble variations.[14] The variations this layering creates are the pool from which potential institutional challenges and alternatives to prevailing meta-value ensembles, institutional arrangements, and GG systems will emerge. Such challenges and alternatives will inevitably emerge because the basis for any given GG system is the relative power of the collectives that created it. Given the structural property that compels humans to form groups which will inevitably compete for resources, all meta-value ensembles, institutional arrangements, and GG systems are subject to decline and demise and therefore are historically situated. There is no "end of history" thesis in realism, because the constant drive among groups to acquire and balance power ensures that the basis for any system of GG is relatively fleeting.[15] And although many individuals and polities might believe in a particular system's efficacy, ultimately no GG system can survive the decline of those powerful collectives who have promoted and defended it.

On the other hand, what provides the constant and dynamic source for new meta-value ensembles, institutional arrangements, and GG systems is the tendency to imitate and layer alternative social practices. This tendency also derives from the human need to form groups and culturally glue them together, but what it produces is continual innovation to and variation in meta-value ensembles and institutions. Some of these new ensemble and institutional variations will prove to be relatively more adept at amassing resources on behalf of their collectives. Hence these will be the basis for new GG systems in the future, as well as the objects of emulation by other collectives. This dynamic process produces ever more interesting and unanticipated social possibilities, since the pursuit of power involves not only the material and technological capacity to amass resources but a collective ideational foundation that sanctions the pursuit of power on behalf of the collective. It is impossible to anticipate the precise parameters that will constitute power in the future, and hence the form that GG will take, because material capacity is always wedded to and authorized by hegemonic beliefs about the moral purpose of the collective that are subject to layered innovation as well. Yet this dynamic process is bounded in recurring and anticipated ways by the human imperative to form collectives that compete for resources. In this way, structure and history interact to ensure that GG is a transhistorical power project whose institutional and normative particulars are constantly and historically in flux.

Studying contemporary GG: imagined dragons and genuine fire-breathers

Since meta-value ensembles vary across time and space and make any particular GG historically contingent, it is essential to distinguish ultimate, structural elements from historical, proximate causes when studying contemporary GG. Reus-Smit provides a reasonably accurate description of the governance of our own times which is based on the belief that "the moral purpose of the modern state lies in the augmentation of individuals' purposes and potentialities," with the source of sovereignty located in the people (1999: 123, 129; see also Reus-Smit 2001). This has given rise to legislative justice and, at the system level, codified international law as the norm of procedural justice for guiding interactions among nation-states. It has been assisted by "a generic institutional form of multilateralism" which, according to Ruggie, "coordinates behavior among three or more states on the basis of generalized principles of conduct," with the internal principles and politics of the powerful being as important to the delineation and propagation of these principles as the fact that they *are* the powerful in a relative sense (1992: 567, 574).

In contrast to much of the "Multilateralism Matters" literature, Reus-Smit argues that the meta-values that produced international law and multilateralism as the basis for inter-group interaction and justice were not simply American but European as well. Certainly Ruggie is also correct that it took American power to ensure its endurance and scope after World War II (Ruggie 1992), but the fact that other relatively powerful groups already shared these meta-values is what provided a receptive climate for them to become the ordering principles of the day.[16] Western Europe's receptivity to contemporary GG was also encouraged by bipolarity (Mearsheimer 1990), and other nation-states and entities increasingly found they *had* to operate within parameters promoted by the meta-values of the powerful, which only furthered the process whereby these became the principles for the global system of collective interaction.

Because scholars and students of IR tend to either choose between structure and history or confuse their effects in the analysis of contemporary GG, there is a tendency to ask all the wrong questions about the content and parameters of the map of contemporary GG. Dragons are seen where there actually are none, and genuine fire-breathers that exist at the edge of the map, and hence at the nexus of structure and history, are overlooked or ignored. Much is made, for example, of disagreements between the United States and other nation-states over such issues as the establishment of an international criminal court, the efficacy of banning land mines, the identification of collective security threats, or the health risks of genetically altered food. These are interesting historical processes and outcomes that underscore the structural centrality of differing social practices, group competition, and balance of power to contemporary GG. Yet such processes are frequently taken to mean that the powerful have somehow been displaced by their own creations and we can therefore stop talking about them and power in general. The drive to cooperate, we are told, takes on a "life of its own" which no longer depends on the original foundation of power to survive and flourish.

Certainly it is the case that such processes and outcomes are only understandable if the historical evolution of any particular system of GG results from a variety of interacting sources. How any particular system of GG evolves is an historical question, however, and it should not be confused with why there is any evolution to systems of GG, which is a structural question. To observe that, having promoted international law as a basic procedural norm of the present GG system, the US frequently now finds itself isolated by those who would use the procedural norm against it, is certainly an interesting historical phenomenon. But it does nothing to displace the relative power that made international law the procedural norm of contemporary GG and which reifies the embedded power of its creators. Such outcomes and processes can only occur because the contemporary system of GG steers potential challenges to it into avenues that are both acceptable to and controllable by the creators of that system.[17] Thus to challenge the United States with its own rules when one is essentially playing by those same rules is not much of a challenge to history and is certainly none to structure.

Similarly one finds an enormous flourishing of NGOs in the world today and about which much is made in theoretical circles, but these obtain legal and economic status only through a system of governance which promotes ordering principles determined by the powerful nation-states. Surely one can argue that NGOs have done much to raise awareness within nation-states about myriad problems, and they have saved the lives of many people in the process. But those are historical effects and should not be confused with the structural parameters of GG which remain firmly rooted in collectives with relative power and an ability to structure time and space for historically contingent social practices. NGOs might affect the latter in particular and unanticipated ways, but they do not directly affect the former, being creatures themselves of a system of contemporary GG that has already determined their status in the world and relative to power.[18] Trying to explain contemporary GG by focussing exclusively on historical processes such as NGOs, civil-society movements, technological change, and economic interdependence is like trying to explain global weather patterns by looking outside your window. It is, as Strange said of the equivalent in the study of regimes, "one of those shifts of fashion not too difficult to explain as a temporary reaction to events in the real world but in itself making little in the way of a long-term contribution to knowledge" (1983: 337).

Most structural perspectives on contemporary GG fare no better, because they tend to ignore the essential role that history plays in the GG transhistorical power project. Contemporary GG is instead treated as if it were a systemic phenomenon separated from the historical, internal meta-value ensembles that made it possible in the first place. This has led to ongoing explanatory problems for realists, liberals, and constructivists alike. In trying to say something meaningful about global politics on the basis of polarity alone, realists have tended to argue that international law and multilateralism are merely rhetorical devices disguising traditional balance of power politics. Such claims are captured in phrases such as "liberal talk, realist thinking" or "organized hypocrisy."[19] Alternatively, liberals and constructivists have tended to treat international institutions and norms as if they could provide the basis for a genuine commitment to *trans*national as opposed to merely national cooperation.[20]

The result is that we end up with surprises all around when powerful nation-states invest time and energy in supporting contemporary GG or when they blatantly ignore and undermine it. Much analytical energy is then expended on explaining these surprises in ways that are equally unsatisfactory, all because the glaring warnings written on the edge of the contemporary GG map, to study it as a phenomenon of co-determination, have been ignored. The normative hypocrisy that appears to be endemic to the contemporary GG system is due to the way in which the content of history and what is structurally transhistorical to human interaction have merged in this particular epoch. Given the content of many historical meta-value ensembles, it does not necessarily follow that all systems of GG involve a contradiction between GG systems and the normative complexes that license them.[21] The contemporary system of GG, however, is based on a meta-value ensemble whose particular content is in normative and practical contradiction with the structural parameters that make any system of GG possible.

To be more specific, the moral purpose of the nation-state involves serving the needs of its individual members, all of whom have been socialized to believe that this is the proper ordering of the universe. What makes this noteworthy is not that the nation-state justifies itself, and its need to amass resources on its own behalf, on the basis of a particular normative complex, since all collectives must do that in some way. It is instead that the nation-state does so on behalf of its *individual* members for whom it is meant to assist a process of actualization, augmentation, and possibly even self-perfection. The result is that the type of ordering mentality we have today is not merely territorially bounded, as so many constructivists and functionalists are apt to highlight (for example, Ruggie 1998). Rather the ordering mentality is territorially bounded on behalf of the collective's smallest constituent unit—the individual—and not vice versa. Hence the nation-state evolved as a political and social institution to help its *own* individual members achieve equal rights and personal fulfillment.

This is the philosophical basis for the nation-state's moral purpose and for most Western nation-states it has produced a genuine commitment to the ideas and language of universal individual augmentation, the equal application of its law, and suffrage for its citizens. To argue as Mearsheimer does that Americans behave as realists but are rhetorically committed to liberalism because it "is so deeply rooted in their culture" is to miss the fact that liberalism *is* their culture (2002: 28). The US and the European nation-states wouldn't exist as "nation-states" today if a genuine commitment to Enlightenment ideas had not plainly informed their own institutional development. The apparent hypocrisy, if it can even be called that, derives instead from the application of this moral purpose to inter-group relations. Modern legitimate statehood involves, as Reus-Smit has observed, "a discourse that seeks to justify territorial particularism on the grounds of ethical universalism" (2001: 520). While it is the case that all meta-value ensembles and GG systems occur within a structural context that demands particularism, the scope and content of the present set of meta-value ensembles involves an ethics of universal individual elevation. When such ethics become the basis for ordering international relations, it contradicts the very legitimacy that nation-states acquire by sustaining these ethics on behalf of their own particular individuals.

There are various sites throughout the global system where we can see this contradiction, and hence the edge of the GG map where the nexus of history and structure lies, most clearly. One such site can be found in the national court systems, where national judges grapple with cases involving the application of and consistency between national and international laws, both of which result from the same norm of procedural justice (see, for example, the Goldstein and Ban chapter in this volume). Another can be found in the immigration policies of liberal societies, which on the whole have proven to be exceedingly illiberal (Hollifield 1992). It is at sites such as these that there is a convergence in the elements of universalism and particularism, in power and possibility, in "metaphysical universals and a realm of becoming, between being and being-in-the-world, the latter having identity and reality only through participation in the former" (Walker 1987: 75).

Even the most imaginative institution builder must therefore contend with the fact (or is cognitively yet unconsciously representative of this mentality in turn) that the nation-state's purpose is to satisfy the needs and wants of the individuals who comprise it. It is for this reason that these individuals have banded together into this type of unit in this moment in time, and it is upon this basis that the nation-state justifies its own actions vis-à-vis other nation-states and other types of entities. For all practical purposes, the only jurors who matter to the evaluation of each nation-state's choices and behaviors are its own leaders and publics, and they do so on the basis of how well it has augmented *them*. The social beings the nation-state creates have licensing mentalities that confirm this as the proper ordering of the cosmos. This is why, despite deep inequalities in the world, that guarantee more people will die each day from poverty than warfare (Zalewski 1996: 351; Murphy 2001), this is only viewed as a "problem" in relation to each nation-state's own individuals. This is why, according to Buzan and Little, "the main centers of supposedly postmodern evolution in North America, Europe, and Japan also remain remarkably parochial, culturally self-centered, and politically inward looking" (2000: 361). And this is why, according to Thomson, "powerful states, which have benefited from participating in a particular practice, ban it when it becomes a threat to themselves" (1992: 198).

Although it is tempting to label such behavior "hypocrisy," and Krasner (1999) is certainly correct that it is an endemic rather than aberrant feature of contemporary GG, to do so is analytically misleading. It suggests that national leaders and the societies they represent are insincere about individual universalism and that they are engaged in a form of premeditated rhetorical duplicity in order to obtain some alternative, hidden goal. In fact, however, the relatively powerful societies that have created contemporary GG are quite sincere about universal augmentation and suffrage for the individuals of their *own* particular collectives. In this there is no duplicity, no double-standard for the polity that is the nation-state. It is a contradiction, however, when it is the basis for a system of GG, because it implies that a structure of authority should act to protect and augment individuals everywhere. Since such a structure of authority does not exist (and will not, given the human imperative to form groups that will compete), contemporary GG encourages the erroneous belief that we can have these universalistic goals without the particularisms that made them possible as a system of GG. As Griffiths and O'Callaghan put it, "suffering…does not correlate with territorial boundaries, but the political capacity to respond to it does. Our cosmopolitan moral sentiments are constantly frustrated by our particularistic political identities as citizens" (2001: 192).

It is an ironic twist of history that the nation-state, as the dominant political unit of the moment, produces a particularly parochial licensing mentality, yet the shared desire for universal suffrage and equality is a direct result of it. The very content of the nation-state's moral purpose encourages the fanciful notion that the nation-state and its moral purpose are mutually exclusive. The effects this self-delusion have had on our scholarship are well documented by Brown, who notes that, "the inability of mainstream American social scientists to understand those many features of the modern world that reflect diversity and difference stems from its universalism" and that "the real irony is that if American social science was *more* parochial it would have a better chance of getting things right" (2001: 216). This self-delusion also runs rampant among national leaders, who continually rely on and promote notions of universal human rights and suffrage, even as they have been elected to protect and defend a very narrow and particular segment of the earth's population.[22]

Perhaps worst of all is that this self-delusion misdirects the energy of activists in a host of transnational issue areas, who have been encouraged to believe that international law and the multilateralism associated with it can emancipate us from the evils of particularism embodied by the nation-state. Unfortunately these are not particularly good vehicles if universal suffrage and equality are your goals. One cannot hope to piggy-back off the nation-state's own moral purpose and norms of justice and then expect to sneak up on and overturn it. Nor can these norms of justice be used as a vehicle to make power, in both its stark utilitarian and its embedded constitutive sense, any less relevant to the conduct of global affairs. As Buzan and Little note, "while some IGOs and INGOs might have achieved significant levels of relative autonomy, it is much less clear either that they have escaped the dominion of the state, or that they are themselves plausible candidates for status as new types of dominant units" (2000: 361). In fact, international law and much of what passes as cooperation these days merely serves to reify both the nation-state as the dominant political unit of the moment and the social practices and licensing mentalities of the powerful nation-states in particular.

Some final thoughts on the future of GG and its study

There is always a temptation to search for solace in the fact that the nation-state will not be the dominant polity in the future and that its demise will somehow provide a resolution in favor of the universalistic principles its GG system has promoted. It is correct that there will be a resolution of sorts, but the particulars of such a resolution hold out no more hope for the final realization of the nation-state's moral purpose on a global scale (absent it as the dominant polity) than the contemporary GG system does now. Thanks to a knowledge of structure, we know that group competition produces a constant evolutionary dynamism to social practice, polity creation and demise, relative power, and GG systems. Hence we know that the nation-state will be replaced with alternative types of dominant polities in the future, and that whatever internal moral purposes justify the existence of these polities will also serve as the basis for future GG systems. The particular set of meta-value ensembles to which we at present subscribe are only the latest justificatory version for collective existence, and there will be other meta-value ensembles and licensing mentalities in the future.

However, those who would search in such a formula for certainty in the content of those meta-value ensembles, licensing mentalities, and hence GG systems will be sorely disappointed. The specific content of any meta-value ensemble results from the historical ways in which group competition, power, and social practice interact and dynamically evolve new and unanticipated contents. That is, we can predict the basic pattern to future institutional evolution, but we cannot predict its content. This is because institutional evolution occurs in a competitive group context that selects polities according to their relative capacity to amass resources effectively on their behalf. What any polity seeks to amass will be defined by and contingent on its own internal meta-value ensembles which are neither entirely static nor entirely novel. It is this melding of institutions and mental horizons that makes possible the alternative hegemonic beliefs that then authorize alternative, innovative means to obtain relative capacity and resource exploitation.

To understand this melding we have to take a bottom-up view of IR and systems of GG, by examining and combining multiple levels of historical analysis. There is excellent work being done in this regard, by scholars such as Checkel (2001), Hopf (2002), Johnston (1995), and Marsh (2003), to name a few. And what this work indicates is that while there will certainly be linkages between the ensembles of the future and those of the past and present, those linkages filter though internal processes and institutions that are causal in their own right. The creation of new moral purposes, and hence licensing mentalities, dominant polities, and GG systems, is contingent on this institutional layering that occurs in the act of competitive imitation. Such layering guarantees that there is never exact replication or stasis in ensembles, institutions, and polities. Hence the ensembles of the future, and the polities and GG systems that will be licensed by them, will not and cannot be those of the present. This means that the demise of the nation-state as the dominant type of polity also spells the demise of its meta-value ensembles and system of GG as well. What will constitute the GG systems of the future will depend on what types of dominant polities emerge from the co-determination of structure and historical process.

To argue that the contemporary GG system can flourish without the type of polity that made it possible is to privilege history over structure and to thereby ignore or analytically deny the very combination that makes the contemporary GG system feasible. Those who believe otherwise are, for all theoretical and practical purposes, confusing process with structure and what is historically contingent with what is transhistorical. Group formation, group dynamics, and power produce transhistorical patterns. Power provides the necessary foundation for a common language of governance to develop among the groups of any given period, be it the language of absolutism or individual suffrage. The governance systems that develop are historically contingent processes, neither culminating nor teleological but reflective of the particularisms of their times. These governance systems define what counts as legitimate group formations and modes of action among groups, but they cannot displace the transhistorical structure derived from power and groups, since these provide the basis for GG to exist at all. The present system of GG affirms the centrality of nation-states and power, even as so many activists work feverishly with international law and existing modes of multilateralism to displace them. Unfortunately these are excellent examples of power and difference as structural parameters for social practice, and we as theorists do a disservice to activists everywhere by failing to tell them that this is so.

It also matters a great deal whether we use a term like "governance" to describe the order, organization, and rules that the powerful have imposed on the cosmos of our time. For most of us the term "governance," like the term "regimes" before it, is "value-loaded in that it takes for granted...that greater order and managed interdependence should be the collective goal" (Strange 1983: 345). Yet this "governance" is merely the internal meta-value ensembles of particular groups, who have proven adept at amassing relative power for themselves in this particular historical moment in time, and who have ordered inter-group relations according to their own particular licensing mentalities. It is a governance system that, as with all other systems that have come before it or will develop in the future, is neither eternal nor equitable in its particulars. Ultimately it will rise and fall with those polities who have, by virtue of their relative power, been able to promote it, because human beings are social creatures who inevitably form groups, and groups inevitably compete for resources and hence power. As with all other governance systems that have come before it or will come in the future, its particulars reinforce the essentiality of power and do nothing to overcome it.

And more to the point of this particular exercise, we should be particularly careful when embarking on the development of new approaches with grand labels such as "global governance" that we do not merely take the historically contingent processes of the moment as the basis for understanding global politics. Since doing so will only reify this particular historical moment and its concomitant but unstated value-biases, we will be left incapable of explaining the world around us. We need instead to confront the puzzle of co-determination and this, I believe, will lead us back to realism; an approach which is hardly new but which leaves us capable of explaining a great deal. This too was one of Strange's dragons and it bears repeating:

> If (as so many books in international relations have concluded) we need better "tools of analysis," it is not because we will be able to dig up golden nuggets with them. Those nuggets—the great truths about human society and human endeavor—were all discovered long ago. What we need are constant reminders so that we do not forget them.
>
> (1983: 351)

The existence of governance on a global scale is itself a constant reminder of these truths, yet we IR scholars may be on the verge of digging it under by trying to develop yet one more "new" analytical approach that will fail miserably to understand it.

Notes

1 For similar criticisms of realism see Wendt (1987); Dessler (1989); Koslowski and Kratochwil (1994); Lebow (1994); Beer and Hariman (1996: 21–2); Halliday (1996: 325); Hobden (1998: 66–90).

2 Constructivists, for example, have tended to actively encourage the belief in "a different logic of transformation, one driven more by self-conscious efforts to change structures of identity and interest than by unintended consequences," which, as Wendt himself then acknowledges, would "seem to contradict the spirit of constructivism" (1992: 418–19). Dunn has observed that, "This is arguably one of the most significant weaknesses of Wendt's and Onuf's international theories, in that they have a tendency to imply that the social world can be reconstituted simply by reconstructing our identity from 'within' (a phenomenological perspective)" (1995: 373). It is a problem which Kratochwil has noted as well (1996: 196).

3 Other theoretical perspectives such as world systems theory or historical materialism have remained committed to structuralism as well, while increasingly attempting to analytically grapple with indeterminacy. As Denemark has observed, this undoubtedly results from a legitimate attempt to "embrace reflectivity and avoid determinism while not abandoning their search to understand historically similar circumstances and structural constraints" (1999: 66). See, for example, the work of Arrighi and Silver (1999) or Thompson and Modelski (1999).

4 See, for example, Gilpin (1981); Buzan, Jones, and Little (1993); Reus-Smit (1999); Buzan and Little (2000).

5 There are many different types of realism, including classical, neo-defensive, tragic, offensive, evil, and neoclassical. For reviews of these differences, see Spirtas (1996); Brooks (1997); Jervis (1999). Neoclassical realists comprise a small contingent interested in exploring the relationship between the anarchic international system, domestic- and individual-level intervening variables, and international outcomes. Rose discusses various neoclassical realists who examine domestic institutions and structures as intervening variables (1998), while others, such as Mercer (1995), Taliaferro (2000/01), or myself (2002), have been more interested in exploring psychology, emotions, and biology as intervening variables.

6 Of these, Hall's treatment of identity and realism remains one of the best examples. His "will-to-manifest-identity" is the link between the individual and the collective, and he explicitly juxtaposes the concept to realism. However, one of Hall's sources for this concept is Bloom (1990), who argues in turn that the need to identify is rooted in species survival and remains a necessity for human infants in this regard.

7 Although there is a clear compatibility between constructivism and "neoclassical" realism, it is possible to find elements of constructivism in neo-realism as well. Inayatullah and Blaney (1996) have pointed out that Waltz's discussion of socialization and his reliance on the play "Who's Afraid of Virginia Woolf?" as analogous to international structure is quite similar to basic constructivist tenets. In arguing that the couple's "activities cannot be understood without considering the system that emerges from their interactions," Waltz is in essence suggesting that interaction creates a structure which none of its participants control but which nonetheless has an unintended impact on norms and behavior (1979: 74). Although Inayatullah and Blaney note that subsequent realist scholarship ignored this point, the implication is that "surely socialization also gives meaning and purpose to our actions and thoughts," and so it would seem "necessary to connect socialization to meanings, as Waltz himself hints" (1996: 69).

8 Ray implies a similar distinction between form/structure and content/history when comparing the inability of IR theorists to predict the end of the Cold War and meteorologists who "understand hurricanes quite well and, in retrospect can explain quite convincingly the process that produces them and why they hit when and where they do. What they cannot do is to predict specifically, years or even months in advance, when and where a major hurricane will occur" (1995: 350).

9 In Mesopotamia it was kingships, in Greece it was city-states, in China it was dynastic empires, in Mesoamerica it was urban empires, in the Islamic world it was tribal empire, and in Medieval Italy it was towns and cities (Ferguson and Mansbach 1996: Chapters 3–14).

10 The governance systems Reus-Smit examines include those created by the Greek city-states (which promoted arbitration), the Italian city-states (which promoted oratorical diplomacy), the absolutist states (which promoted old diplomacy), and the nation-state (which promote international law and multilateralism). See also Reus-Smit (2001).

11 Or, as Dunne has put it, "International society exists as a social fact. Like all social structures it is unobservable but its effects are real. The structure embodies rules of identifying who gets to count as a member, what conduct is appropriate, and what (if any) consequences follow from acts of deviancy" (2001: 89).

12 See, for example, Gilpin (1981) or Schweller and Priess (1997).

13 As Buzan, Jones, and Little (1993) have argued, however, technology and interaction capacity have made it increasingly difficult to isolate oneself from systemic effects.

14 For more extended expositions on this phenomenon, see Sterling-Folker (2002: 76–92) or (2001: 90–100).

15 Contrast, for example, Fukuyama (1989) with Gilpin (1981), Kennedy (1989), Schweller and Priess (1997).

16 Indeed, given that the principles upon which multilateralism rests are, according to Ruggie (1993) and other contributors to the "Multilateralism Matters" literature, a mixture of American self-interest and socially constructed perspectives on politics and world order, the term "multilateralism" to describe this phenomenon sounds more than a little contradictory and self-serving.

17 Smith provides a good example in his study of the evolution of humanitarian laws of war which, thanks to pressure from the powerful, now legitimize a new sort of violence "that licenses hi-tech states to launch wars as long as their conduct is deemed just," and allows hi-tech states to "defend hugely destructive, essentially unopposed, aerial bombardments by citing the authority of seemingly secular and universal legal standards" (2001: 356, 370).

18 See, for example, Fowler (1996) or Clark, Friedman, and Hochstetler (1998).
19 See Krasner (1999) and Mearsheimer (2002, 2001).
20 For example Zacher (1992) or Wendt (1999; Chs 6–7).
21 In fact, Reus-Smit's discussion of the GG system promoted by absolutist states under-scores that normative complexes, GG systems, and the structural demands of particularism can be nearly synonymous (1999; Ch. 5).
22 Which leads, in turn, to on-going attempts to actually implement universal ethics across a variety of global issue areas. Small wonder, then, that Ottaway finds, despite a genuine commitment "in theory" to reconstruct post-conflict countries according to a democratic model, that the international community "lacks the political will to really try" (2003: 315). Indeed her findings that – "the result is a growing discrepancy between the model that is propounded and the policies that are actually practiced" – is a descriptive statement of fact for contemporary GG.

References

Arrighi, G. and Silver, B.J. (1999) *Chaos and Governance in the Modern World System*, Minneapolis: University of Minnesota Press.

Beer, F.A. and Hariman, R. (eds) (1996) *Post-realism: The Rhetorical Turn in International Relations*, East Lansing: Michigan State University Press.

Bloom, W. (1990) *Personal Identity, National Identity, and International Relations*, Cambridge, UK: Cambridge University Press.

Brown, C. (2001) "Fog in the Channel: Continental International Relations Theory Isolated (or an Essay on the Paradoxes of Diversity and Parochialism in IR Theory," in R.M.A. Crawford and D.S.L. Jarvis (eds) *International Relations: Still an American Social Science? Toward Diversity in International Thought*, Albany, NY: State University of New York Press.

Brooks, S.G. (1997) "Dueling Realisms," *International Organization*, 51: 445–78.

Buzan, B. (1996) "The Timeless Wisdom of Realism?," in S. Smith, K. Booth, and M. Zalewski (eds) *International Theory: Positivism and Beyond*, Cambridge, UK: Cambridge University Press.

Buzan, B and Little, R. (2000) *International Systems in World History: Remaking the Study of International Relations*, Oxford: Oxford University Press.

Checkel, J.T. (2001) "Why Comply? Social Learning and European Identity Change," *International Organization*, 55: 553–88.

Clark, A.M., Friedman, E.J. and Hochstetler, K. (1998) "The Sovereign Limits of Global Civil Society: A Comparison of NGO Participation in UN World Conferences on the Environment, Human Rights and Women," *World Politics*, 51: 1–35.

Crawford, N.C. (2000) "The Passion of World Politics: Propositions on Emotion and Emotional Relationships," *International Security*, 24: 116–56.

Denemark, R.A. (1999) "World System History: From Traditional International Politics to the Study of Global Relations," *International Studies Review*, 1: 43–76.

Dessler, D. (1989) "What's at Stake in the Agent-Structure Debate?," *International Organization*, 43: 441–73.

Dunne, T. (1995) "The Social Construction of International Society," *European Journal of International Relations*, 1: 367–89.

—— (2001) "Sociological Investigations: Instrumental, Legitimist and Coercive Interpretations of International Society," *Millennium: Journal of International Studies*, 30: 67–91.

Ferguson, Y.H. and Mansbach, R.W. (1996) *Polities: Authority, Identities, and Change*, Columbia, SC: University of South Carolina Press.

Fowler, A. (1996) "Assessing NGO Performance: Difficulties, Dilemmas and a Way Ahead," in M. Edwards and D. Hulme (eds) *Beyond the Magic Bullet: NGO Performance and Accountability in the Post-Cold War World*, West Hartford, CT: Kumarian Press.

Fukuyama, F. (1989) "The End of History?," *The National Interest*, 16: 3–18.

Gilpin, R. (1981) *War and Change in World Politics*, Cambridge, UK: Cambridge University Press.

Griffiths, M. and O'Callaghan, T. (2001) "The End of International Relations?" in R.M.A. Crawford and D.S.L. Jarvis (eds) *International Relations—Still an American Social Science? Toward Diversity in International Thought*, Albany, NY: State University of New York Press.

Guzzini, S. (1998) *Realism in International Relations and International Political Economy: The Continuing Story of a Death Foretold*, London: Routledge.

Hall, R.B. (1999) *National Collective Identity: Social Constructs and International Systems*, New York: Columbia University Press.

Halliday, F. (1996) "The Future of International Relations: Fears and Hopes," in *International Theory: Positivism and Beyond*, Cambridge, UK: Cambridge University Press.

Hobden, S. (1998) *International Relations and Historical Sociology: Breaking Down Boundaries*, London: Routledge.

Hollifield, J. (1992) *Immigrants, Markets, and States*, Cambridge: Cambridge University Press.

Hopf, T. (2002) *Social Construction of International Politics: Identities and Foreign Policies, Moscow, 1955 and 1999*, Ithaca, NY: Cornell University Press.

—— (1998) "The Promise of Constructivism in International Relations Theory," *International Security*, 23: 171–200.

Ikenberry, G.J. and Kupchan, C. (1990) "Socialization and Hegemonic Power," *International Organization*, 44: 283–315.

Inayatullah, N. and Blaney, D.L. (1996) "Knowing Encounters: Beyond Parochialism in International Relations Theory" in Y. Lapid and F. Kratochwil (eds) *The Return of Culture and Identity in IR Theory*, Boulder, CO: Lynne Rienner Publishers.

Jervis, R. (1999) "Realism, Neoliberalism and Cooperation: Understanding the Debate," *International Security*, 24: 42–63.

Johnston, A.I. (1995) *Cultural Realism: Strategic Culture and Grand Strategy in Chinese History*, Princeton, NJ: Princeton University Press.

Kennedy, P. (1989) *The Rise and Fall of the Great Powers: Economic Change and Military Conflict from 1500–2000*, London: Fontana.

Koslowski, R. and Friedrich, V.K. (1994) "Understanding Change in International Politics: The Soviet Empire's Demise and the International System," *International Organization*, 48: 215–48.

Kowert, P. and Jeffrey, L. (1996) "Norms, Identity, and Their Limits: A Theoretical Reprise" in P. Katzenstein (ed.) *The Culture of National Security*, New York: Columbia University Press.

Krasner, S.D. (1999) *Sovereignty: Organized Hypocrisy*, Princeton, NJ: Princeton University Press.

Kratochwil, F. (1996) "Citizenship: On the Border of Order" in Y. Lapid and F. Kratochwil (eds) *The Return of Culture and Identity in IR Theory*, Boulder, CO: Lynne Rienner Publishers.

Kubalkova, V., Onuf, N., and Paul, K. (eds) (1998) *International Relations in a Constructed World*, Armonk, New York: M.E. Sharpe.

Lapid, Y. (1996a) "Culture's Ship: Returns and Departures in International Relations Theory" in Y. Lapid and F. Kratochwil (eds) *The Return of Culture and Identity in IR Theory*, Boulder, CO: Lynne Rienner Publishers.

—— (1996b) "Nationalism and Realist Discourses of International Relations" in F.A. Beer and Robert Hariman (eds) *Post-Realism: The Rhetorical Turn in International Relations*, East Lansing, MI: Michigan State University Press.

Lapid, Y and Kratochwil, F. (1996) "Revisiting the 'National': Toward and Identity Agenda in Neorealism?" in Y. Lapid and F. Kratochwil (eds) *The Return of Culture and Identity in IR Theory*, Boulder, CO: Lynne Rienner Publishers.

Lebow, R.N. (1994) "The Long Peace, the End of the Cold War, and the Failure of Realism," *International Organization*, 48: 249–78.

Marsh, C. (2003) "Learning From Your Comrade's Mistakes: The Impact of the Soviet Past on China's Future," *Communist and Post-Communist Studies*, 35(3, September).

Mearsheimer, J.J. (2002) "Liberal Talk, Realist Thinking", *University of Chicago Magazine*, 94(3, February): 24–8.

—— (1991) *The Tragedy of Great Power Politics*, New York: W.W. Norton and Company Inc.

——(1990) "Back to the Future: Instability in Europe After the Cold War", *International Security*, 15: 5–56.

Mercer, J. (1995) "Anarchy and Identity," *International Organization*, 49: 229–52.

Modelski, G. and Thompson, W.R. (1999) "The Long and the Short of Global Politics in the Twenty-first Century: An Evolutionary Approach," *International Studies Review* 1(2): 109–40.

Murphy, C.N. (2001) "Political Consequences of the New Inequality", *International Studies Quarterly*, 45: 347–56.

Onuf, N.G. (1989) *World of Our Making: Rules and Rule in Social Theory and International Relations*, Columbia, SC: University of South Carolina Press.

Ottaway, M. (2003) "Promoting Democracy After Conflict: The Difficult Choices," *International Studies Perspective* 4(3): 314–22.

Ray, J.L. (1995) "Promise or Peril? Neorealism, Neoliberalism, and the Future of International Politics," in C.W. Kegley, Jr. (ed.) *Controversies in International Relations Theory: Realism and the Neoliberal Challenge*, New York: St. Martin's Press.

Rose, G. (1998) "Neoclassical Realism and Theories of Foreign Policy," *World Politics*, 51(October): 144–72.

Reus-Smit, C. (1999) *The Moral Purpose of the State: Culture, Social Identity, and Institutional Rationality in International Relations*, Princeton, NJ: Princeton University Press.

—— (2001) "Human Rights and the Social Construction of Sovereignty," *Review of International Studies*, 27(4): 519–38.

Ruggie, J.G. (1992) "Multilateralism: The Anatomy of an Institution," *International Organization*, 46(3): 561–98.

—— (ed.) (1993) *Multilateralism Matters: The Theory and Praxis of an Institutional Form*, New York: Columbia University Press.

—— (1998) *Constructing the World Polity: Essays on International Institutionalization*, New York: Routledge.

Schweller, R.L. and Priess, D. (1997) "A Tale of Two Realisms: Expanding the Institutions Debate," *Mershon International Studies Review*, 41(May): 1–32.

Spegele, R.D. (2001) "Out With Theory—In with Practical Reflection: Toward a New Understanding of Realist Moral Skepticism," in Robert M.A. Crawford and Darryl S.L. Jarvis (eds) *International Relations: Still an American Social Science? Toward Diversity in International Thought*, Albany, NY: SUNY Press.

Spirtas, M. (1996) "A House Divided: Tragedy and Evil in Realist Theory," in B. Frankel (ed.) *Realism: Restatements and Renewals*, London: Frank Cass.

Spruyt, H. (1994) *The Sovereign State and Its Competitors: An Analysis of Systems Change*, Princeton, NJ: Princeton University Press.

Sterling-Folker, J. (2001) "Evolutionary Tendencies in Realist and Liberal IR Theory," in William R. Thompson (ed.) *Evolutionary Interpretations of World Politics*, New York: Routledge.

—— (2002) *Theories of International Cooperation and the Primacy of Anarchy: Explaining U.S. International Monetary Policy-making After Bretton Woods*, Albany, NY: SUNY Press.

Strange, S. (1983) "*Cave! hic dragones*: A Critique of Regime Analysis," in S.D. Krasner (ed.) *International Regimes*, Ithaca, NY: Cornell University Press.

Taliaferro, J.W. (2000/01) "Security-seeking Under Anarchy: Defensive Realism Revisited," *International Security*, 25(Winter).

Thomson, J.E. (1992) "Explaining the Regulation of Transnational Practices: A State-building Approach," in J.N. Rosenau and E.O. Czempiel (eds) *Governance Without Government: Order and Change in World Politics*, Cambridge, UK: Cambridge University Press.

Walker, R.B. J. (1987) "Realism, Change, and International Political Theory," *International Studies Quarterly*, 31: 65–86.

Waltz, K. (1979) *Theory of International Politics*, New York: McGraw-Hill.

Wendt, A. (1987) "The Agent-Structure Problem in International Relations Theory," *International Organization*, 41: 335–70.

—— (1999) *Social Theory of International Politics*, Cambridge, UK: Cambridge University Press.

—— (1992) "Anarchy is What States Make of It: The Social Construction of Power Politics," *International Organization*, 46: 391–25.

Zacher, M.W. (1992) "The Decaying Pillars of the Westphalian Temple: Implications for International Order and Governance," in J.N. Rosenau and E. Czempiel (eds) *Governance Without Government: Order and Change in World Politics*, Cambridge, UK: Cambridge University Press.

Zalewski, M. (1996) " 'All These Theories Yet the Bodies Keep Piling Up': Theory, Theorists, Theorising," in S. Smith, K. Booth, and M. Zalewski (eds) *International Theory: Positivism and Beyond*, Cambridge, UK: Cambridge University Press.

3 Global governance, class, hegemony

A historical materialist perspective

Henk Overbeek

Introduction

Global governance has become a buzzword since the early 1990s (the publication of Rosenau and Czempiel 1992 was a watershed event). This is not the place to consider in detail the genesis of the concept or survey all the various meanings that the concept has acquired (for a good overview, see Behrens 2002). There are enduring definitional problems with both elements of the concept, i.e. with the meaning of *global* and with the meaning of *governance*. Both are diffuse and elusive notions that defy precise definition exactly because they have been developed to capture diffuse and elusive phenomena. So, for the moment we should be satisfied with a loose approximation, where *global* roughly means 'of planetary dimension', 'world-wide', 'globe-spanning' (or at least the potentiality of those qualities), and *governance* has connotations with 'regulation', 'co-ordination', and 'authoritative allocation of values' (all possibly encompassing 'government' without, however, being limited to it).

The definition of global governance that is probably quoted more often than any other is the one by the Commission on Global Governance: 'The sum of the many ways individuals and institutions, public and private, manage their common affairs. It is a continuing process through which conflicting or diverse interests may be accommodated and co-operative action may be taken' (CGG 1995: 2). There are at least three key problems with this type of definition. First, the definition has little analytical or theoretical meaning. Rather, it has a strong normative bias. 'Governance' is seen as a consensual process of accommodation between parties whose highest purpose is to reconcile possible conflict co-operatively. This normative dimension is not necessarily all bad: it reflects a desire for a more equitable and just world order and as such can potentially contribute to a reformist, or even to a counter-hegemonic, project. In fact, it is often understood in this way. However, by exclusively emphasizing the cooperative element this definition in fact eliminates any possible connotation of domination and force, which of course is also part of 'governance'. This de-politicizing tendency is strengthened further by a second problem. The definition of the CGG implies an actor-oriented approach, and its disaggregating line of reasoning exposes it to the pitfalls of *pluralism*, i.e. of taking the plurality of actors, interests and partial structures (or 'spheres of authority', e.g. Rosenau 2002) as being the essence of things, and as being essentially undetermined, unbiased, 'neutral', rather than seeing this plurality as set in a wider hierarchical configuration of social power. Thirdly, it is ahistorical in that it abstracts from the concrete historical conjuncture in which the concept has emerged. It thus implies that 'global governance' is of all times. However, concepts only acquire their full meaning and complexity if the abstract contours, which may be true for all time, are coloured in with the specificities of the historical epoch to which they are applied.[1] In this essay, I argue that we need a definition that is more analytical, founded in a theoretical framework that enables us to see how the current conceptualization of global governance in fact neuters any critical content that the concept might have originally contained when it was first coined in response to the perceived need to deal with global problems.

An abstract analytical definition of global governance might be arrived at by first looking at the two component words of the concept, namely 'governance' and 'global'. An abstract definition of '*governance*' may refer to, or incorporate, the following shorthand definitions found in some of the key sources in the literature: 'order plus intentionality' (Rosenau 1992: 5), or 'organizing collective action' (Prakash and Hart 1999: 2), or 'interactions in which public as well as private actors participate' (Kooiman 2003: 4), or 'authoritative allocation of resources and exercise of control and co-ordination' (Rhodes 1996: 652). An abstract definition of 'global' would have to refer to the specific quality of the phenomenon under consideration, which is (potentially at least) 'of planetary dimension', 'world-wide' or 'globe-spanning'. Putting these two together we might tentatively define 'global governance' as follows: 'Global governance refers to the authoritative allocation (by a variety of means) of values in policy areas that potentially affect the world as a whole and its component parts.' However analytical such a definition is, it does not resolve the third problem: it is still ahistorical. In this essay, the aim is to outline a historically specific understanding of 'global governance'. Such an approach ought to address the three issues mentioned above: it must be an analytical approach rather than a primarily normative one; it must avoid the pitfalls of pluralism; and it must be grounded in a historical understanding. In this essay, these objectives are met, or at least that is the contention here, by situating the approach in the tradition of transnational historical materialism.[2] Although it is not possible to discuss the full foundations of this approach in the context of this essay, it is necessary for our purposes to outline five key elements of this approach at the outset so that our argument about global governance will retain its coherence.

The first point to make, picking up on the issue of making our concepts historically specific, is to stress the importance of the Marxian method of abstraction as outlined in the *Grundrisse*. In Marx's own words, 'even the most abstract categories, despite their validity – precisely because of their abstractness – for all epochs, are nevertheless, in the specific character of this abstraction, themselves likewise a product of historic relations, and possess their full validity only for and within these relations' (1973: 105). Thus, analytical concepts need to carefully separate abstract and invariant properties from historically specific ones. Concretely, the concept of 'global governance', even if it became fashionable only in the 1990s, refers in an abstract sense to forms of regulation of social and economic interactions that we can also discern in earlier epochs. To understand why it is that the concept gained currency in the 1990s, and to understand how the concrete forms of global governance of the current epoch are related to those earlier ones, the method of abstraction is uniquely useful. Without it, we will not be able to come to terms conceptually with the sequence of episodes[3] that emerges from the consideration of these historical similarities and differences.

If we accept that the historical process produces breaks, transformations, we need a theory of social change. In historical materialism, this theory is grounded in the concept of *dialectics*. Fundamentally, this theory sees social reality as a dynamic totality and as a unity of opposites. Social development occurs through the unfolding of the contradictions that are in fact inherent in the social structures in question, and are not due to 'exogenous factors'. In the words of Lucien Sève, 'when the attempt to grasp the essence of things leads us invariably to contradiction, it is because contradiction is the essence of things' (1975: 676; my translation).

From this dialectical perspective, Marx equated the history of mankind – and this *dictum* has come to live a life of its own – with the history of class struggle. This statement can give rise (and has done so) to intense debate. Here, what needs to be highlighted is the specific meaning of the concept of social class. From the standpoint of historical materialism, any analysis of the world we live in must be grounded in an understanding of the way in which human beings have organized the production and reproduction of their material life. This in fact is what Marx understood by 'social': the totality of all activity undertaken by human beings towards the (re-)production of their existence.[4] The centrality of *class* can be established on the basis of this understanding. Class should thus not be seen as a narrow and exclusive concept that relegates the 'non-economic' to insignificance. On the contrary, class is a broad and inclusive concept that refers to the situation of human beings in the social relationships through which they structure the production and reproduction of their existence, and by which in turn they are constituted *as social beings*. These social relations of (re-)production are hierarchical and exploitative. They are furthermore guaranteed by the state: in the era of the dominance of *capitalist social relations*, they are guaranteed by the capitalist state. Although 'class' as an organizing concept is a broad and inclusive one, it does nevertheless enable us to escape the weaknesses of pluralism by relating 'politics' to the underlying social power structures.[5]

When next we consider the translation of 'class' into politics, the adoption of Gramsci in transnational historical materialism is of crucial importance. In developed and complex capitalist societies, the political power of the ruling class does not rest exclusively or primarily on the control of the coercive apparatus of the state, but is diffused and situated in myriad institutions and relationships in civil society. This form of class rule, hegemony, is based on consent, backed up only in the last instance by state coercion. Ideological and moral elements play a crucial role in cementing the historic bloc[6] and its hegemony in wider society (Gramsci 1971: 161, 168). Organic intellectuals of the dominant social groups formulate and disseminate these intellectual and moral ideas, transforming them into 'universal' ones that bind subordinate groups into the existing social order (e.g. Gramsci 1971: 181–2). The concept of hegemony thus defined is of key importance in discussions of 'global governance', since hegemony refers to exactly the same apparent plurality of 'sites of governance' that is recognized in much of the global governance literature but explicitly links this plurality to an underlying class-based exploitative hierarchy.

The final element of transnational historical materialism that is crucial to an understanding of the phenomenon of contemporary global governance is its emphasis on the transnational character of the capitalist system. What is meant here by *transnational?* Transnational processes, this essay maintains,[7] are *constituted in a social space transcending national borders* (i.e. their dynamics are not fundamentally defined by the existence of national boundaries; in the words of Samuel Huntington (1991) they take place 'in relative disregard of national borders') and take place *simultaneously* in subnational, national *and* international arenas. The 'national' thus ceases to be the primary constitutive dimension of social relations: an overarching and increasingly dominant globe-spanning network of social relations encapsulates local, national, international, and regional structures, dynamics and realities. In this sense, the traditional divide between 'domestic' and 'international' politics is less and less helpful in the analysis of contemporary politics.

In the remainder of this essay, I will attempt to offer some building blocks for a historical materialist analysis of global governance, in which the relationship between structure and process, between the structural condition and the agency of social forces in the global political economy, is understood as a dialectical one rather than as an either–or question. First, I present a brief historical overview of the development of modes of global governance in the capitalist world economy. Then in the following section I turn to a theoretization of the contemporary mode of *neo-liberal* global governance, before finally attempting to draw out some more general theoretical implications of the analysis of neo-liberal governance. By way of empirical example, each of these sections will refer to the evolving ways in which the issue of business taxation has been dealt with at the global level, as this issue presents a perfect illustration of the dynamics and determining factors I wish to highlight.

Historical modes of global governance

Global governance, we might say in a shorthand definition, is governance in the age of globalization. Globalization has been defined in a thousand and one ways, mostly highlighting one or the other epiphenomenal aspect. However, at a more abstract level, 'globalization' is about *commodification*, i.e. the process of transforming objects and activities into products and services that are sold on a market, thus into commodities. The decades since the late 1970s have shown a sudden and unprecedented process of deepening commodification, expressed in:

- the quantitative growth of existing forms of commodification (e.g. the growth of international trade and finance);
- the expansion of the market into previously non-market sectors in the capitalist economies (e.g. privatization of state firms);
- the incorporation of new politico-geographic regions into the capitalist world market and its networks of commodified interaction (the demise of the planned socialist economies);
- the subordination to market forces of spheres of human activity and existence that were hitherto not commodified in any real sense of the word at all (human reproduction, intellectual property, traditional medicine, etc.).

After decades of privatization and marketization, very few spheres of life on this planet remain shielded from the pursuit of private profit. Ultimately, this process is driven by capital's ceaseless search for profit: its search for cheap sources of circulating capital and labour, for new markets, for differential profit rates, for an escape from the internal contradictions of the capital–wage labor relation.

Commodification is not new to the world. In the past five hundred years it is possible to identify three episodes of intensified market expansion and deepening commodification: the episode of the original creation of the world market, which I will call the period of *mercantile globalization* (1492–1648); the expansion of industrial capital and the rise of imperialism in the second half of the nineteenth century, which I will call the era of *laissez-faire globalization* (1840s–1914); and finally the present episode of *neo-liberal globalization* characterized by the global expansion of transnational capital (1980s–present).[8] The best way to look at these episodes is as distinct periods characterized by intensified change in an historical process of much longer duration, namely the process of capitalist development that has engulfed the globe since the fifteenth century. Each of these waves of globalization has produced its own mode of (liberal) 'global governance' (e.g. Murphy 1994).

Modes of global governance in this chapter are viewed as *historical structures*, that is as

> particular combination[s] of thought patterns, material conditions, and human institutions which has a certain coherence among its elements. These structures do not determine people's actions in any mechanical sense but constitute the context of habits, pressures, expectations, and constraints within which action takes place.
>
> (Cox 1996: 97)[9]

A starting point guiding further analysis of these modes of global governance is the distinction between various fractions of capital and the particular hegemonic projects associated with such fractions. In volume 2 of *Capital* Marx considers the different functional forms that capital assumes in the circuits composing the overall reproductive circuit of capital: commodity capital, money capital and productive capital. In terms of concrete firms, merchant houses, financial firms and industry approximate these fractions.[10] Underlying this fractionalization is the even more fundamental distinction between fixed capital and circulating capital (loosely identifiable with productive capital and money capital respectively) (cf. Shortall 1986). In turn, this process of fractionalization of capital shapes class fractions which share common orientations, interest definitions and collective experiences. These provide ingredients for a coalition of interests aspiring to represent the 'general interest' of a class, supported by a broader social hegemony incorporating subordinate classes and social forces. In modern politics in capitalist societies, private and fractional interests tend to coagulate around

> largely implicit, but no less definite, common programs, or *comprehensive concepts of control*. Such concepts are political formulas that lend cohesion and cogency to the rule of particular classes and fractions of classes by translating idealized class and fractional viewpoints into a strategic orientation for society as a whole. Their capacity to be presented as a necessary and/or legitimate expression of the general interest derives from their basis in pivotal positions in the economy, which at particular junctures in the process of capital accumulation and social development acquire a relevance beyond this mere 'function'.
>
> (Van der Pijl 1989: 7–8)

These concepts of control are constituted around two prototypes, the money capital concept and the productive capital concept (reflecting the distinction between fixed and circulating capital). Usually those groups assert themselves most effectively whose specific group interests at a given juncture most closely correspond with the prevailing objective state of capital accumulation and class struggle (van der Pijl 1984: 33–4).

We must now see how the changing balance of forces between fractions of capital, the related succession of correspondingly dominant comprehensive concepts of control and the scale of operation of these various fractions of capital (in other words, the spatial coordinates of their specific reproductive cycles) interact to define the main characteristics of global capitalism in specific historical episodes. While money capital, abstractly as total capital, concretely as 'high finance', has operated on a cosmopolitan plane ever since the Middle Ages, production under its influence has operated on an only gradually widening scale. When the typical, or 'paradigmatic', scale of operation of industry coincided with the national state in the most important countries, a historically unique situation developed. Internationally operating money capital was subordinated to nationally operating productive capital, a development that reached its zenith in the 1930s and was only phased out slowly over the period 1945–1975.

Table 3.1 Paradigmatic scales of operation of capital and hegemonic concepts of control in modern capitalism

	Paradigmatic scale of operation#		Hegemonic concept
	Money capital	Productive capital	
1820s–1870s	cosmopolitan*	local	liberal internationalism
1870s–1914	cosmopolitan*	national	
1920s	cosmopolitan	national*	state monopolism
1930s	national	national*	
1950s	national	Atlantic*	corporate liberalism
1960s & 1970s	cosmopolitan	Atlantic*	
1980s & 1990s	cosmopolitan*	global & regional	neo-liberalism

Source: Overbeek and Van der Pijl 1993, p. 7.

Notes
* The asterisks mark the prevailing perspective (money or productive) in the hegemonic concept of control.
# Although both 'cosmopolitan' and 'global' indicate that the paradigmatic scale of operation encompasses the whole world, the difference is that money capital can disengage itself almost completely from any form of nation-state control, whereas productive capital, however globally operative, is always, at any particular moment in time, bound to specific physical/geographical locations, and therefore subject to state control.

Prior to this stage of the mobilization of the 'principle of social protection' in the context of the national state, industry operated on a subnational scale. Its output was marketed on a world market dominated by British industry, commerce and transport to such an extent that notions of universal free trade and harmony developed in Britain were also embraced in countries whose capacity to compete was undermined by unmitigated exposure. The era of the Pax Britannica spawned a comprehensive concept of control expressing and idealizing this state of affairs. Normalcy and the 'general interest' were predominantly defined therefore in terms of an abstract and cosmopolitan money capital perspective. The hegemonic concept of this era was *liberal internationalism*.

In the crisis of the 1970s, finally, a struggle ensued which resulted in the triumph of *neo-liberalism*. Neo-liberalism reaches back to the abstract and cosmopolitan money capital perspective so prominent in liberal internationalism, but industry has meanwhile outgrown its national confines. The paradigmatic scale of operation of industrial capital today is global, at least in tendency. At the same time we witness a relative disintegration of the national framework into multiple local and regional frameworks.

To illustrate the emerging mode of liberal global governance in this era, let us consider briefly the emergence of the transnational regulation of business taxation. During the late nineteenth and early twentieth centuries states were confronted for the first time with the impact of increased capital mobility on their tax systems. On the one hand, states began to introduce various schemes of direct taxation to finance their growing expenditures, while on the other hand capital internationalized rapidly (finance in particular, but productive capital as well). This brought to the fore the problem of *double taxation*, i.e. the same income being taxed by the country of residence as well as by the host country (where the income was being generated). Business pressure, through the International Chamber of Commerce in Paris, put the issue on the agenda of the Fiscal Committee of the League of Nations. In the early 1920s the Fiscal Committee commissioned a report, funded by the Rockefeller Foundation, to propose action (Picciotto 1991: 54–5). The report considered two alternative ways of approaching the problem, *formula apportionment* and the *arm's length principle*.

Formula apportionment entails the shared taxation of the total profits of a corporation, with a formula stipulating the respective shares for home and host (or capital exporting and capital importing) countries' governments. This approach was rejected in the report because it posed too many politically sensitive issues and would require a multilateral international agreement. The arm's length principle, which was the report's preferred solution, means that the activities by subsidiaries of corporations are considered essentially as separate businesses to be taxed by the host government. This principle thus requires negotiations between corporate officials and host government bureaucrats, which in many cases reinforces the already skewed balance of forces between weak governments and strong global corporations. The arm's length principle would eventually become the basis for the post-World War II international corporate taxation regime (Picciotto 1991: 55).

In the period from World War I to the 1950s the productive capital perspective (Polanyi's (1957) principle of social protection) was dominant at the national level; in this era, the hegemonic concept of control was that of *state monopolism*. Money capital was still principally engaged in international operations, but the crisis of the 1930s led to its curtailment by state authorities. Given the near collapse of the global economy, it is no surprise that the proposals of the Fiscal Committee of the League of Nations for the regulation of international business taxation were put on hold during this period. Regulation was primarily undertaken at the national level, in any case much more so than either before 1930 or after 1945.

Gradually, and definitely following World War II, (US) industry expanded on an Atlantic plane, albeit in a highly regulated setting. A welfare state concept, the highest form of Polanyi's principle of social protection constructed around the productive capital viewpoint, combined aspects of expanding production with a measure of reliberalization in the international sphere. Liberalization, however, was mostly restricted to trade in industrial products. Trade in agricultural products, and more importantly in services, as well as financial flows, were and remained heavily regulated and restricted. In theoretical terms, we may conclude that during this episode the hegemony of the productive capital view was overwhelming and subordinated the money capital perspective. The comprehensive concept defining the new normalcy and general interest at this stage was *corporate liberalism*. The new system of international business taxation accompanying corporate liberalism was eventually initiated with the wartime tax treaty concluded between the United States and the United Kingdom. This became the model after which a rapidly expanding network of bilateral taxation treaties was erected, primarily between and among the US, the UK, the English-speaking Commonwealth countries, and the major West European states. The co-ordination of this system, based on intergovernmental bilateralism mixed with the informal involvement of corporate lobby groups, was eventually entrusted not to a United Nations organ, but to the Fiscal Committee of the OECD (Braithwaite and Drahos 2000: 96–7). The structure of this system in many ways resembles and complements the structures of the Lockean heartland created in the second part of the nineteenth century in the form of the old Commonwealth and its symbiosis with the United States (cf. Van der Pijl 1989, 1998). The new system functioned without great difficulties in the era of 'embedded liberalism' (Ruggie 1998: 62–84) as corporate liberalism has also become known.

What interim conclusions can we draw from this brief exposition on historical modes of global governance? What is crucial to emphasize once more is that in our view a mode of global governance as historical structure captures the dialectic between structural properties of the global order on the one hand and the impact of the strategic agency of social forces, guided by comprehensive concepts of control, on the other. Nowhere can this better be illustrated than in the analysis of the latest mode of global governance, the neo-liberal one.

Neo-liberal global governance

In this section, I turn to an analysis of the conditions under which the global governance concept has risen to such ubiquitous popularity, and which social forces have 'hijacked' the notion and defined its politicized (neo-liberal) meaning. First I will take a brief look at the rise of neo-liberalism to hegemony in the 1970s and 1980s, if not globally then at least within the developed capitalist parts of the world, i.e. roughly speaking in the OECD world. Second, in order to analyse neo-liberal global governance a bit more theoretically, I look at some of the relevant concepts proposed by Robert Cox and Stephen Gill. Finally, I will again illustrate the main points through a brief exposé on the development of the global regime for business taxation in this period.

To trace the emergence of neo-liberalism and the latest globalization wave, we must go back to the 1970s (see also Overbeek and van der Pijl 1993 on this). With the crises in the 1970s of Fordism and the Keynesian welfare state as the catalysts, and with the rise of new technologies in transport, communication and information as enabling factors, a process of rapid internationalization of financial and productive capital was set in motion. This internationalization drive was pushed forward by successive state-led liberalization and deregulation offensives explicitly aimed at subordinating the global economy as well as the various national economies to the discipline of 'the markets'. The comprehensive concept of control that emerged as a response to this crisis has become known as *neo-liberalism*. Neo-liberalism elevates identifiable fractional interests to the level of a claimed 'general' interest: it expresses the outlook of *transnational circulating capital*, primarily international money capital but also an increasing proportion of the capital embodied by transnational industrial corporations as these became more and more dominated internally by financial managers rather than production engineers. The key to understanding the 'solution' to the crisis offered by neo-liberalism lies in the role that *money capital* as capital in general plays in the restructuring of both the spatial and technical aspects of production and the social relations of production, in order to adjust production to consumption, and restore profitability by raising the rate of exploitation and the mass of surplus value. Capital had to be liberated from all unnecessary constraints on its mobility before this restructuring could be undertaken. This 'general' capitalist interest was reasserted through the adoption of monetarism.

Monetarism holds that by making money scarce, inflation can be combated effectively and sound microeconomic reasoning can be forced upon the state and society as a whole. Although unpopular since the 1920s, it had always continued to attract the support of some economists, journalists and government officials, particularly in the USA and Britain. After 1945, it was propagated by a number of private transnational groups such as the Mont Pèlerin Society (inspired by Friedrich Hayek and Milton Friedman), and as the crisis of the 1970s deepened, its voice grew louder and succeeded in winning over more and more influential bodies. The monetarists scored important victories in Chile (with the rise to prominence of the 'Chicago boys' in 1975) and Britain (with Margaret Thatcher's emergence as the country's leader in 1979). The decisive turning point came when, also in 1979, Paul Volcker was appointed chairman of the US Federal Reserve Board and initiated a strict monetarist regime that drove up real interest rates in the US and the world economy. This rise of monetarism resulted in a rapid shift in the class structure away from the corporate-liberal pattern to an individualist one in which the interests of the rentier and the 'venture capitalist' were predominant. Rentier incomes rose, stock ownership was popularized through privatization and bank profits increased relative to those of industry. Investment banking and financial services became the hottest industries. In reaction to the tenets of the disintegrating corporate-liberal or Keynesian consensus of the years 1945–1971, neo-liberalism extolled the virtues of the free market and the withdrawal of the state from the management of the economy. Its core concepts and precepts (liberalization, privatization, deregulation and internationalization) as well as its new individualist ethic gradually became hegemonic and eclipsed traditional social democracy. The victory of neo-liberalism was even interpreted as the 'End of the Social-Democratic Century' (Dahrendorf 1990).

This process is not as straightforward as it might seem from this account. In fact, there is a complex and dialectical relationship between neo-liberalism as *process* and neo-liberalism as *project*. Certainly, there is such a thing as a neo-liberal project that is consciously and purposefully pushed by its protagonists (organic intellectuals, entrepreneurs and politicians, organizational representatives, etc.). This is where the agency of individuals such as Milton Friedman and organizations such as the Mont Pèlerin Society was crucial during the 1970s and 1980s, and this is where agents such as the *World Economic Forum* and others carried forward the neo-liberal onslaught in the 1990s (cf. van der Pijl 1998). But of course, as critics of this approach will quickly point out, these programmes have never been simply put into practice lock, stock and barrel. A hegemonic project or comprehensive concept of control is shaped, and continuously reshaped, in a process of struggle, compromise and re-adjustment, resulting in 'a succession of negotiated settlements, of concessions to the rigidities and dynamics of structures as well as the political possibilities of the moment' (Drainville 1994: 116). Eventually we have seen a form of *consolidation* of neo-liberalism, internationally as well as within the advanced industrial countries. Any notion of an alternative to the global rule of capital became utterly 'unrealistic' and discredited and neo-liberal reforms were 'locked-in' and 'normalized'. The significance of the demise of real socialism in this respect cannot be overstated (Mishra 1999: 111–112): until its definitive discomfiture and disintegration the mere existence of an alternative economic and social system provided an incentive for the capitalist class in the West to accommodate the working class. With the demise of real socialism this incentive lost its force, opening up political space for a more radical overhaul of the structures of corporate-liberalism (see also Overbeek 2003).

In terms of theoretically grasping the new structure of the global system and the nature of neo-liberal global governance, a convenient and inspiring reference point is the concept of the 'internationalization of the state' (Cox 1996: 107). In this article Cox analysed the mechanisms for maintaining hegemony in the era of *Pax Americana* and argued that the internationalization of the state is associated with the expansion of international production. He later defined it as the process through which 'the nation state becomes part of a larger and more complex political structure that is the counterpart to international production' (Cox 1987: 253). The process can be expressed in three points:

- a process of interstate consensus formation regarding the needs or requirements of the world economy that takes place within a common ideological framework;
- participation in this consensus formation is hierarchically structured;
- the internal structures of states are adjusted so that each can best transform the global consensus into national policy and practice, with 'state structure' both referring to the machinery of government and to the historic bloc (the

alignment of dominant and acquiescent social groups) on which the state
rests.

(Cox 1987: 254)

It is, says Cox, 'increasingly pertinent to think in terms of a global class structure
alongside or superimposed upon national class structures' (Cox 1996: 111; emphasis
added). At the apex of this emerging global class structure is the 'transnational
managerial class' situated in the higher echelons of the Trilateral Commission,
the World Bank and IMF, and the OECD. The members develop a common
framework of thought and guidelines for policies that are disseminated through
the process of the internationalization of the state (Cox 1996: 111; see also
Sklair 2001 for a recent study). In peripheral areas the financial power exercised
by the IMF and the World Bank, which was tremendously intensified after
the debt crisis of the 1980s, often serves to impose or restore the discipline of the
market where it is lacking or weakening. The collapse of the Soviet Union and
the subsequent transformation of the global state system have eliminated many
obstacles to the further expansion of markets through the enhanced global reach
of transnational capital. The priorities of economic and social policies world-
wide have been recast to reflect the new dominance of investors. International
institutions (such as OECD, IMF, World Bank and WTO) and groupings of
dominant states (G7) are engaged in the legal and political reproduction of this
disciplinary neo-liberalism and ensure through a variety of regulatory, surveillance
and policing mechanisms that neo-liberal reforms are *locked in* (cf. Gill 1995; the
disciplinary dimensions of neo-liberal global governance are also central to
Duffield's recent study, Duffield 2001). In the core areas of the world economy
this discipline appears in the shape of 'voluntary' programs of competitive
deregulation and austerity that are codified in such arrangements as the EMU
stability pact or the WTO liberalization regime. Stephen Gill refers to the
erosion of democratic control implied in this process as *New Constitutionalism*, '...
the move towards construction of legal or constitutional devices to remove
or insulate substantially the new economic institutions from popular scrutiny or
democratic accountability' (Gill 1992: 165).

Again, developments in the area of global business taxation may serve as
illustration. In the 1970s the first cracks began to appear in the international
fiscal system. The spread of multinational corporations posed increasing problems for national fiscal authorities (cf. Murray 1975). These difficulties were
intensified by the growing importance of tax havens. Tax havens in a sense
emerged in the 1920s as a consequence of some states, primarily Switzerland,
not following in the footsteps of the other industrial countries in joining the
emerging international fiscal order (cf. Palan & Abbott 1996; Palan 1998;
Picciotto 1999). At that time, 'tax havens' really were anachronistic phenomena.
However, after the collapse of the Bretton Woods system in 1971 and the relax-
ation of capital controls, new tax havens and other 'off-shore financial centers'
were created, primarily in the Caribbean but in Europe as well (Jersey, Gibraltar,
and Luxembourg). As tariffs on imports fell under the impact of successive

GATT trade liberalizations, the incentives to compete through taxes increased further (Tanzi 1996). Under these changing conditions being a 'tax haven' became a deliberate strategy for state-like entities and statelets whose survival in the inter-state system is now reproduced and expanded by interested parties and indeed by the state system itself (Palan 1998).

The logic of the international tax competition that ensued threatened to destabilize the 'orderly' conduct of transnational business (for instance by facilitating the increasing penetration of the international financial system by organized transnational crime) and would indeed ultimately lead to the complete elimination of corporate taxation. In response, governments in the OECD area agreed that something would have to be done to eradicate the worst abuses and protect the legitimacy of the tax system. Both in the EU and in the OECD this resulted in discussions over a 'voluntary' code of conduct for governments. The OECD published a report on the issue in 1998 (OECD 1998), and held a conference in December 1998 to consider measures to curb 'harmful tax competition' in the form of a voluntary code of conduct (cf. Nettinga 1999, and Weiner and Ault 1998). In its follow-up report (OECD 2000) the OECD made a beginning with identifying 'uncooperative' tax havens and with listing possible countermeasures. In itself, this line of action is not very impressive: voluntary codes of conduct in the regulation of global business are generally characterized by ineffectiveness and mostly serve a legitimating function (van der Pijl 1993). They do illustrate however that neo-liberal de-regulation leads to re-regulation of a specific kind, involving a new mix of public, semi-public and private actors and institutions that are brought together in national, regional and global forums and networks (Picciotto 1999: 64–6; see also Cerny 1991). This system tends to 'legitimize the continued existence of the offshore system for avoidance which has not been stigmatized, especially tax. However, tax avoidance depends on facilities such as corporate and banking secrecy, which undermine regulatory cooperation on other matters' (Picciotto 1999: 70). Such policy convergence as does take place within the OECD area comes about primarily through emulation rather than international agreement. It continues to be based on the arm's length principle that ignores the integrated nature of transnational corporations and thus continues to place them in a privileged position vis-à-vis the tax authorities.

Some final theoretical considerations

The concept of global governance has acquired its popularity in the years of intensifying globalization since the early 1980s. The previous sections have argued that our understanding of this concept must be historicized and must be made 'class sensitive'. Our shorthand definition of global governance (governance in the age of globalization) must therefore be expanded by reference to a number of historically specific characteristics to make it applicable to an analysis of the *contemporary* wave of globalization.

Governance in the contemporary global political economy is increasingly characterized by *informalization* and *transnationalization* or, put differently, by the creation of additional formal and informal structures of authority and sovereignty besides and beyond the state. Institutions such as the International Monetary Fund and the World Trade Organization have achieved a considerable degree of autonomy from the national governments that nominally control their executives, while more informal organizations such as the G-7 or the World Economic Forum play a crucial role in formulating longer-term strategic policy orientations. Equally striking is the multiplicity of governance sites and modes involving any combination of intergovernmental and trans-governmental regulation, 'public-private' regimes, and forms of private authority and self-regulation.[11] The emergence of these new structures, often combining public and private forces, has led Robert Cox to his famous phrase of a global *nébuleuse* (Cox 1996: 298).

The role of international organizations such as the OECD, the IMF and others in providing direction to this *nébuleuse* is noteworthy. These organizations more frequently than not have no formal regulatory powers, they cannot impose their will on states (not on non-members, but neither on their own member states), and they have few or no sanctioning powers. Nevertheless their influence and prestige are enormous and most governments in the world are willing, albeit reluctantly, to comply with their 'recommendations'. Their primary role often is that of progenitor of ideas, which they successfully spread through bringing together senior civil servants, business executives, and technical specialists in working groups and conferences that give real substance to the concept of epistemic community (Strange 1996: 62). The role of civil servants of international organizations in this context is also striking. For instance, the role of top officials in the IMF's Fiscal Affairs Department (Vito Tanzi, Howard Zee) in the campaign in favor of the establishment of an International Tax Organization to regulate global tax competition and look after the states' fiscal soundness is a case in point. It indeed provides an eloquent illustration of the role that Kees van der Pijl sees the *cadre class* (the social stratum of managers both in the private business world and in public service) playing:

> The cadres are oriented, by definition, to sustaining social cohesion and the integrity of the social [...] substratum exploited by capital. Even if, as in neo-liberalism, the dominant orientation is towards deepening the discipline of capital, the function of providing cohesion cannot be abandoned.
>
> (Van der Pijl 1998: 163)

Elsewhere (see Pellerin and Overbeek 2001) we have attempted to clarify in some detail what functions these informal and quasi-formal forums (or 'processes') perform. It would seem that these include at least the following:

- *Communication*: they serve as channels for communication between policy-makers, experts, and interested third parties. This is especially important for those countries (e.g. several of the CIS countries) whose officials have little or no direct contact with their counterparts in the OECD world;

- *Socialization*: they further serve to socialize the officials, experts and policy-makers of peripheral states into the existing global epistemic communities;
- *Institutionalization*: they help to secure the desired (neo-liberal) policy reforms within the (semi-) peripheral states (this process is called *locking in*);
- *Integration*: in the case of the relationship between the OECD and the European Union on the one hand and a number of the Central and East European states on the other, these forums are clearly complementary to the ongoing accession process and prepare the ground for ultimate full membership of the EU and the wider OECD world.

Contemporary global governance is not just process; it is also substance. It is *neo-liberal* global governance. Its 'social purpose' (Ruggie 1998: 62–72) is dictated by the imperatives of capital accumulation on a world scale. This social purpose transpired clearly in the example of the governance of international business taxation. As we have seen, the international system of tax regulation, which emerged in the 1920s and served its purpose relatively well until the 1970s, has in recent decades come under increasing competitive pressures. The existing system heavily privileges mobile (especially financial) capital and allows transnational capital to circumvent or evade taxation practically without sanction. Such regulation as does exist is based on voluntary forms of self-regulation, while no formal international organization exists with regulatory powers to impose a decent tax ethic on capital. The requirements of global freedom of movement for capital dictate the shape and form of global governance in the tax sphere, in which various inter-governmental and international non-governmental organizations play key roles.

In sum: our explorations have shown that neo-liberal global governance in large part functions to make market reforms irreversible through inscribing them into, and anchoring them deeply in, the legal systems of most countries. Global governance constitutionalizes private property rights, guarantees the unhindered mobility of capital, and controls and subordinates potentially rebellious social forces and states. The concept of global governance thus has suffered the same fate of other initially progressive normative concepts such as 'new international economic order' or 'sustainable development': it has been hijacked by social forces that have emptied it of its counter-hegemonic content and redefined it in such a way that the concept in fact supports the further consolidation of the world-wide rule of capital.

Notes

1 'The principle of historical specificity', wrote C. Wright Mills (commenting on Marx), 'leads us to see that conceptions and categories are not eternal, but are relative to the epoch which they concern' (1977: 39).
2 A more extended account of transnational historical materialism can be found in Overbeek (2000). See also Gill (1993) and Rupert and Smith (2002). The term was originally coined by Gill and Law (1988).
3 I try to avoid using terms like 'cycles', 'stages' or 'phases' which are all tainted with connotations leading us into debates that are not pertinent for our present purposes.

For an excellent collection of essays precisely on these questions see Albritton *et al.* 2001.

4   This is brought out very clearly in *The German Ideology*: 'The first presupposition of all human history is of course the existence of living human individuals. ... [Human beings] begin to distinguish themselves from the animals as soon as they begin to *produce* their means of existence. ... The creation of life, current life through labor and new life through procreation, immediately reveals itself as a social relation – social in the sense that it implies the collaboration of various people, irrespective of the conditions, the manner and the objective' (Marx and Engels, 1974: 21, 30; my translation).

5   Historical specificity, dialectics and the primacy of social relations are the key ingredients of Robert Cox's notion of *historical structures* to which I will return below (Cox 1996: 85–123).

6   In Cox's words, 'historic bloc' refers to 'a configuration of social forces upon which state power rests' (1987: 105; also 6 and 409, n. 10).

7   This interpretation was developed at somewhat greater length in a recent article (see Overbeek 2003).

8   This periodization is derived from various other periodizations in the literature, such as those by Mandel in his *Late Capitalism* (1975) or by Zürn (1995), which are roughly similar though certainly not the same. See Lysandrou (forthcoming) for a similar approach.

9   The concept thus reminds us of Marx's statement that men make their own history, but that they do so in conditions that are not of their own choosing.

10 Cf. Van der Pijl 1984: 1–20 and 1998, 49–63; also Overbeek 1990: 23–29, 176–181.

11 For recent overviews of the role of private authority in global governance see Cutler *et al.* 1999; Higgott *et al.* 2000; Hall and Biersteker 2002.

References

Albritton, R., Itoh, M., Westra, R. and Zuege, A. (eds) (2001) *Phases of Capitalist Development. Booms, Crises and Globalizations*, Houndmills: Palgrave.

Behrens, M. (ed.) (2002) *Global Governance: Probleme, Konzepte, Kritik*, Hagen: Fernuniversität.

Braithwaite, J. and Drahos, P. (2000) *Global Business Regulation*, Cambridge: Cambridge University Press.

Cerny, P.G. (1991) 'The limits of deregulation: transnational interpenetration and policy change', *European Journal of Political Research*, 19: 173–196.

Commission on Global Governance (1995) *Our Global Neighborhood*, Oxford: Oxford University Press.

Cox, R.W. (1987) *Production, Power, and World Order. Social Forces in the Making of History*, New York: Columbia University Press.

Cox, R.W., with Sinclair, T.J. (1996) *Approaches to World Order*, Cambridge: Cambridge University Press.

Cutler, A.C., Haufler, V. and Porter, T. (eds) (1999) *Private Authority and International Affairs*, Albany: State University of New York Press.

Dahrendorf, R. (1990) *Reflections on the Revolution in Europe*, London: Chatto and Windus.

Drainville, A. (1994) 'International political economy in the age of open Marxism', *Review of International Political Economy*, 1: 105–132.

Duffield, M. (2001) *Global Governance and the New Wars. The Merging of Development and Security*, London: Zed Books.

Gill, S.R. (1992) 'Economic globalization and the internationalization of authority: limits and contradictions', *Geoforum*, 23: 269–283.

—— (1993) *Gramsci, Historical Materialism and International Relations*, Cambridge: Cambridge University Press.

—— (1995) 'Globalisation, market civilization and disciplinary neoliberalism', *Millennium: Journal of International Studies*, 24: 299–423.

Gramsci, A. (1971) *Selections from the Prison Notebooks*, New York: International Publishers.

Hall, R.B. and Biersteker, T.J. (eds) (2002) *The Emergence of Private Authority in Global Governance*, Cambridge: Cambridge University Press.

Held, D. and McGrew, A. (eds) (2002) *Governing Globalization. Power, Authority and Global Governance*, Oxford: Polity Press.

Higgott, R.A., Underhill, G.R.D. and Bieler, A. (eds) (2000) *Non-state Actors and Authority in the Global System*, London: Routledge.

Holman, O., Overbeek, H. and Ryner, M. (eds) (1998) 'Neoliberal hegemony and the political economy of European restructuring' (2 vols), *International Journal of Political Economy*, 28(1–2).

Huntington, S.P. (1991) 'Transnational organizations in world politics', in R. Little and M. Smith (eds) *Perspectives on World Politics*, London: Routledge.

Kooiman, J. (2003) *Governing as Governance*, London: Sage.

Lake, D.A. (1999), 'Global governance: a relational contracting approach', in A. Prakash and J.A. Hart (eds) *Globalization and Governance*, London: Routledge.

Lysandrou, P. (forthcoming) 'Globalization as commodification', *Cambridge Journal of Economics*.

Mandel, E. (1975) *Late Capitalism*, London: Verso Books.

Marx, K. (1973) *The Grundrisse*, Harmondsworth: Penguin.

—— (1979) *Capital*, Harmondsworth: Penguin.

Marx, K. and Engels, F. (1974) *De Duitse Ideologie deel 1*, Nijmegen: SUN.

Mills, C. W. (1977) *The Marxists*, Harmondsworth: Penguin.

Mishra, R. (1999) *Globalisation and the Welfare State*, Cheltenham: Edward Elgar.

Murphy, C.N. (1994) *International Organization and Industrial Change. Global Governance since 1850*, Cambridge: Polity Press.

Murray, R. (1975) *Multinational Companies and Nation States*, Nottingham: Spokesman Books.

Nettinga, M. (1999) 'Conference discusses initiatives to curb harmful tax competition', *European Taxation*, 39: 37–39.

OECD (Organization for Economic Cooperation and Development) (1998) *Harmful Tax Competition: An Emerging Global Issue*, Paris: OECD.

—— (2000) *Towards Global Tax Co-operation. Report to the 2000 Ministerial Council Meeting and Recommendations by the Committee on Fiscal Affairs*, Paris: OECD.

Overbeek, H.W. (ed.) (1993) *Restructuring Hegemony in the Global Political Economy: the Rise of Transnational Neo-liberalism in the 1980s*, London: Routledge.

—— (2000) 'Transnational historical materialism: theories of transnational class formation and world order', in R.P. Palan (ed.) *Global Political Economy. Contemporary Theories*, London: Routledge.

—— (2003) 'Transnational political economy and the politics of European (un)employment: introducing the themes', in H.W. Overbeek (ed.) *The Political Economy of European Employment: European Integration and the Transnationalization of the (Un)employment Question*, London: Routledge.

Overbeek, H.W. and van der Pijl, K. (1993) 'Restructuring capital and restructuring hegemony: neo-liberalism and the unmaking of the post-war order', in H.W. Overbeek (ed.) *Restructuring Hegemony in the Global Political Economy: the Rise of Transnational Neo-liberalism in the 1980s*, London: Routledge.

Palan, R.P. (1998), 'Trying to have your cake and eating it: how and why the state system has created offshore', *International Studies Quarterly*, 42: 625–644.

Palan, R.P. and Abbott, J., with P. Deans (1996) *State Strategies in the Global Political Economy*, London: Pinter.

Picciotto, S. (1991) 'The internationalisation of the state', *Capital and Class*, 43: 43–64.

—— (1999) 'Offshore: the state as legal fiction', in M. Hampton and J. Abbott (eds) *Offshore Finance Centres and Tax Havens: The Rise of Global Capital*, Houndsmill: Macmillan.

Polanyi, K. (1957) *The Great Transformation: The Political and Economic Origins of Our Time*, Boston: Beacon Press.

Pijl, K. van der (1984) *The Making of an Atlantic Ruling Class*, London: Verso Books.

—— (ed.) (1989) 'Transnational relations and class strategy,' *International Journal of Political Economy*, 19(3).

—— (1993) 'The sovereignty of capital impaired: social forces and codes of conduct for multinational corporations', in H. Overbeek (ed.) *The Political Economy of European Employment. European Integration and the Transnationalization of the (Un)employment Question*, London: Routledge.

—— (1998) *Transnational Classes and International Relations*, London: Routledge.

Rhodes, R.A.W. (1996) 'The new governance: governing without government', *Political Studies*, 44: 652–657.

Rosenau, J.N. (1992) 'Governance, order, and change in world politics', in J. Rosenau and E.-O. Czempiel (eds) *Governance Without Government: Order and Change in World Politics*, Cambridge: Cambridge University Press.

—— (2002) 'Governance in a new global order', in D. Held and A. McGrew (eds) *Governing Globalization. Power, Authority and Global Governance*, Oxford: Polity Press.

Rosenau, J.N., and Czempiel, E.-O. (eds) (1992) *Governance Without Government: Order and Change in World Politics*, Cambridge: Cambridge University Press.

Ruggie, J.G. (1998) *Constructing the World Polity. Essays on International Institutionalization*, London: Routledge.

Rupert, M. and Smith, H. (eds) (2002) *Historical Materialism and Globalisation*, London: Routledge.

Sève, L. (1975) 'De methode in de ekonomiese wetenschap', *Te Elfder Ure*, 17: 671–690 (translated from the French original in *La Nouvelle Critique*, 71, Feb. 1974, 27–36).

Sklair, L. (2001) *The Transnational Capitalist Class*, Oxford: Blackwell.

Strange, S. (1996) *The Retreat of the State. The Diffusion of Power in the World Economy*, Cambridge: Cambridge University Press.

Tanzi, V. (1996) *Globalization, Tax Competition and the Future of Tax Systems*, IMF Working Paper 96/141–EA.

Weiner, J.M., and Ault, H.J. (1998) 'The OECD's report on harmful tax competition', *National Tax Journal*, 51: 601–608.

Zürn, M. (1995) 'The challenge of globalisation and individualisation: a view from Europe', in H.H. Holm and G. Sørensen (eds) *Whose World Order? Uneven Globalisation and the End of the Cold War*, Boulder: Westview.

4 Global governance and hegemony in the modern world system

Giovanni Arrighi

Global governance in world-systems perspective

In world-systems analysis the notion of "governance" (global or otherwise) has been used to designate the purposive regulation and direction that particular states and international organizations have exercised on interstate relations. As such, governance is an integral aspect of the concept of "world hegemony" understood in the Gramscian sense of the additional power that accrues to a dominant group by virtue of its capacity to lead society in a direction that serves the dominant group's interests but is perceived by subordinate groups as serving also a more general interest (Gramsci 1971: 181–2). World hegemonies thus understood have been key ingredients in the formation, reproduction, and eventual transformation of the modern world system from a regional (that is, European) system into a global system. As the system became global (starting in the nineteenth century), so did governance (Arrighi 1994; Arrighi and Silver 1999 and 2001).

Within the world-system perspective, this Gramscian conceptualization is the exception rather than the rule. The rule remains Immanuel Wallerstein's conceptualization of the modern world system as a quantitatively expanding but structurally invariant anarchic/competitive system. In this conceptualization, hegemonies neither transform the system nor involve governance (cf. Wallerstein 1984 and Arrighi and Silver 1999: 22–6). In this respect, the concept of world hegemony that my co-authors and I have been deploying within world-systems analysis resembles the concept of hegemony that a great variety of scholars have derived from Antonio Gramsci (see, among others, Cox 1983, 1987; Gill 1986, 1993; Gill and Law 1988; Overbeek 1993; Rupert 1995; Robinson 1996; Soederberg 2005). Nevertheless, unlike these scholars, we concur with Wallerstein that the structures and processes of the contemporary world system can only be understood in light of the system's entire lifetime, from its earliest beginnings in early modern Europe to the present.

As we shall see in the next sections of the essay, our particular variant of world-systems analysis generates an account of system-wide hegemonies and governance that departs in key respects from the accounts generated within the tradition that Henk Overbeek (2003) calls "transnational historical materialism."

Like theorists working within this tradition we find it useful to conceive of the modern world system as a capitalist system. We nonetheless find that patterns typical of contemporary capitalism—most notably, processes of so-called financialization and interstate competition for mobile capital—have characterized the modern world system long before world capitalism became a mode of production, as it did in the late eighteenth and early nineteenth centuries. In order to subject these patterns to a comprehensive analysis, we find it more useful to define world capitalism not as a mode of production—as transnational historical materialism scholars do—but as a mode of accumulation and rule that at a particular stage of its development became also a mode of production.

In outlining the main features of this particular account of the nature, origins and evolution of world capitalism as mode of accumulation and rule, I shall begin by focussing on the main structural characteristics of the successive hegemonies with which world capitalism has been associated. These structural characteristics include, first, the scale, scope, and complexity of the successive regimes of accumulation in which the expanding European (and eventually global) interstate system has been embedded, and second, the particular historic bloc of governmental and business organizations that exercised a hegemonic role in the formation and regulation of these regimes. I shall then turn in the following section to outline the processes through which each of these regimes emerged, consolidated, and was eventually superseded by regimes of greater scale, scope, and complexity. On the basis of this analysis, in the concluding section I will assess the nature and likely future trajectories of whatever global governance is extant in the contemporary world.

The structures of governance in the modern world system

System-level governance on an increasing and eventually global scale has been a fundamental enabling condition of the enlarged reproduction of the modern world system. This expansion of the scale of system-level governance has not been a continuous process. Rather, it has come about through fundamental transformations in the organization of the modern world system itself—that is, in the way in which the system has been structured and in the governmental and business institutions that have provided whatever regulation and direction were necessary for the system to reproduce itself on an increasing scale. I shall later discuss the dynamic of these transformations. For now I will focus exclusively on the distinct agencies and structures that have succeeded one another in promoting systemic expansion.

As argued in detail elsewhere, the recurrence of alternating phases of material expansion—in the course of which capital accumulates primarily through investment in trade and production—and phases of financial expansion—in the course of which capital accumulates primarily through investment in property titles and other claims on future incomes—enables us to identify four successive "systemic cycles of accumulation," each characterized by a distinct leading

agency and organization. A comparison of these distinct agencies and organizations reveals, not only that they are different, but also that the sequence of these
differences describes an evolutionary pattern towards regimes of increasing size,
scope and complexity (Arrighi 1994). This evolutionary pattern is summed up in
Figure 4.1 (Figure 4.1 and what follows in this section are taken from Arrighi and
Silver 2001: 264–68). The first column of Figure 4.1 focuses on the "containers
of power"—as Anthony Giddens (1987) has aptly characterized states—that
have housed the "headquarters" of the leading capitalist agencies of the successive regimes: the Republic of Genoa, the United Provinces, the United
Kingdom, and the United States.

At the time of the rise and full expansion of the Genoese regime, the Republic
of Genoa was a city-state small in size and simple in organization, which
contained very little power indeed. Yet, thanks to its far-flung commercial and
financial networks the Genoese capitalist class, organized in a cosmopolitan dias-
pora, could deal on a par with the most powerful territorialist rulers of Europe,
and turn the relentless competition for mobile capital among these rulers into a
powerful engine for the self-expansion of its own capital. At the time of the rise
and full expansion of the Dutch regime of accumulation, the United Provinces
was a hybrid kind of organization that combined some of the features of the
disappearing city-states with some of the features of the rising nation-states. The
greater power of the Dutch state relative to the Genoese enabled the Dutch capitalist class to do what the Genoese had already been doing—turn interstate
competition for mobile capital into an engine for the self-expansion of its own
capital—but without having to "buy" protection from territorialist states, as the
Genoese had done through a relationship of political exchange with Iberian
rulers. The Dutch regime, in other words, "internalized" the protection costs that
the Genoese had "externalized" (see Figure 4.1, column 4).

At the time of the rise and full expansion of the British regime of accumulation, the United Kingdom was not only a fully developed nation-state. It was also
in the process of conquering a world-encompassing commercial and territorial
empire that gave its ruling groups and its capitalist class a command over the
world's human and natural resources without parallel or precedent. This
command enabled the British capitalist class to do what the Dutch had already
been able to do—turn to its own advantage interstate competition for mobile
capital and "produce" all the protection required by the self-expansion of its
capital—but without having to rely on foreign and often hostile territorialist
organizations for most of the agro-industrial production on which the profitability of its commercial activities rested. If the Dutch regime relative to the
Genoese had internalized protection costs, the British regime relative to the
Dutch internalized production costs as well (see Figure 4.1, column 5). As a
consequence of this internalization, world capitalism continued to be a mode of
accumulation and rule but became also a mode of production.

Finally, at the time of the rise and full expansion of the US regime of accumulation, the US was already something more than a fully developed
nation-state. It was a continental military-industrial complex with sufficient

Figure 4.1 Evolutionary Patterns of World Capitalism

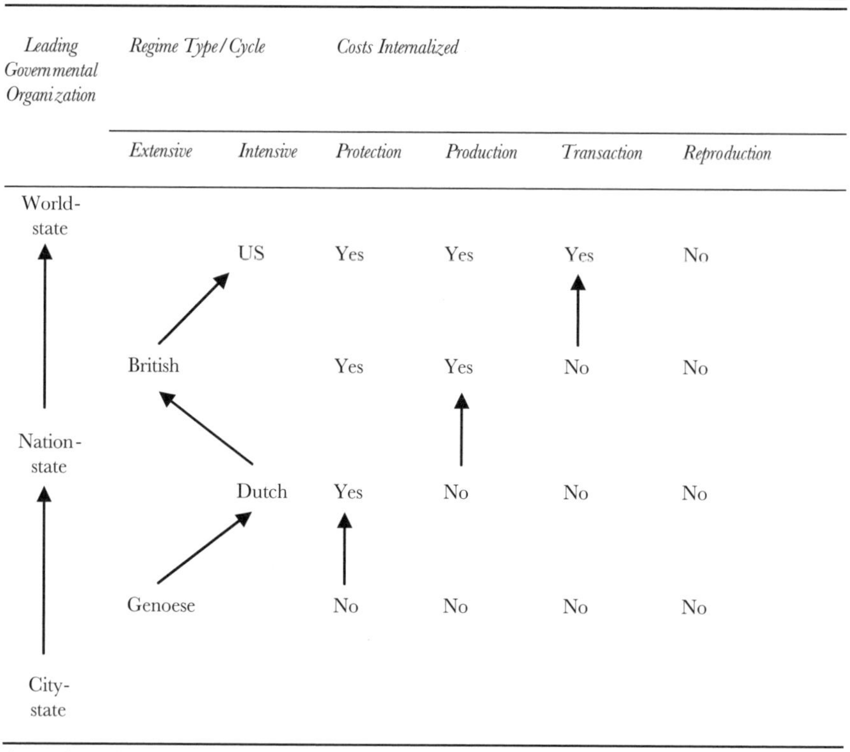

Leading Governmental Organization	Regime Type/Cycle		Costs Internalized			
	Extensive	Intensive	Protection	Production	Transaction	Reproduction
World-state		US	Yes	Yes	Yes	No
	British		Yes	Yes	No	No
Nation-state						
		Dutch	Yes	No	No	No
	Genoese		No	No	No	No
City-state						

Source: Arrighi and Silver (2001: 265)

power to provide a wide range of subordinate and allied governments with effective protection and to make credible threats of economic strangulation or military annihilation towards unfriendly governments anywhere in the world. Combined with the size, insularity, and natural wealth of its domestic territory, this power enabled the US capitalist class to internalize not just protection and production costs—as the British capitalist class had already done—but transaction costs as well, that is to say, the markets on which the self-expansion of its capital depended (see Figure 4.1, column 6).

This steady increase in the size, scope and complexity of successive regimes of capital accumulation on a world scale is somewhat obscured by another feature of the temporal sequence of such regimes. This feature is a double movement, forward and backward at the same time. For each step forward in the process of internalization of costs by a new regime of accumulation has involved a revival of governmental and business strategies and structures that had been superseded by the preceding regime. Thus, the internalization of protection costs by the Dutch regime in comparison with the Genoese regime occurred through a revival of the strategies and structures of Venetian state monopoly capitalism that the Genoese regime had superseded. Similarly, the internalization of production costs by the British regime in comparison with the Dutch regime occurred through a revival in new and more complex forms of the strategies and structures of Genoese cosmopolitan capitalism and Iberian global territorialism. And the same pattern recurred once again with the rise and full expansion of the US regime, which internalized transaction costs by reviving in new and more complex forms the strategies and structures of Dutch corporate capitalism (see Figure 4.1, columns 1 and 2).

This recurrent revival of previously superseded strategies and structures of accumulation generates a pendulum-like movement back and forth between "cosmopolitan-imperial" and "corporate-national" organizational structures, the first being typical of "extensive" regimes—as the Genoese–Iberian and the British were—and the second of "intensive" regimes—as the Dutch and the US were. The Genoese–Iberian and British "cosmopolitan-imperial" regimes were extensive in the sense that they have been responsible for most of the geographical expansion of the modern world system. Under the Genoese regime, the world was "discovered," and under the British it was "conquered." The Dutch and the US "corporate-national" regimes, in contrast, were intensive in the sense that they have been responsible for the geographical consolidation rather than expansion of the modern world system. Under the Dutch regime, the "discovery" of the world realized primarily by the Iberian partners of the Genoese was consolidated into an Amsterdam-centered system of commercial entrepots and joint-stock chartered companies. And under the US regime, the "conquest" of the world realized primarily by the British themselves was consolidated into a US-centered system of national states and transnational corporations.

This alternation of extensive and intensive regimes blurs our perception of the underlying, truly long-term, tendency towards the formation of regimes of increasing size, scope and complexity. When the pendulum swings in the direction of extensive regimes, the underlying trend is magnified, and when it swings in the direction of intensive regimes, the underlying trend appears to have been less significant than it really was. Nevertheless, once we control for these swings by comparing the two intensive and the two extensive regimes with one another—the Genoese–Iberian with the British, and the Dutch with the US—the underlying trend becomes unmistakable.

The development of historical capitalism as a world system has thus been based on the formation of ever more powerful cosmopolitan-imperial (or corporate-national) blocs of governmental and business organizations endowed with the capacity to widen (or deepen) the functional and spatial scope of the world capitalist system. And yet, the more powerful these blocs have become, the shorter the life-cycle of the regimes of accumulation that they have brought into being—the shorter, that is, the time that it has taken for these regimes to emerge out of the crisis of the preceding dominant regime, to become themselves dominant, and to attain their limits as signaled by the beginning of a new financial expansion. Relying on Braudel's dating of the beginning of financial expansions, this time was less than half both in the case of the British regime relative to the

Genoese and in the case of the US regime relative to the Dutch (Arrighi and Silver 1994: 216–17).

This pattern of capitalist development, whereby an increase in the power of regimes of accumulation is associated with a decrease in their duration, calls to mind Marx's contention that "*the real barrier* of capitalist production is *capital itself*" and that capitalist production continually overcomes its immanent barriers "only by means which again place these barriers in its way on a more formidable scale" (1962: 244–5). But the contradiction between the self-expansion of capital on the one side, and the development of the material forces of production and of an appropriate world market on the other, can in fact be reformulated in even more general terms than Marx did. For historical capitalism as world system of accumulation became a "mode of production"—that is, it internalized production costs—only in its third (British) stage of development. And yet, the principle that the real barrier of capitalist development is capital itself, that the self-expansion of existing capital is in constant tension, and recurrently enters in open contradiction, with the expansion of world trade and production and the creation of an appropriate world market—all this was clearly at work already in the Genoese and Dutch stages of development, notwithstanding the continuing externalization of agro-industrial production by their leading agencies.

In all instances the contradiction is that the expansion of world trade and production was a mere means in endeavors aimed primarily at increasing the value of capital and yet, over time, it tended to drive down the rate of profit and thereby curtail the value of capital. Thanks to their continuing centrality in networks of high finance, the established organizing centers are best positioned to turn the intensifying competition for mobile capital to their advantage, and thereby reflate their profits and power at the expense of the rest of the system. From this point of view, the reflation of US profits and power in the 1990s follows a pattern that has been typical of world capitalism from its earliest beginnings (Arrighi and Silver 1999: 272–5). Does the persistence of this long established pattern mean that the still-dominant US regime is in the process of being replaced by another regime, as all its predecessors sooner or later were? In order to answer this question, we must turn to the dynamics of hegemonic transitions, focussing specifically on the novelties of present transformations.

The dynamics of systemic transformations

The exercise of system-level governance by the agencies and through the structures depicted in Figure 4.1 has been a highly discontinuous process that has waxed and waned with the rise and decline of world hegemonies. My co-authors and I have developed a model of this process by comparing three successive hegemonic transitions from four distinct angles of vision: geopolitics, business organization, social conflict, and inter-civilizational relations. According to this model (see Figure 4.2), hegemonic states *lead* and *govern* a system which they *reconstruct* after a period of fundamental and seemingly irremediable disorganization—what we call "systemic chaos" (for a detailed discussion of the model, see Arrighi and Silver 1999: 26–35; and Arrighi and Silver 2001: 261–71).

Historically, particular states have been able to play this hegemonic role—as the United Provinces did in the mid-seventeenth century, the United Kingdom in the early nineteenth century, and the United States in the mid-twentieth century— under two conditions. First, the dominant groups of these states had developed the capacity to lead the system in the direction of new forms of interstate cooperation and division of labor that enabled the system's units to break out of what Waltz has called "the tyranny of small decisions"— that is, to overcome the tendency of the separate states to pursue their national interest without regard for system-level problems that required system-level solutions (1979: 108–9). In other words, they were the bearers of an effective "supply" of world-governance capabilities. And second, the system-level solutions offered by the would-be hegemon addressed system-level problems that had become so acute as to create among the system's extant or emergent dominant groups a deeply and widely felt "demand" for systemic governance. When these supply and demand conditions were simultaneously fulfilled, the would-be hegemonic state could play the role of "a surrogate of government" in promoting, organizing, and managing an expansion of the collective power of the system's dominant groups (cf. Waltz 1979: 196).

As Figure 4.2 shows, each systemic expansion has been the outcome of the interplay of two different kinds of leadership, which jointly define hegemonic situations: a systemic reorganization by the hegemonic state, which promotes expansion by endowing the system with a wider or deeper division of labor and specialization of functions; and an emulation of the hegemonic state, which provides the separate states with the motivational drive needed to mobilize energies and resources in the expansion. There is always a tension between these two tendencies because a wider and deeper division of labor and specialization of functions involves cooperation among the system's units, while emulation is based on and fosters their mutual competition. Initially, emulation operates in a context that is predominantly cooperative and thereby acts as an engine of expansion. But expansion increases what Emile Durkheim has called the "volume" and "dynamic density" of the system, that is, the number of socially relevant units that interact within the system and the number, variety, and velocity of transactions that link the units to one another (1964: 115; 1984: 200–5). Over time, this increase in the volume and dynamic density of the system tends to intensify competition among the system's units beyond the regulatory capacities of existing institutions. When that happens, the tyranny of small decisions regains the upper hand, the power of the hegemonic state declines, and a hegemonic crisis sets in.

As shown in Figure 4.2, hegemonic crises are characterized by three distinct but closely related processes: the intensification of interstate and inter-enterprise competition; the escalation of social conflicts; and the interstitial emergence of new configurations of power. The form that these processes take and the way in which they relate to one another in space and time vary from crisis to crisis, as we shall see. But some combination of the three processes can be detected in

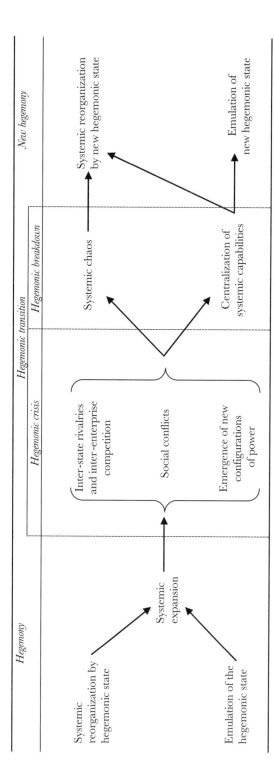

Figure 4.2 The Dynamics of Hegemonic Transitions

Source: Arrighi and Silver (1999: 29)

each of the two, so-far-completed hegemonic transitions—from Dutch to British and from British to US hegemony—as well as in the present transition from US hegemony to a yet unknown destination. Moreover, differences in form and in spatio-temporal configuration notwithstanding, in all three hegemonic crises — Dutch, British and US—the three processes have been associated with a pattern which we take as the most evident manifestation of the capitalist nature of the modern world system. This pattern is the recurrence of lengthy periods of system-wide financial expansion.

Financial expansions are symptoms of an underlying and unresolved crisis of over-accumulation that transforms the capitalist game on a world scale from a positive-sum into a negative-sum game. At the same time they have also been an integral aspect of hegemonic crises, both past and present, as well as of the eventual transformation of past hegemonic crises into hegemonic breakdowns (see especially Arrighi 1994: 214–38; Arrighi and Silver 1999: 258–64). The impact of financial expansions on the tendency of crises to turn into breakdowns is ambivalent. Initially, they hold it in check by temporarily inflating the power of the declining hegemonic state. To paraphrase Fernand Braudel, they are the "autumn," not just of major capitalist developments, but also of the hegemonic regimes in which these developments are embedded (Braudel 1984: 246). Thanks to its continuing centrality in networks of high finance, the declining hegemon can turn the competition for mobile capital to its advantage and thereby contain, at least for a time, the forces that challenge its continuing dominance. Over time, however, financial expansions strengthen these same forces by widening and deepening the scope of interstate and inter-enterprise competition and social conflict, and by reallocating capital to emergent structures that promise greater security or higher returns than the dominant structure. Declining hegemonic states are thus faced with the Sisyphean task of containing forces that keep rolling forth with ever-renewed strength. Sooner or later, even a small disturbance can tilt the balance in favor of the forces that wittingly or unwittingly are undermining the already precarious stability of existing structures, thereby provoking a breakdown of systemic organization.

This is what eventually happened in past hegemonic transitions. In the present transition, it is possible that the bursting of the "new economy" bubble and September 11 will be seen in retrospect as premonitory signs of a subsequent breakdown of US hegemony. But whether they will or not, the US-centered financial expansion of the last thirty years or so presents striking similarities, not just with the British-centered financial expansion of the late nineteenth and early twentieth centuries as many observers have noted, but also with the Dutch-centered financial expansion of the mid-eighteenth century. These similarities make the present expansion and the attendant reflation of US power signs of a hegemonic crisis comparable to those of 100 and 250 years ago. Once we actually compare the three financial expansions and the underlying hegemonic crises, however, we can detect major novelties in the present transition. Three such novelties are especially germane to an understanding of the present and possible futures of global governance.

Geopolitically, the most important novelty of present transformations is a bifurcation of military and financial capabilities that has no precedent in earlier hegemonic transitions. In all past transitions, financial expansions were characterized by the interstitial emergence of governmental-business complexes that were (or could be plausibly expected to become) more powerful both militarily and financially than the still-dominant governmental-business complex—as the US complex was relative to the British in the early twentieth century, the British complex relative to the Dutch in the early eighteenth century, and the Dutch relative to the Genoese in the late sixteenth century. In the present transition, in contrast, no such emergence can be detected. As in past transitions, the declining but still dominant US complex has been transformed from the world's leading creditor into the world's leading debtor nation. Unlike in past transitions, however, military resources of global significance have become more than ever concentrated in the hands of the still-dominant complex. The declining hegemon is thus left in the anomalous situation that it faces no credible military challenge—a circumstance that makes war among the system's great powers less likely than in past transitions—but it does not have the financial means needed to solve system-level problems that require system-level solutions—a circumstance that may very well lead to a hegemonic breakdown even in the absence of world wars among the system's great powers (Arrighi and Silver 1999: 88–96, 263–70, 275–8, 286–9).

Just as important is the social novelty of present transformations. In past hegemonic transitions, system-wide financial expansions contributed to an escalation of social conflict. The massive redistribution of rewards and social dislocations entailed by financial expansions provoked movements of resistance and rebellion by subordinate groups and strata whose established ways of life were coming under attack. Interacting with the interstate power struggle, these movements eventually forced the dominant groups to form a new hegemonic social bloc that selectively included previously excluded groups and strata. In the transition from Dutch to British hegemony, the aspirations of the European propertied classes for greater political representation and the aspirations of the settler bourgeoisies of the Americas for self-determination were accommodated in a new dominant social bloc. With the transition from British to US hegemony—under the joint impact of the revolt against the West and working-class rebellions—the hegemonic social bloc was further expanded through the promise of a global New Deal. The working classes of the wealthier countries of the West were promised security of employment and high mass consumption. The elites of the non-Western world were promised the right to national self-determination and development (that is, assistance in catching up with the standards of wealth and welfare established by Western states). It soon became clear, however, that this package of promises could not be delivered on. Moreover, it engendered expectations in the world's subordinate strata that seriously threatened the stability and eventually precipitated the crisis of US hegemony (Arrighi and Silver 1999: 153–216).

Here lies the peculiar social character of this crisis in comparison with earlier hegemonic crises. The crisis of Dutch hegemony was a long drawn-out process in which a system-wide financial expansion came late and system-wide social conflict later still. The crisis of British hegemony unfolded more rapidly but the system-wide financial expansion still preceded system-wide social conflict. In the crisis of US hegemony, in contrast, the system-wide explosion of social conflict of the late 1960s and early 1970s preceded and thoroughly shaped the subsequent financial expansion. Indeed, in a very real sense the present financial expansion has been primarily an instrument—to paraphrase Wallerstein (1995: 25)—of the containment of the combined demands of the peoples of the non-Western world (for relatively little per person but for a lot of people) and of the Western working classes (for relatively few people but for quite a lot per person). The financial expansion and associated restructuring of the global political economy have undoubtedly succeeded in disorganizing the social forces that were the bearers of these demands in the upheavals of the late 1960s and 1970s. At the same time, however, the underlying contradiction of a world capitalist system that promotes the formation of a world proletariat but cannot accommodate a generalized living wage (that is, the most basic of reproduction costs), far from being solved, has become more acute than ever (Arrighi and Silver 1999: 282–6).

Social pressures for the internalization of reproduction costs within the structures of world capitalism have not been eliminated. And yet, the bifurcation of military and financial power and the decentralization of financial power in otherwise politically weak states do not augur well for an easy or imminent accommodation of those pressures through the emergence of more effective institutions of global governance. This does not mean that there are no solutions to the crisis of over-accumulation that underlies the ongoing financial expansion. Rather, it means that the crisis has more than one possible solution, and which particular solution will eventually materialize depends on an on-going process of struggle that for the most part still lies in front of us.

To complicate things further, this process of struggle can be expected to be shaped by a third major novelty of present transformations: the shift of the epicenter of the global economy to East Asia—a region that unlike all previous organizing centers of world capitalism lies outside the historical boundaries of Western civilization. It is this shift above all else that has led Samuel Huntington (1993) to advance his highly influential thesis of a coming "clash of civilizations." In reality, a clash between Western and non-Western civilizations has been a constant of the historical process through which the European capitalist system became a global system. The transition from Dutch to British hegemony was marked by the violent conquest or destabilization of the indigenous world systems of Asia. The transition from British to US hegemony was marked, first, by a further extension of Western territorial empires in Asia and Africa, and then by a general revolt against Western domination (Arrighi and Silver 1999: 219–63).

Under US hegemony, the map of the world was redrawn to accommodate demands for national self-determination. By and large this new map reflected the legacy of Western colonialism and imperialism, including the cultural hegemony that led non-Western elites to claim for themselves more or less viable "nation-states" in the image of the metropolitan political organizations of their former imperial masters. There was nonetheless one major exception to the rule: East Asia. Except for some states on its southern fringes (most notably, Indonesia, Malaysia, the Philippines and the city-states of Hong Kong and Singapore), all the region's most important nations that were formally incorporated in the expanded Westphalia system—from Japan, Korea, and China to Vietnam, Laos, Kampuchea, and Thailand—had all been nations long before the European arrival. What's more, they had all been nations linked to one another, directly or through the Chinese center, by diplomatic and trade relations and held together by a shared understanding of the principles, norms, and rules that regulated their mutual interactions as a world among other worlds (Arrighi *et al.* 2003).

This geopolitical relict was as difficult to integrate into the US Cold War world order as into the British world order. The fault-lines between the US and Soviet spheres of influence in the East Asian region started breaking down soon after they were established—first by the Chinese rebellion against Soviet domination, and then by the US failure to split the Vietnamese nation along the Cold War divide. Then, while the two superpowers escalated their competition in the final embrace of the Second Cold War, the various pieces of the East Asian puzzle reassembled themselves into the world's most dynamic regional economy. Suffice it to mention that in 1960, at the height of US hegemony, East Asia's Gross National Product (GNP) was only 35 percent of the North American GNP. By 1990, in contrast, it was almost as large (91 per cent). In the 1990s, the combination of US resurgence and Japanese collapse slowed down but did not reverse the shift—the East Asian GNP relative to the North American rose further, to 92 per cent by 1998, thanks primarily to continuing rapid growth in the "China Circle" (mainland China, Singapore, Hong Kong, and Taiwan). The shift, however, is even more significant than these figures imply. For persistent current-account surpluses in the balance of payments of Japan and the China Circle on the one side, and large and growing US current-account deficits on the other, have further deepened the reversal of positions of East Asia and the United States in the international credit system (Arrighi *et al.* 2003). The problems for effective global governance due to the bifurcation of military and financial power are thus compounded by the "migration" of the latter outside the boundaries of Western civilization.

Prospects for global governance

The geopolitical, social, and civilizational novelties of ongoing transformations of the global political economy make the exercise of global governance extremely difficult. From this point of view, the unparalleled and unprecedented concentration of military power of global significance in the hands of the United States and its closest allies, as well as the formation of a transnational capitalist class emphasized by some authors working within the tradition of transnational historical materialism, are undeniable but misleading. They are misleading because the real issue confronting the prospects of global governance is not the *absolute* level of US military power or of the combined economic power of whatever transnational capitalist class is actually emerging. The real issue is whether these powers—however great they might be by historical standards—are the bearers of a credible solution of the geopolitical, social, and inter-civilizational problems that underlie the crisis of US hegemony, or are instead a factor of the ongoing tendency towards the transformation of international relations from a positive-sum into a negative-sum game and of a possible breakdown of the world system as instituted under US hegemony.

As David Calleo has suggested, the "international system breaks down not only because unbalanced and aggressive new powers seek to dominate their neighbors, but also because declining powers, rather than adjusting and accommodating, try to cement their slipping pre-eminence into an exploitative hegemony" (Calleo 1987: 142). In Gramscian terms, Calleo's "exploitative hegemony" corresponds to what Ranajit Guha has called "dominance without hegemony" (Guha 1992: 231–2). Bearing this in mind, Calleo's distinction is very useful in tracking a fundamental change in the mechanisms of hegemonic decline.

Thus, our comparison of past hegemonic transitions shows that the role of aggressive new powers in precipitating systemic breakdowns has decreased from transition to transition, while the role of exploitative domination by the declining hegemon has increased. Dutch world power was already so diminished in the declining decades of its hegemony that Dutch resistance played only a marginal role in the systemic breakdown in comparison with the role played by the emerging, aggressive empire-building nation-states, first and foremost Britain and France. By the time of its own hegemonic decline, in contrast, Britain remained powerful enough to transform its hegemony into exploitative domination. Although the emergence of aggressive new powers—first and foremost Germany—still played a major role in the breakdown of the British-centered world system, Britain's resistance to adjustment and accommodation was also crucial.

Today we have reached the other end of the spectrum. There are no credible aggressive new powers that can provoke the breakdown of the US-centered world system but the United States has even greater capabilities than Britain did a century ago to convert its declining hegemony into an exploitative domination. If the system eventually breaks down, it will be primarily because of US resistance to adjustment and accommodation. And conversely, US adjustment and accommodation primarily, but not exclusively, to the rising economic power of the East Asian region is an essential condition for a non-catastrophic transition to a new world order.

For the time being there are few signs that such an adjustment and accommodation are actually in the making. On the contrary, US reactions to 9/11 (and to the prior bursting of the new economy bubble) point to a blind reliance on force—military force in particular—to compensate for a growing deficit in the consent component of US hegemony. Indeed, if we had at our disposal minimally valid and reliable measurements of the "force" and "consent" components of US global power—which we do not have—we would probably find such a precipitous decline in the consent component of US power in the wake of the

war on Iraq that we should no longer speak of US hegemony but of US dominance without hegemony.

Under these circumstances, the prospects of any kind of global governance in
the near future are dim. The most likely scenario is one of increasingly severe
and seemingly irremediable systemic disorganization, that is, of systemic chaos.
Whether, when, and how this new period of systemic chaos—like the ones that
have characterized previous hegemonic transitions—will result in the establishment of a new hegemony and a new period of global governance, is hard to tell.
All we can predict with some confidence is that such a hegemony will be possible
only if it can provide a minimally credible solution to the geopolitical, social, and
inter-civilizational contradictions that underlie the crisis of US hegemony but
have hardly begun to receive the attention they deserve.

References

Arrighi, G. (1994) *The Long Twentieth Century: Money, Power, and the Origins of Our Time.*
London: Verso.
Arrighi, G. and Silver, B.J. (1999) *Chaos and Governance in the Modern World System.*
Minneapolis, MN: University of Minnesota Press.
Arrighi, G and Silver, B.J. (2001) "Capitalism and World (Dis)order," *Review of International
Studies* 27: 257–79.
Arrighi, G., Hamashita, T., and Selden, M. (2003). "Introduction," in G. Arrighi, T.
Hamashita, and M. Selden (eds) *The Resurgence of East Asia: 500, 150 and 50 Year Perspec-
tives.* London: Routledge.
Arrighi, G., Hui, P., Hung, H., and Selden, M. (2003) "Historical Capitalism East and
West," in G. Arrighi, T. Hamashita, and M. Selden (eds) *The Resurgence of East Asia:
500, 150 and 50 Year Perspectives.* London: Routledge.
Braudel, F. (1984) *Civilization and Capitalism, 15th–18th Century, III: The Perspective of the
World.* New York: Harper & Row.
Calleo, D. (1987) *Beyond American Hegemony: The Future of the Western Alliance.* New York:
Basic Books.
Cox, R. (1983) "Gramsci, Hegemony, and International Relations: An Essay in Method,"
Millennium: Journal of International Relations XII, 2: 162–75.
—— (1987) *Production, Power, and World Order: Social Forces in the Making of History.* New York:
Columbia University Press.
Durkheim, E. (1964) *The Rules of Sociological Method.* New York: Free Press.
—— (1984) *The Division of Labor in Society.* New York: Free Press.
Giddens, A. (1987) *The Nation-State and Violence.* Berkeley: University of California Press.
Gill, S. (1986) "Hegemony, Consensus, and Trilateralism," *Review of International Studies*
XII: 205–21.
—— (ed.) (1993) *Gramsci, Historical Materialism, and International Relations.* Cambridge:
Cambridge University Press.
Gill, S. and Law, D. (1988) *The Global Political Economy: Perspectives, Problems and Policies.*
Baltimore, MD: The Johns Hopkins University Press.
Gramsci, A. (1971) *Selections from the Prison Notebooks.* New York: International Publishers.
Guha, R. (1992) "Dominance Without Hegemony and Its Historiography," in R. Gupta
(ed.) *Subaltern Studies IV.* New York: Oxford University Press, 210–305.
Huntingon, S. (1993) "The Clash of Civilizations?" *Foreign Affairs* LXXIII, 3: 22–49.

Marx, K. (1962) *Capital*, Vol. III. Moscow: Foreign Languages Publishing House.

Overbeek, H. (1993) *Restructuring Hegemony in the Global Political Economy: The Rise of Transnational Neo-liberalism in the 1980s*. London: Routledge.

—— (2003) "Class, Hegemony, and Global Governance: A Historical Materialist Perspective," paper presented at the International Studies Association Meeting, Portland, Oregon, February 26– March 1.

Robinson, W. (1996) *Promoting Polyarchy. Globalization, US Intervention, and Hegemony*. Cambridge: Cambridge University Press.

Rupert, M. (1995) *Producing Hegemony: The Politics of Mass Production and American Global Power*. Cambridge: Cambridge University Press.

Soederberg, S. (2005) *The Politics of the New Financial Architecture: Reimposing Neoliberal Domination in the Global South*. London: Zed Books.

Wallerstein, I. (1984) *The Politics of the World-economy. The States, the Movements and the Civilizations*. Cambridge: Cambridge University Press.

—— (1995) "Response: Declining States, Declining Rights?" *International Labor and Working-class History* XLVII: 24–7.

Waltz, K. (1979) *Theory of International Politics*. Reading, MA: Addison-Wesley.

5   Global governance

An English School perspective[1]

Tim Dunne

Governance is a relatively new word for an old idea. It suggests the possibility of a relatively stable order among interdependent actors despite the absence of a legitimate enforcer. In other words, the absence of world government is not a barrier to the realization of forms of governance. The discourse and practice of governance is therefore counter to the stark dualism associated with classical realism that counters order within the state to the state of war among them. Governance implies that common interests and values can be realised within a framework of rules and institutions that has been constructed by sovereign states but is not reducible to them. In this respect, there are striking parallels between the governance paradigm and the idea of international society which came to dominate international-relations thinking in Britain after 1945.

The belief that states form a society is based on two connected claims about common interests and shared values. At the most basic level, states take into account the impact their decisions have on other members of their society. Failure to do this could jeopardise the survival of the system as a whole, on which their independence is predicated. At a deeper level, international society can signify the presence of intricate patterns of social interaction, evident in the balance of power and in their general fidelity to the rules of the game. This does not mean that states will always act in accordance with agreed rules and conventions, only that this is the regular pattern and not the exception.

Despite the fact that so-called English School theorists and adherents of the global-governance paradigm share similar views of the world, there has not been a great deal of dialogue between these two academic perspectives. This chapter sets out to explore the basis of this dialogue from an English School perspective. It will do so in response to the following questions:

1   What is distinctive about an English School view of world politics? What is international society and how do we know it exists?
2   To what extent is recent work by English School theorists compatible with global governance and what are the key points of divergence?
3   Looking at world politics after 9/11, what dynamics of international order would be emphasised by the English School?

The English School of international relations

For some time now, the English School of international relations has been distinguished by its commitment to the idea that the societal domain constitutes an important (and overlooked) dimension of world politics. The guiding thought here is that just as the behaviour of individuals is regulated and conditioned by institutions and rules or laws, states are also members of a society that in large measure is the source of their identity and their obligations.

According to leading figures in post-1945 British international relations, international society was incompatible with both the dominant alternatives of realism *and* idealism. For writers such as C.A.W. Manning, Martin Wight, Hedley Bull, Adam Watson and R.J. Vincent, there was 'more to international relations than the realist suggests but less than the cosmopolitan desires' (Linklater 1996: 95). The work produced by these writers became known as the English School, a history that has received considerable attention in recent times (Dunne 1998; Suganami 2003). While the writings associated with the first wave of the English School continue to be published (Wight 1991; Watson 1992; Alderson and Hurrell 2000), there is an emerging English School literature that is more inclined to engage with new currents of thinking in the American heartland of international relations, engaging with constructivism (Reus-Smit, 2002) and global governance (Armstrong 1998; Hurrell 1999).

If the challenge for macro-sociological research international relations is 'how the world hangs together', as Ruggie so neatly argued, then the picture that begins with an English School account of international society needs less justification today than it did at any time in the last two decades. Such a change of fortune can be discerned from comparisons with earlier historiographical debates in international relations. In reflections on the 'state of the discipline' in the 1980s, the English School was nowhere to be seen (Banks 1984; Smith 1989), neither did it figure in early representations of the debate between neorealism and its critics – what many have termed the 'third debate' (Keohane 1988; Lapid, 1989). By the mid- to late 1990s, interest in the English School was on the increase. Many influential textbooks began to include it as an alternative approach to the subject, placing it alongside realism, liberalism and various critical approaches (Der Derian 1995; Brown 1997; Roberson 1998; Jackson and Sorensen 1999). Added to these, weighty monographs and doctoral dissertations proliferated, all taking the English School as their point of departure (*inter alia* Armstrong 1993; Welsh 1995; Neumann 1996; Korman 1997; Almeida 2000).

This sense of a resurgent English School paradigm was heightened by theoretical developments in the North American mainstream. As the new debate was constructed around the rationalist/constructivist fissure (Katzenstein 1998) the English School found itself represented as a form of constructivism. The leading rationalist Stephen Krasner referred to it as 'the best known sociological perspective' in international relations (in Buzan 2004: 46). Similarly, those who self-identified with constructivism openly acknowledged the insights of classical English School theory (Finnemore 1996; Reus-Smit 1999; Wendt 1999). The extent to which both 'old' and 'new' institutionalism can learn from one another has been extensively debated in the field (Dunne 1995; Wæver 1998; Reus-Smit 2002).

Such momentum prompted an attempt to pull together the diverse strands in English School theorising into a coherent research programme, led by Barry Buzan and Richard Little. Buzan's agenda-setting paper 'The English School: an under-exploited resource in IR' was published in the *Review of International Studies* in 2001 as the lead article in a forum on the English School (Buzan 2001: 465–513). This agenda has also been debated in other journals, most recently in a Special Issue of *International Relations* in which the editor's foreword speaks of how the School has 'flourished' in recent years (Cox 2003: 251–252).

While the English School has produced a significant body of work on international society, there is much that can be learned from other approaches to the institutional context of international relations. Just as one can study norms without being a constructivist, or the material basis of the international system without being a neo-realist, it is possible to theorise international society without being a member of the English School. By decoupling English School theory from international society we are able to open up the macro-institutional context to a range of theoretical perspectives. The 'driver' of this agenda should not be to vindicate one paradigm over another, but to understand the social totality we call international society and its dynamics. This endeavour requires engaging with English School writings but it also demands a dialogue with a wider literature in international relations and beyond. In the paragraphs below, I sketch some fault-lines *within* recent English School work, and hint at fault-lines *between* the English School and the global-governance literature.

International society 'meets' global governance

In their introduction to this volume, the editors point out the various meanings that have been given to the term global governance. The English School is also characterised by a deep ambiguity in respect to whether its central concept of international society signifies an empirical claim about 'what the world is and how it works' or whether it reveals a disciplinary location. Is international society 'outside' in the world, or 'inside' the academy of international relations? As I have argued elsewhere, international society should be thought of as the co-constitution of practices and institutions: crucially, different theoretical frameworks provide alternative understandings of how states, purposes and institutions relate to one another. Just as one does not have to be a constructivist to theorise norms (Wendt 1999), one does not have to be a member of the English School to theorise international society (Dunne 2002).

Aside from this shared ambiguity, perhaps the most important overlap between the English School and global governance is that both try to theorise 'how the world hangs together'. Neither approach is geographically bounded. One might also add to this list of convergences the importance attached to institutions, although what global governance and the English School mean by the term institutions quickly becomes contested.

If we take governance in general to mean 'the establishment and operation of social institutions' (Young 1997: 4), then global governance ought to date back as far as the emergence of sovereign states and the rudimentary institutions established to regulate their conduct. Yet, while the English School go back to Westphalia (Bull/Watson) and earlier Augsburg (in the case of Martin Wight), the orthodox account of the emergence of governance comes much later. Craig Murphy (1994) identified the emergence of global governance with 'the inter-imperial order' from 1814 to 1914. The main reason why this period is associated with the development of the idea of governance is the multilateral conference system associated with the Concert of Europe. In addition, the nineteenth century witnessed the development of explicit regimes for telecommunications and the laws of war. Yet, the idea of large-scale conferences dates back at least to the treaties of Münster and Osnabrück that constitute the Peace of Westphalia. Similarly, international conventions associated with diplomatic and ambassadorial rights and privileges originated in the Italian city-state system in the Renaissance period (Frey 1999).

State-centrism and its critics

The English School is frequently criticised for being overly state-centric in its ontology of world order. If this were the case, it would be at odds with the mainstream global governance literature. To take an authoritative voice in the global-governance camp, James Rosenau has for many years pointed out that non-state actors operate within the international rule structure. Moreover, governance exists at a variety of different levels, with authority seeping upwards to international institutions and leaking downwards to groups within transnational civil society (Rosenau 1995: 16–19). There is no prima facie reason why global-governance theorists and advocates of the society of states cannot learn from each other on the question of agency.

Bull's classical definition in *The Anarchical Society* argues that a society of states is constituted 'when a group of states, conscious of certain common interests and common values, form a society in the sense that they conceive themselves to be bound by a common set of rules in their relations with one another, and share in the working of common institutions' (1977: 13). At first glance, such a definition is open to the charge of *state-centrism*, something that the global-governance paradigm has from the outset sought to avoid. Even though Bull acknowledged the fact that states defined as 'independent political communities' pre-dated the emergence of modern sovereign states (1977: 9), what the English School account of international society lacks is an adequate theorisation of *how* states are capable of social relations.

This touches upon the issue that international society should be thought of in ontological terms (as a social structure) and agential terms (a capacity for action). The former refers to powers, tendencies, emergent properties and rules that take the form of enablements and constraints on action. The latter captures the residual truth that nothing happens in international society without something being done by those who act in the name of governments (*and* what predecessors in these roles have done). Agency captures the way in which representatives of 'international society' have clarified and codified rules about diplomatic immunity, the laws of war, principles of co-existence following a breakdown in order, and so on.

No major event happens in world politics without a politician or activist calling for the 'international community'[2] to 'do something'. New problems generate calls for international action across a vast range of issue areas from security, to trade, to global communications networks. This implies that international society has certain competences, ranging from agreements in the form of international treaties and concerted diplomatic pressure on one end of the spectrum to imposing its will through the collective use of force on the other. That said, international society is not reducible to the question of agency; in other words, its structure exists even when it is not manifested in observable processes of collective action.

More work needs to be done on the question of agency. In the global-governance literature, it is not clear who is the actor, and how 'it' is to be held accountable. In the English School literature, it is important not to regard states as pre-formed units as Bull implies. In the history of international society, membership has been ascribed to dynastic monarchies, imperial states, states that meet 'a standard of civilisation'. It has been denied to 'backward' peoples, secessionist groups, and latterly to authoritarian states that are suspected of acquiring weapons of mass destruction. In the early twenty-first century, we need to escape from the prison of sovereignty such that the terms of debate about the state are irrevocably changed. Rather than lining up on opposite sides of the 'decline of the state' thesis, what needs to be put in its place is a more nuanced agenda about how new challenges are being met by new kinds of state actors. Political economy is still being shaped by regulatory institutions controlled by states, but often the negotiating representatives are not 'sovereigns' or even foreign ministers, rather, the key individuals are trade officials.

The danger with taking states for granted is that we have implicitly answered one of the central questions of international politics, namely, where does authority lie and how is it exercised. The danger of ignoring states is also very real, especially the great powers. Fred Halliday has criticised 'most writing on global governance' for implying that action takes place on a multilateral basis (Halliday: 2003: 490). The history of international relations suggests a different model, namely, one in which great powers create and enforce an order convenient to themselves. This begs the question how rules and institutions come to be 'shared', and the various mechanisms and instruments by which new members (and recalcitrant ones) are socialised into the prevailing norms of international society. Historically, force, calculation and persuasion have all played a part (Wendt 1999). Arguably, the English School is well placed to understand the relationship between power, interest and norms, avoiding the twin pitfalls of denying the legal-normative domain any independent validity (as realists do), or underestimating the extent to which power creates a normative framework convenient to itself (as cosmopolitan inclined global-governance thinkers are prone to).

System, society and world society

The debate about membership of international society slides into the question of 'boundaries': in other words, what lies *outside* this vexatious entity we call international society? Bull was absolutely clear that international society was only 'one element' in the reality of world politics. It co-existed uneasily with systemic forces such as war and conquest, and transnational economic and social forces. Self-styled globalists (Held and McGrew 2003),[3] while not dismissive of the inter-state realm, nevertheless argue that this is not the place to begin our analysis of world order in the twenty-first century. Across various sectors – cultural, economic, military – interactions are not being driven by territorially bounded units. Putting this into language more familiar to the English School, world society has displaced international society as being the dominant domain.

The classical English School literature is ambiguous as to whether it is seeking to provide an account of the relationship *between* the three elements, or whether its aim is the vindication of the societal dimension. Within recent English School literature, this ambivalence has become an issue that divides those who are more inclined to holistic accounts of the social world (Jackson 1990: 112; Hurrell 1998; Almeida 2003) from those inclined to analytical disaggregation (Buzan and Little 2000; Little 2000; Buzan 2003). In the former camp are those who believe it is increasingly problematic to distinguish between system, society and world society. Bull's initial configuration of a system, suggesting mere contact between states in the absence of shared rules, lacks plausibility given the high degree of interdependence today: 'All relations between human beings – including people who speak and act in the name of states – necessarily rest on mutual intelligibility and communication' (Jackson 1990: 112). Such an observation leads Robert Jackson to argue that we should abandon the system/society distinction (see also James 1993).

What Jackson means here is that international society is an essentially normative business, in contrast to the 'the abstract logic of the system of states' (Bull in Alderson and Hurrell 2000: 25) that characterises Waltzian neorealism. We know international society exists, according to Jackson, because it is present in the 'normative vocabulary' of practitioners (Jackson 2000: 5). The society of states is a human construct which is produced and reproduced by the activities of statespeople and other representatives of institutions. Bull's view is closer to a realist ontology. Agreed, international society exists in the minds of men and women, but crucially, his position is that *it is not reducible to them*. Social facts – norms, expectations, habits – *do* exist 'out there' in that they will endure even if individuals resist or dispute them. On this account, there is an international social reality which is composed of structures that are unobservable yet constrain and compel actors. The theoretical task is to show how properties of international society such as legal rules, enable certain actions, such as the legitimacy of colonial possessions overseas in one historical era and proscribe them in another. This requires a causal account of how 'really existing' social structures operate.

Although Jackson and Bull implicitly work with different ontologies, they share the view that international society is a permanent feature of world politics.

As Bull wrote in his *magnum opus*, 'the element of a society has always been present, and remains present, in the modern international system' (1977: 41). Such a position is mature in the sense that it recognises that the 'darker' forces in world politics are also *social*. War and inter-state violence are only intelligible in the context of competition among sovereign states for rewards which are valued inter-subjectively be they priced in territory, status, security or wealth. Moreover, this competition takes place within an established framework of rules and practices. An understanding of war without an understanding of this wider context would be like trying to explain the meaning of a five-pound note without providing an account of the social system of production and exchange.

The difficulty with the macro-social version of international society is that too much is folded into this account. International society is repeated in the hope that each iteration will make it come true. Blind faith is no substitute for an account of how an institutional order emerged, is reproduced and has potentiality (or not) for transformation. The kind of sociological functionalism that often underpins a holistic account of international society is partly responsible. Functionalism blurs differentiation and causation, goals become causes and description merges imperceptibly with normative adequacy. At a minimum, an adequate theorisation of international society needs to be able to disentangle emergent properties from their consequences.

Barry Buzan has for some time been an eloquent exponent for analytically disaggregating international society from other domains. While his early work focused on the system/society boundary (1993), his recent book (2004) examines at great length the world society dimension of English School theorising. His motivation for this shift is to re-position the School in a manner that enables it to deal with the increasing density of inter-state/society relations under conditions of globalisation. It is important to dwell on Buzan's argument both because of its intrinsic merit as a statement of grand theory, and because he articulates a position that is open to objections from those wanting to resist disaggregating the *via media*.

Buzan sets out his stall with a great sense of purpose. As he tells the reader at a number of junctures, the 'three pillars' of the English School 'triad' – system, society and world society – must be preserved because of their explanatory potential. The problem lies in the fact that the connections between the pillars have not been properly worked through. Taking the system/society boundary first, we see that a marked shift in his thinking has occurred. Buzan argued previously, in his co-authored book with Richard Little, that we need to draw a distinction between shared ideas (belonging to the societal sector), and the kind of mechanistic material power that Waltz and fellow neo-realists regard as an attribute of the system (Buzan and Little 2000: 103–105). The influence of Wendtian constructivism has led Buzan to revise his position. As Wendt argues in *Social Theory of International Politics*, materialist theories of society can explain cooperation, just as shared ideas and norms explain war (1999: 253).

The central thrust of Buzan's argument is not about the system/society boundary so much as the international/world society boundary. He rightly points out that traditional English School thinking in this area is 'both incoherent and underdeveloped' (2003: 143). In terms of 'actors', world society has often been treated as a 'residual category' in which we place all kinds of entities that do not fit into the system or societal sectors. This problem is compounded by the fact that too much writing on world society has been framed around normative theoretical concerns about the rights of states versus the rights of individuals replaying an old debate between positive and naturalist conceptions of international law (Bull 1966). In the context of today's human rights culture, the effect of this move is the 'merging' of the two pillars, to the detriment of analytical progress (Buzan 2003: 107). By way of example, the sector where shared values and institutions are most in evidence is political economy (particularly in a regional context). The tendency to frame the question of the degree of convergence of values in terms of pluralism and solidarism has further impaired our vision of the boundary between international and world society.

Buzan's reconstructive surgery of the English School rests on the following moves. Abandoning the category of the system on constructivist grounds, Buzan focuses on the interstate/world society boundary. Each side of this divide is subject to extensive rethinking. Interstate society is opened up to a spectrum of variations, from 'thin' to 'thick'. In addition, it is a layered phenomenon where the global institutional order is accompanied by sub-global structures, each of which can be mapped according to the degree of social solidarity on the thin–thick spectrum. The global and regional macro-social structures are held together by an admixture of coercion, calculation and belief. Using these analytical categories, it is possible to see how the international social structure has changed historically, something that Buzan hints at in his conclusion.

Buzan's re-working of the English School might hold great interest to those working within a global-governance paradigm. In particular, many may find fertile his opening up of world society into a distinction between the transnational domain and the inter-human domain (the society of peoples). The point at which Buzan's reconstruction overlays with the classical English School agenda is over the vital question about how the domains relate to one another. What connects and infuses them are the underlying meta-values and moral purposes (Reus-Smit 1999). The question then becomes whether the best way to access these principles is through a structural theory or by way of a historical-cum-normative enquiry. Buzan is right to argue that we can gain much in this regard from constructivist work although the over-reliance on Wendt's statist interpretation of constructivism might hinder rather than further this goal.

Buzan's *From International to World Society?* has set out a new point of departure for the English School. Greater analytical clarity has been the result and new avenues have been untapped: there is no doubt that the domain of world society has been enriched by his reinterpretation. What is striking about his book, however, is the lack of attention to the system/society boundary. As the final section of this chapter argues, this is an area where the English School have a great deal to offer, particularly to adherents of the global-governance paradigm.

The normative basis of international society

For much of the 1990s the normative debate within the English School fractured along a normative divide, with communitarian minded 'pluralists' at odds with cosmopolitan minded 'solidarists'. As Nick Wheeler argued at the beginning of that decade, the vexed question of humanitarian intervention threw the divide into sharp relief (1992: 463–464). When should we respect the pluralist norm of non-intervention, and under what conditions should states suspend the norm in accordance with the solidarist injunction that states be 'burdened with the guardianship of human rights everywhere' (Bull 1966: 63)? Leading members of the English School engaged in a heated debate on this question, with Jackson (2000) making the case for upholding pluralist norms and Wheeler (2000) setting out a constructivist case for intervention. The relevance of this debate is twofold: first, it illustrates the centrality of ethical theory to the English School, and second, ethical contestation within the School reflects the existence of deep tensions in world politics about the appropriate level of normative ambition. At the risk of generalisation, the global-governance literature tends to be infused with a singular kind of liberalism, one that is unreflective about the cultural and historical genealogy of liberal values. As the paragraphs below indicate, the same cannot be said for the English School.

The pluralist-solidarist debate of the 1990s brought ethical considerations to the fore and, in doing so, further underlined the different enterprises that realism and the English School are embarked upon. More significantly, both sets of protagonists were addressing the same central question: is the purpose of inter-national society to maintain inter-state order (even if it is unjust) or is the goal to provide for the conditions of justice everywhere (the only stable order)? As many have remarked, Bull's answer to this question was ambivalent (Linklater 1996; Wheeler and Dunne 1996). Those inclined to a more solidarist understanding of the moral connectedness of international society to the global community of humankind point to passages in his writings where world order becomes the litmus test for the moral adequacy of international society (Dunne 1998: 145–146). If we accept this formulation, there is a moral audit to be done.

One example of just such an undertaking is Paul Keal's new book *European Conquest and the Rights of Indigenous Peoples* (2003). He declares international society to be 'morally backward'. Over five centuries, its language, institutions and rules have enabled the destruction and dispossession of indigenous culture and terri-tory. An English School account of the relationship between the European and the non-European world is capable of reinventing itself but never fully escaping the exclusionary terms of its construction.

Writers such as Keal and Keene (2002) present a different reading of history to that which is found in the classical literature on the development of interna-tional society (Bull and Watson 1984; Mayall 1990). Keal reminds us that expansion and dispossession were two sides of the same coin: 'the expansion of Europe resulted in a progressive erosion and denial of the rights of indigenous peoples' (2003: 35). In classical political thought, erosion and denial came about through a double movement: to escape the state of nature, rights had to be transferred to a sovereign who would protect the natural right of individuals to security and property. Outside of Europe, the absence of 'evidence' of individual property rights led Locke and others to argue that indigenous inhabitants had no legitimate title to their land.

Where Keene and Keal are in agreement is in the intimate relationship between international society and domination. Failure to adequately represent this connection in previous English School writings leads us to wrongly conclude that international society is now 'universal'. Drawing on insights from critical theory, Keal shows us that the expansion story is incomplete for the reason that an estimated 250–300 million indigenous peoples have not been accorded self-determination. Until this is achieved, the legitimacy of international society is in question. Such a line of thought leads to a further question about whether the politics of autonomy and recognition of indigenous peoples needs to be pursued in opposition to a statist concept of world order. But as Keene shows, international society has invented many diverse forms of divided sovereignty in its history – we should not therefore presume its inability to accept (and protect) a non-territorial account of self-determination that is acceptable to indigenous peoples.

Society and hierarchy

The classical international society literature of the mid- to late twentieth century regarded decolonisation as the main challenge to international society. In the wake of September 11 and the 'war on terror', we have to pose the question of whether the main threat today would appear to be a revolt against the institutions of international society by the United States and its allies.

To begin to answer this question we first need to reflect on why a concentration of power in the hands of a single actor (be it a sole superpower or empire) is a threat to international society? The answer to this question takes us straight to the origins and purpose of international society. From the earliest consciousness of the idea of common rules and institutions agreed to by sovereign states, the primary justification has been anti-hegemonic in character. International society exists to protect diverse political communities from being overrun by more powerful neighbours.

In the absence of a world government, it is up to the great powers and other institutions to ensure the rights of sovereign states are protected. The fact that Bull referred to the great powers as one of the institutions of international society suggests that he was very aware of the ambiguous relationship between law and power: law needs to act as a constraint upon those states looking to act in ways that are contrary to the greater good, while at the same time law requires enforcement, a burden that falls disproportionately on the shoulders of the great powers. The members of international society generally accept that order has to be managed. This explains why it is that in a system of legal equality, certain privileges are nevertheless accorded to great powers. In the UN system, the

Security Council is responsible for international peace and security, and that Council is dominated by the permanent members. More broadly, as noted previously, all the major peace settlements since Westphalia have been dominated by the great powers (Clark 2005).

Hierarchy is not something that is new in international politics – in fact, sovereign equality is a thin veneer masking the vast inequalities of power that exist in the international system (Krasner 1999). So what makes *this* challenge to international society different from the threat posed by other hegemonic powers? In the case of classical European international society, the members agreed to accept the legitimate nature of the hierarchical order *and* extended the same privileges reciprocally. What is potentially different today is that international society does *not* appear to accept the special privileges that the United States now demands.

In a recent article, I presented two clusters of reasons for this tension (Dunne 2003). First, if we look at the dynamics of international society at the beginning of the twenty-first century, we find many abnormalities. In a system characterised as anarchic, order requires a stable distribution of power and a commitment on the part of the great powers to manage the system. An anarchical society therefore requires some inequality but not to such an extent that, in Vattel's words, one state is able to 'lay down the law to others'. The actions of the United States in the build-up to the war against Iraq suggests that the United States is both willing and capable of laying down the law to those it sees as rogue states, even when it has conspicuously failed to persuade the majority of Security Council representatives.

It is plausible to argue that cooperation among great powers is not a necessary condition for international order. The Cold War is an example where there was little evidence of concerted action but a fragile international society was able to persist because of a general balance of power that dictated mutual respect for strategic parity and a broad agreement on the respective spheres of influence. A key characteristic of the post-September 11 order is the absence of effective countervailing institutions against the primacy of American power, exacerbated by the fact that maintaining such an imbalance has become a goal of United States grand strategy.[4]

The combination of the growth in United States military power and its post-September 11 doctrine of pre-emption together signal the emergence of a hierarchical pattern of power and authority. This does not mean that the United States will oppose the rules and institutions of international society in all respects but it will retain an option to disregard the rights of other members. Like a suzerain power, it will seek to conduct international relations bilaterally while overseeing the multilateralism of others. The right of states to remain neutral should no longer be taken for granted, and with it, the debate between pluralists and solidarists is being recast.

The existence of hierarchy does not mean the end of international society. In part this is because the 'supersize' power will continue to engage with other sovereign states in accordance with the settled norms, particularly in relation to low politics issues. The motivation to co-operate on trade stems from the extraordinarily high levels of economic and financial integration on which American prosperity depends. But over questions about vital national interests, concerned with the use of force and the management of world order, we see that hierarchy represents a threat to international society and a source of on-going tension. We should also leave open the possibility that disagreement over large-scale questions about international order might trigger a reverse spillover effect, such that the consensus in low political issue areas comes under strain and possibly unravels.

This brief analysis of world order after 9/11 implies that the 'governance' literature is in danger of underestimating two trends in the international system. First, the way in which war continues to be 'a basic determinant of the shape the system assumes at any one time' (Bull 1977: 187). What separates the English School from a realist account is that the system is only one domain of international action; the other two domains along which international social action proceeds is international society and world society. It is in this latter domain that one can identify a second key difference between the two approaches. Central to the English School is a belief in the power of critique, evident in the concern expressed in recent writings that the leading great powers are acting, in Bull's words, like 'great irresponsibles'.

Conclusion

The resurgence of English School theorising had added considerably to the body of knowledge generated by earlier exponents. In light of developments in social theory, we know more about the integrative forces in international society, in particular how norms emerge and become accepted or contested. New histories of international society have explored the relationship between global social formations and patterns of domination. And further thinking on ethics continues to draw our attention to the question of moral adequacy and normative change.

It is clear from the preceding discussion that theoretical innovation has been a dual-track process. There is evidence of an on-going conversation within the English School, where ideas first mooted in British Committee discussions are resurrected and innovatively applied to a different context; the debate about pluralism and solidarism is a case in point (Wheeler 2000). Alongside, we find a parallel track in which new theories have been imported from other fields in order to refine knowledge about complex processes such as socialisation or the formation of institutions. A deeper engagement with the governance literature is likely to enhance the prospects for theoretical advancement, particularly in regard to the domain of world society.

Buzan's *From International to World Society?* is an example of theoretical innovation. He strips the classical English School tradition of its philosophical idealism – out goes the Wightean dialogue between realism, rationalism and revolutionism. In its place he puts a reconfigured structural theory that seeks to identify connections between global and regional dynamics. His theory downgrades the importance of states and brings in the dense web of economic interactions among states, corporations and individuals. While Bull often remarked about the need to take political economy seriously, Buzan has actually done so in his recon-figuration of English School theory. In doing so, he has brought the analytical wing of the English School much closer to global-governance theory.

Other contemporary English School writers are less interested in the analyt-ical theorising adopted by Buzan (and shared by global-governance thinkers). Instead, in a manner that might appear too interpretive for North American globalists, their focus has been the history of ideas which constituted European international society and the process of global isomorphism. This explains why Welsh (1995), Hurrell (1998), Keene (2002), Suganami (2003) and others privi-lege a hermeneutic method recovering the meaning of a global order structured by shared rules and institutions. Once meanings have been recovered, the task becomes political and normative – why should we value this arrangement? Should it be measured against a transcendental moral standard, or an immanent standard? If it is failing, what is to be done?

There is much that can be gained by a dialogue between the analytical and normative wings of the English School; in this respect Buzan is right to argue they are different but not incompatible. Outside of this dual-track process of intellec-tual regeneration, it is important to note that changes in the world – spectacular events such as September 11 – also trigger new readings of old ideas. Given the dark period of world politics that we have entered, we are likely to see realist sentiments creep back into the English School. While the humanitarian agenda focused our attention on the international society/world society border, there may now be a good case for bringing the system back in. To the extent that the United States has contracted out of certain shared rules, it could be said to be in the system but not in the society, rather like the Americas in the sixteenth century.

While the web of institutions and networks that regulate the global order has not changed significantly in the last few years, the English School would claim that the cohesiveness of the societal domain has been significantly undermined by the actions of a single state. The United States is trying to manage interna-tional order on realist principles, in which it is above the laws it creates and enforces, as against the accepted norms of the society of states in which all sovereigns are bound by the rules. By bringing the system back in, the English School can accommodate this challenge to its theoretical framework; it remains to be seen how adherents of global governance will account for systemic change.

Notes

1 I am deeply grateful to the editors for their enduring patience as well as their supportive comments on an earlier draft. I would also like to thank other participants in the workshop, whose papers and comments have been enlightening. Lastly, I would like to thank Alex Bellamy and Oxford University Press for allowing me to draw upon my chapter in *International Society and its Critics* (Dunne 2005).

2 It is important to add here that what practitioners understand by the term interna-tional community is remarkably similar to Bull's definition of international society.

3 Globalists argue there has been a structural change in world order and global social life. 'Three aspects of this are identified in the globalist literature; namely, the transformation of dominant patterns of socio-economic organization, of the territorial principle, and of power' (Held and McGrew, 2002, p. 7).

4 New thinking on the Cold War suggests that maintaining this imbalance has always been part of United States grand strategy. If this is the case, then 9/11 represents a moment in which the pursuit of global dominance becomes more entrenched. I am grateful to Theo Farrell for this point.

References

Alderson, K. and A. Hurrell (eds) (2000) *Hedley Bull on International Society*, London: Palgrave.

Almeida, J. (2003) 'Challenging Realism by Returning to History: The British Committee's Contribution to IR Forty Years On', *International Relations* 17: 253–272.

Armstrong, D. (1993) *Revolution and World Order: The Revolutionary State in International Society*, Oxford: Clarendon Press.

—— (1998) 'Globalization and the Social State', *Review of International Studies* 24: 461–478

Banks, M. (1984) 'The Evolution of International Relations Theory', in M. Banks (ed.), *Conflict in World Society: A New Perspective on International Relations*, London: Harvester Wheatsheaf.

Brown, C. (1997) *Understanding International Relations*, Basingstoke: Macmillan.

Bull, H. (1977) *The Anarchical Society: A Study of Order in World Politics*, Houndmills: Macmillan.

Bull, H. and A. Watson (eds) (1984) *The Expansion of International Society*, Oxford: Clarendon Press.

Buzan, B. (1993) 'From International System to International Society: Structural Realism and Regime Theory Meet the English School', *International Organization* 47: 327–352.

——. (2001) 'The English School: an Underexploited Resource in IR', *Review of International Studies* 27: 471–488.

—— (2004) *From International to World Society? English School Theory and the Social Structure of Globalisation*, Cambridge: Cambridge University Press.

Buzan, B. and R. Little (2000) *International Systems in World History: Remaking the Study of International Relations*, Oxford: Oxford University Press.

Clark, I. (2005) *Legitimacy in International Society*, Oxford: Oxford University Press.

Cox, M. (2003) 'Editor's Introduction', *International Relations* 17: 251–252.

Der Derian, J. (1995) *International Theory: Critical Investigations*, London: Macmillan.

Dunne, T. (1995) 'The Social Construction of International Society', *European Journal of International Relations* 1: 367–389.

—— (1998) *Inventing International Society: A History of the English School*, London: Macmillan.

—— (2001) 'New Thinking on International Society', *British Journal of Politics and International Relations* 3: 223–242.

—— (2002) 'After 9/11: What Next for Human Rights?', *International Journal of Human Rights* 6: 93–101.

—— (2003) 'Society and Hierarchy in International Relations', *International Relations* 17: 303–320.

—— (2005) 'The New Agenda', in A. Bellamy (ed.), *International Society and its Critics*, Oxford: Oxford University Press.

Finnemore, M. (1996) *National Interests in International Society*, Ithaca: Cornell University Press.

Halliday, F. (2003) 'Global Governance: Prospects and Problems', in D. Held and A. McGrew (eds), *The Global Transformations Reader: An Introduction to the Globalization Debate*, Cambridge: Polity.

Held, D. and A. McGrew (2003) 'The Great Globalization Debate – An Introduction', in D. Held and A. McGrew (eds), *The Global Transformations Reader: An Introduction to the Globalization Debate*, Cambridge: Polity.

Hurrell, A. (1998) 'Society and Anarchy in International Relations' in B.A. Roberson (ed.), *International Society and the Development of International Relations Theory*, London: Continuum, pp. 17–42.

—— (1999) 'Security and Inequality' in A. Hurrell and N. Woods (eds), *Inequality, Globalization, and World Politics*, Oxford: Oxford University Press, pp. 248–271.

Jackson, R.H. (2000) *The Global Covenant: Human Conduct in a World of States*, Oxford: Oxford University Press.

—— (1995) 'The Political Theory of International Society', in K. Booth and S. Smith (eds) *International Relations Theory Today*, Cambridge: Polity, pp. 110–128.

Jackson, R. H. and G. Sorensen, (1999) *Introduction to International Relations*, Oxford: Oxford University Press.

James, A. (1993) 'System or Society?', *Review of International Studies* 19: 269–288.

Katzenstein, P.J. (ed.) (1996) *The Culture of National Security: Norms and Identity in World Politics*, New York: Columbia University Press.

Keal, P. (2003) *European Conquest and the Rights of Indigenous Peoples: The Moral Backwardness of International Society*, Cambridge: Cambridge University Press.

Keene, E. (2002) *Beyond the Anarchical Society: Grotius, Colonialism and Order in World Politics*, Cambridge: Cambridge University Press.

Keohane, R.O. (1988) 'International Institutions: Two Approaches', *International Studies Quarterly* 32: 379–396.

Korman, S. (1996) *The Right of Conquest: The Acquisition of Territory by Force in International Law and Practice*, Oxford: Clarendon Press.

Lapid, Y. (1989) '"Quo Vadis" International Relations? Further Reflections on the Next Stage of International Relations Theory', *Millennium* 18: 77–88.

Linklater, A. (1996) 'Rationalism' in S. Burchill *et al.* (eds) *Theories of International Relations*, London: Macmillan.

Little, R. (2000) 'The English School's Contribution to the Study of International Relations', *European Journal of International Relations* 6: 395–422.

Mayall, J. (1990) *Nationalism and International Society*, Cambridge: Cambridge University Press.

Murphy, C. (1994) *International Organization and Industrial Change: Global Governance since 1850*, Oxford: Oxford University Press.

Neumann, I.B. (1996) *Russia and the Idea of Europe: A Study in Identity and International Relations*, London: Routledge.

—— (1999) *The Uses of the Other: The 'East' in European Identity Formation*, Minneapolis: Minnesota University Press.

Reus-Smit, C. (1999) *The Moral Purpose of the State: Culture, Social Identity and Institutional Rationality in International Relations*, Princeton: Princeton University Press.

—— (2002) 'Imagining Society: Constructivism and the English School', *British Journal of Politics and International Relations* 4: 487–509.

Roberson, B.A. (1998) *International Society and the Development of International Relations Theory*, London: Pinter.

Rosenau, J.N. (1995) 'Governance in the Twenty-first Century', *Global Governance* 1: 13–43.

Smith, S. (1989) 'Paradigm Dominance in International Relations' in H. Dyer and L. Mangasarian (eds), *The Study of International Relations: The State of the Art*, London: Macmillan.

Suganami, H. (2003) 'British Institutionalists, or the English School, 20 Years On', *International Relations* 17: 253–272.

Wæver, O. (1998) 'Four Meanings of International Society: A Transatlantic Dialogue' in B.A. Roberson (ed.), *International Society and the Development of International Relations Theory*, London: Pinter, pp. 80–144.

Watson, A. (1992) *The Evolution of International Society: A Comparative Historical Analysis*, London: Routledge.

Welsh, J. (1995) *Edmund Burke and International Relations*, London: Macmillan.

Wendt, A. (1999) *Social Theory of International Politics*, Cambridge: Cambridge University Press.

Wheeler, N.J. (1992) 'Pluralist or Solidarist Conceptions of International Society: Bull and Vincent on Humanitarian Intervention', *Millennium* 21: 463–487.

—— (2000) *Saving Strangers: Humanitarian Intervention in International Society*, Oxford: Oxford University Press.

Wheeler, N.J. and T. Dunne (1996) 'Hedley Bull's Pluralism of the Intellect and Solidarism of the Will', *International Affairs* 72: 91–107.

Young, O.R. (ed.) (1997) *Global Governance: Drawing Insights from the Environmental Experience*, Ithaca: Cornell University Press.

6 Regime theory and the quest for global governance[1]

Oran R. Young

Introduction

Twenty-five years ago, none of us anticipated that regime theory—or the new institutionalism more generally—would develop into a major movement in the study of international relations (Young 1994). Yet in retrospect, it is not hard to identify several factors that converged to bring about this unanticipated occurrence. What many now call neo-liberal institutionalism arose, in part, to explain how cooperation could survive and even thrive at the international level—especially in fields like trade and monetary relations—in the face of the declining capacity of the United States to act as an effective hegemon. As Robert Keohane's seminal account—set forth in his 1984 book entitled *After Hegemony*—makes clear, issue-specific regimes can prove beneficial for all parties concerned, whether or not these actors constitute a privileged group in the Olsonian sense.[2]

Additionally, regime theory proved effective in taking up the slack in an intellectual environment in which much of mainstream thinking in the fields of international law and organization had been marginalized by a preoccupation with formal structures—particularly the various elements of the United Nations system—that seemed increasingly ineffectual and incapable of meeting the demand for governance arising in international society. As the essays collected in *International Regimes*—an influential volume edited by Stephen Krasner and published originally in 1982 as a special issue of the journal *International Organization*—made clear, those concerned with international governance were not confined to the repetition of uninspiring and increasingly shopworn proposals aimed at organizational reforms in the United Nations System (Krasner 1983).

More generally, the study of international regimes merged into and gained strength from the new institutionalism spreading throughout the social sciences in the 1970s and 1980s (Rutherford 1994; Scott 1995). Particularly in the variants associated with the fields of economics and public choice, this movement offered a theoretically attractive framework for those seeking new intellectual capital to energize thinking about governance at the international level. What has emerged from this effort is a conception of governance as a social function centered on steering social systems in such a way as to enhance social welfare together with a realization that issue-specific regimes can create islands of governance even in the absence of anything resembling an overarching government at the international level (Rosenau and Czempiel 1992).

What follows is an account of the regime-theoretic perspective on global governance as seen through the lens of my personal involvement with the new institutionalism in international relations. It is clear that my work has evolved over the last twenty-five years along with the new institutionalism in international relations more generally (Young 1983, 1989, 1994, 1999b). Without a doubt, I have been influenced by the work of others in this connection. But it is fair to conclude as well that my work has influenced the direction this intellectual movement has taken in several areas. I make no claim that this commentary constitutes a comprehensive and even-handed account of the past, present, and future of regime theory.[3] But it does reflect an effort on the part of one who was present at the creation and who has been active in the development of regime theory ever since to assess the contributions of this movement to the study of global governance and to offer some suggestions about growth areas for the future that others may find of some interest.

Structure: regimes as sources of global governance

Most regime theorists—deliberately for the most part—have adopted the individual regime as their principal unit of analysis. This strategy has contributed substantially to the success of this stream of research over the last two decades. Individual regimes are typically more or less self-contained arrangements that can be identified with reasonable precision and examined in depth as discrete entities. What is more, the universe of cases containing issue-specific regimes is large enough to allow for a variety of forms of comparative analysis.[4] Much remains to be done in this realm, and there is every reason to believe that increases in analytic sophistication and the growth of accessible databases will stimulate comparative studies that add substantially to our knowledge of issues arising in the study of individual regimes (Breitmeier *et al.* 1996).

As a number of British scholars have forcefully reminded us, however, there are substantial costs associated with any strategy that ignores the links between issue-specific regimes, on the one hand, and international society, on the other (Evans and Wilson 1992; Buzan 1993; Hurrell 1993; Dunne 2001). When we turn our attention to this set of relationships, it becomes clear immediately that two distinct clusters of concerns deserve careful consideration. Individual regimes operate within the social setting created by international society. Accordingly, we must examine the impact of this embedded character of regimes in any effort to construct comprehensive accounts of regime formation and effectiveness (Young 1999b: Ch. 8). But at the same time, the operation of individual regimes produces broader consequences or, in other words, impacts that go well beyond the confines of specific problems to generate more or less significant impacts on international society as a whole (Underdal and Young 2004). This observation has led, among other things, to a number of insights about the role of issue-specific regimes as mechanisms that can respond to the demand for governance in an anarchical and decentralized social setting of the sort exemplified by international society (Bull 1977).

The creators of individual regimes ordinarily assume—implicitly if not explicitly—that these arrangements rest on and reflect the defining characteristics of international society. This assumption has a range of implications for our understanding of issue-specific regimes. Among the most important of these are the propositions that (1) the formal members of international regimes are ordinarily states, (2) the provisions of regimes are not legally binding on members unless and until they have ratified or otherwise explicitly consented to them, (3) regimes seldom have access to significant material resources of their own, and (4) there are few mechanisms available to provide authoritative interpretations regarding the provisions of regimes in cases where individual members disagree about their content.

Clearly, international society does provide constitutive rules that are important to the operation of specific regimes. By comparison with most domestic arrangements, however, international regimes must be able to function on a relatively self-contained basis. They cannot rely on overarching societal mechanisms to monitor, much less enforce, compliance with their provisions. They cannot turn to a central government to provide the funds needed to carry out their functions. They cannot hand over disagreements or disputes about the operational meaning of their provisions to a society-wide mechanism in the expectation of obtaining authoritative interpretations that the parties involved will acknowledge as binding.

A number of observers have pointed out as well that it is not easy to fit the full range of issue-specific regimes into the conventional model of international society construed as a society of states (von Moltke 1997). There are significant regimes in which some—or even all—of the members are non-state actors (Keck and Sikkink 1998; Florini 2000; Haufler 2001). The international insurance regime is a striking case in point (Haufler 1997). This regime began in the nineteenth century as an arrangement in which states were relatively unimportant and has evolved over the last century into a complex arrangement featuring extensive interactions between states and non-state actors. Similarly, we are witnessing today the development of regimes that violate or at least modify some of the constitutive rules of international society. Some regimes, like the emerging arrangement for the protection of biological diversity, have become vehicles that actors use to launch initiatives leading to substantial interventions into the domestic affairs of member states. Others, like the regime for whales and whaling, rely on decision rules that make it possible to arrive at important decisions in the absence of genuine consensus among their members. Still others feature efforts to develop funding mechanisms that do not require regular contributions from their members.

What are we to make of this situation? Real institutions are always more complex and messy than our simple models would lead one to believe, and there is no doubt that the growth of international regimes constitutes an innovative force at the international level. Yet it remains appropriate—at least as a point of departure—to look upon regimes as institutional arrangements created to respond to demands for governance in a society in which states are still essential actors and in which there is no central public authority

For the most part, interested parties create individual regimes to solve specific problems, such as what to do about the depletion of stratospheric ozone or how to lower or eliminate protective tariffs. This makes it appropriate to evaluate individual regimes in terms of their success in the realm of problem solving. Taken together, however, regimes are beginning to generate broader consequences affecting the overarching society within which they operate. Partly, this is a matter of reforming the states system through such measures as finding appropriate roles for non-state actors, curtailing the more extreme manifestations of state sovereignty, and devising ways to address important problems, even when it is difficult to achieve consensus among member states. In part, the development of a growing collection of issue-specific regimes has become a driving force in the emergence of what many have begun to call global civil society (Lipschutz 1996; Wapner 1996; Wapner 1997; Keane 2003). Because the decentralized character of international society makes it hard to bring about reforms framed in general terms, those seeking to alter particular features of this society often find it helpful to introduce innovations at the level of issue-specific regimes and then to work hard to promote the diffusion of these institutional innovations to other regimes and ultimately to international society as a whole. It follows that some observers will judge the effectiveness of regimes, at least in part, in terms of their broader consequences (Underdal and Young 2004). Observers may regard specific regimes as effective in terms of these broader consequences, even when their performance leaves a good deal to be desired in terms of solving specific problems.

One of the most interesting issues raised by these observations concerns the role that regimes play as suppliers of governance in international society. Governance, on this account, becomes an important concern whenever interdependencies give rise to collective-action problems or, in other words, individualistic behavior leads to a loss of social welfare. The demand for governance in this sense at the international (and transnational) level is rising steadily. Yet the absence of anything resembling a government in this society has long been regarded as a decisive impediment to supplying governance in world affairs (Young 1999b). Throughout the last century, many sought to remedy this defect by advocating the creation of a world government (Suganami 1989). But the movement to establish an overarching public authority in international society is no closer to achieving its goal today than it has been in the past. We are now increasingly aware as well of the costs governments impose on societies not only in material terms but also in terms of more intangible factors like the suppression of civil liberties.

This has led, in recent years, to a rapid rise of interest in the idea that a growing collection of issue-specific regimes can and will prove successful in supplying governance without government in international society (Rosenau and

Czempiel 1992).[5] Clearly, it is important not to jump to naive conclusions in this realm. Although effective regimes have emerged in a number of issue areas, there is much less progress to report in others. Regimes vary dramatically in terms of their capacity to solve specific problems, much less to produce desirable broader consequences. There are major gaps in the availability of mechanisms to resolve disputes or even respond to allegations regarding non-compliance arising in connection with specific regimes. Still, the emergence of a growing collection of regimes is surely significant from the point of view of global governance, and the vision underlying the idea of governance without government is undoubtedly an appealing one. There is much to be said, under the circumstances, for devoting sustained attention to these broader consequences of regimes, even as we continue to analyze questions pertaining to regime formation, evolution, and effectiveness *per se*.

Processes: regime formation and the pursuit of effectiveness

Of course, the observation that institutions serve to overcome or at least to alleviate collective-action problems (Schelling 1960, 1978), thereby supplying a measure of governance in the decentralized setting of international society, simply opens up a new range of questions (Levy *et al.* 1995). What exactly are regimes, and how do they come into existence? Why do regimes arise to deal with some situations involving interactive decision-making but not others? How do regimes operate to guide the behavior of those engaged in interactive decision-making? Why are some regimes more successful than others in solving the problems that lead to their creation in the first place? The effort to answer these and a number of related questions has spawned a large and vibrant literature among students of international relations.[6] In this section, I single out two major strands of this literature—studies of regime formation and regime effectiveness—that I have worked with and that seem particularly significant to me.

Regime formation

Early contributors to regime theory were preoccupied, for the most part, with the subject of regime formation (Ruggie 1975; Young 1977; Oye 1986; Haggard and Simmons 1987; Hasenclever *et al.* 1997). The explanation for this orientation is straightforward. There is a sense in which institutions themselves are public goods—or "bads" as the case may be (Kindleberger 1988). They commonly exhibit the defining attributes of (1) non-excludability—it is hard to exclude individual members of a group from enjoying the benefits produced by regimes once they come on stream—and (2) non-rivalness—providing the benefits associated with a regime to individual members normally does not reduce the supply available to others.[7] This suggests that free riding should be a common occurrence when it comes to the creation of institutional arrangements, so that the supply of regimes will be suboptimal.[8] Guided by the analytic apparatus of game theory and neo-classical microeconomics, moreover, early research on regimes often assumed that success in forming a regime and success in problem solving were, for all practical purposes, one and the same thing.[9] On both accounts, the processes involved in forming regimes loom as a critical topic for analysis.

Not surprisingly, many students of international politics responded to this interest in regime formation by deploying arguments about the role of power in the material or structural sense as a determinant of outcomes resulting from interactive behavior at the international level. As Susan Strange asserted, in a widely quoted passage, an understanding of these matters "is more likely to be captured by looking not at the regime that emerges on the surface but beneath, at the bargains on which it is based" (1983: 354).[10] Going a step further—and building on Charles Kindleberger's account of the causes of the Great Depression—many realists and neo-realists developed an argument (often characterized as hegemonic stability theory) to the effect that the presence of a single dominant actor or, in other words, a hegemon possessing the capacity and the will to act in a given issue area constitutes a necessary—if not a sufficient—condition for success in efforts to create international regimes (Kindleberger 1973, 1981).[11]

As numerous contributors to regime theory have pointed out, this line of thinking cannot be sustained empirically, despite its analytic appeal as a parsimonious perspective on regime formation (Snidal 1985). There are many instances of success in regime formation where it is impossible to point to the work of a hegemon, even in the limited sense of an actor dominant in a particular issue area. In fact, studies of regime formation involving natural resources and the environment make it clear that there are a good many cases in which success in processes of regime formation has required a concerted effort on the part of others to persuade a reluctant hegemon—usually the United States in recent years—to acquiesce in the establishment of a new regime (e.g. the climate-change regime) or the strengthening of an existing regime (e.g. the biodiversity regime).

My own work on regime formation has focussed on three interlocking themes—processes of regime formation, institutional bargaining, and stages of regime creation. Early on, I sought to answer questions about regime formation by differentiating among spontaneous, negotiated, and imposed regimes (Young 1983). Spontaneous or self-generating regimes, as analysts like Friedrich Hayek (1973), Robert Axelrod (1984), and Robert Ellickson (1991) have taught us, are routinized or, as some would say, institutionalized patterns of behavior that arise in the absence of any conscious effort and that succeed in coordinating the behavior of group members in the absence of explicit compliance mechanisms. Imposed regimes, as many realists and neo-realists think of them, are arrangements that a dominant actor—or in some cases a dominant elite or alliance—articulate and pressure others to accept either through coercion in the ordinary sense of the term or through some form of cognitive, or Gramscian, hegemony (Gill 1993). Negotiated regimes lie between these extremes; they involve conscious efforts on the part of actors that are autonomous, though seldom equal, to arrive at mutually acceptable rules and decision-making procedures through some sort of bargaining process.

Today, I have come to realize that these distinctions regarding processes of regime formation are analytic in nature. Most cases involve elements of all three, so that it is pointless to argue whether we can safely ignore one or another of the three processes. Even so, I remain persuaded that regime formation in the setting provided by international society ordinarily involves a substantial element of bargaining. The major players in international society lack the cultural homogeneity, much less the sense of community that typically underlies self-generating institutional arrangements in other social domains.[12] Except in cases involving coordination problems where there are no incentives to cheat, moreover, actors in international society generally prefer to see rules and the commitments that go with them spelled out in formal—though not necessarily legally binding—agreements (Stein 1983; Abbott and Snidal 2001). Conversely, even unusually powerful actors generally find it easier, and less costly, to engage in negotiations about the provisions of regimes than to rely on coercion, pure and simple, to induce others to accept their institutional preferences, much less to comply with the resultant rules on an ongoing basis. There is as well much more to dominance at the international level than the assertions of those who speak of hegemony would lead one to believe. Numerous cases occur, under real-world conditions, in which seemingly powerful actors find it extremely hard to force others to accept their preferences regarding regimes, and seemingly weak actors manage to exert considerable influence in processes of regime formation (Young 1994; Miles *et al.* 2002).

If this means that interactions describable in a general way as negotiation constitute a particularly prominent feature of processes of regime formation at the international level, however, it does not ensure that bargaining over the terms of international regimes or, in other words, the provisions of constitutional contracts will fit neatly into the models of bargaining familiar to those who work in the traditions of game theory or microeconomics.[13] One of my most significant contributions to the study of regimes encompasses what I call institutional bargaining (Young 1994). This type of bargaining is distinctive in at least three major respects. It occurs under conditions of considerable uncertainty not only about the outcomes likely to flow from the selection of various combinations of strategies but also about the range of feasible strategies themselves. Participants therefore have incentives to engage in integrative (or productive) in contrast to distributive (or positional) bargaining (Walton and McKersie 1965; Cross 1969). The goal of institutional bargaining is normally to create maximum winning coalitions—and preferably coalitions of the whole—in contrast to the minimum winning coalitions widely discussed in theories of legislative bargaining (Riker 1962). In addition, the typical processes occurring in this sort of bargaining feature the development of negotiating texts which are gradually refined into explicit agreements that all, or at least most, of the participants are prepared to sign and recommend to their colleagues back home for ratification and implementation. We lack formal models capable of explaining, much less predicting, outcomes flowing from institutional bargaining at the international level. Nonetheless, a good deal of knowledge about this form of bargaining is accumulating from careful studies of a growing universe of cases.[14]

More recently, I have come to believe that it is useful to divide processes of regime formation into distinct stages. On this account, negotiation remains the central element of these processes. But the negotiation stage is normally bracketed by a stage of agenda formation that precedes negotiation and a stage of operationalization that follows negotiation (Young 1998). Agenda formation encompasses the processes through which an issue emerges as a policy concern, is framed for consideration in policy arenas, and rises to a high enough level on the international agenda to justify the initiation of negotiations (Tversky and Kahneman 1981; Kahneman and Tversky 2000). Operationalization, by contrast, includes the processes through which agreements make the transition from paper to practice both internationally and within the domestic systems of participating states (Mitchell 1994). The point of introducing these distinctions arises from the fact that the forces at work in each of the three stages are far from identical (Young 1998). While the role of interest-based bargaining is particularly prominent during the negotiation stage, for instance, ideas and other cognitive forces figure more prominently during the stage of agenda formation.[15] I do not see this development as detracting from my earlier work on processes of regime formation in general and on institutional bargaining more specifically. But it does mean that we should be skeptical about claims purporting to identify propositions applying uniformly across the entire process of regime formation.

Regime effectiveness

Much remains to be learned about regime formation. But the development of research on regime formation into a form of normal science has led some of us to turn our attention elsewhere in search of new areas of inquiry (Kuhn 1970). A key observation arising from this search is that regimes vary markedly in terms of the extent to which they succeed in solving the problems that lead their members to create them in the first place. This realization launched the study of what we now call regime effectiveness (Young 1992). Almost immediately following the acceptance of effectiveness as an important issue for regime theory came the recognition that there are major challenges facing those who seek to differentiate between the roles regimes play and the impacts of a variety of other determinants of collective outcomes at the international level. Exemplified by the question "do regimes matter?" (Haas 1989), this range of concerns has now coalesced into a second broad and enduring component of regime theory (Young 1992, 1999a, 1999b; Haas *et al.* 1993; Victor *et al.* 1998; Weiss and Jacobson 1998; Wettestad 1999; Underdal and Hanf 2000; Social Learning Group 2001; Miles *et al.* 2002; Underdal and Young 2004).

The most intuitively appealing way to think about effectiveness is to say that regimes succeed to the extent that they solve the problems that lead to their creation (Young 1994). But this formulation is fraught with complications. Problem solving is not an all-or-nothing affair. Regimes may range from slightly effective to decisive, and they may become more or less effective with the passage of time. Similarly, regimes may serve to manage problems in the sense of preventing them from becoming more severe in contrast to solving them. In all these cases, moreover, it is extremely difficult to determine the proportion of the observed variance that is reasonably attributable to the operation of regimes in contrast to other forces. Many collective outcomes are best understood as products of clusters of driving forces that are highly interactive and hard to separate in any meaningful sense (Young 2002b). These complications have given rise to two alternative approaches to assessing effectiveness. One focusses on actor behavior in contrast to problem solving and asks whether the operation of any given regime has produced demonstrable changes in the behavior of some or all of the actors whose behavior is relevant to the problem (Young 1999a). The other directs attention to implementation and compliance and seeks to monitor how well regulatory rules are implemented by regime members and whether subjects conform to the requirements of these rules in going about their business (Victor *et al.* 1998; Raustiala and Slaughter 2002). These alternatives have obvious attractions in terms of their methodological implications. But a moment's reflection will suffice to make it clear that they are not full-fledged substitutes for an approach to effectiveness that emphasizes problem solving. The obvious solution is to encourage researchers to work with all three approaches, comparing and contrasting the results wherever possible. The upshot is a conception of effectiveness that largely maps onto the distinctions—familiar to students of public policy—among outputs, outcomes, and impacts (Easton 1965).

Assuming that we can get past these conceptual complications, the next logical step in the study of regime effectiveness is to deploy familiar techniques of variation finding analysis in search of generalizations about the determinants of effectiveness (Dessler 1992). Here effectiveness becomes the dependent variable and any of a wide range of factors figure as independent variables in conjectures about effectiveness. Researchers working in this area have come up with numerous hypotheses about sources of effectiveness, ranging from the importance of a dominant actor or hegemon committed to the success of a regime to the need for an informal network or community of supporters (Reinicke 1998; Young 1999b: Ch. 6). The catch is that it is relatively easy to find specific cases that contradict or, at least fail to confirm, virtually every specific hypothesis. Of course, situations of this sort are common in social-science research, and the normal response among those employing variation finding techniques is to subdivide the universe of cases in order to control for various factors thought to be relevant or to deploy a battery of multivariate statistical procedures in the interests of attaching weights to several factors operating at the same time (Miles *et al.* 2002). The problem with this response in the study of international regimes is that the universe of cases is both relatively small and characterized by considerable internal variation. This does not rule out the use of multivariate statistics entirely. But no one has succeeded so far in using such techniques to advance our understanding of regime effectiveness significantly.

Given this set of complications, what recourse is available to scholars seeking to reveal the determinants of regime effectiveness (Underdal and Young 2004)? The answer that I and a team of researchers working with me have arrived at is that progress in this area requires a concerted effort first to identify the behavioral mechanisms or pathways through which regimes affect the behavior of their members (and those operating under the jurisdiction of members) and then to examine individual cases systematically in order to illuminate the role of these mechanisms in specific regimes (Young 1999a). Perhaps the most obvious mechanisms rest on the assumption that the relevant actors are unitary utility maximizers. In the hands of Robert Keohane and his colleagues, this has resulted in the identification of the three "Cs" (Haas *et al.* 1993). Regimes can affect behavior by intensifying concern about a problem, by improving the contractual environment among the relevant players, or by building capacity to deal with the problem. Beyond this obvious tack, however, the specification of behavioral models makes it possible to investigate other pathways through which regimes can affect the behavior of actors (Young 1999c). Even retaining the assumption of unitary actors, we can examine the impacts of regimes as bestowers of authority or legitimacy, as mechanisms that influence role definitions, and as facilitators of social learning.[16] If we go a step further and relax the assumption of unitary actors, a range of issues involving the effects of regimes on domestic or, more broadly, internal politics come into focus (Putnam 1988).

It is obviously desirable to spell out these behavioral mechanisms with some precision at the outset and then to examine actual cases systematically in search of evidence of their operation. The result is not a mode of analysis that can be described as testing hypotheses empirically, much less a process that features the effective use of statistical procedures. Yet the development of these causal models to guide the empirical examination of actual cases leads to important insights about the determinants of regime effectiveness. At this early stage, it is apparent that regimes, which are not actors in their own right, not only do make a difference but also impact the behavior of those who are actors in a number of distinct ways. It is apparent as well that individual behavioral mechanisms can and often do come into play simultaneously. This should alert us to the dangers associated with the use of models that are highly restrictive with respect to their behavioral assumptions. At the same time, it holds the promise of yielding results that are more useful to policymakers than contingent generalizations that suffer from a lack of specificity regarding the conditions under which they can be expected to hold.

Next steps: extending the reach of regime theory

This, then, is the basic logic of regime theory as an approach to global governance, especially as developed by those of us whose intellectual roots are planted firmly in theories of collective action. There is clearly a large agenda of additional research to be carried out within this paradigm. Among other things, the processes through which regimes change over time—a topic that has received only marginal attention to date[17]—seems likely to become increasingly prominent during the near future (Young 1999b: Ch. 7). Regime change may well join the problems of regime formation and regime effectiveness during the foreseeable future as a third major strand of the mainstream of regime theory. Yet it has become increasingly apparent as well that major contributions are being made to the new institutionalism in international relations by those employing intellectual capital that differs significantly from the mainstream of collective-action theories (Reinicke 1998). This observation opens up an important set of issues that are likely to become increasingly prominent during the near future. It is hazardous, of course, to generalize about the various forms that this development will take. But in my own work, I have found it particularly helpful to think in a sustained fashion about three sets of concerns that extend beyond the reach of collective-action theories in their normal forms: regime tasks, the links between actors and institutions, and the distinction between collective-action models and social-practice models (Young 1999b, 2002a).

Starting from the logic of collective action, it seems natural to think of regimes in regulatory terms (Chayes and Chayes 1995). The essential role of these arrangements is to supply rules or codes of conduct whose purpose is to mitigate the well-known tendency for actors to generate Pareto inferior outcomes under conditions of interactive decision-making. Important as this regulatory function is, however, it does not constitute the only function of regimes in international society. I have found it increasingly useful to identify several other roles—I call them procedural, programmatic, and generative roles—and to differentiate them from the idea of regimes as regulatory mechanisms (Young 1999b).

Procedural roles center on the creation and operation of arrangements that allow the members of regimes to make social or collective choices about a variety of matters. Whereas rules spell out prescriptions that are expected to govern behavior on an ongoing basis, procedural arrangements allow actors to reach agreement on matters of common concern, including issues that (1) are both recurrent and non-recurrent in nature, (2) were unforeseen at the stage of regime formation, and (3) involve alterations in the regulatory rules themselves.

Programmatic roles center on efforts on the part of regime members to coordinate their actions or to combine their resources in the interests of undertaking projects expected to generate benefits for all the participants. Coordinated efforts to reduce pollution in shared lakes and rivers and unitization schemes governing the exploitation of shared pools of oil or gas are prominent examples of such roles.

Generative roles, by contrast, feature processes of social learning in which regime members gain new knowledge regarding the nature of the problems to be solved, develop new ideas about policy instruments available to solve these problems, or acquire new norms regarding appropriate behavior in connection with the issues at stake (Social Learning Group 2001). The role of the European long-range transboundary air pollution regime both in raising consciousness about the dangers of acid rain and in devising new ways of thinking about the problem (e.g. the idea of critical loads) constitutes a striking example of the generative role that regimes can play (Underdal and Hanf 2000).

These roles are by no means mutually exclusive. Many regimes combine regulatory and procedural functions, for instance, and the combination of programmatic and generative roles is a common occurrence. Even so, regimes do tend to become known in international circles for the primary roles they play. The ozone regime, for example, is essentially a regulatory arrangement (Parson 1993; 2003). The Great Lakes water-quality regime has a pronounced programmatic orientation (Botts and Muldoon 1996). The most important role of the regime governing trade in endangered species is procedural (Sand 1997). The point of drawing such distinctions is not to suggest that any one of these roles is more important than the others. The important thing is to recognize that the requirements for success differ significantly depending upon the particular role or combination of roles a regime is expected to play. Understandably, issues relating to compliance loom large in conjunction with regulatory activities. Procedural arrangements at the international level focus attention on the nature of consensual decision-making and on options allowing individual members to opt out of specific decisions, concerns that make compliance *per se* relatively unimportant in thinking about regimes of this type. For their part, programmatic regimes typically direct attention to matters of coordinated planning and funding in contrast to matters involving compliance with regulatory rules.

Theories of collective action routinely assume that actors exist *ex ante* and that these actors have fully specified utility functions that they seek to maximize through a stream of choices involving the selection of well-defined courses of action. This leads naturally to a contractarian perspective on regimes in which actors weigh the benefits and costs of joining regimes as well as living up to their commitments once they become members. This is a powerful perspective with an impressive intellectual pedigree in many areas of enquiry (Rawls 1971; Buchanan 1975). But it is not the only useful way to think about the nature of regimes in international society. This realization leads to a number of valuable insights, often associated with the work of those who call themselves constructivists but by no means limited to any particular line of analysis.[18] For starters, there is the issue of the relationship between agents and structures (Wendt 1987). The essential point here is that social structures, including international regimes, sometimes influence the identities of their members in contrast to emerging as products of interactions among actors whose identities are fully defined at the outset. It requires little thought to see the relevance of this process both at the level of international society as a whole and at the level of individual regimes (Wendt 1999). As many "new" states established in the postwar era have discovered, membership in a society of states can become a powerful socializing force (Falk 1970; Jackson 1990). More modestly, participants in issue-specific regimes, like the arrangements governing whales and whaling or trade in endangered species, often find themselves acting in ways they would never have anticipated prior to becoming regime members (Friedheim 2001).

These observations raise fundamental questions about how we think of the members of international regimes and the forces that drive their regime-related behavior. The assumption that actors are unitary utility maximizers is a powerful one. It has produced impressive results, and there are good reasons to expect that many studies of regimes will continue to use this assumption to good advantage during the foreseeable future. Nevertheless, it seems apparent that we must also devote time and energy to understanding a variety of behavioral mechanisms that are largely abstracted away in models rooted in the logic of collective action. Three distinct phenomena deserve particular attention in this connection: discourses, norms, and routinized behavior. Discourses serve to structure both the ways in which we conceptualize problems and the cognitive constructs that guide the search for solutions to them (Litfin 1994; Dryzek 1997). They address a deeper level of analysis than most utilitarian assessments in the sense that a shift from one discourse to another may change the way in which we define a problem as well as the way in which we identify alternatives to be considered from a utilitarian or benefit/cost point of view. As the recent revival of interest in the role of norms at the international level makes clear, there is considerable scope for normative considerations to enter into the operation of regimes, particularly in settings characterized by severe limits on available information.[19] Faced with uncertainties regarding not only options for solving problems but also the fundamental character of the problems themselves, actors often fall back on normative principles as guides to action. What is more, routinization—roughly the equivalent of socialization at the level of individual behavior—is an important determinant of the behavior of states and other collective entities involved in the formation and operation of regimes. Exemplified by the development of standard operating procedures (SOPs) on the part of government agencies responsible for implementing the provisions of regimes, routinization ordinarily accounts for the bulk of day-to-day behavior on the part of those responsible for the activities that regimes seek to govern (Allison 1971).

Interestingly, these forces need not be thought of as contradicting the dictates of rational choice construed as utility-maximizing behavior. In a complex world in which numerous issues require attention simultaneously and high levels of uncertainty with regard to individual issues are typical, rational actors routinely rely on rules of thumb and make use of a variety of shortcuts (Tversky and Kahneman 1974). From this point of view, the existence of a coherent discourse that serves to structure thinking about a problem is apt to seem attractive, and the development of standard operating procedures is an unavoidable necessity. Even so, these differentiable perspectives on the sources of behavior have given rise to several distinct approaches to modeling the processes associated with international regimes. In my judgment, it makes sense to group these approaches, in a rough and ready fashion, into two broad clusters that I call collective-action models and social-practice models (Young 2001, 2002a).

Collective-action models rest on utilitarian premises in the sense that they treat the actors in social settings as unitary utility maximizers weighing the benefits and costs associated with alternative choices in situations involving interactive decision-making (Rutherford 1994; Sandler 1997). Regimes, in these models, are first and foremost regulatory arrangements created to solve or manage social dilemmas (Dawes 1990). Behavioral prescriptions—often characterized as the rules of the game or as codes of conduct—are the essential elements of institutions, and implementation coupled with the achievement of compliance with these prescriptions is critical to their success. The essential link in this chain of reasoning is clear: the role of institutions is to prevent individualistic behavior from leading to Pareto inferior outcomes or, in other words, outcomes that are worse for all participants than feasible alternatives under conditions of strategic interaction. Recently, an interesting debate has arisen among those who think in these regulatory terms about the extent to which compliance is better understood as a matter of management in contrast to a matter of enforcement (Chayes and Chayes 1995; Downs *et al.* 1996; Koh 1997; Mitchell 1998; Raustiala 2000; Raustiala and Slaughter 2002). The issue here concerns the relative importance of sanctions—rewards and punishments—in contrast to various forms of debate, normative pressure, material assistance, capacity building, and institutional enmeshment as sources of behavior in institutional settings. But this does not alter the fact that the focus of collective-action models is on the identification of factors that determine the extent to which the actual behavior of actors conforms to the requirements of regulatory prescriptions.

Social-practice models, by contrast, treat institutions—including international regimes —as arrangements that engender patterned practices which play a role in shaping the identities of participants and feature the articulation of normative discourses, the emergence of informal communities, and the encouragement of social learning (Scott 1995). These models direct attention to processes through which actors become enmeshed in complex social practices that subsequently influence their behavior through *de facto* engagement in belief systems and normative preferences rather than through conscious decisions about compliance with regulatory rules. In the process, they emphasize the relationships that develop between institutions proper and the broader sociocultural settings— some would say communities (Singleton and Taylor 1992)—within which they operate. In these models, regimes guide the course of human interactions with both natural and social environments by influencing the ways in which participants perceive their interests, enmeshing them in practices that give rise to routinized or (as some say) institutionalized behavior, and generating ongoing activities that encourage social learning, even when levels of compliance with their formal prescriptions leave a lot to be desired (Haas and Haas 1995; Social Learning Group 2001).

Is one of these approaches to modeling more appropriate than the other as a basis for research on international regimes? Although it complicates efforts to devise a unified theory—undoubtedly a desirable goal over the long run—there is much to be said for pursuing both lines of analysis at this stage. Each approach points to a distinct set of questions arising from a different way of thinking about the behavioral mechanisms underlying the operation of regimes. While collective-action models are concerned with matters of compliance and the development of incentive-compatible policy instruments to be deployed in regulatory settings, for example, social-practice models direct attention to the routinization of behavior and to the role of community as factors affecting the success of regimes. Additionally, each approach draws on the intellectual capital of a distinct segment of the overall community of social scientists interested in institutions. Collective-action models are largely the work of economists and those interested in public choice; social-practice models grow out of the work of sociologists and social anthropologists. So long as we treat the two sets of models as complementary analytic constructs rather than as competing positions in an ongoing sectarian battle, I am convinced that regime theory will stand to benefit from the insights generated by both sets of models.

Conclusion: the future of regime theory

The last twenty-five years have witnessed a remarkable, though largely unanticipated, rise in the influence of regime theory. What began as a North American effort to think about ways to sustain international cooperation in the face of a (perceived) decline in the relative dominance of the United States has become a worldwide movement broadly linked to the emergence of the new institutionalism in the social sciences. European scholars are now in the vanguard of those seeking ways to identify the determinants of regime effectiveness (Rittberger 1993; Victor *et al.* 1998; Wettestad 1999; Social Learning Group 2001; Miles *et al.* 2002). There are clear indications that this mode of analysis is catching on in East and Southeast Asia.[20] Everywhere, analysts report that they have found regime theory useful as a way of organizing their thinking about contemporary public issues.

Ultimately, however, the future of regime theory will hinge on two sets of considerations: (1) the development of usable knowledge about regimes as such and (2) the growth of insights about the capacity of regimes to supply governance in the decentralized setting of international society. Both factors are important. If regime theorists cannot produce cumulative knowledge about regimes treated as a well-defined universe of cases, analysts will lose interest in this stream of research and drift off into the pursuit of alternative research programs. If regime theory cannot shed light on the overarching problem of meeting the growing demand for global governance, on the other hand, it will become a narrow research program of interest only to specialists dealing with certain specific problems at the international level.

To meet the first of these challenges, regime theory needs to resolve lingering questions about procedures for identifying regimes in operational terms, to find ways to specify and track the causal mechanisms through which regimes affect collective outcomes at the international level, and to meld the insights flowing from what I have described as collective-action models and social-practice models.[21] I do not envision this effort leading to the development of a sizable collection of propositions that spell out either necessary or sufficient conditions for regimes to form and become effective and that can be translated into straightforward design principles to be used by those responsible for creating specific regimes.[22] International regimes are affected by a sizable number of factors that interact with one another in what Charles Ragin (1987) calls a combinatorial or conjunctural fashion. What this means in practice is that we must examine individual situations in depth in order to devise regimes that will prove effective under the particular combination of conditions prevailing in each instance rather than turning to a collection of predetermined designs and choosing one that seems superficially appropriate (Barrett 2002).

Some may find this conclusion disappointing. It does not offer an approach to institutional design that anyone can follow with little need for expert advice. But in my judgment, this reaction is unwarranted. Creating a regime is somewhat akin to building a bridge or treating an illness. We would not ask an engineer to design a bridge without a thorough assessment of the particular conditions prevailing in the case at hand. Nor would we ask a physician to prescribe a treatment for a patient in the absence of a careful consideration of the full range of conditions—including environmental factors—at play in the case at hand. The role of experts in such situations is not to provide simple recipes that any intelligent person can use to produce desired results. Much like engineers and physicians, regime analysts will succeed to the extent that they can provide careful assessments of specific cases that lead to the development of designs that are well adapted to the circumstances at hand.

Meeting the challenge regarding the role of regimes as sources of global governance is equally important. It is essential, in this connection, to avoid being misled by unrealistic expectations. Governments vary dramatically in their capacity to supply governance without producing negative side-effects that swamp their achievements as suppliers of governance. Not surprisingly, much the same is true of issue-specific international regimes treated as arrangements designed to produce governance in limited areas. Actual regimes vary in terms of effectiveness, ranging from dead letters that have little to offer in terms of governance to highly successful arrangements that produce generally acceptable outcomes on an ongoing basis. An attractive feature of issue-specific regimes construed as governance systems is that corrupt regimes operating as discrete entities are less likely to produce profoundly negative side-effects poisoning the whole system than governments that become corrupt. The flip side of this observation, however, is that governance without government is apt to (1) be patchy or uneven, (2) lack well-developed mechanisms for resolving problems arising from interactions among distinct regimes, and (3) leave certain crosscutting functions, like the provision of authoritative interpretations, underdeveloped. Clearly, relying on a growing collection of issue-specific arrangements to meet the rising demand for governance in international society is not a panacea. Nonetheless, it may constitute the best option available during the foreseeable future. To the extent that this is the case, those concerned with governance in world affairs will find that they have strong incentives to launch more systematic efforts to understand the broader consequences of international regimes.

Notes

1 This is an expanded and substantially restructured version of an essay published originally in Japanese in Akio Watanabe and Jitsuo Tsuchiyama (eds) (2001) *Global Governance*, Tokyo: Tokyo University Press, 18–44.

2 A privileged group, in Olson's sense, is a group in which one member places such a high value on a collective good that the benefits outweigh the costs for this dominant member, even when it must bear the entire burden of supplying the good in question (Olson 1965).

3 For an effort to present a more balanced view of the past, present, and future of regime theory, see Young 1999b: Ch. 10.

4 For a helpful comparison of a number of different types of comparative analysis, see Ragin (1987).

5 For a parallel assessment of the evolution of governance systems at the local level, see Ostrom 1990.

6 To trace the evolution of this rapidly growing body of literature, consult Krasner 1983, Rittberger 1993, Levy *et al.* 1995; Hasenclever *et al.* 1997; Martin and Simmons 1998; and Simmons and Martin 2002.

7 In fact, the effectiveness of a regime may increase as more members of the relevant group join.

8 It is understandable, under the circumstances, that creators of institutions sometimes devote energy to the development of exclusion mechanisms in order to strengthen incentives to contribute to their establishment and operation (Frohlich *et al.* 1971).

9 Games in normal form, for example, are over once the players select their strategies and the outcome is determined (Luce and Raiffa 1957; Sandler 1997).

10 A more recent expression of similar sentiments appears in Mearsheimer 1994/1995. See also Gruber 2000.

11 In the terminology of collective action, a situation of this sort would give rise to a privileged group (Olson 1965).

12 For an argument emphasizing the importance of community in small-scale systems, see Singleton and Taylor 1992.

13 For a survey of game-theoretic and microeconomic models of bargaining, see Young 1975.

14 One useful starting point in this context is what Kahneman and Tversky (1979) have called prospect theory.

15 As a result, the role of leadership changes substantially from the stage of agenda formation to the stage of negotiation (Young 1991).

16 The distinction between the logic of consequences and the logic of appropriateness, introduced by March and Olson 1998, is helpful in this connection.

17 Exceptions include Keohane and Nye 1977 and Gehring 1994.

18 For a helpful review of recent writings in the constructivist mode, see Checkel 1998.

19 For a review of recent work on the role of norms in international society, see Raymond 1997.

20 The edited volume (in Japanese) in which the earlier version of this essay appeared has gone into a second printing.

21 Two long-term efforts to address this challenge that have occupied a good deal of my attention in recent years are: (1) the development of an International Regimes Database (Breitmeier *et al.* forthcoming) and (2) the creation of an international project on the Institutional Dimensions of Global Environmental Change (Young *et al.* 1999, Young 2002).

22 Compare the design principles for dealing with the management of common pool resources (CPRs) set forth in Ostrom 1990.

References

Abbott, K. W. and Snidal, D. (2000) "Hard and Soft Law in International Governance," *International Organization*, 54: 421–456.

Allison, G. T. (1971) *Essence of Decision: Explaining the Cuban Missile Crisis*, Boston: Little, Brown.

Axelrod, R. (1984) *The Evolution of Cooperation*, New York: Basic Books.

Barrett, S. (2002) *Environment and Statecraft: The Strategy of Environmental Treaty-making*, Oxford: Oxford University Press.

Botts, L. and Muldoon, P. (1996) *The Great Lakes Water Quality Agreement: Its Past Successes and Uncertain Future*, Hanover: Institute on International Environmental Governance.

Breitmeier, H., Levy, M. A., Young, O. R., and Zürn, M. (1996) "The International Regimes Database as a Tool for the Study of International Cooperation," IIASA Paper WP-96-160.

Breitmeier, H., Young, O. R. and Zürn, M. (forthcoming) *Analyzing International Regimes: from Case Study to Database*.

Buchanan, J. M. (1975) *The Limits of Liberty*, Chicago: University of Chicago Press.

Bull, H. (1977) *The Anarchical Society: A Study of Order in World Politics*, New York: Columbia University Press.

Buzan, B. (1993) "From International System to International Society: Structural Realism and Regime Theory Meet the English School," *International Organization*, 47: 327–352.

Chayes, A. and Chayes, A. H. (1995) *The New Sovereignty: Compliance with International Regulatory Agreements*, Cambridge: Harvard University Press.

Checkel, J. T. (1998) "The Constructivist Turn in International Relations Theory," *World Politics*, 50: 324–348.

Cross, J. G. (1969) *The Economics of Bargaining*, New York: Basic Books.

Dawes, R. (1980) "Social Dilemmas," *Annual Review of Psychology*, 32: 169–193.

Dessler, D. (1992) "The Architecture of Causal Analysis," paper presented at the Center for International Affairs, Harvard University.

Downs, G. W., Rocke, D. and Barsoom, P. (1996) "Is the Good News about Compliance Good News about Cooperation?" *International Organization*, 50: 379–406.

Dryzek, J. S. (1997) *The Politics of the Earth: Environmental Discourses*, Oxford: Oxford University Press.

Dunne, T. (2001) "Sociological Investigations: Instrumental, Legitimist and Coercive Interpretations of International Society," *Millennium: Journal of International Studies*, 30: 1–25.

Easton, D. (1965) *A Systems Analysis of Political Life*, New York: Wiley.

Ellickson, R. C. (1991) *Order without Law: How Neighbors Settle Disputes*, Cambridge: Harvard University Press.

Evans, T. and Wilson, P. (1992) "Regime Theory and the English School of International Relations," *Millennium*, 21: 329–351.

Falk, R. A. (1970) *The Status of Law in International Society*, Princeton: Princeton University Press.

Florini, A. M. (ed.) (2000) *The Third Force: The Rise of Transnational Civil Society*, Tokyo and Washington: Japan Center for International Exchange and Carnegie Endowment for International Peace.

Friedheim, R. L. (ed.) (2001) *Toward a Sustainable Whaling Regime*, Seattle: University of Washington Press.

Gehring, T. (1994) *Dynamic International Regimes: Institutions and International Environmental Governance*, Frankfurt: Lang.

Gill, S. (ed.) (1993) *Gramsci, Historical Materialism and International Relations*, Cambridge: Cambridge University Press.

Gruber, L. (2000) *Ruling the World: Power Politics and the Rise of Supranational Institutions*, Princeton: Princeton University Press.

Haas, P. M. (1989) "Do Regimes Matter? Epistemic Communities and Mediterranean Pollution Control," *International Organization*, 43: 377–403.

Haas, P. M. and Haas, E. B. (1995) "Learning to Learn: Improving International Governance," *Global Governance*, 1: 255–284.

Haas, P M., Keohane, R. and Levy, M. (eds) (1993) *Institutions for the Earth: Sources of Effective International Environmental Protection*, Cambridge: MIT Press.

Haggard, S. and Simmons, B. (1987) "Theories of International Regimes," *International Organization*, 41: 491–517.

Hasenclever, A., Mayer, P. and Rittberger, V. (1997) *Theories of International Regimes*, Cambridge: Cambridge University Press.

Haufler, V. (1997) *Dangerous Commerce: Insurance and the Management of International Risk*, Ithaca: Cornell University Press.

—— (2001) *A Public Role for the Private Sector: Industry Self-regulation in a Global Economy*, Washington, D.C.: Carnegie Endowment for International Peace.

Hayek, F. A. (1973) *Rules and Order*, vol. 1 of *Law, Legislation, and Liberty*, Chicago: University of Chicago Press.

Hurrell, A. (1993) "International Society and the Study of Regimes," in Volker Rittberger (ed.) *Regime Theory and International Relations*, Oxford: Oxford University Press, 49–72.

Jackson, R. H. (1990) *Quasi-States: Sovereignty, International Relations, and the Third World*, Cambridge: Cambridge University Press.

Kahneman, D. and Tversky, A. (1979) "Prospect Theory: An Analysis of Decision Under Risk," *Econometrica*, 47: 263–291.

—— (eds) (2000) *Choices, Values, and Frames*, New York: Cambridge University Press.

Keane, J. (2003) *Global Civil Society*, Cambridge: Cambridge University Press.

Keck, M. E. and Sikkink, K. (1998) *Activists Beyond Borders: Advocacy Networks in International Politics*, Ithaca: Cornell University Press.

Keohane, R. O. (1984) *After Hegemony: Cooperation and Discord in the World Political Economy*, Princeton: Princeton University Press.

Keohane, R. O. and Nye, J. (1977) *Power and Interdependence: World Politics in Transition*, Boston: Little, Brown.

Kindleberger, C. P. (1973) *The World in Depression, 1929–1939*, Berkeley: University of California Press.

—— (1981) "Dominance and Leadership in the International Economy," *International Studies Quarterly*, 25: 242–254.

—— (1988) *The International Economic Order: Essays on Financial Crisis and International Public Goods*, Cambridge: MIT Press.

Koh, H. H. (1997) "Why Do Nations Obey International Law?" *Yale Law Journal*, 106: 2598–2659.

Krasner, S. D. (ed.) (1983) *International Regimes*, Ithaca: Cornell University Press.

Kuhn, T. S. (1970) *The Structure of Scientific Revolutions*, 2nd edn, enlarged. Chicago: University of Chicago Press.

Levy, M. A., Young, O. and Zürn M. (1995) "The Study of International Regimes," *European Journal of International Relations*, 1: 267–330.

Lipschutz, R. (1996) *Global Civil Society and Global Environmental Governance*, Albany: SUNY Press.

Litfin, K. T. (1984) *Ozone Discourses: Science and Politics in Global Environmental Cooperation*, New York: Columbia University Press.

Luce, R. D. and Raiffa, H. (1957) *Games and Decisions*, New York: Wiley.

March, J. G. and Olson, J. (1998) "The Institutional Dynamics of International Political Orders," *International Organization*, 52: 943–969.

Martin, L. and Simmons, B. (1998) "Theories and Empirical Studies of International Institutions," *International Organization*, 52: 729–757.

Mearsheimer, J. (1994/1995) "The False Promise of International Institutions," *International Security*, 19: 5–49.

Miles, E. L., Underdal, A., Andresen, S., Wettestad, J., Skjaerseth, J. and Carlin, E. (2002) *Explaining Regime Effectiveness: Confronting Theory with Evidence*, Cambridge: MIT Press.

Mitchell, R. B. (1994) *Intentional Oil Pollution at Sea: Environmental Policy and Treaty Compliance*, Cambridge: MIT Press.

—— (1998) "Adversarial and Facilitative Approaches to On Site Inspection in Arms Control and Environmental Regimes," paper presented at the annual meeting of the International Studies Association, Minneapolis, March 17–21.

Olson, M. (1965) *The Logic of Collective Action*, Cambridge: Harvard University Press.

Ostrom, E. (1990) *Governing the Commons: The Evolution of Institutions for Collective Action*, Cambridge: Cambridge University Press.

Oye, K. (ed.) (1986) *Cooperation under Anarchy*, Princeton: Princeton University Press.

Parson, E. (1993) "Protecting the Ozone Layer," in P. M. Haas, R. Keohane, and M. A. Levy (eds) *Institutions for the Earth: Sources of Effective International Environmental Protection*, Cambridge: MIT Press, 27–73.

—— (2003) *Protection of the Global Ozone Layer*, New York: Oxford University Press.

Putnam, R. (1988) "Diplomacy and Domestic Politics: The Logic of Two-Level Games," *International Organization*, 42: 427–460.

Ragin, C. C. (1987) *The Comparative Method: Moving Beyond Qualitative and Quantitative Strategies*, Berkeley: University of California Press.

Rapoport, A. (1960) *Fights, Games and Debates*, Ann Arbor: University of Michigan Press.

Raustiala, K. (2000) "Compliance and Effectiveness in International Regulatory Cooperation," *Case Western Reserve Journal of International Law*, 32: 387–440.

Raustiala, K. and Slaughter, A. (2002) "International Law, International Relations, and Compliance," in W. Carlsnaes, Thomas Risse, and B. A. Simmons (eds) *Handbook of International Relations*, London: Sage Publications, 538–558.

Raymond, G. (1997) "Problems and Prospects in the Study of International Norms," *Mershon International Studies Review*, 41: 205–245.

Rawls, J. (1971) *A Theory of Justice*, Cambridge: Harvard University Press.

Reinicke, W. (1998) *Global Public Policy: Governing without Government*, Washington, D.C.: Brookings Institution Press.

Riker, W. (1962) *The Theory of Political Coalitions*, New Haven: Yale University Press.

Rittberger, V. (ed.) (1993) *Regime Theory and International Relations*, Oxford: Clarendon Press.

Rosenau, J. and Czempiel E. (eds) (1992) *Governance without Government: Order and Change in World Politics*, Cambridge: Cambridge University Press.

Ruggie, J. (1975) "International Responses to Technology: Concepts and Trends," *International Organization*, 29: 557–583.

Rutherford, M. (1994) *Institutions in Economics: The Old and the New Institutionalism*, Cambridge: Cambridge University Press.

Sand, P. H. (1997) "Commodity or Taboo? International Regulation of Trade in Endangered Species," in H. O. Bergesen and G. Parmann (eds) *Green Globe Yearbook 1997*, Oxford: Oxford University Press, 19–36.

Sandler, T. (1997) *Global Challenges: An Approach to Environmental, Political, and Economic Problems*, Cambridge: Cambridge University Press.

Schelling, T. C. (1960) *The Strategy of Conflict*, Cambridge: Harvard University Press.

—— (1978) *Micromotives and Macrobehavior*, New York: W.W. Norton.

Scott, W. R. (1995) *Institutions and Organizations*, Thousand Oaks, CA: Sage Publications.

Simmons, B. and Martin, L. (2002) "International Organizations and Institutions," in W. Carlsnaes, Thomas Risse, and B. A. Simmons (eds) *Handbook of International Relations*, London: Sage Publications, 192–211.

Singleton, S. and Taylor, M. (1992) "Common Property: Collective Action and Community," *Journal of Theoretical Politics*, 4: 309–324.

Snidal, D. (1985) "The Limits of Hegemonic Stability Theory," *International Organization*, 39: 579–614.

Social Learning Group (2001) *Learning to Manage Global Environmental Risks: A Comparative History of Social Responses to Climate Change, Ozone Depletion, and Acid Precipitation*, Cambridge: MIT Press.

Stein, A. A. (1983) "Coordination and Collaboration: Regimes in an Anarchic World," in S. D. Krasner (ed.) *International Regimes*, Ithaca: Cornell University Press, 115–140.

Strange, S. (1983) "*Cave! hic dragones:* A Critique of Regime Analysis," in S. D. Krasner (ed.) *International Regimes*, Ithaca: Cornell University Press, 337–354.

Suganami, H. (1989) *The Domestic Analogy and World Order Proposals*, Cambridge: Cambridge University Press.

Tversky, A. and Kahneman, D. (1974) "Judgment under Uncertainty: Heuristics and Biases," *Science*, 185: 1124–1131.

—— (1981) "The Framing of Decisions and the Psychology of Choice," *Science*, 211: 453–458.

Underdal, A. and Hanf, K. (eds) (2000) *International Environmental Agreements and Domestic Politics: The Case of Acid Rain*, Aldershot: Ashgate.

Underdal, A. and Young, O. (eds) (2004) *Regime Consequences: Methodological Challenges and Research Strategies*, Dordrecht: Kluwer Academic Publishers.

Victor, D., Raustiala, K. and Skolnikoff, E. (eds) (1998) *The Implementation and Effectiveness of International Environmental Commitments*, Cambridge: MIT Press.

Von Moltke, K. (1997) "Institutional Interactions: The Structure of Regimes for Trade and the Environment," in O. R. Young (ed.) *Global Governance: Drawing Insights from the Environmental Experience*, Cambridge: MIT Press, 247–272.

Walton, R. and McKersie, R. (1965) *A Behavioral Theory of Labor Negotiations*, New York: McGraw-Hill.

Wapner, P. (1996) *Environmental Activism and World Civic Politics*, Albany: SUNY Press.

—— (1997) "Governance in Global Civil Society," in O. R. Young (ed.) *Global Governance: Drawing Insights from the Environmental Experience*, Cambridge: MIT Press, 65–84.

Watanabe, A. and Tsuchiyama, J. (eds) (2001) *Global Governance* (in Japanese), Tokyo: Tokyo University Press.

Weiss, E. and Jacobson, H. (eds) (1998) *Engaging Countries: Strengthening Compliance with International Environmental Accords*, Cambridge: MIT Press.

Wendt, A. (1987) "The Agent-Structure Problem in International Relations Theory," *International Organization*, 41: 335–370.

—— (1999) *Social Theory of International Politics*, Cambridge: Cambridge University Press.

Wettestad, J. (1999) *Designing Effective International Regimes: The Key Conditions*, Cheltenham: Edward Elgar.

Young, O. (ed.) (1975) *Bargaining: Formal Models of Negotiation*, Urbana: University of Illinois Press.

—— (1977) *Resource Management at the International Level: The Case of the North Pacific*, London: Frances Pinter.

—— (1983) "Regime Dynamics: The Rise and Fall of International Regimes," in S. D. Krasner (ed.) *International Regimes*, Ithaca: Cornell University Press, 93–113.

—— (1989) *International Cooperation: Building Regimes for Natural Resources and the Environment*, Ithaca: Cornell University Press.

—— (1991) "Political Leadership and Regime Formation: On the Development of Institutions in International Society," *International Organization*, 45: 281–309.

—— (1992) "The Effectiveness of International Institutions: Hard Cases and Critical Variables," in J. N. Rosenau and Ernst-Otto Czempiel (eds) *Governance without Government: Order and Change in World Politics*, Cambridge: Cambridge University Press, 160–194.

—— (1994) *International Governance: Protecting the Environment in a Stateless Society*, Ithaca: Cornell University Press.

—— (1998) *Creating Regimes: Arctic Accords and International Governance*, Ithaca: Cornell University Press.

—— (ed.) (1999a) *The Effectiveness of International Environmental Regimes: Causal Connections and Behavioral Mechanisms*, Cambridge: MIT Press.

—— (1999b) *Governance in World Affairs*, Ithaca: Cornell University Press.

—— (1999c) "Hitting the Mark: Why Are Some International Environmental Agreements More Successful Than Others?" *Environment*, 41(8): 20–29.

—— with contributions from Arun Agrawal, Leslie A. King, Peter H. Sand, Arild Underdal, and Merrilyn Wasson (1999) *The Institutional Dimensions of Global Environmental Change (IDGEC) Science Plan*. Report No. 9. Bonn: IHDP.

—— (2001) "The Behavioral Effects of Environmental Regimes: Collective-action vs. Social-practice Models," *International Environmental Agreements*, 1: 9–29.

—— (2002a) *The Institutional Dimensions of Environmental Change: Fit, Interplay, and Scale*, Cambridge: MIT Press.

—— (2002b) "Are Institutions Intervening Variables or Basic Causal Forces: Causal Clusters vs. Causal Chains in International Society," in M. Brecher and F. Harvey (eds) *Millennium Reflections on International Studies*, Ann Arbor: University of Michigan Press.

7 What's global about global governance?

A constructivist account

Matthew J. Hoffmann

A number of chapters in this volume grapple with how to conceive global governance (GG), parsing the concept into its component parts, global and governance, in an attempt to bring some analytic rigor to bear on what often seems an ephemeral concept. This academic grappling parallels the ongoing struggles of multiple actors attempting to live with and address issues, phenomena, and problems that are of the globe. Most attention is focussed on the governance aspect of the phrase. However, there has always been governance and the creation of rules, rule, institutions, patterns, and authority structures have always been the focus of politics and at the center of our studies. The novel and interesting aspect of GG is in many ways the adjective that precedes governance—global. Global is interesting precisely because it has numerous potential meanings when it modifies governance. One possibility is governance *of* the globe. However, other than perspectives that focus on global government, most GG studies are not concerned with the emergence of a political unit that covers the globe. Instead, most who use the GG phrase intend to convey the notion of governance *on* the globe—management of problems/phenomena that do not fit nicely into the boundaries of existing political units. This understanding of global is virtually unlimited. There exists no *a priori* or ahistorical configuration of actors that is the natural or right or best means through which to address problems on the globe. Participation in *global* governance is thus socially constructed and how our understanding of global is constructed has enormous ramifications for the rules, rule, institutions, patterns, and authority structures—governance—that emerge in world politics.

In this chapter, I offer a constructivist perspective on GG with an eye toward examining what global means and implies for governance on the globe in a specific instance—the attempt to address climatic change. I first discuss social constructivism in general and as a perspective on GG. I then discuss how understandings of global are constructed in the attempt to address climate change and how these understandings influence the governance of climate change. I conclude with some thoughts on the implications of this argument on what is global about GG.

Social constructivism and GG

Social constructivism is not a singular discourse and within the boundaries of this perspective there exists enormous diversity (Adler 1997; Checkel 1998). Individual constructivists differ on epistemology, the relative importance of agency versus structure, change versus continuity, and the operationalization of key theoretical elements (see, e.g., Hollis and Smith 1991; Wendt 1991; Jabri and Chan 1996; Adler 1997; Guzzini 2000; Checkel 2001; Sending 2002; Jacobsen 2003). However, in the contours of thought agreeable to most constructivists there are insights into a constructivist contribution to understanding GG.

Constructivists have in common a philosophy that "the manner in which the material world shapes and is shaped by human action and interaction depends on dynamic normative and epistemic interpretations of the material world" (Adler 1997: 322). There is a world of meanings and knowledge as well as an objective, material world. This intersubjective world—a world of shared knowledge where objects require human agreement to exist—is where the important "action" of world politics takes place.

In this worldview, knowledge structures or intersubjective meanings enable practices or actions. Behavior can only be understood (both by actors and observers) and is only undertaken within an intersubjective context of shared knowledge about the world. Actors exist and behave in a world where limits and possibilities are bounded and defined by intersubjective meanings or knowledge structures. Intersubjective meanings render actions "plausible or implausible, acceptable or unacceptable, conceivable or inconceivable, respectable or disreputable" (Yee 1996, quoted in Adler 1997: 327).

Of course the causal action is not unidirectional. While intersubjective knowledge constitutes actors' identities, interests, and behavior, social structures themselves are the aggregation and accretion of actors' actions. "Intersubjective" indeed implies the need for continual actions in the reproduction and modification of social structures. Social facts like money, borders, states, international law, treaties, and the rules of GG (however conceived) only exist when actors instantiate them through their actions and beliefs (Searle 1995). Thus mutual constitution is at the core of social constructivism. Agent practices create the social structures of consensual and shared knowledge that organize and define the social world, while simultaneously those knowledge structures constitute the actors undertaking the practices.

A broadly defined social-constructivist approach to world politics has gained in popularity in recent years. It is, however, a somewhat odd perspective for a volume that explores contending perspectives on GG as social constructivism is not really a perspective on GG. Regarding the questions that guided the preparation of this volume, social constructivism has very few unequivocal answers. A priori, it has very little to say about the form of GG, the existence of GG, trends in GG, the actors involved in GG, or the amount of GG existing in the world. Constructivism is agnostic at best on most of these questions.

A constructivist chapter also fails to fit comfortably in either Part I or Part II. Is constructivism a traditional approach to world politics or is it a new approach? Constructivism has gained a foothold in the pantheon of international-relations theory by challenging more established approaches (Wendt 1987, 1992). In this sense, constructivism argues for a new approach to world politics. However, this call for change in thinking is not directly tied to the emergence of the GG or globalization phenomena as are the calls from approaches highlighted in Part II. Social constructivists apply their insights to GG, but the dynamics of GG or globalization did not catalyze the development of constructivism—thus the inclusion in Part I.

Further, constructivists are wishy-washy on the question of world order. We can (and do) easily fit into both of the camps identified in the introductory chapter—the approach makes no assumptions as to whether the structure of GG is a single, coherent system of order or a series of multiple-rule systems. Depending on the constructivist asked, GG as noun could represent a project, a matter of hegemonic control, a series of regimes, or spheres of authority. The form of GG is epiphenomenal and multiple instantiations are possible.

However, that being said, the discomfiture with which constructivism fits the categories discussed in this volume does not lessen the importance of this approach to GG. Constructivism (and this particular constructivist) has a great deal to say about the structure of GG, considering it to be more generic social structures that can take on any number of forms (norms, rules, institutions, norm complexes, world orders). Further, constructivism has concrete notions about the *nature* of GG as noun. The structure of GG is ideational—ideas, meanings, and social knowledge define and constitute the structure of GG. Further, constructivists have spent a great deal of time ruminating on what this volume calls the process of GG. In fact, social constructivism is best considered a theory of social process rather than as a theory of world politics. At its core, constructivism lacks substantive assumptions about world politics—who the important actors are, what these actors want, how they interact—and instead provides insights into the mutually constitutive processes that dynamically link and constitute actors and structures. Social constructivism is thus very explicit about GG as verb; in whatever form, GG is constructed, maintained, and changed through the process of mutual constitution. A constructivist perspective is thus a welcome corrective to GG studies that on the one hand stress new dynamism in world politics and on the other too often concentrate on outcomes, actors, and issues to the exclusion of the processes of governance. Constructivists, ambivalent as to how GG looks, provide a number of important insights into how governance unfolds.

Ideational structure of GG

The flexibility inherent in constructivist thought manifests in the constructivist comfort with all of the versions of GG as noun discussed in this volume. In each case, constructivism could be used to explore how these structures have emerged and how they might change.[1] However, flexibility aside, constructivist assumptions have important content for GG as well. If, as Rosenau (1997) claims, governance consists of steering mechanisms, rules, orders, institutions, and orga-nizations, then the contribution of social constructivism, or its perspective on the structure of GG, is understanding the ideational foundation of GG.

Consider any number of governance activities cited in this volume that fall under the GG rubric—multilateral negotiations, decisions of international organi-zations, social movement lobbying, the actions of private bond-raters, hegemonic decrees, regime development, or the project(s) of global capital. Constructivism considers that all of these are under-girded by ideational structures; intersubjective knowledge defines who can/should take actions, what those actors want, and what actions they find conceivable. For instance, in multilateral negotiations, ideational structures determine which actors negotiate, define the problems over which they negotiate, and bound possible/plausible negotiation solutions.

Constructivists consider these ideational factors differently than the "ideas matter" literature (Goldstein and Keohane 1993). Where this neoliberal litera-ture focusses almost exclusively on the regulative rules that shape actors' behaviors, constructivism considers that norms and discourses serve to *both* regu-late governance and constitute it (Searle 1995; Ruggie 1998). Norms thus shape actors' beliefs, interests, and behaviors in pursuit of governance, and they consti-tute, define, or "create the very possibility" of undertaking an activity (Ruggie 1998: 871).[2] These constitutive norms are the rules that "specify *what counts as*" the activity in question (Ruggie 1998: 871, emphasis in original). They define what counts as governance (however conceived) or what counts as the appro-priate response to transnational problems.

Thus for constructivism the structure of GG consists of deeper social struc-ture—the norms and knowledge that provide the contours for more recognizable governance activities. Meanings, knowledge, and norms are the stuff of governance and they fundamentally shape the very conditions for governance activities—however conceived and at whatever scope. Therefore understanding GG requires exploring its ideational foundations and the social norms, ideas, and discourses that constitute them—what they are, how they emerge, change, and influence politics.

Returning to the specific theme of this chapter, social norms and other ideational forces also provide definitions and understandings of global. They shape what all actors consider to be appropriate courses of action and possible outcomes in pursuing governance on the globe. They define how the global in GG is conceived. Understanding the construction of global is crucial because this idea conditions and constrains more concrete governance activities—bargaining among states, institutional effects of the UN and other international organizations, and influence of non-state actors. Understanding GG begins with understanding the social construction of the idea of global.

The mutually constitutive process of GG

As discussed in the introductory chapter, the recent self-labeled GG literature has justified its break from mainstream approaches by asserting that world politics is dynamic and filled with rules or rule systems. The claim is that we have moved away from a world where powerful states, due to their power alone, set the rules of world politics. Rather, rule systems result from the dynamic actions and inter-actions of many actors in different contexts (Rosenau 1997; Held and McGrew 2002). Unfortunately, this literature has produced less clear insights into the processes by which rule systems are dynamically constructed. For example, in his discussion of global environmental governance, Peter Haas claims, "The evolu-tion of global governance has been driven by combinations of scientific understanding, international institutional guidance, market forces, national lead-ership, and mass concern." He goes on to claim that these forces "have accumulated to form a coherent set of expectations about national behavior and, to a lesser degree, a common set of actual practices exercised by governments and companies" (1995: 346). The GG literature is rife with similar studies that delineate *important factors* in the emergence of governance—a crucial undertaking to be sure. However, we are too often left to wonder *how* the emergence and evolution takes place.

A constructivist perspective appears to be a natural solution. Essentially, the central puzzle running through the GG "literature" is the same as social constructivism's common theme—the actor/rules or agent/structure relation-ship. Constructivists ask how ideas (both regulative and constitutive) become intersubjectively understood and how interactions (persuasion, coercion, social-ization) lead to the emergence/reification of rules, norms, and institutions. According to Rosenau (1997: 147):

> The evolution of intersubjective consensus based on shared fates and common histories, the possession of information and knowledge, the pres-sure of active or mobilizable publics and/or the use of careful planning, good timing, clever manipulation, and hard bargaining—either separately or in combination—foster control mechanisms that sustain governance without government.

If governance unfolds through complex, dynamic interactions like those envi-sioned by Rosenau, then social constructivism can provide concrete mechanisms and insights that will illuminate how this takes place. The mechanism is mutual constitution.

A deceivingly simple concept, mutual constitution is merely one way to link agents and social structures (or actors and their social context). The simplicity is in the logic. Actors create or constitute their own social context—the social facts, norms, institutions, mores, laws, patterns, customs, culture—through their actions and interactions. However, these acts of creation (or reification or change) are themselves shaped (or constituted) by extant social structures—the results of prior actions and interactions. While the logic is simple, the simultaneity of the consti-tution has created challenges for constructivist attempts to operationalize mutual constitution in an analytically useful way. Some critics do not even see such opera-tionalization as possible. For instance, Michael Taylor argues that "with no analytical separation between the two [agents and structures] (or between culture and action), I do not see how it is possible to unravel the causal interaction of action and structure over time and hence to explain social change"(1989: 22).

Notwithstanding the challenges and critics, constructivists have developed frameworks that explicate mutual constitution by focussing on the emergence, evolution, and impact of social norms and other social structures like discourses at the foundation of governance. Some frameworks, like Finnemore and Sikkink's (1998) norm life cycle or Bernstein's (2001) socio-evolutionary approach detail the emergence and evolution of social norms. Other frameworks, like the socialization model developed by Risse *et al.* (1999), Checkel's (2001) persuasion framework, and Johnston's (2001) work with socialization, focus on how ideas and social norms constitute actors.

While these analytic frameworks differ significantly in the details of how they operationalize mutual constitution, more important are the similarities in the general flow of the process whereby social structures or norms emerge, influence actors, and evolve. This process, combined with assumptions about the ideational structure of GG, provides the contours of a constructivist approach to GG.

However conceived, governance begins with intersubjective understandings. Actors involved in managing global problems know what they want, who should be participating, what the problem is, and what possible outcomes consist of. Social norms and other ideas provide these understandings. As governance unfolds over time, actors reify or transform the foundational understandings through their actions and interactions. Over time, new ideas about who should participate, what should be done, and how governance should proceed can arise in the system. Governance processes will change if actors are convinced of the appropriateness of the new ideas.[3] Actors' beliefs and actions thus constantly re-create the context of governance as they learn from, follow (or break), and transform (or reify) the knowledge structures and social norms that structure the opportunities and obstacles for GG. Social constructivists consider that this generic social process is at the heart of GG, providing a foundation of knowledge for actors to recognize and address problems on the globe.

Constructing global

Participation in governance on the globe

Constructivists have made their living by explaining what others take for granted and showing how those phenomena not only influence politics, but can change over time (see e.g. Wendt 1992; Finnemore 1996; Price and Tannenwald 1996; Price 1997). They have shown how ideas and norms matter and how they co-evolve with actors through mutual constitution. In this section I apply constructivist insights and briefly examine what is too often taken for granted in the study of GG: what is global about GG. Raising this unasked question is important because understandings of what it is to be global are constantly evolving with enormous ramifications for how GG plays out in any particular issue.

But what is global? In considering governance on the globe, global delineates the scope of the problem and the actors who should participate in managing it. In other words our understanding of global tells us who participates in governance on the globe. This *global* participation in governance activities is not obvious—most if not all global issues can be dealt with by diverse configurations of actors[4]—nor are appropriate or "optimal" participation levels deducible from the scientific or technical characteristics of the issue at hand. Instead, participation is an inherently path-dependent (Pierson 2000) and *political* concern. It is governed by social norms.

That being said, we can consider participation and what counts as a global response or GG in two ways. First, some perspectives begin with fundamental assumptions about which actors are important and thus whose actions constitute GG. For instance, traditional international-relations approaches tend to be state-centric and would consider any definition of the global in GG to concern states.[5] This perspective is by no means unchallenged. The private-authority literature discusses the ways in which the domain of state authority has shrunk, giving rise to actors with market, moral, and illicit authority (Sinclair 1994; Hall and Biersteker, 2002). Rosenau has delineated the emergence of a multi-centric world, parallel to the state-centric world (1990). Others have explored the role of civil society, social movements, and NGOs in influencing the governance process (O'Brien *et al.* 2000).

Constructivism provides a second approach to participation and global, claiming that other perspectives' assumptions about important actors are drawn from the observable implications of sedimented processes of mutual constitution—we can fruitfully focus on particular actors in GG and say that actions by a set of actors counts as GG because processes of social construction have solidified their role in certain GG processes. What these perspectives hold constant, constructivism examines, exploring how global is constructed so as to authorize certain actors. It provides a way to trace how different actors become authoritative participants in GG processes. How do NGOs and other civil-society actors come to have influence in the IMF and World Bank (O'Brien, this volume; O'Brien *et al.* 2000)? How do bond-rating agencies come to have influence over the rules and patterns of sovereign debt (Sinclair 1994; this volume)? How do transnational courts come to have influence over the governing of states (Goldstein and Ban, this volume)? Social constructivism claims that there is a common process underlying the answers to all three of these GG examples—the process through which normative understandings about who should participate emerge and evolve.

These considerations of participation are not academic trivia. One lesson from the recent GG literature is that we cannot assume the answers to "what is global?" and "who participates?" because this literature has shown that such answers can change over time and across issues. At the very least the list of authoritative actors whose actions count as global governance is not stable. Perhaps more importantly, the participation question has enormous ramifications for how GG unfolds and what it looks like. The configuration of actors that participate in the formation, maintenance, and alteration of the structures of GG intimately influences the content of those structures. If states are the (only) authoritative participants in GG, whatever the issue being addressed, this shapes how the issue is dealt with—what interests are involved, what solutions are pursued, and how the process unfolds. Other actors bring other characteristics to the table, fundamentally altering how governance proceeds. The prevailing understanding of what "global" entails thus structures how a problem is envisioned and how it will be managed.

Climate change: a problem of the globe

Global environmental problems represent relatively tough cases for a constructivist argument about the meaning of global. Modifying environmental problems with the adjective "global" is thought to signify self-evident or scientifically based ideas about participation in governance processes. Yet it is a mistake to leave "global" unquestioned when examining even the issue of climate change, a quintessential problem of the globe.

Climate change results from the greenhouse effect whereby various gases (carbon dioxide, methane, CFCs, water vapor and others) absorb solar radiation that would otherwise be reflected back to space from the Earth. This greenhouse effect itself is not a problem. Indeed, it keeps the planet warm and allows life to flourish in the forms we are familiar with. The carbon dioxide and other gases in our atmosphere that form the greenhouse keep the earth 34 degrees centigrade warmer than it would be in the absence of substantial carbon dioxide levels (Rathgens 1991: 155). The greenhouse effect potentially becomes a problem because of the effects from anthropogenic emissions of carbon dioxide and other gases in the last 150 years. Emissions since the industrial revolution, and especially in the last 50 years, have caused dramatic increases in atmospheric concentrations of carbon dioxide—most arising from the burning of fossil fuels. Though the effects of changes in carbon-dioxide concentrations are not fully understood, most scientists agree that warming will occur and that warming has the potential to alter climatic patterns—melting polar ice-caps, affecting everyday weather, increasing the frequency and severity of storms, and altering long-standing temperature patterns. These altered climatic conditions promise the potential of sea-level rise, crop damage, destruction of biological diversity (as species will be unable to adapt to quickly changing environmental conditions), and altered disease patterns.[6]

Perhaps like no other problem (environmental or otherwise with the possible exception of ozone depletion), climate change has a global scope—it is a problem of the globe. The potential effects of climate change are not going to be the same everywhere, but it promises to have an impact on the whole globe. This is well recognized in science and policy circles.[7] With only rare exceptions, every discussion of climate change includes a line claiming that climate change is a *truly* global problem and thus requires a global response. The response to climate change has indeed been impressive in some ways—virtually all states have played a role in the multilateral negotiations designed to address climate change; thousands of NGOs are working at multiple levels to change the behavior of governments, corporations, and publics; thousands of scientists work to raise the level of climate knowledge and climate change awareness; and the climate issue has engaged multiple international organizations. It has become a cliché to say that climate change is a global problem that requires a global response, and because it is a cliché too little attention has been paid to explaining how a global response has been constructed—how we have defined what it means to be global and how our understandings of "global" affect the response to climate change.

Governance on the globe: how to address climate change

Contrary to conventional wisdom and perceptions, there is little mystery to the successful governance of climate change—create a set of rules that lead to a decrease in carbon dioxide and other greenhouse gas emissions. Accomplishing this is slightly more complex. Climate change is relatively well established as a problem of the globe with potentially far-reaching consequences and thus a natural target for governance. Yet, as detailed below, what constitutes a "global" response—who should participate in governance—has been a contested and changing idea. We see this contest and evolution in examining two aspects of participation: the potential erosion of the primacy of multilateral negotiations as the means of governance and state-participation dynamics.

Global as multilateral negotiations

Governance never starts from scratch and the governance of climate change is no exception. Theoretically, any number of actors could undertake the governance of climate change—any number of responses could count as global. However, though climate change is an unprecedented problem, somehow people knew the procedure for governing it—we knew what counted as governance on the globe for this problem of the globe even as we realized that attaining effective rules for addressing this problem would be challenging. When the governance of climate change is discussed, most thoughts turn immediately to the multilateral process that produced the Framework Convention on Climate Change (FCCC) in 1992 and the Kyoto Protocol in 1997. The story of GG in climate change is most often told through a state-centric lens that follows the development of UN-supervised, multilateral negotiations (see, e.g., Bodansky 1994; Rowlands 1995; Harris 2000; Andresen and Agrawala 2002; Barret 2002; Hoffman 2005). This is not surprising, for what counts as a global response in many issues is negotiations between sovereign states.

As Ruggie (1998: 871) makes abundantly clear, most theories of international relations

> explain virtually nothing that is constitutive of the very possibility of conducting international relations: not territorial states, not systems of

states, not any concrete international order, nor the whole host of institutional forms that states use, ranging from promises to treaties to multilateral organizing principles.

Practitioners of these other approaches are not blind—there are often good reasons to take states and their relations as unproblematic. State-centric theories can exist and thrive precisely because there exist constitutive rules (norms) that stabilize expectations and constitute actors' understanding of their political context.

Indeed, constructivists see a coherent world order in the sense that there exists a set of constitutive norms that determine what counts as global governance—negotiation among sovereign political units. Notions such as the social contract, sovereignty, international society, international law, anarchy, and the foreign–domestic dichotomy reify the notion that while states are bound to take care of issues that arise within their borders, issues that transcend borders have to be dealt with through the interaction of states. An anarchic political order guarantees that there is no central authority above states, making states the authoritative actors to deal with transnational issues like climate change.

When climate change began to be addressed in the late 1980s, the World Meteorological Organization and the United Nations Environment Program (UNEP)—intergovernmental organizations set up by states as a mechanism for addressing transnational problems—were the catalysts of a global response. They organized the scientific panels, the ministerial discussions, and eventually the multilateral negotiations that have come to be synonymous with the governance of this issue. States engaged in negotiations from 1991 to 1992 to produce the Framework Convention on Climate Change at the Earth Summit in 1992. States continued to refine the global response beyond the FCCC through the 1990s with multiple meetings of the parties to the FCCC designed to produce a climate-change protocol with concrete steps for addressing climate change. This protocol was achieved in Kyoto in 1997.

This state-centric story is the one most-often told when the governance of climate change is discussed (see, e.g., Rowlands 1995; Andresen and Agrawala 2002; Barret 2002; Hoffmann 2005). The stories focus on bargaining between states (both between the US and EU and between the North and South), the role of scientific uncertainty, mechanisms for implementation of governance outcomes and more. This is the "stuff" of governance for climate change. What constructivism reminds us, however, is that this "stuff" is pre-conditioned by the underlying constitutive norms that designate that this is what counts as governance. The counterfactual is intriguing. What if states were not the primary authoritative actors responsible for transnational problems like climate change?

Such a counterfactual is not as fanciful as the above discussion of the constitutive norms of the inter-state system may suggest. While the norms that constitute the states system are still coherent, they are not static nor is the primacy of the states system necessarily permanent. As constructivists highlight, the norms at the foundation of governance activities are dynamic entities and the process of mutual constitution not only reifies embedded understandings, it can also change them.

Constructivists stress that the notion of global as multilateral is a socially constructed order, not a natural state of affairs. Even though the notion of GG through state interaction is deeply embedded, we cannot make the mistake of thinking that it is somehow the way things have to be. Consider that the governance of climate change could take place in a variety of ways:

- Publics could change their behavior.
- Corporations could negotiate and impose rules on themselves in various sectors.
- Subnational groups could undertake rules (together or in isolation).
- A centralized environmental organization, akin to the World Trade Organization, could impose rules for addressing climate change.

These possibilities seem unlikely as the primary means of creating rules and institutions—i.e. governance—on their face because the constitutive rules that under-gird the international states system are also at the foundation of the governance of climate change. Yet each of these activities is currently ongoing or at least being discussed, challenging the primacy of a state-centric understanding of GG for climate change.

The stable expectations that governance occurs through the interactions of states may indeed be eroding. The authors in Part II of this volume document the emergence and increasing importance of non-state actors so it is not necessary to do so in detail here. However, as these actors gain in authority and are accepted by states as authoritative actors, this erodes the constitutive principles that under-gird the understanding of *global* governance as negotiation among sovereign actors.

This erosion is well documented in the governance of climate change in the growing NGO presence at the multilateral meetings, in terms of accredited NGO participants, NGO members of state delegations, and the now ubiquitous NGO fora (as Rosenau documents in this volume) that accompany most major environmental negotiations (see also, Auer 2000). Additionally, there is a growing trend towards alternative forms of a global response to climate change. Wapner (1996) details this in his analysis of how global civil society actors work above, below, and between states to not only influence state behavior, but also to develop governance on their own.[8] Global governance as multilateral negotiations may not be the dominant understanding for long.

Global as universal participation

While the state-centric notion of global—that governance on the globe is to be undertaken by states—may be eroding, states still do play the most important roles in the governance of climate change. But even if we focus solely on states, the construction of what it means to be global is still at issue—state-centrism does not put the question of "what is global?" to rest. Conventionally, invoking the global label implies that all states should participate in governance processes—universal participation. The idea of universal participation is, in fact, so embedded in our analyses and consciousness that it is rarely questioned or examined when considering problems like climate change; it is simply a *de facto* characteristic of these problems.

This is curious. Across global environmental problems, there has been a wide diversity of state participation requirements and understandings. Rather than there being a single and obvious way to approach environmental problems with geographically expansive scope, deciding which states should participate in governance processes is actually a contested and inherently dynamic concern. Taking for granted this facet of the governance of climate change is a mistake. The governance of climate change (as multilateral negotiations) cannot be separated from fundamental understandings of who should participate and thus neither can our explanations of governance (as multilateral negotiations) be separated from an explanation of state participation.

But is it really that surprising that climate change is understood to require universal participation? Was such an understanding not inevitable given the worldwide causes and potential consequences of the problem? Curiously, the answer to both of these questions is yes. Beyond blindly accepting the conventional wisdom that problems of the globe require universal participation, there is a dearth of reasons to expect universal participation and many good reasons to be skeptical that the governance of climate change had to take place this way.

First, there are a growing number of "global" problems like poverty, arms control, terrorism, development, and health that have causes and consequences worldwide that do *not* require universal participation. Universal participation is not a universal response to global problems. Second, universal participation in climate change (and other issues) is antithetical to hallowed findings in international relations about the importance of small numbers for collective action (Olsen 1968; Sebenius 1983; Oye 1986). Large-scale negotiations have never been considered rational.

Further, we cannot rely on hegemonic influence and strategy to explain the emergence of universal participation in climate change. Certainly the US did desire to stall the negotiations, thus making it potentially rational for the US, as hegemon, to call for universal participation. Yet, the US was actually a late-comer to universal participation. This idea was embedded in UNEP and other global environmental negotiations in the late 1980s (see below)—the US was actually socialized to this norm. In addition, both those actors that wanted to pursue significant actions (like the EU and small island nations) and those opposed to such actions (US, Japan, Russia) defined climate change as requiring universal participation.

Finally, we cannot forget science. Conventional wisdom holds that scientific characteristics of a problem can tell us who should participate. As climate change is a problem with a global scope, it is natural to address it through universal participation. This logic falls short as well. Putting aside questions about the ability of "science" to objectively inform governance activities (see Litfin 1994), the science of climate change does not necessitate a particular level of participation. While the whole globe is affected by climate change, a relatively small number of states (US, EU, China, India, Brazil, Russia, Japan) contribute an overwhelming percentage of the problem. Science tells us about both aspects of the climate-change problem, leaving questions of participation up in the air.

But let us be clear, inevitable or not, from the very beginning of the policy response to climate change, this problem was considered to be a global problem requiring universal participation. Over one hundred states participated in each of the negotiation sessions that led to the FCCC and Kyoto Protocol (UNGA 1991a; 1991b; 1991c; 1991d; 1992; UNFCCC 1995; 1996; 1997) and all involved were convinced that the only way to approach climate change was through universal participation. A constructivist analysis again considers that this universal participation is a social construction—there was a norm in force that shaped how actors perceived the climate-change problem.

Universal participation was not a conscious choice in any meaningful sense; it was an underlying understanding that preceded any strategizing about how to approach climate change. In fact, universal participation became part of how climate change was even defined. All actors considered universal participation to be required and it was not even possible to consider approaching the problem in any other way even though other options may have been better (Sebenius 1991; Downs *et al.* 1998). The foundation of governance activities was the understanding that climate change requires universal participation.

Rather than being inevitable, the requirement of universal participation was socially constructed. This is perhaps made most clear when we consider that universal participation has not always been the "natural" way to approach global environmental problems like climate change. Five years before the FCCC negotiations began, the first ozone depletion agreement, the Vienna Convention, was negotiated almost exclusively by Northern states.[9] A North-only participation norm reigned in the early ozone depletion negotiations and negotiations were routinely attended by fewer than 40 states. Universal participation emerged in 1987–89 as a new idea about how to address ozone depletion arose in the negotiations that produced the Montreal Protocol (see Hoffmann 2005). The idea that Southern states should participate in global environmental negotiations destabilized the extant understanding of North-only participation. As a number of Southern states began participating and Northern states began expecting their participation, a universal participation norm emerged.[10]

The ozone depletion negotiations were crucial in the development of an understanding that some environmental problems require the active participation of all (or most of) the nations of the world. During the course of these negotiations, the international community constructed a new global response to ozone depletion, defining the problem in a new way such that Southern states became full participants in governance processes. "Global" came to be associated with a requirement for universal participation and the ramifications of this change were felt in the governance of climate change.

The implications of the switch to universal participation were enormous. First, the negotiations, if not the outcomes, have been relatively equitable. Southern issues have been prominent on the agenda. Southern states have played a major role in most aspects of the negotiations. Without an underlying norm specifying that climate change should be addressed through universal participation, it is not clear that such equity would be evident in the negotiations and even that Southern participation would be so prominent.

Second, both the FCCC and Kyoto negotiations proved to be enormously complex and characterized by US recalcitrance that was facilitated by universal participation. The complexity of the negotiations was and continues to be caused both by the complex nature of climate change as well as by the myriad interests represented by the participating states. Universal participation put a multitude of interests into play. Additionally, universal participation shaped how states strategized to pursue their interests. For instance, as has been extensively reported in the media and in the academic literature, the US has been loath to take significant actions to address climate change. Universal participation defined how the US perceived the governance of climate change and thus US strategy. The strategy was to dispute European calls for binding and significant actions to reduce greenhouse emissions combined with accepting the principle of assisting Southern states with their efforts at addressing climate change, while arguing with the South about the practical implementation and conditions of such assistance. Crucially, these strategic actions were predicated on the understanding that climate change would be addressed through universal negotiations and responses. Without the underlying norm of universal participation, the US may still have been recalcitrant, but its strategy would have been different.

While the norm of universal participation has structured the governance of climate change since the inception of the multilateral negotiations, this does not imply that universal participation is a permanent aspect of our understanding of global. Constructivism does not provide a static account of the ideational foundations for the governance of climate change. Universal participation is not natural; it is not how the governance of global environmental problems has always proceeded; and it may not be the way that the governance of climate change will proceed in the future. The universal participation norm may be evolving or eroding.

In the post-Kyoto negotiations, there has been evident contestation over the meaning of universal participation. In other words, it is fine and good to say that climate change requires universal participation, but states have also been concerned about *how* different states should participate. This has led to significant debate over whether Northern states should take the first steps to solve a problem that they hold historical responsibility for, or Southern states should undertake significant actions now for a problem that they are destined to contribute a great deal to in the future. This debate dominated both the discussions leading up to Kyoto and those that have taken place since Kyoto. The understanding of "global" participation is very much in flux as the debate provided part of the justification for the US withdrawal from the Kyoto process in early 2001. Such acrimony in the governance of climate change—such a fundamental rift in the ideational foundation of governance activities—forces the question of whether the governance of climate change is likely to proceed through smaller-scale regimes or even through uncoordinated individual responses.

Constructing the governance of climate change

A couple of key notions stand out from this analysis. First, at any point in time, people knew how to approach the governance of climate change. In the 1990s governance proceeded through negotiations universally attended by states. Yet, while everyone knows how governance should take place, there is nothing natural about it. Instead, underlying, constitutive ideas about governance (both the identity of participants and the number of participants) shape how actors perceive the problems they face and solutions they devise. Second, the constitutive norms are not static. State centrism is eroding as is universal participation. The ideas that constitute "global" have and will continue to evolve. When NGOs and insurance companies and corporations begin acting as if they are participants in global governance, this alters what is considered the global part of global governance and a global response to climate change. When different configurations of states have different notions of what an appropriate response to climate change should be, this alters what is considered the global part of GG. Third, these underlying ideas have real consequences for how governance plays out. In determining what counts as governance (or who participates in it), these norms determine what interests are at play, what solutions are deemed possible, and what strategies actors pursue. Understanding the continual construction of global helps us to understand the continuing quest for GG in climate change.

The place of constructivism as GG perspective

In the abstract constructivism cannot provide insight into what GG will likely look like, which actors are likely to be important, or how GG is likely to evolve over time. This characteristic sets constructivism apart from other approaches represented in this volume. Constructivism only has assumptions about the nature of social structure—ideational—and the process through which politics (as a subset of social dynamics in general) plays out—mutual constitution.

This generality is an advantage in an era that many have described as one of great change. If the authors in Part II are correct that we are seeing fundamental changes in world politics, constructivism can readily analyze these dynamics. In fact, constructivists have been undertaking "GG" studies and many self-labeled GG scholars are implicitly or explicitly adopting a constructivist approach. The flexibility inherent in constructivism is crucial in a number of ways for analyzing the "new" dynamics of GG.

First, constructivism is agnostic on the type and identity of actors involved in global governance processes—NGOs, individuals, IGOs, states, international financial institutions, MNCs, global civil society, social movements, and others all play prominent roles in constructivist work. Because constructivism is a theory of process rather than a theory of world politics, it does not have to delineate "important" actors—instead constructivism is flexible enough to study a range of actors and their influence on GG processes. Constructivism does not attempt to make generalizations about state (or any other actors') behavior. Rather it is concerned with the processes that link actors and a larger social context. It thus can incorporate both Murphy's observation that "we are not going to be able to explain the nature of global governance without understanding the ways in which powerful states construct and pursue their grand strategies" (2000: 797) and the strident demands in the GG literature to move beyond traditional state-centrism.

Second, by its very nature constructivism is focussed on rules and rule systems (Rosenau, this volume and 1997), discussed through most of the literature as norms, culture, or structures. Intersubjective understandings (rules) structure the manner in which actors view the world, significantly influencing their identities, preferences and behavior. In turn the actions and interactions of those actors create the structures of world politics—actors create their own social context. Rules play a prominent part in most major constructivist approaches, whether as structures in the more sociologically oriented approaches (Finnemore 1996; Katzenstein 1996) or as the medium of interaction between agents and structures (Onuf 1989, 1998).

Finally, constructivism is inherently dynamic and thus fully able to embrace the dynamism and change that has led many to call for new thinking. World order is created, maintained, and altered through the dynamic process of mutual constitution that puts all the parts of social life in motion. Actors are dynamic, as their wants, actions, and even perceptions are affected by the changing (sometimes slowly) context in which they find themselves (their intersubjective environment constitutes them). Structures are also dynamic as the rules of the game and notions of appropriateness are instantiated only by the actions and interactions of the actors—even status quo or robust structures require continual action in their reproduction.[11]

Conclusion

Constructivism is a powerful tool for studying GG, even if it is not wholly a perspective on GG. The GG "content" to be found in social constructivism concerns the ideational foundations of politics and the process of mutual constitution. Taken together these constructivist insights do provide a baseline understanding of GG as noun and verb and a way to analyze the dynamics of GG. Constructivism is valuable because it forces us to consider the understandings and meanings that bring governance at any level to life. With GG, constructivism asks us to consider the implications of invoking the label "global," arguing that our understanding of what constitutes global is crucially important for understanding what emerges as GG.

Notes

1　Of course, the authors may vehemently disagree that a social-constructivist approach actually captures the essence of the various structures because social constructivism relies on assumptions that are antithetical to many of the approaches in this volume.
2　Now of course, constitutive regulative norms do not represent a strict dichotomy. Even the canonical examples (see Searle 1995; Ruggie 1998) of the rules of chess (for constitutive) and driving on a particular side of the road (regulative) contain aspects of both constitution and regulation. The rules of chess not only constitute the game of chess, but also regulate how the pieces move. Similarly, driving on the left-hand side of the road is a rule that regulates driving in Britain, but it also constitutes what it means to drive and even to be British.
3　There is a large and growing debate on how this transformation takes place—why actors change their beliefs or ideas about what is appropriate (see, e.g., Guzzini 2000; Checkel 2001; Johnston 2001; Sending 2002; Jacobsen 2003).
4　In addition, there is likely no optimal participation for "effective" governance.
5　Sterling-Folker's contribution to this volume is an important exception to this general rule.
6　Of course, not everyone agrees that all or even most of this will come to pass.
7　Even George W. Bush has recently admitted that climate change is a real problem of global scope.
8　For other analyses of global civil society see Lipshutz (1996); O'Brien (this volume).
9　For a comprehensive account of the ozone depletion negotiations, see Benedick (1991) and Tolba (1998).
10　As in the case of climate change, the switch to universal participation in ozone depletion was not inevitable or even expected. See Hoffmann (2005).
11　To be clear—dynamism does not necessarily imply change.

References

Adler, E. (1997) "Seizing the Middle Ground: Constructivism in World Politics," *European Journal of International Relations*, 3: 319–363.

Andresen, S. and Agrawala, S. (2002) "Leaders, Pushers and Laggards in the Making of the Climate Change Regime," *Global Environmental Change*, 12: 41–51.

Auer, M. (2000) "Who Participates in Global Environmental Governance? Partial Answers from International Relations Theory," *Policy Sciences*, 33: 155–180.

Barrett, S. (1992) *Convention on Climate Change: Economic Aspects of Negotiations*, Paris: OECD.

Bodansky, D. (1994) "Prologue to the Climate Change Convention," in I. Mintzer and J. A. Leonard (eds) *Negotiating Climate Change: The Inside Story of the Rio Convention*, Cambridge: Cambridge University Press.

Benedick, R. (1991) *Ozone Diplomacy: New Directions in Safeguarding the Planet*, Cambridge: Harvard University Press.

Checkel, J. (1998) "The Constructivist Turn in International Relations Theory," *World Politics*, 50: 324–348.

—— (2001) "Why Comply? Social Learning and European Identity Change," *International Organization*, 55: 553–588.

Downs, G., Rocke, D. and Barsoom, P. (1998) "Managing the Evolution of Multilateralism," *International Organization*, 52: 397–419.

Finnemore, M. (1996) *National Interests in International Society*, Ithaca: Cornell University Press.

Finnemore, M. and Sikkink, K. (1998) "International Norm Dynamics and Political Change," *International Organization*, 50: 887–918.

Goldstein, J. and Keohane, R. (1993) *Ideas and Foreign Policy*, Ithaca: Cornell University Press.

Guzzini, S. (2000) "A Reconstruction of Constructivism in International Relations," *European Journal of International Relations*, 6: 147–182.

Haas, P. (1995) "Global Environmental Governance," in *Issues in Global Governance: Papers Written for the Commission on Global Governance*, Cambridge: Kluwer Law International.

Hall, R. B. and Biersteker, T. (2002) *The Emergence of Private Authority in Global Governance*, Cambridge: Cambridge University Press.

Harris, P. (ed.) (2000) *Climate Change and American Foreign Policy*, New York: St. Martin's Press.

Held, D. and McGrew, A. (eds) (2002) *Governing Globalization*, London: Polity Press.

Hoffmann, M. J. (2005) *Ozone Depletion and Climate Change: Constructing a Global Response*, Albany: SUNY Press.

Hollis, M. and Smith, S. (1991) "Beware of Gurus: Structure and Action in International Relations," *Review of International Studies*, 17: 393–410.

Jabri, V. and Chan, S. (1996) "The Ontologist Always Rings Twice: Two More Stories about Structure and Agency in Reply to Hollis and Smith," *Review of International Studies*, 22: 107–110.

Jacobsen, J. K. (2003) "Dueling Constructivisms: a Post-mortem on the Ideas Debate in Mainstream IR/IPE," *Review of International Studies*, 29: 39–60.

Johnston, I. (2001) "Treating Institutions as Social Environments," *International Studies Quarterly*, 45: 487–516.

Katzenstein, P. (ed.) (1996) *The Culture of National Security: Norms and Identity in World Politics*, New York: Columbia University Press.

Lipshutz, R. (1996) *Global Civil Society and Global Environmental Governance*, Albany: SUNY Press.

Litfin, K. (1994) *Ozone Discourses*, New York: Columbia University Press.

Murphy, C. (2000) "Global Governance: Poorly Done and Poorly Understood," *International Affairs*, 76: 789–803.

O'Brien, R., Goetz, A. M., Scholte, J. A., and Williams, M. (2000) *Contesting Global Governance: Multilateral Economic Institutions and Global Social Movements*, Cambridge: Cambridge University Press.

Olsen, M. (1968) *The Logic of Collective Action*, New York: Schocken.

Onuf, N. (1989) *World of Our Making: Rules and Rule in Social Theory and International Relations*, Columbia, SC: University of South Carolina Press.

—— (1998) "Constructivism: A User's Manual," in V. Kubalkova, N.Onuf, and P. Kowert (eds) *International Relations in a Constructed World*, Armonk, NY: ME Sharpe.

Oye, K. (1986) "Explaining Cooperation Under Anarchy," in K. Oye (ed.) *Cooperation Under Anarchy*, Princeton: Princeton University Press.

Pierson, P. (2000) "Increasing Returns, Path Dependence, and the Study of Politics," *American Political Science Review*, 94: 251–268.

Price, R. (1997) *The Chemical Weapons Taboo*, Ithaca: Cornell University Press.

Price, R. and Tannenwald, N. (1996) "Norms and Deterrence: The Nuclear and Chemical Weapons Taboo," in P. Katzenstein (ed.) *The Culture of National Security: Norms and Identity in World Politics*, New York: Columbia University Press.

Rathgens, G. (1991) "Energy and Climate Change," in J. T. Matthews (ed.) *Preserving the Global Environment*, New York: WW Norton Company.

Risse, T., Ropp, S. and Sikkink, K. (eds) (1999) *The Power of Human Rights: International Norms and Domestic Change*, Cambridge: Cambridge University Press.

Rosenau, J. N. (1990) *Turbulence in World Politics: A Theory of Change and Continuity*, Princeton: Princeton University Press.

—— (1997) *Along the Foreign-Domestic Frontier*, Cambridge: Cambridge University Press.

Rowlands, I. (1995) *The Politics of Global Atmospheric Change*, New York: Manchester University Press.

Ruggie, J. (1998) "What Makes the World Hang Together? Neoutilitarianism and the Social Constructivist Challenge," *International Organization*, 52: 855–885.

Searle, J. (1995) *The Construction of Social Reality*, New York: Free Press.

Sebenius, J. (1983) "Negotiation Arithmetic: Adding and Subtracting Issues and Parties," *International Organization*, 37: 281–316.

—— (1991) "Designing Negotiations Toward a New Regime: The Case of Global Warming," *International Security*, 15: 110–148.

Sending, O. J. (2002) "Constitution, Choice and Change: Problems with the 'Logic of Appropriateness' and its Use in Constructivist Theory," *European Journal of International Relations*, 8: 443–470.

Sinclair, T. (1994) "Passing Judgment: Credit Rating Processes as Regulating Mechanisms of Governance," *Review of International Political Economy*, 1: 133–160.

Taylor, M. (1989) "Structure, Culture, and Action in the Explanation of Social Change," *Politics and Society*, 17 (2): 116–162.

Tolba, M. (1998) *Global Environmental Diplomacy: Negotiating Environmental Agreements for the World, 1973–1992*, Cambridge: The MIT Press.

UNGA (1991a) *Annotated Provisional Agenda of the INC First Session, January 18, 1991* (A/AC.237/1/Add.1).

—— (1991b) *Provisional Agenda, INC Second Session, May 22, 1991* (A/AC.237/Misc.1/Add.1).

—— (1991c) *Report of the Second Session of the INC/FCCC, August 8, 1991* (A/AC.237/9).

—— (1991d) *Report of the Third Session of the INC/FCCC, October 25, 1991* (A/AC.237/12).

—— (1992) *Report of the Fourth Session of the INC/FCCC, January 29, 1992* (A/AC.237/29).

UNFCCC (1995) *Report of the Conference of the Parties on its First Session.* 5/24/95 (FCCC/CP/7).

—— (1996) *Report of the Conference of the Parties on its Second Session.* 10/29/96 (FCCC/CP/1996/15).

—— (1997) *Report of the Conference of the Parties on its Third Session* (FCCC/CP/1998/7).

Wapner, P. (1996) *Environmental Activism and World Civic Politics*, Albany: SUNY Press.

Wendt, A. (1987) "The Agent–Structure Problem in International Relations," *International Organization*, 41: 335–370.

—— (1991) "Bridging the Theory/Meta-Theory Gap in International Relations," *Review of International Studies*, 17: 383–392.

—— (1992) "Anarchy is What States Make of It: The Social Construction of Power Politics," *International Organization*, 46: 391–425.

Yee, A. (1996) "The Causal Effect of Ideas on Policies," *International Organization*, 50: 69–108.

Part II

Global governance as catalyst for new perspectives

8   Global governance as disaggregated complexity

James N. Rosenau

In focusing on the structures and processes of global governance (GG) one has to be wary of proceeding from an initial presumption that there is a single empirical reality out there to be investigated. Since it suggests desirable and compelling values that ought to be promoted, GG invites wishful thinking, an unexamined premise that somehow our messy, tension-ridden world must be undergoing governance on a global scale marked by a modicum of coherence that can and should be analyzed.

My perspective on this "reality" derives from an understanding of how GG became an overarching concept central to the discourse on world affairs. Its emergence requires recognizing that widespread use of the word "governance" is essentially a recent phenomenon—indeed, it did not exist in some languages (e.g., German)—and that its increasing usage has paralleled the acceleration of globalization. With but few exceptions, in fact, governance tends to be employed only when it is modified by the adjective "global." Otherwise, for scales short of the global—whether local, provincial, or national—"government" is usually treated as the entity through which order is sought and goals framed and implemented. And why have "global" and "governance" become inextricably linked in public discourse? The answer strikes me as stemming from three sources. One involves the need to refer to the exercise of authority beyond national borders and the implausibility of doing so by referring to global government inasmuch as such a structure neither exists nor hovers on the horizon. Second, the need to speak of transnational authority was intensified by the Apollo picture of the earth taken from outer space that depicted a lonely spheroid in a vast universe and thereby served to heighten a keen awareness of humankind as sharing a common fate.[1] Third, for a long time the world was described as increasingly interdependent, but not until the Cold War ended were people freed up to fully recognize that the dynamics of interdependence tended to have consequences that are global in scope. The problem of global warming, for example, knows no boundaries and reaches into every corner of the globe. Likewise, genocidal policies and practices in Rwanda and Kosovo have been experienced as challenges to all of humankind, as have financial crises and a growing gap between the rich and poor in developing countries. As such processes accelerated at a seemingly ever more rapid rate, and as new electronic technologies facilitated a collapse of time and distance, the notion quickly spread that interdependence is characteristic of the world as a whole. Accordingly, persuaded that many problems cannot be allowed to fester and endanger the well-being of people everywhere, and eager to bring a modicum of order and direction to the uncertainties and dislocations inherent in the vast degrees of interdependence, analysts have quite naturally begun to talk of the need for GG and the structures and processes that might foster and sustain it.

At first glance everything seems in place for a surge toward effective GG. Both publics and their governments are keenly aware the world is a messy place—the "organized irresponsibility that rules the globe" (Sachs 2002: 9)—and they all aspire to bringing some order and progress to it. A plethora of international and transnational organizations have come into being for this purpose, and there is no shortage of good minds and decent people working hard at framing ideas for improving existing institutions and founding new ones that may move the world along the path to more effective GG. A huge and ever-growing literature, a seemingly endless spate of conferences, an outpouring of commitments by corporate boards and religious organizations, a flurry of activity by public officials in myriad issue areas, and a turn toward new courses and programs in the academic world testify to the continuing expansion of the surging preoccupation with how effective GG might be realized.

Put differently, at first glance much of the world appears to have moved collectively from a fragmented NIMBY (not in my backyard) syndrome to a keen awareness of an integrated future symbolized by the aforementioned picture of the earth from outer space. Backyards remain marked by extensive local variation that cannot be ignored, but such differences are now somewhat more likely to be framed in a global context.

A post-international perspective

Despite the explosion of literature on the subject, none of the approaches to GG strikes me as adequate. Too wedded to existing theories such as realism and liberalism, most formulations tend to underplay, even ignore in some cases, the messiness of the current world scene and the consequences of a growing interdependence on a global scale that is at the same time marked by undiminished local variations. Accordingly, I have developed my own theoretical perspective, one that stresses the changing nature of world affairs by treating the emergent structures and processes as post-international (Rosenau 1990). Such a perspective is rooted in the premise that the world is undergoing a profound transformation wherein three of its basic parameters have become variables rather than constants. One is at the micro level and involves the acquisitions of new skills by people everywhere. A second is a macro parameter that posits a bifurcation of global structures such that the long-standing state-centric world now has to contend with a multi-centric world composed of diverse and numerous collectivities such as NGOs, corporations, professional societies, etc.

The third is a micro–macro parameter that focuses on how the links between people at the micro level and collectivities at the macro level give rise to pervasive authority crises within most collectivities.

Structure-spheres of authority

The major structural consequence of the transformations that mark post-international politics is the advent of an ever-greater number of spheres of authority (SOAs) that, in effect, amount to a vast disaggregation of the mechanisms through which GG is exercised. In effect, therefore, the global stage has become increasingly dense and crowded, thereby lessening the probability that governance on a global scale can be effective. There are just too many centers of power and authority.

Yet, notwithstanding the huge extent to which the global stage has become crowded with diverse actors at every level of community who take positions and pursue policies that may have widespread repercussions beyond the scope of their authority, most discussions of GG start at the level of reforming international institutions and then note how the reforms have to be implemented by national and local governments. To be sure, the vulnerability of international institutions to the wishes of the member governments that created them is fully acknowledged and bottom-up solutions thereby hinted; but whether the solutions are top-down or bottom-up, they posit vertical flows of authority. The repeated calls for a World Environmental Organization similar to the World Trade Organization exemplify the vertical perspective (French 2000: 159; Sachs 2002: 65). Such a perspective has led quite naturally to a widespread presumption that GG is founded on a coordinated structure, as if governance on a global scale involves a singular form of activity, or at least a set of activities that are in harmony with one another. No one quite says it that way, but the implication always seems to underlie GG formulations. More than that, GG is usually posited as a good thing, as consisting of desirable activities and outcomes. To be sure, simplistic approaches to GG are relatively scarce. Most analysts do acknowledge the complexity, but nonetheless they usually presume it is a manageable complexity, one that is potentially coherent and all-encompassing.

In short, efforts to develop viable solutions to GG problems are still cast in the context of traditional approaches to the nature of authority. They ignore the ways in which collectivities in both the public and private sectors sustain authority flows horizontally through networks as well as vertically through hierarchical structures, almost as if allowance for horizontal, network-like flows is just too complex to contemplate. Lip service is paid to the role of NGOs and publics and their modes of interaction, but in the end allowance for such dynamics is essentially limited. The state continues to be posited as the prime, if not the only, wielder of effective authority. Thus, still rooted in the notion that compliance involves those at the top persuading, instructing, or ordering that those down the chain of command conduct themselves in specified ways, no allowance is made for requests and suggestions that evoke compliance through non-hierarchical structures. In effect, the NIMBY syndrome has been elevated to the national level, thereby minimizing the extent to which we are sensitive to the variability that still prevails at local levels. Put differently, our concern for the global problems posed by our recognition of the earth as a lonely spheroid in a vast universe serves to block our appreciation of the relevance of authority being exercised in local networks. The disaggregation of authority sustained is thus a major reason why the challenges of GG are so daunting. In the words of one observer,

> So dominant in contemporary consciousness is the assumption that authority must be centralized that scholars are just beginning to grapple with how decentralized authority might be understood. ... [T]he question of how to think about a world that is becoming "domesticated" but not central-ized, about a world after "anarchy," is one of the most important questions today facing not only students of international relations but of political theory as well.
>
> (Wendt 1999: 308)

If the world is conceived to be a disaggregated multiplicity of SOAs that collectively constitute a new global order, the key to understanding their various roles in GG lies not so much in focusing on their legal prerogatives, but rather in assessing the degree to which they are able to evoke the compliance of the people whom they seek to mobilize through the directives they issue. Achieving compliance is the key to leadership and politics, and it is not readily accom-plished. The more complex societies and the world become, the more difficult it is to get people to respond to efforts to generate their compliance. States have an advantage in this regard because they have the legitimate right to employ force if their citizens fail to comply. But to stress this distinctive quality of states is to ignore the underpinnings of compliance. Most notable perhaps, it ignores the large degree to which compliance is rooted in habit, in an unthinking readi-ness to respond to directives issued by the authorities to which one has been socialized to be committed, responsive, and loyal, and the large degree to which such habits are no longer encompassed by the clear-cut province of states. With the proliferation of SOAs that span long-standing conventional boundaries, with the emergence of alternative authorities to which people can be responsive, analytic attention needs to focus on the ways in which compliance habits may be undergoing transformation.

It is not a simple matter to grasp GG as a congeries of diverse collectivities, only some of which are governments and states while most are nongovernmental organizations (NGOs), private groups, corporations, and a host of other boundary-spanning entities. Such a proliferation of transnational actors requires one to wrench free of the unquestioned premise that the boundaries separating countries are firm and impassable without permission of the states that preside over them. This wrenching task is not easily accomplished. Our analytic capaci-ties are rooted in methodological territorialism (Scholte 2001: 56–58), in a long-standing, virtually unconscious habit of probing problems in a broad, geographic or spatial context. This habit poses an acute problem because of the ever-growing porosity of domestic–foreign boundaries (Rosenau 1997) that has rendered territoriality much less pervasive than it used to be even as all the social sciences construct their inquiries, develop their concepts, formulate their hypotheses, and frame their evidence-gathering procedures through spatial lenses. Nor are officials free to think in alternative contexts: as one analyst put it, "Trapped by the territoriality of their power, policy makers in traditional settings often have little choice but to address the symptoms rather than the causes of public problems" (Reinicke 1999–2000: 45).

Yet, breaking out of the conceptual jail imposed by methodological territorialism is imperative because the processes of disaggregation so readily span foreign–domestic boundaries, thus making it difficult for states to exercise control over the flows of ideas, money, goods, pollution, crime, drugs, and terrorists; and they have only slightly greater control over the flow of people. Why? Because their capacities have been weakened by an ever-greater complexity embedded in some eight dynamics (outlined below) that have greatly increased transborder flows and rendered domestic–foreign boundaries ever more porous. With the collapse of time and distance, subnational organizations and governments that once operated within the confines of national boundaries are now so inextricably connected to far-off parts of the world that the legal and geographic jurisdictions in which they are located matter less and less. What matters, instead, are the spheres of authority to which their members are responsive.

Put differently, with the United States committed to a policy of pre-emption and thus acting as if it has accumulated most of the world's power and authority, it is not easy to accept the possibility that the world is becoming ever more disaggregated. Preferring a tidier, less complex conception of how global affairs are structured, all too many analysts are inclined to reject the conception of GG as disaggregated centers of authority. They argue that positing the global stage as ever more crowded with SOAs amounts to such a broad conception as to make it "virtually meaningless both for theory construction and social action" (Väyrynen 1999: 25). As the foregoing discussion suggests, however, here this argument is found wanting. Opting for a narrow conception may facilitate analysis, but doing so is also misleading in that it ignores the vast proliferation of SOAs that have emerged as a prime structural characteristic of the system of GG subsequent to the end of the Cold War.

Process –fragmegration

If disaggregation is the major structural consequence of the transformations presently under way, the prime process generated by the changes involves the confluence of two major and contrary dynamics. One involves all those forces that press for centralization, integration, and globalization, and the other consists of those forces that press for decentralization, fragmentation, and localization. In turn, these polarities can be viewed as either philosophical premises or as empirical processes. As philosophical premises, they amount to forms of either localism or globalism, both of which consist of mind sets, of orientations, of worldviews, with localism pertaining to those mental sets that value the familiar and close-at-hand arrangements located within conventional community and national boundaries, and with globalism involving orientations toward the distant circumstances that lie beyond national boundaries. But localism and globalism can usefully be distinguished from localization and globalization, which I conceive to be empirical processes rather than mind sets, processes that are boundary-spanning in the case of globalization and that either contract within conventional boundaries or do not span them in the case of localization.

Whether globalism and localism are viewed as orientations toward or as processes of integration and fragmentation, they are best conceived as a singular phenomenon wherein the foregoing polarities converge. Indeed, it is the dominant phenomenon of the epoch that has emerged subsequent to the Cold War, so much so that I have coined a word designed to capture the inextricable links between the individual and societal tendencies to integrate across boundaries that are the hallmark of globalization and the counter-tendencies toward fragmentation that are fomented by localizing resistances to boundary-spanning activities. My label is that of "fragmegration," an ungainly and contrived word that has the virtue of capturing in a single phrase—and thus of arresting our attention to—the extraordinary complex phenomena that sustain the endless interactions between the forces of fragmentation and integration. I dare to suggest that by viewing the world through fragmegrative lenses one can discern the underlying dynamics of our epoch with a clarity that is not otherwise available (Rosenau 1997).

In short, globalization and localization feed off each other, stimulate responses to each other, in endless interactions at every level of community. At times the interactions are cooperative, but often they are conflictual and underlie many of the issues on the global agenda. Hence, it is not far-fetched to assert that many increments of globalization give rise to increments of localization, and vice versa, so thoroughly are the two contrary orientations and processes interconnected. Needless to say, the tasks of GG are enormously confounded by the pervasiveness of fragmegrative processes.

Sources of fragmegrative processes

In order to probe the underpinnings of GG as disaggregated complexity I find it useful to identify eight major sources of fragmegration that shape attitudes and behavior at four levels of aggregation—the micro level of individuals, the macro level of collectivities and states, the micro–macro level at which individuals and collectivities shape and interact with each other, and the macro–macro level wherein collectivities interact and influence each other. Both the eight sources and the four levels are set forth in Table 8.1, with the cell entries being crude hypotheses that suggest some—though surely not all—the possible consequences that may flow at each level in response to each of the various sources.

Many more hypotheses could be listed if space permitted. None of the hypotheses have been tested. Intuitively they make sense, and they are consistent with much of the literature on globalization, but I welcome any research efforts that employ systematic empirical data to establish or refute their validity. For present purposes, however, the ensuing analysis is confined to elaborating briefly on the eight sources and noting some of their more conspicuous consequences at the several levels as a means of depicting the complexity of GG.[2]

It must be emphasized that the eight sources are interactive, that each has consequences for the others. Innovative microelectronic technologies, to cite but one example, serve to expand the skills of people, the formation and strengthening of organizations, the weakening of territoriality, states, and sovereignty, and thus the potential for authority crises. Indeed, so interactive are the various sources that any attempt to trace their causal potency is very much an unsolvable chicken-and-egg problem that complexity theory may some day be able to solve; but all we can do here is note that they are all relevant and suggest some of the consequences that each fosters.

Microelectronic technologies

Among the consequences that may flow from the Internet, mobile phones, and fax machines is an ever more effective capacity to mobilize like-minded people on behalf of shared goals. It is a capacity that serves those committed to localism as well as those inclined toward globalism. Equally important, such technologies level the playing field. Mobilization in local communities is facilitated by word of mouth as well as electronic technologies, but the latter make it possible to reach and mobilize the like-minded across national boundaries and great distances. The image of Marcos, the Zapatista commander, under a tree in the jungle with a laptop seeking support from leaders and publics around the world (Olesen 2005) is but a microcosm of how these technologies can be used to generate support and give rise to fragmegrative tensions. Indeed, the Internet has been a major factor in the surging and repeated expansion of anti-globalization protests. As an organizer of the Seattle protests put it, "The Internet has become the latest, greatest arrow in our quiver of social activism."[3]

Skill revolution

Elsewhere I have argued at length that people everywhere—elites, activists, ordinary folk in rural areas and urban centers—have expanded their skills at dealing with the challenges and crises that mark our accelerated epoch.[4] It is no longer plausible to take publics for granted, to assume they can be led by their officials to support any course of action. Rather, equipped with a deeper understanding and more clear-cut values than, say, their great grandparents, today they are more ready to take action in response to circumstances they find wanting. This greater readiness is perhaps especially evident with respect to environmental issues, sensitivities to which have greatly increased in recent decades as polluted air has enveloped cities and a host of

Table 8.1 Some sources of fragmegration at four levels of aggregation

Sources of Fragmegration	Levels of Aggregation			
	Micro	Macro	Micro-macro	Macro-macro
Micro-electronic Technologies	enable like-minded people to be in touch with each other anywhere in the world	render collectivities more open, connected, and vulnerable; empowers them to mobilize support	constrain governments by enabling opposition groups to mobilize more effectively	accelerate diplomatic processes; facilitate electronic surveillance and intelligence work
Skill Revolution	expands people's horizons on a global scale; sensitizes them to the relevance of distant events; facilitates a reversion to local concerns	enlarges the capacity of governmental agencies to think "out of the box," seize opportunities, and analyze challenges	constrains policy making through increased capacity of individuals to know when, where, and how to engage in collective action	multiplies quantity and enhances quality of links among states; solidifies their alliances and enmities
Organizational Explosion	facilitates multiple identities, subgroupism, and affiliation with transnational networks	increases capacity of opposition groups to form and press for altered policies; divides publics from their elites	contributes to the pluralism and dispersion of authority; heightens the probability of authority crises	renders the global stage ever more transnational and dense with non-governmental actors
Bifurcation of Global Structures	adds to role conflicts, divides loyalties, and foments tensions among individuals; orients people toward local spheres of authority	facilitates formation of new spheres of authority and consolidation of existing spheres in the multi-centric world	empowers transnational advocacy groups and special interests to pursue influence through diverse channels	generates institutional arrangements for cooperation on major global issues such as trade, human rights, the environment
Mobility Upheaval	stimulates imaginations and provides more extensive contacts with foreign cultures; heightens salience of the outsider	enlarges the size and relevance of sub-cultures, diasporas, and ethnic conflicts as people seek new opportunities abroad	increases movement across borders that lessens capacity of governments to control national boundaries	heightens need for international cooperation to control the flow of drugs, money, immigrants, and terrorists

Continued overleaf

Continued

Sources of Fragmegration	Levels of Aggregation			
	Micro	*Macro*	*Micro-macro*	*Macro-macro*
Weakening of Territoriality, States, and Sovereignty	undermines traditions and national loyalties; increases distrust of governments and other institutions	adds to the porosity of national boundaries and the difficulty of framing national policies	lessens confidence in governments; renders nationwide consensuses difficult to achieve and maintain	increases need for interstate cooperation on global issues; lessens control over cascading events
Authority Crises	redirect loyalties; encourage individuals to replace traditional criteria of legitimacy with performance criteria	weaken ability of both governments and other organizations to frame and implement policies	facilitate the capacity of publics to press and/or paralyze their governments, the WTO, and other organizations	Enlarge the competence of some IGOs and NGOs; encourage diplomatic wariness in negotiations
Globalization of National Economies	swells ranks of consumers; promotes uniform tastes; heightens concerns for jobs; widens gap between winners and losers	complicates tasks of state governments vis-à-vis markets; promotes business alliances	increases efforts to protect local cultures and industries; facilitates vigor of protest movements; polarizes communities	intensifies trade and investment conflicts; generates incentives for building global financial institutions

other environmental crises have marred the course of events. The recurrent anti-globalization protests are again illustrative in this regard, as many of the protestors give voice to concerns about the environment and, in so doing, intensify the clash of global and local forces. Stated in the words of one analyst, "The local efforts of citizens have always been crucial to the environmental movement. Grassroots activism is the seedbed of more organized and enduring efforts and institutions" (Thiele 1999: 28). Furthermore, the skill revolution along with the new technologies has heightened people's sense of identity and their capacity to shoulder multiple identities. Put differently, both reflective analysis and virulent environmentalism can be traced to the greater awareness that has accompanied the skill revolution.

Organizational explosion

A central pattern of this accelerated epoch is the proliferation of organizations at every level of community, local, national, and transnational. Spurred in good part by environmental and human rights issues but for many other reasons as well, organizations are forming and expanding at startling rates. The data eloquently tell this proliferation story. The number of NGOs working across international borders soared during the last century, climbing from just 176 in 1909 to more than 230,000 in 1998. The reach of the organizational explosion is further exemplified by the finding that, "in 1984, the Citizens Clearinghouse for Hazardous Waste worked with 600 community groups, and the figure would rise to 8,000 groups by the mid-1990s" (Thiele 1999: 18). Nor is the reach of the organizational explosion a singular process. On the contrary, at least in the United States—and doubtless elsewhere—beginning in the 1980s the environmental movement underwent a "two-pronged mainstreaming"—"from the top down through the large national organizations and from the bottom up through dispersed grassroots efforts" (Thiele 1999: 19).

No less important, due largely to the Internet and the fax machine, many of the proliferating organizations are horizontally as well as vertically structured. Networks have supplemented hierarchies as an organizational form, and more than a few of the new organizations are conspicuously lacking in hierarchy. Combined with the processes of localization, the organizational explosion is thus enabling people to find common cause with others in their community and to come together when the need to do so arises. The shifting balance between hierarchical and network forms of organization, between vertical and horizontal flows of authority, is an important dynamic that can both facilitate and hinder GG. Assisted by the growth of the Internet, people now converge electronically as equals, or at least not as superiors and subordinates. They make plans, recruit members, mobilize support, raise money, debate issues, frame agendas, and undertake collective action that amount to steering mechanisms founded on horizontal rather than hierarchical channels of authority. Indeed, it has been argued, with reason, that

> the rise of network forms of organization—particularly "all channel networks," in which every node can communicate with every other node— is one of the single most important effects of the information revolution for all realms: political, economic, social, and military. It means that power is migrating to small, nonstate actors who can organize into sprawling networks more readily than can traditionally hierarchical nation-state actors.
>
> (Arquilla and Ronfeldt 1997: 5)

In other words, not only has the advent of network forms of organization undermined the authority of states, but in the context of our concern with GG, it has also had even more important consequences. Most notably, networks have contributed to the disaggregation of authority as well as the formation of new collectivities not founded on hierarchical principles.

If the notion that new rule systems can be founded on horizontal as well as vertical structures of authority seems awkward, it warrants reiterating that the core of effective authority lies in the compliance of those toward whom it is directed. If people ignore, avoid, or otherwise do not heed the compliance sought by "the authorities," then it can be said that for all practical purposes they are authorities in name only, that their authority has evaporated. Authority is thus profoundly relational. It links—or fails to do so, or does so somewhat—those who issue directives and those for whom the directives are intended. It is useful, therefore, to treat authority as a continuum wherein at one extreme full compliance is evoked and at the other extreme it is not. The viability of all collectivities can be assessed by ascertaining where they are located on the continuum. The closer they are to the compliance extreme, the greater will be their viability and effectiveness, just as the nearer they are to the noncompliance extreme the greater is the likelihood that they will be ineffective and falter.

Bifurcation of global structures

Beginning sometime after World War II the overall structure of world politics began, as previously noted, to undergo change, to bifurcate, with the flourishing of innumerable actors other than states clambering up on to the world stage and undertaking actions with consequence for the course of events. As a result, what I call a "multi-centric" world evolved that consists of a great variety of collectivities and that has come to rival the long-standing, anarchical state-centric system. One can reasonably assert that overall global structures are today marked by two worlds of world politics, two worlds that sometimes cooperate, oft-times conflict, and endlessly interact (Rosenau 1990: 246–296). The bifurcated evolution of the global system serves to intensify fragmegrative dynamics in the sense that it contributes to the long-term process whereby authority is undergoing disaggregation. Consequently, the multi-centric world now provides avenues for local groups to articulate their needs and goals as they join with each other in persuading governments in the state-centric world to heed—or at least to hear—their claims.

It is noteworthy that the bifurcation of global structures has undergone institutionalization since the two worlds of world politics converged and interacted at the 1992 environmental conference in Rio—with 160 governments represented and some 1,500 accredited NGOs at the Earth Summit and thousands more at the parallel Earth Forum—which was then followed by comparable events that focused on human rights in Vienna, on population problems in Cairo, on social development in Copenhagen, on women's rights in Beijing, on cities in Istanbul, on trade, finance, and other aspects of globalization in Seattle, Washington, D.C., Davos, Genoa, Johannesburg, and numerous other locales. It is hard to imagine any future gathering of leaders of the state-centric world that is not accompanied by a simultaneous and adjacent gathering of organizations and individuals from the multi-centric world, a reality that is profoundly and thoroughly expressive of the dynamics of fragmegration.

Mobility upheaval

Due in part to the advent of jet aircraft and a steady lessening of the costs to travel in them, the accelerated epoch has witnessed a vast movement of people—everyone from the tourist to the terrorist, from the business executive to the immigrant, from illegal aliens seeking work to those fleeing persecution, from students studying abroad to artists and other professionals advancing their careers. To cite one example, there were 635 million international tourist arrivals in 1998, whereas the figure for 1950 was 25 million (French 2000: 29). In many ways this mobility upheaval, as I call it, has contributed to the integrative dimension of fragmentation, but in one important way it has served to intensify fragmentation. In many countries the migrant, legal as well as illegal, has fostered strong negative reactions in the host society. Immigrants and migrants represent the "stranger" and many people in the recipient communities are uneasy about what these strangers may do to them and their ways of life. The friend and the enemy are known entities, but the stranger is not and is widely seen as a threat to long-standing traditions. Australia's handling of this problem, its refusal to let boatloads of migrants disembark on its shores, is a classic instance of this fragmegrative dynamic, but numerous other Western countries have also tried to curb this aspect of the mobility upheaval.

Weakening of territoriality, states, and sovereignty

As technologies shrink the world, as people become increasingly skillful, as organizations proliferate, as the multi-centric world expands, and as the mobility upheaval sustains vast movements of people, the meaning of territory becomes less compelling and states and their sovereignty become weaker. This is not to forecast the end of the state as a central political structure. Rather it is to stress that states have increasing difficulty controlling the flow of ideas, money, goods, drugs, crime, pollution, and people across their borders, thus contributing substantially to the processes whereby authority is undergoing disaggregation on a worldwide scale. The fragmegrative consequences of these processes are considerable. Most notably perhaps, local communities and groups are acquiring greater autonomy and a heightened readiness to contest the integrative forces of globalization through street protests and other means.

Authority crises

As noted earlier in connection with the transformation of the micro–macro parameter, the processes of disaggregation have contributed to a proliferation of authority crises on the part of governments, local as well as national. Such crises are most conspicuous when protesters crowd the streets and make strident demands, but an even more common form of authority crisis involves the inability of governments to frame goals and move toward them. Stalemate and paralysis, in other words, amount to authority crises, and they are pervasive.

Japan's inability to confront and surmount the long-term decline of its economy and the persistence of widespread corruption and unemployment in China are illustrative of authority crises that derive their strength from stalemated political systems. Much the same can be said about most other governments throughout the world. There may be increasing numbers of democratic systems, but few of these have majorities that are able to rule effectively. One need only recall how the U.S. government closed and locked its doors twice late in 1995 to appreciate the extent to which authority crises have come to mark the prevailing global scene. Nor are these crises limited to governments. NGOs, churches, unions, and a variety of other institutions are also going into one or another form of paralysis and upheaval. Even the Mafia has experienced an authority crisis rooted in its young members defying the dictates of its seniors. Needless to say, pervasive authority crises bear importantly on the world's capacity to evolve effective GG. If in fact it can be said that GG does exist, then it is surely undergoing a severe authority crisis.

It might be wondered whether pervasive authority crises and the advent of bifurcated structures implies that states are in a process of disintegration. Not at all. Doubtless the interstate system will continue to be central to world affairs for decades and centuries to come. To stress that collectivities other than states have emerged as important SOAs is not in any way to suggest that states are headed for demise. Analysts differ over the degree to which the national state has been weakened by the dynamics of fragmegration, but few contend that the weakening amounts to a trend line that will culminate in total collapse. States are still among the main players on the global stage, but they are no longer the only main players.[5] Many of them are deep in crisis, in cross-cutting conflicts that paralyze their policy-making processes and result in stalemate and stasis, in the avoidance of decisions that would at least address the challenges posed by a fragmegrative world undergoing vast and continuous changes. Yet, most states still control their banking systems and maintain legitimate monopoly over the use of force. And while states have undergone transformation into managerial entities, they are still able to exercise a measure of control over the course of events. But for all its continuing authority and legitimacy, key dimensions of the power of the modern state have undergone considerable diminution. In the words of one analyst, "As wealth and power are increasingly generated by private transactions that take place across the borders of states rather than within them, it has become harder to sustain the image of states as the preeminent actors at the global level" (Evans 1997: 65).

Globalization of national economies

The turn toward free-enterprise economic systems and a lessening of trade barriers has had a number of fragmegrative consequences. On the integrative side the emergence of a global economy has led to a greater variety of goods and services being available to more and more people, processes that have also contributed to an ever-greater interdependence among groups and societies. On the fragmenting side, the globalization of national economies has also served to widen the gap between rich and poor both within and between countries. It has also highlighted the role of transnational corporations, thereby generating conditions for a wide variety of fragmegrative situations, from protests against the world's economic institutions—the World Bank, the IMF, the WTO, the G8—to boycotts of the goods of corporations that are considered to skew progress toward GG.

The convergence of structure and process

Elsewhere I have suggested that the core of governance involves a convergence of structure and process through rule systems in which steering mechanisms are employed to frame and implement goals that enable organizations and communities to move in the directions they wish to go or that enable them to maintain the institutions and policies they wish to maintain (Rosenau 1995). Governance is not the same as government in that the rule systems of the latter are rooted in formal and legal procedures, while those of the former are also marked by informal rule systems (Rosenau 1992). It follows that the achievement of a modicum of governance on a global scale requires the development of steering mechanisms that evoke compliant actions, not just words, on the part of the innumerable individual and collective actors whose activities shape the course of events within and among communities throughout in the world.

Three key challenges here are especially noteworthy. One concerns myriad local variations that resist overall global solutions. Some problems are global in scope, but the circumstances of different communities and issues can vary considerably, with the result that GG involves the exercise of authority in a host of diverse conditions. To aspire to transnational institutions that are relevant to situations everywhere is to drastically misread the governance problem. Needs at the local level must be met without encouraging or reinforcing the NIMBY syndrome.

The second challenge involves the fact that political entities are not the only ones that engage in governance. It is now commonplace to speak of market governance, of corporate governance, of environmental governance, of governance by NGOs, of media governance (Siochrú and Girard 2002), and so on across all the types of collectivities that may exercise authority on the global stage. It follows that an adequate conception of GG needs to incorporate all the various forms of extant governance. Not to do so would be to miss central features of the pervasive complexities that mark GG.[6]

The third challenge is posed by the aforementioned nature of compliance, of getting relevant actors to put aside habitual responses and, instead, to yield to authorities who set new, more globally compatible standards for the systems of which they are a part. The challenge is huge not only because GG is a highly complex, disaggregated and minimally coordinated system of governance comprising the sum of the hundreds of thousands of formal and informal rule systems at all levels of the world's communities, but also because of an inclination not to confront the complexity it represents and, instead, to favor a more streamlined system that is hierarchically aggregated.

In short, since fragmegrative processes sustain authority flows that are not neatly structured and go every which way, emanating from a vast array of actors whose rule systems seek to evoke compliance through a variety of means, GG involves crazy-quilt arrangements wherein authority is exercised partly by hierarchical structures, partly by horizontal networks, and partly by oblique links among overlapping vertical and horizontal SOAs. Taken in its entirety, the prevailing system of global governance is comparable to a mobius strip or web. It is a system marked by patterns that unfold when the impetus to steer a course of events derives from networked and hierarchical interactions across levels of aggregation among transnational corporations (TNCs), NGOs, intergovernmental organizations (IGOs), states, elites, mass publics, and local or provincial communities, interactions that are elaborate and diverse enough to constitute a hybrid structure in which the dynamics of governance are so overlapping among the several levels as to form a singular, web-like process that is continuous and, like a mobius, neither begins nor culminates at any level or at any point in time. A mobius web is top-down, bottom-up and side-by-side governance all at once (Rosenau, 2002a: 81–83).

Needless to say, the growing numbers of SOAs immensely complicate the challenges they face in evoking compliance. SOAs proliferate because increasingly people are capable of shouldering and managing multiple identities that lessen their allegiance to their states. As they get involved in more and more networks in the multi-centric world, so may their loyalties fracture and become issue- and object-specific. To be sure, history in this era of fragmegration does record pockets of successful coordination among states in the state-centric world and among the diverse nongovernmental collectivities in the multi-centric world that are able to generate meaningful compliance. Even though SOAs vary widely in their ability to evoke compliance and thus in their contributions to the processes of governance at a global scale, some do manage to gain a measure of control over fragmegrative tensions. Rule systems developed through negotiation among national governments—such as the United Nations, the Kyoto Protocol on Climate Change, the World Trade Organization, or the European Union—have the widest scope and, consequently, make perhaps the most substantial contribution to governance processes globally. Steering mechanisms maintained by SOAs in the multi-centric world—such as the calculations of credit-rating agencies that estimate the reliability of national economies, the rulings of truth commissions designed to enable countries racked by civil strife to heal their wounds, or the practices of the insurance industry to offset climate changes (Carlsson and Stripple 2000), and a host of other mechanisms (Cutler *et al.* 1999)—exemplify effective instruments of governance with respect to specific issues. To repeat, no less important are the many successful efforts at GG that result from cooperation among collectivities in the state- and multi-centric worlds. In the words of one knowledgeable observer, "global regimes are increasingly the product of negotiations among state and nonstate actors" (Zacher 1999: 48).

For every example of rule systems in world politics that achieve meaningful coordination and compliance, however, innumerable cases can be cited in which efforts to maintain effective steering mechanisms fail to generate the compliance necessary for effective governance. Indeed, such failures may well be more the rule than the exception in world affairs today. Our messy world is littered with paralyzed or stalemated governments and nongovernmental SOAs that fall far short of evoking the compliance appropriate to their goals and policies.

The governance of a fragmented world

Given a disaggregated and fragmegrative system of GG in which the global stage is dense with actors, large and small, formal and informal, economic and social, political and cultural, national and transnational, international and subnational, aggressive and peaceful, liberal and authoritarian, there is a serious question of whether the world can be effectively governed and thereby facilitate movement to a more sane and orderly global system. To be sure, the disparate collectivities in the two worlds of world politics have in common that all of them sustain rule systems that range across the concerns of their members and that constitute the boundaries of their SOAs (Rosenau 2003: Ch. 13). Clearly, however, this commonality may not be sufficient to allow for progress toward effective governance. The challenge is to insure that fragmegrative dynamics do not rupture evolving mobius forms of governance among two or more of the actors. The challenge is not easily met, as the tensions between integrative and fragmenting tendencies continually pose the possibility of rupture.

Put differently, there is no lack of either variety or number in the extant systems of governance. It is difficult to overestimate how crowded the global stage has become as the world undergoes a multiplication of all kinds of governance, from formal to multilevel governments, from formally sanctioned entities such as arbitration boards to informal SOAs, from emergent supranational entities such as the European Union to emergent issue regimes, from regional bodies to IGOs, from TNCs to neighborhood associations, from humanitarian groups to ad hoc coalitions, from certifying agencies to social movements, and so on across an ever-widening array of activities and concerns.

Of course, notwithstanding the increasing difficulty of generating compliance posed by the world's greater complexity, not every fragmegrative situation on the global agenda lacks governance. Some mobius webs are harmoniously structured and capable of resisting rupture. There are innumerable situations involving localizing responses to globalizing stimuli that are marked by a high, or at least an acceptable, quality of governance and that thus need not be of concern here. The vast proliferation of rule systems in recent decades includes a trend to devolve governance so that its steering mechanisms are closer to those who experience its policies. This trend is most conspicuously marked by the evolution of what has been called "multilevel" governance, a form of rule system in which authority is voluntarily and legally dispersed among the various levels of community where problems are located and local needs require attention. The

European Union exemplifies multilevel governance, as does Scotland, Wales, the French provinces, U.S. welfare programs, and many other federal systems in which previously centralized authority has been redistributed to provincial and municipal rule systems. Such systems are not lacking in tensions and conflicts, but relatively speaking the quality of governance is such that the tensions do not lead to violence, the loss of life, the deterioration of social cohesion, or the degradation of people. In short, fragmegrative process are not inherently negative or destructive.

For all kinds of reasons, however, numerous fragmegrative situations are fragile, deleterious, violence-prone, and marked by publics who resent, reject, or otherwise resist the intrusion of global values, policies, actors, or institutions into their local affairs. It is these situations that pose the main problems for worldwide governance. To be sure, some of the global intrusions can be, depending on one's values, welcomed and applauded. The world's intrusion into the apartheid rule system, for example, was clearly worthwhile. But in a large number of cases—in those where fragmegrative situations involve local reactions to globalizing dynamics that result in internal fighting, external aggression, intensified crime, repressed minorities, exacerbated cleavages, sealed boundaries, glorified but exclusionary ideals, pervasive corruption, and many other patterns that run counter to human dignity and well-being—corrective steering mechanisms that upgrade the quality of governance seem urgently needed.

Part of the problem of achieving governance over deleterious fragmegrative situations, of course, is that often they require the use of external force against local authorities, a practice that has long been contrary to international law and only lately undergone revision, most notably with respect to Kosovo and, more recently, Iraq. But international military interventions into domestic arenas are only one part—and a small one at that—of the challenge of establishing rule systems for unwanted fragmegrative conditions. There are many situations in which organized violence is not the response to globalizing dynamics but which are nonetheless woefully lacking in appropriate steering mechanisms and thus in need of enlightened rule systems. The list of such circumstances is seemingly endless: they can involve situations in which boundaries are sealed, minorities silenced, crime tolerated, majorities deceived, societies ruptured, law flouted, tyrants enhanced, corruption ignored, oppositions jailed, people trafficked, pollution accepted, elections rigged, and thought controlled—to cite only the more conspicuous practices that are often protected by the conventions of sovereignty and that one would like to see subjected to a modicum of effective and humane mechanisms of GG. The thwarted aspirations of the Falun Gong, the people of Burma, and the recurring wars and pervasive poverty in Africa are only among the more conspicuous of many examples of continuing fragmegrative situations that elude efforts toward steerage in enlightened directions,

Nor are the protections of sovereignty the only hindrance to effective GG. Mobius governance on a global scale is also difficult because the globalizing and localizing interactions often occur across both cultures and issue areas. For instance, while national governments can address—though not necessarily alleviate—the fears of their workers over the loss of jobs resulting from foreign trade with relative ease because they have some jurisdiction over both the well-being of their workers and the contents of trade regulation, the global scale of fragmegrative dynamics can also involve situations in which the parties to them are not located in the same jurisdiction, with the result that any attempt to steer them must be undertaken by diverse authorities that often have different interests and goals. Indeed, not infrequently a globalizing political or economic stimulus can provoke localizing cultural reactions far removed from the country, region, or issue area in which the stimuli were generated; contrariwise, local events such as protest marches, coups d'état, or severe economic downturns, can have widespread consequences in distant places. The rapid spread of currency crises, for example, often seems ungovernable because authority for coping with the crises is so widely dispersed in this issue area and because much of the action takes place beyond the reach of any extant governments, in cyberspace. Put more strongly, the processes of imitative, emulative, and isomorphic spread, as well as those that are direct and not circuitous, are so pervasive and powerful that developing steering mechanisms that prevent, or at least minimize their unwanted consequences, seems a staggering task under the best of circumstances.

Leadership

Some analysts contend that the dangers of rupture and disarray are not as great as they may seem, that tendencies in these directions are held in check—and in some cases reversed—by the leadership of the United States as the dominant actor in the post-Cold War arrangement of world politics. Frequently referred to as "hegemonic stability," a "unipolar structure," or an emergent empire the dominance of the United States and the democratic values it espouses is conceived to be a form of GG. It is a conception that presumes the capabilities of the U.S. are so unrivaled that it can generate the compliance necessary to preserve stability on a global scale even as it promotes human rights, democracy, and open markets. As I see it, such an approach is misguided. Not only does it ignore the reluctance of the American people to play an active role in the processes of GG—a reluctance which takes the form of not paying in full its dues to the United Nations or otherwise not participating in numerous international rule systems to which most countries have agreed—but even more important it is a perspective that takes no account of the large degree to which authority is undergoing disaggregation. If the preceding analysis is correct that the global stage is ever more crowded with SOAs capable of independently pursuing their goals, then obviously hegemonic leadership can neither flourish nor endure. Much as many people in the U.S., ordinary citizens as well as leaders, might prefer to pursue unilateral policies, in most situations the country is forced to work within and through multilateral institutions and, in so doing, it often has to accept modification of its goals. And when it does not accept any modifications, when it proceeds unilaterally, its policies tend to flail aimlessly at best, or fail at worst. The world is simply too interdependent, and authority is too dispersed, for any one country to command the global scene as fully as earlier empires did.

Conclusions

Of course, to a large degree conclusions reached on the potential of GG depend on one's temperament—on whether one pessimistically stresses the disarray inherent in weakened states or optimistically focuses on humankind's capacities for innovation and adaptation. Although basically an optimist, I am inclined to reiterate some pessimistic responses followed by a couple of upbeat observations that may offset at least some of the downbeat interpretations. My bleak assessment of the prospects for effective GG derives from the crazy-quilt nature of global structures and processes, along with the failure to conceptually allow for them. For processes founded on effective authority that inches the world toward sanity, a wide variety of numerous actors, both individuals and collectivities, have to be coordinated and their differences at least minimally subordinated to the interests of their great grandchildren. More than that, given the boundary-spanning nature of fragmegrative dynamics, all concerned have to recognize that people everywhere have an interest in your grandchildren as well as their own.

The chances of such mobius webs being fashioned as effective rule systems seem very slim indeed. Too many actors can intrude ruptures in the webs. Whether they are corporate executives who sacrifice the well-being of future generations for the sake of immediate profits, states that pursue economic goals at the expense of sustainable environments, sovereignty-protective officials who are oblivious to the great grandchildren of publics other than their own, NGOs that put their narrow interests ahead of collective policies, the United States that withdraws from treaties, individuals whose corrupt practices undermine efforts to hasten economic development, or bureaucrats and analysts mired in conceptual confusion who do not fully appreciate the numerous local foundations of global structures—to mention only a few of the ways in which the diverse actors on the global stage can divert movement toward a sane world—the coordination needed to implement GG seems unlikely to surmount the disaggregated authority structures on which GG rests.

This is not to suggest that GG accords all actors a veto over the pace of reform and progress. Rather, it is to highlight the extraordinary complexity and barriers that confront efforts to move a world marked by highly disaggregated SOAs in meaningful and desired directions.

Nor is it to suggest that no progress toward effective GG lies ahead. In the environmental field, for example, there has already been a proliferation of environmental regimes: "fourteen different global environmental agreements [were] concluded in the rather short period between 1985 and 1997" (Anderson 2001: 117), though, to be sure, the record of compliance with these treaties has been, at best, spotty. Equally relevant, there is no lack of good, knowledgeable leaders and activists who expend a lot of energy on behalf of decent goals. Pockets of progress will thus doubtless occur as some countries, corporations, and NGOs sign on to constructive rule systems designed to advance GG as the skill and organizational revolutions lead to public pressures on recalcitrant collectivities. One observer expresses the difficulty of coming to a conclusion on whether progress or decline lie ahead by asking an upbeat question and then offering a downbeat answer relative to the environment:

> Is the world witnessing the beginning of such a phase shift [toward GG] in the antiglobalization protests, in the unprecedented initiatives undertaken by both private corporations and local communities, in the growth of NGOs and their innovations, in scientists speaking up and speaking out, and in the outpouring of environmental initiatives by the religious community? We must certainly hope so. The alarms sounded 20 years ago have not been heeded, and soon it will be too late to prevent an appalling deterioration of the natural world.
>
> (Speth 2002: 76)

My own view is that, on balance, the dynamics that underlie the disaggregated character of GG seem likely to thwart movement toward a viable and worldwide coherence. It was neither an accident nor pervasive malevolence that prevented earlier treaty commitments from being implemented. The pervasive inaction appears, rather, to be inherent in the structural constraints and conceptual blocks that currently prevail in the global system.

Yet, I am inclined to cling to my inveterate optimism by noting three aspects of an upbeat answer that may prove operative if one is willing to look beyond the immediate present.

In the first place, more than a little truth attaches to the aphorism that there is safety in numbers. That is, the more pluralistic and crowded the global stage gets with SOAs and their diverse steering mechanisms, the less can any one of them, or any coalition of them, dominate the course of events and the more will all of them have to be sensitive to how sheer numbers limit their influence. Every rule system, in other words, will be hemmed in by all the others, thus conducing to a growing awareness of the virtues of cooperation and the need to contain the worst effects of deleterious fragmegration.

Secondly, there is a consciousness of and intelligence about the processes of globalization that is spreading widely to every corner of the earth. What has been designated as "reflexivity" (Giddens and Pierson 1998: 115–117) and what I call "the globalization of globalization" (Rosenau 2002b) is accelerating at an extraordinary rate—from the ivory towers of academe to the halls of government, from the conference rooms of corporations to the peasant homes of China (where the impact of the WTO is an intense preoccupation), people in all walks of life have begun to appreciate their interdependence with others as time and distance shrink. For some, maybe even many, the rush into a globalized world may be regrettable, but few are unaware that they live in a time of change and thus there is likely to be a growing understanding of the necessity to confront the challenges of fragmegration and of being open to new ways of meeting them. Put more positively, an endlessly explosive literature on globalization reflects substantial evidence that good minds in government, academe, journalism, and the business community in all parts of the world are turning, each in their own way, to the task of addressing the challenges posed by fragmegrative dynamics. It is difficult to recall another period of history when so many thoughtful people concentrated their talents on the human condition from a worldwide perspective.

Third, the advent of networks and the flow of horizontal communications have brought many more people into one or another aspect of the ongoing dialogue. The conditions for the emergence of a series of global consensuses never existed to quite the extent they do today. The skills of individuals and the orientations of the organizations they support are increasingly conducive to convergence around shared values. To be sure, the battle of Seattle and subsequent skirmishes between advocates and critics of globalization—quintessential instances of fragmegration—point to a polarization around two competing consensuses, but aside from those moments when their conflicts turn violent, the very competition between the opposing camps highlights a potential for dialogue that may lead to compromises and syntheses. Already there are signs that their critics have arrested the attention of international institutions such as the World Bank, the World Economic Forum, the WTO, and the IMF and that they are pondering the challenges posed by the growing gap between rich and poor people and nations.

None of this is to suggest, however, that nirvana lies ahead. Surely it does not. Surely fragmegration will be with us for a long time and surely many of its tensions will intensify. But the collective will to preserve and use the new, horizontal forms of authority is not lacking and that is not a trivial conclusion.

Notes

1 For a cogent analysis of how the outer-space image of the earth has heightened awareness of a common fate, see Jasanoff (2001).
2 Both the contents of Table 8.1 and parts of the ensuing discussion of the eight sources of fragmegration are adapted from Rosenau (2003: Ch. 3).
3 Mike Dolan, quoted in French (2000: 163).
4 For an initial discussion of the skill revolution as a micro dynamic, see Rosenau (1990: Chaps. 9 and 13). For an updated elaboration of the concept, see Rosenau (2003: Chap. 10).
5 Some analysts suggest that conceptions of the state trace a pendulum-like pattern that swings back and forth between notions of strong and weak states. See, for example, Evans (1997: 83), who cites Dani Rodrik as observing that "excessive optimism about what the state would be able to accomplish was replaced by excessive pessimism."
6 For a typological formulation that attempts to account for the diversity of governance forms, see Rosenau (2002a).

References

Anderson, W. T. (2001) *All Connected Now: Life in the First Global Civilization*, Boulder: West-view Press.

Arquilla, J and Ronfeldt, D. (1997) "A New Epoch—and Spectrum—of Conflict," in J. Arquilla and D. Ronfeldt (eds) *In Athena's Camp: Preparing for Conflict in the Information Age*, Santa Monica: RAND.

Carlsson, S. and Stripple, J. (2000) "Climate Governance beyond the State—Contributions from the Insurance Industry," a paper presented at the International Political Science Association (Quebec City: August 1–5).

Cutler, A. C., Haufler, V., and Porter, T. (eds) (1999) *Private Authority in International Affairs*, Albany: State University of New York Press.

Evans, P. (1997) "The Eclipse of the State? Reflections on Stateness in an Era of Globalization," *World Politics*, 50(1): 62–87.

French, H. (2000) *Vanishing Borders: Protecting the Planet in the Age of Globalization*, New York: W.W. Norton.

Giddens, A. and Pierson, C. (1998) *Conversations with Anthony Giddens: Making Sense of Modernity*, Cambridge: Polity Press.

Jasanoff, S. (2001) "Image and Imagination: The Formation of Global Environmental Consciousness," in P. Edwards and C.A. Miller (eds) *Changing the Atmosphere: Science and the Politics of Global Warming*, Cambridge: The MIT Press.

Olesen, T. (2005) *International Zapatismo: The Construction of Solidarity in the Age of Globalization*, London: Zed Books.

Reinicke, W. H. (1999–2000) "The Other World Wide Web: Global Public Policy Networks," *Foreign Policy*, 117(Winter): 44–57.

Rosenau, J. N. (1990) *Turbulence in World Politics: A Theory of Change and Continuity*, Princeton: Princeton University Press.

—— (1992) "Governance, Order, and Change in World Politics," in J.N. Rosenau and E.O. Czempiel (eds) *Governance without Government: Order and Change in World Politics*, Cambridge: Cambridge University Press.

—— (1995) "Governance in the 21st Century," *Global Governance*, 1: 13–43.

—— (1997) *Along the Domestic–Foreign Frontier: Exploring Governance in a Turbulent World*, Cambridge: Cambridge University Press.

—— (2002a) "Governance in a New Global Order," in D. Held and A. McGrew (eds) *Governing Globalization: Power, Authority and Global Governance*, Cambridge: Polity Press.

—— (2002b) "The Globalization of Globalization," in M. Brecher and F. Harvey (eds) *Millennium Reflections on International Studies*, Ann Arbor: University of Michigan Press.

—— (2003) *Distant Proximities: Dynamics Beyond Globalization*, Princeton: Princeton University Press.

Sachs, W. (2002) *The Jo'burg Memo: Fairness in a Fragile World*, Berlin: Heinrich Boll Foundation.

Scholte, J.A. (2000) *Globalization: A Critical Introduction*, London: Macmillan Press.

Siochrú, S.Ó. and Girard, B. (2002) *Global Media Governance: A Beginner's Guide*, Lanham: Rowman & Littlefield.

Speth, J.G. (2002) "Recycling Environmentalism," *Foreign Policy*, 131(July/August): 74–76.

Thiele, L.P. (1999) *Environmentalism for a New Millennium: The Challenge of Coevolution*, New York: Oxford University Press.

Väyrynen, R. (ed.) (1999) *Globalization and Global Governance*, Lanham, MD: Rowman and Littlefield.

Wendt, A. (1999) *Social Theory of International Politics*, Cambridge: Cambridge University Press.

Zacher, M. (1999) "Uniting Nations: Global Regimes and the United Nations Systems," in R. Väyrynen (ed.) *Globalization and Global Governance*, Latham: Rowman and Little-field.

9 The European human-rights regime as a case study in the emergence of global governance

Leslie Friedman Goldstein and Cornel Ban

Preface

Many of the chapters in this collection see "global governance" as a reference to the way the whole global system is governed—in other words, as the way that so-called "international," or inter-state systems are ordered the world over. This chapter, by contrast, fits into that group of chapters (which includes those by Young, and O'Brien) that see "global governance" as about saying and seeing that governance takes place on the globe to an increasing degree (not only by state and interstate actors, but also) by suprastate, non-state, and substate actors. This chapter examines the strengthening of one of these "disaggregated spheres of authority" (in the phrase of James Rosenau), namely, the European Court of Human Rights (hereafter ECtHR, or the Court, or "Strasbourg"), a trans-state actor that now regulates human behavior in an arena previously monopolized by state sovereigns.

We see the world-wide "structure" of global governance as in fact an absence of structure linking these disaggregated spheres, but one can nonetheless identify the structure of each particular global governance sphere of authority and the processes of governance within it. This chapter zeroes in on one example of the now-several recently emerged or currently emerging trans-state legal regimes. By this, we mean regimes constructed and governed by transnational courts, the norms legitimating them and the norms they propound, and the actors and institutions that implement these norms. We do so in order to address this question: By what processes do trans-state legal regimes manage to take hold?[1] The vantage point from which we examine the growth and entrenchment of this trans-state regime is that of public law. This chapter focuses on a single trans-state, rule-of-law regime, one implemented by a mix of trans-state actors of the Council of Europe (COE) and of domestic actors from political and legal institutions of its member states, all of whom are charged with making and enforcing the law of the European Convention on Human Rights (hereafter ECHR).

A number of scholars in international relations (IR) have already noted that a major factor facilitating the development of the capacity of trans-state judicial regimes to acquire the ability to alter the behavior of erstwhile sovereign states is the prior existence of a well-entrenched domestic culture committed to the rule of law. While we acknowledge the helpfulness of such a culture for nurturing the trans-state judiciaries that have been proliferating and growing in strength around the turn of the twenty-first century, our research uncovered a number of other elements that played important roles in the process by which the ECHR regime took hold. Indeed, these other elements were in a number of instances enough to compensate for a relatively weak rule-of-law culture. These included, at the domestic level, strong political leadership—whether on the part of judges on constitutional courts or by members of executive or legislative branches— and, at the trans-state level, (1) the political mood (across Europe) among elected member-state leaders particularly during the mid- to late 1980s and (2) the incentive structure provided by the European Union (EU), a body separate from, and with a membership different from but partly overlapping with, the COE.

Introduction

The ECHR

The European Court of Human Rights was founded in 1959 within the structure of the Council of Europe, a group of European countries committed to the protection of human rights (originally, Belgium, Denmark, France, Ireland, Italy, Luxembourg, the Netherlands, Norway, Sweden, and the United Kingdom). The ECtHR was to function as interpreter of the 1953 European Convention of Human Rights. The Convention regime began designedly gradually, with a cumbersome enforcement system, an enforcing Court that met only temporarily, and, probably most important, many opportunities for member nations to opt out of the ECHR system on particular rights. (For details on these procedural mechanisms, see Goldstein and Ban 2003.) The COE was to dramatically strengthen this enforcement system in the 1990s, as explained below.[2] Not until the early 1970s did the ECtHR even begin to issue decisions with real teeth in them—i.e., decisions that produced prompt policy corrections by offending governments (Goldstein and Ban 2003).

By the end of 1998, however, the ECtHR became a permanent Court and the right of individuals to petition the Court for violations, which had not even existed until 1994, now became mandatory on all COE member countries. Thus the ECtHR became an effective co-director of the ECHR legal regime, in unofficial partnership with the European Court of Justice (ECJ), the court of the European Union, whose own doctrine obliges it to honor the ECHR whenever the Convention is relevant.

This transnational regime has frequently increased its extent, most notably in the 1970s and the 1990s. The 1970s wave of enlargement moved largely southward, taking in (among other states) three recent dictatorships: Greece, Spain (a dictatorship from 1939 to 1975) and Portugal (a dictatorship from 1933 to 1974). The latter two, upon replacing fascist or authoritarian rule with democracy, signed the Convention on the day of their entry into the Council of Europe, on 24 November 1977 and 22 September 1976, respectively. Greece, recently plagued by periods of instability and dictatorship, had signed onto the Convention in 1950, but did not ratify it and then withdrew in 1969, giving it practical effect only in 1974.[3]

The second (and massive) wave took place between 1991 and 2003, when all former communist states, including Russia, were admitted to the COE. After fifty to seventy years of open disregard for the values professed by the Convention, particularly for the rule of law, these countries formally adopted an alternative political and legal paradigm for the protection of human rights. The number of COE members grew from 23 at the end of 1989 to 46 in 2003, and the total population of the member states grew from 451 to 800 million. The number of applications (i.e., challenges to a particular government practice) to the Court grew from 1,013 in 1988 to 10,486 (Report 2001: 4). By contrast, the EU, all of whose members are in the COE and whose court (the ECJ) accepts ECHR rules as binding, had only fifteen members as of 2003.

Research question and methodology

Despite the variegated mosaic of democratic and legal traditions amassed under the aegis of the COE, the ECHR regime by the late 1990s was being acclaimed as a strikingly successful transnational framework for the protection of fundamental human rights and liberties (Gearty 1997: x–xv). Its very success raises intriguing questions, questions whose answers shed light on the processes by which at least one of the "spheres of authority" that engages in "global governance" has come into being: What holds it together? How do the common rule-of-law standards outlined by the ECtHR in fact apply to countries as different as England and Romania? Is this regime embedded uniformly or unevenly in the domestic order of the signatory members of the Convention? If it is indeed unevenly embedded, what explains the variations?[4]

By applying a blend of IR approaches with public-law analyses, as recommended in recent years by a number of influential IR and international-law scholars of differing theoretical approaches (Abbot 1989; Koskenniemi 1990; Slaughter 1993; Finnemore 1996, 139–143; Koh 1997; Reus-Smit 1997; Keohane 1997 and 2000; Slaughter *et al.* 1998; Byers 2000), this chapter examines the extent to which rules derived from this Convention have become embedded in the domestic legal order of the member states. To do so, we employ the analytical framework of an international regime, extending our gaze beyond the traditional international-law studies of the ECtHR that confine their research focus to its legal doctrine (e.g., Delmas-Marty 1992; Yourow 1996; Clements *et al.* 1999). This chapter views the Convention and the Court as part of the broader European human-rights regime, which includes other organizations with which the Court cooperates closely (the Committee of Ministers of the COE) or loosely (the ECJ and the European Commission of the EU). This approach provides a more complete picture of the forces at work in creating a rule of law for Europe than would be available merely through analysis of judicial doctrine.

We view the set of rules and the organizational structure created around the Convention as a transnational legal regime. The Preamble of the Convention explicitly acknowledges its legal character by identifying as its foundation Europe's "common heritage of political traditions, ideals, freedom and *the rule of law*" (www.coe.int; emphasis added).[5] The regime tracks the rule of law in the sense that it aims to uphold the principle that the relationships of the individual with the state should be regulated by a framework of legal rules whose interpretation and application are in the hands of independent judges and are to be applied even-handedly (Merrills 1993). This principle permeates all the articles of the Convention and of its 11 additional protocols.

Within the IR literature, a commonly cited definition of international regimes is that of Stephen Krasner: they are sets of issue-bounded "implicit or explicit principles, norms, rules and decision-making procedures around which actors' expectations converge" (1983: 2). We can offer a concrete example to give the reader a feel for the kinds of "norms" that the ECtHR produces for this regime: one of the guiding principles utilized by the Court is the doctrine of a "national margin of appreciation"; it states that the priority of a given Convention rule must be weighed against national interests and thus may be restricted to the degree "necessary in a democratic society" (*Lawless v. Ireland*, ECtHR 1981).

We label the ECHR regime (i.e., the regime created around the Convention and the Court) transnational rather than international because its rules, norms, and procedures are not confined to interstate interaction. For instance, the parties to the Convention explicitly commit to a variety of concrete and specific due process measures in Articles 5, 6, and 7. These states thereby pre-commit themselves to allow third-party transnational institutions to hold their otherwise sovereign institutions liable for compensatory damages, to this degree abrogating sovereign prerogatives. Clearly, there is a hierarchical arrangement in which the combined forces of the ECtHR and the Committee of Ministers, which supervises the implementation of the ECtHR rulings, sit above the domestic courts and domestic political actors who implement the ECtHR rulings. This structure contrasts sharply with the sheer intergovernmentalism that typifies purely international institutions. The ECHR regime orders not simply state-to-state relations but multiple patterns of interaction—those between individuals and the state, between elements of civil society and state, between domestic courts and national political constituencies, between the EU and individual states, and between the ECtHR/Committee of Ministers and each of the aforementioned categories. The Convention is operationalized primarily through the medium of domestic law and courts (de Bruyn *et al.* 1997: 2–6), and few aspects of domestic policymaking pertaining to human rights evade the reach of the Convention and its protocols. Within the ECHR regime, states by now routinely act upon these limitations of their own sovereignty by consciously shaping their policies into patterns adapted to ECtHR jurisprudence.

As we began to address these questions, our inquiry was shaped by the observation that the COE countries sensibly might be grouped by the fact that some (the long-time members) had to undergo only the transition from a system of state to supra-state governance, while others were undergoing a dual transition—that from state governance to supra-state governance and that from a dictatorship to a rule-of-law, representative democracy. We expected that those states facing the challenge of a dual transition in governance would take longer to embed ECHR principles firmly into domestic law. Not only was their adjustment a more complicated one, but also this expectation was fortified by the growing literature that began in the mid-1990s both on general IR theory and specifically on EU integration that points to the importance of liberal, rights-respecting, rule-of-law-cultures for easing the acceptance of suprastate judiciaries (Seurin 1994: 625–36; Weiler 1994; Moravscik 1995; Slaughter 1995; Alter 1996, 476; Shaw 1996; Goldstein 1996; 1997; 2001: 158–60; Helfer and Slaughter 1997). Moreover, although the ECtHR and the ECJ both began around the same time, the ECJ successfully and actively began to assert its authority as a suprastate court in the early 1960s, long before the ECtHR did, which fact gave the long-time members of the COE who also belonged to the EEC/EC/EU decades of experience entrenching principles of legitimacy that transfer sovereign power to supranational institutions (Alter 2001; Goldstein 2001).

For these reasons, we judged that a useful picture of how the governance system of the ECtHR took hold should span a range of countries that varied in the timing and in the degree of complexity of their transition into the ECHR regime. We divided our cases into three categories, as follows:

1   *Longtime COE (and EU) member states*—France, Germany, and the Netherlands. These all have a long rule-of-law tradition, albeit one punctuated in the case of Germany (and for a much shorter time Vichy France) by its Fascist/Nazi periods and a lengthy experience with supranational legal/political institutions.

2   *States that became COE members in the 1970s (and EU members in the 1980s)*— Portugal, Greece, and Spain. These states experienced decades-long discontinuities in the rule of law and missed the formative period of early European Community membership.

3   *Members of the Council of Europe from outside Western Europe (i.e. states of the former Soviet bloc)*—Romania. When they joined the Council of Europe in the early 1990s, these countries had endured fifty years of totalitarian political abuses and an abysmal record of rule-of-law performance. Romania joined the COE in 1993, ratified the Convention in June 1994, submitted its application for EU membership in June 1995, and began EU accession negotiations on 15 February 2000.[6]

We compare below both the rate and the thoroughness with which each of these countries accepted ECHR norms into their own legal systems as constraints on their own sovereignty. We examine a number of variations among the seven countries as to formal constitutional and legal structure and both political and legal processes. For all seven we look at the following: (1) ECHR compatibility with texts of national constitutions with particular attention to the hierarchical relation between international (or transnational) law and domestic law; (2) the reception of the ECHR regime by the judiciary; and (3) implementation of ECtHR doctrine by the legislative and executive branches. We expected to find the category one states ahead of the category two states, and both groups ahead of Romania. The reality proved more complicated.

The reader should be aware that the ECtHR treats not only the text of the Convention but also its own doctrinal output as "the law of the Convention" (Shapiro and Stone Sweet 2002: 2; Goldstein and Ban 2003). This aspect of ECtHR doctrine merits attention because some national courts used to claim, and others still do (at considerable expense in treasure and credibility), that they were/are bound only by the text of the Convention and by those ECtHR decisions in which their country was a defendant. Thus, in the analysis that follows, we treat such practices as evidence of incompleteness of the entrenching of the ECHR regime.

Transnational forces pushing ECHR acceptance

All the states we examined experience transnational pressure to honor the ECHR in their internal legal systems. Pressure came from two transnational regimes, that of the COE (bound together by the ECHR) and that of the EU (bound by the various EU formative treaties and accession procedures). However, while all seven equally experience pressure from the structures and processes of the COE, the pressure exerted by the EU structures and processes varies significantly as between members of the EU (such as our first six cases) and applicant members (such as Romania). The arrangements are as follows.

EU member states have been bound since 1975 by the Convention because the ECJ asserted then that the ECHR is a fundamental source of rights within the European Community *(Rutili v. Ministry of the Interior* 1975). More recently, the (EU) Treaty of Amsterdam (Article 6) and the recently adopted EU Charter of Fundamental Rights and Freedoms (Article 47) mandated deference to the Convention and to the ECtHR. The ECJ, in contrast to the ECtHR, issues binding interpretations of EU law in Preliminary Rulings at the request of member state courts; the ECtHR has no similar institutionalized process allowing it to communicate directly with national courts and, as a consequence, faces more difficulty in constructing its own legal regime. In the EU member countries not only does the ECtHR benefit from the general socialization of judges into the practice of referring domestic cases for interpretation by the ECJ and to making judgments bounded by (EU) transnational law norms, but it also benefits from the repeated endorsement by the ECJ of the ECHR (Alston and Weiler 1999: 3; Harmsen 2000: 34).

EU applicant states, including Romania, while not yet under the direct jurisdiction of the ECJ, nonetheless undergo significant pressure from EU accession processes. In the applicant countries the Commissioner for EU enlargement directly supervises reform. Each applicant state is required to integrate huge swaths of the European legal order structured in 30 negotiation chapters, one of which is on "justice and domestic affairs" and has a rubric on human-rights violations. The European Commission of the EU annually reports on the state of the judiciary (specifically on issues of judicial independence and corruption) and of human rights, utilizing the technique of shaming (backed up by post-ponement of EU membership) for any failures to make reasonable and timely changes. Finally, the Commission disburses significant amounts of money to EU applicant countries to enforce democracy and the rule of law, mainly by funding judicial reform.

The Council of Europe has its own structure of pressures to push its member states to implement the ECHR, and these operate on all seven of our cases. After the ECtHR hands down a decision against a signatory member of the Convention, the only immediate concrete compulsion that the state confronts is its obligation to pay the "just satisfaction" awarded by the ECtHR to the indi-vidual applicant, an obligation states fulfill more or less on time, in light of the fact that each complainant functions as a highly motivated "monitor" until the payment is made. Having paid the compensatory penalty, however, the state is not then utterly free to preserve its domestic legal order intact and to persist in the same human-rights violations.

The obligation to reform its statutes and legal practices, implicit in its signing on to the Convention, is enforced thereafter in a gentle and gradualist fashion by the Committee of Ministers of the COE. This Committee meets every few months and consists of the foreign ministers of all the member countries. This Committee of Ministers receives a report of each ECtHR judgment and responds to each with a Resolution indicating the type of reform within the member country that is needed to satisfy the Court's judgment—e.g., elimination of a particular penal statute, or the reform of a particular police practice. The state is held accountable at future meetings for reporting on what progress has been made to meet the standards set forth in these Resolutions. In effect, the Committee of Ministers acts as the administrative arm of the ECHR regime to implement, via public shaming, the rules implicit in the judgment of the ECtHR. Should the state drag its feet for an unreasonably long period of time, the Committee sanctions it by adopting interim resolutions that provide informa-tion about the lack of progress in improving implementation (www.coe.int/intro/e-rules-46.htm).

Finally, the ECtHR itself plays a role in speeding legislative reform by the way it words its decisions. In general, the Court refrains from directly stigmatizing a domestic norm as a per se violation and, therefore, from prescribing specific policy reforms (Merrills 1993: 104). Nonetheless, in certain landmark cases, the ECtHR took a more assertive stance and noticeably adopted the role of agenda-setter. In one instance, after having conceded, "The state has a choice of various means," it added that a specific domestic norm violated the Convention (*Marcks vs. Belgium* 1979). The state correctly grasped that this amounted to a strong recommendation to change that law. The ECtHR announces such prescriptive decisions for the fulfillment of positive obligations when the domestic order lacks regulations aimed at protecting the rights outlined in the Convention (*X & Y v. Netherlands* 1985) or when the state has demonstrated neglect for the protection of individual rights (*Platform Artze fur das Leben v. Austria* 1992; Merrills 1993: 102–6).

These reform-generating processes of the COE as of the turn of the twenty-first century have proved remarkably effective. COE member states typically engage in extensive legislative and executive branch reform to implement ECtHR rulings. To redress and prevent future violations of the Convention, legislatures and executive organs adopt new laws or legislative amendments, undertake systematic screening of draft legislation, and send circular letters to law-enforcement agencies to bring their practices into compliance with the standards of ECtHR case-law. Additional executive action has included ordering inclusion of the Convention and of its case-law in the curricula of law schools, disseminating information concerning the Court to the public at large, implementing measures to ensure the independence and the professional prestige of the judiciary, and, finally, training in human rights for sectors responsible for law enforcement.

Within this evolving transnational regime, what, then, are the mechanisms pushing the so-called sovereign states to adopt legislative change and administrative reforms? First, the rationally calculating state, aware of the financial consequences looming in the potential stream of follow-up complaints ("repetitive applications") that may be filed in Strasbourg, may decide that the costs of the "just reparation" payments to be made would outweigh both the material and the non-material benefits of preserving the successfully challenged legal domestic norm. Secondly, the state may abandon its resistance and reform the law after the painstaking and prolonged ordeal faced by its representatives, obliged to justify its resistance three or four times a year in legal language understood by the other members of the Committee of Ministers. These psychic and political costs are particularly high for EU applicant countries, but even member countries are aware that in the extreme situation, a non-complying country could get booted out of the COE.

The seven states

France

Constitutional text and judicial doctrine

The French Constitution of 1958 does not privilege the Convention above other international legal instruments, but it does privilege international obligations in general. Under Article 55, treaties "prevail" over national laws (but not over the Constitution). Nonetheless, the *Conseil Constitutionnel* (the court of France that has a specialized monopoly on constitutional interpretation for purposes of judicial review) in a famous decision on 15 January 1975, although acknowledging this primacy in principle, refused to review the compatibility of international treaties with national law, grounding its refusal on its claim that treaty law is "contingent," as Article 55 puts it, "subject to its application by the other party," thereby declining to enforce the Convention (Coccozza 1996: 714–15; Steiner 1997). In a later case that same year (on 23 July) the *Conseil Constitutionnel* refused specifically to review a French statute legalizing abortion for compatibility with the Convention (Article 2) provision protecting the right to life of every human person. Here the *Conseil* said simply that its jurisdiction was limited to clashes between the Constitution and statutes and did not include treaty interpretation, and the judges ruled the statute constitutional (Troper 2003: 42).

Next, France's supreme appellate court for ordinary law, the *Cour de Cassation*, picked up the ball. In 1975, shortly after the abortion decision this court starting striking down French laws that conflicted with the treaty law of the European Community, or with the ECHR (Troper 2003; Steiner 1997: 281, n. 58). From this court's action evolved the doctrine that all French courts have the duty to strike down a statute that conflicts with treaty law—"convention-based" judicial review (Troper 2003). One scholar characterizes these early forays into ECHR jurisprudence, however, as erratic and marked by ambivalence (Steiner 1997).

In 1981 France legislatively accepted the right of individual petition to the ECtHR, and in 1988 the Secretary-General of the *Conseil Constitutionnel*, Bruno Genevois, admitted that the Convention had constitutional value in France and could not be considered as "contingent" (Genevois 1988; Alter 2001: 158–59). Finally, the *Conseil Constitutionnel* in the late 1980s officially acknowledged its duty under Article 55 of the Constitution to enforce international law supremacy over ordinary domestic statutes, in general, and eventually enforced the Convention in particular (Goldstein and Ban 2003). These prominent shifts by the *Conseil Constitutionnel* evidently helped persuade the *Conseil d'Etat* (France's supreme court for administrative law) by 1989 to abandon its earlier prominent hostility to enforcing international treaties (Steiner 1997: 280; Goldstein and Ban 2003). Moreover, once the *Conseil Constitutionnel* changed its stance toward the ECHR, the *Cour de Cassation* followed along enthusiastically. Between 1987 and 1997 this court issued more than 700 decisions pertaining to the applicability of the Convention and ECtHR case-law (Fabre and Gouron-Mazel 1998), altering its own jurisprudence in case after case following a French defeat at the ECtHR.

Still, the record of the *Cour de Cassation* has been uneven. One can point to numerous cases, where this court has faithfully applied ECtHR standards to alter French law. But in several cases which are sensitive to the creation of European rule-of-law standards such as the right to defense counsel and the right to file for appeal, the *Cour de Cassation* has mounted a "rebellion" against the ECtHR, by refusing to consider explicit case law outlined by the ECtHR in judgments issued against the French state itself (Marguenaud 2001; de Gouttes 2002; Goldstein and Ban 2003).

French lower courts have tended since 1988 to use the Convention more extensively than before, even following the ECHR in preference to explicit French statute law, and copying ECtHR reasoning almost verbatim, although often without acknowledging its source (Lembert 1999: 345; Margenaud 2001: 5–7). Still, they seem to limit their preference for ECHR law to situations where

French law (statutory and/or case-law) either confirms or is silent about particular Convention provisions (Lembert 1999: 349–50; Gouttes n.d.).

Notably, the willingness of the three French high courts to conform to ECtHR rulings has been largely limited to cases in which France played a direct role as respondent state. In other words, these courts have not, as a general matter, treated ECtHR precedents from other countries as creating rules binding on France.

Despite this incompleteness of judicial implementation, it is fair to say that by the late 1980s formal constitutional doctrine in France gave the Convention priority over French statute law, if not over the French Constitution. This was no small change in a country with as strong a tradition of parliamentary sovereignty as France had.

Executive and legislative cooperation with ECHR

We found in France, as in six of the seven countries examined, a mixed picture with respect to legislative and executive implementation of the ECHR regime. One can cite numerous instances of extremely prompt corrective action by the executive and/or legislature, but one can also find, for all the cases except Spain, instances of pronounced foot-dragging, where as many as four or five years elapsed with no corrective action.

No doubt, the 1981 legislative adoption of the right of individual petition to the ECtHR was instrumental in fostering the alteration of constitutional doctrine by the French high Courts. Then, when a French petition for the first time produced an adverse decision at the ECtHR on 24 April 1990, the legislature passed a law correcting the problem within a year (10 July 1991). On at least one occasion it amended legislation upon the mere lodging of a complaint at the ECtHR, even before the Court handed down a decision: France altered its criminal procedure law in January 1993, to prevent breaches of the principle of the presumption of innocence and allow for rectifying measures, well in advance of *Allenet de Ribemont v. France*, ECtHR 10 February 1995. And the French Parliament, faced with the erratic behavior of its *Cour de Cassation*, eventually intervened in deference to the ECtHR, to abrogate article 588 of *Le Code de Procédure Pénale* (regarding the pre-trial length of detention time), which had supplied a number of cases lost by France at the ECtHR (Steiner 1997: 293–4).

On the other hand, one can point to cases of blatant foot-dragging, such as *Letellier v. France*, ECtHR 26 June 1991, which did not produce appropriate legislative reform until 30 December 1996.

Germany

Constitutional text and judicial doctrine

The terms of the German Constitution (Art. 59) accord the Convention no higher rank than any federal statute. Only the German Constitution and general principles of international law are privileged above statutes. Nonetheless, the

German Constitutional Court (*Bundesverfassungsgericht* or BVerfG), which, as in France has a monopoly on constitution-based judicial review, moved on its own in 1987 to grant higher-law status to the ECHR. Pointing to the constitutional principle that the interpretation that conforms to international law must prevail, the BVerfG ruled that its interpretation of those Convention rights that are listed in the German Constitution would follow both the Convention and the case-law of the ECtHR (Decision of 26 March 1987; Schlette 1996). Moreover, the BVerfG (explicitly appointed guarantor of human rights in Germany by the Constitution) ruled that ordinary German statutes must be "interpreted" wherever possible to conform to the ECHR, no matter whether the legislation were prior or subsequent to the Convention (Voss 1997: 155–6). The BVerfG also created a special appeal founded on the principle of equal protection before the law, which was to operate whenever the ECHR was applicable and had been disregarded by ordinary courts (Frowein 1992: 122). This ruling encouraged the ordinary courts to take care to use the ECHR in order that their judgments would not be overturned on appeal. In sum, despite a constitutional text that accorded no special status to the Council of Europe treaty or to the Convention as such, the high constitutional court of Germany by 1987 elevated the ECHR and its related jurisprudence to supremacy over German statutes.

It bears attention that this move by the German Constitutional Court was roughly contemporaneous both with the movement in the same direction by the French *Conseil Constitutionnel*, and with the adoption of the Single European Act of 1987 by the European Community (greatly reducing permission for each member state of the EC to veto an EC policy). The political mood in Western Europe of the late 1980s, irrespective of substantial differences in the treatment of international treaties in the two constitutions, seems to have pushed both these countries' constitutional doctrine with respect to the transnational ECHR regime.

In Germany's ordinary courts, the practice of applying ECtHR jurisprudence as a direct source of law is relatively rare because of the widespread belief among German judges that the fundamental rights listed in their Federal Constitution are wider in scope than those found in the Convention (Voss 1997: 158; Burkhard 2000). But there are numerous exceptions, because the detailed guarantees of Articles 5 and 6 of the ECHR do not appear in the German Constitution. German courts in a number of instances struck down prevailing rules of pre-trial criminal proceedings on the grounds that they exceeded the standards of reasonable detention time (Article 6.1) set by the ECtHR (Frowein 1992: 126; Goldstein and Ban 2003) and have altered other rights-restrictive domestic statutes, enforcement practices, or case-law to make them conform to ECtHR rulings under these articles even where neither the legislature nor the BVerfG had taken corrective action (Frowein 1992: 126).

Executive and legislative cooperation with the ECHR

As with France, one can point in Germany to instances of prompt legislative reform pushed by an ECtHR decision, but also to foot-dragging. The 28

November 1978 ECtHR judgment on payment for costs of court interpreters produced legislative amendments to both the Court Costs Act and the Code of Criminal Procedure by 18 August 1980. On the other hand, in the matter of payment for interpreters in administrative hearings demanded by the ECtHR decision of 21 February 1984, Germany did not change its law until 15 June 1989, more than five years later (Goldstein and Ban 2003).

Netherlands

Constitution and judicial doctrine

Of our seven countries, the Constitution of the Netherlands most clearly subordinates national law to the ECHR regime. Article 94 of the Dutch Constitution unequivocally provides that domestic regulations shall not be applied unless they are in conformity with provisions of treaties and "resolutions of international institutions" once the latter have been published, implicitly incorporating the ensemble of ECtHR case-law within this category of "resolutions," and placing both the Convention and its case-law above domestic law. As early as 1980 the *Hoge Raad* (Dutch Supreme Court) acknowledged this supremacy not only over national laws, but even over the Dutch Constitution. In the same case it ruled that these ECHR rules take "direct effect" in Dutch law—i.e., no prior Dutch legislative or administrative implementation is required in order to give them the force of law (judgment of 23 September 1980). Within the Netherlands, the *Hoge Raad* actively led the judiciary toward involvement with the ECtHR; its opinions contain three-fourths of all the Dutch judicial citations of ECtHR case-law (Vervaele 1992: 211–14; Klerk and de Jonge 1997).

This Dutch constitutional framework requires all Dutch judges to refuse to apply any domestic statutory provisions or provisions of the Constitution that conflict with the Convention (or other international treaty) even though none of the judges, not even on the Supreme Court, are supposed to rule on conflicts between statutes and the Constitution. Unlike four of the countries in our sample, the Dutch do not have a special constitutional court that monopolizes the power of constitution-based judicial review. Constitution-based judicial review (in contrast to international-law-based judicial review) is forbidden in the Dutch Constitution, Art. 111 (Klerk and de Jonge 1997: 111–12).

Even before the *Hoge Raad* decision of 1980, lower courts in this country, empowered by Article 94 to apply provisions of treaties or decisions of international institutions, were treating the Convention as Dutch law, beginning with its first application by the appeals court of Arnhem in 1978–9. Today, recourse to the ECHR and ECtHR jurisprudence is standard procedure for Dutch judges (Corstens 2000). These courts have grown highly sophisticated in making judgments based on the Convention and incorporating skillfully the doctrinal guidelines of the ECtHR such as the rule for a national margin of appreciation (Vervaele 1992: 223).

On many occasions, Dutch low-level courts ordered a human-rights protection very shortly after the ECtHR standards for it were laid out—not only when the decision directly concerned the Netherlands as defendant, but also when it dealt with a challenge to some other country's practices. For instance, the ECtHR ruling in *Abdulaziz, Cabales and Balkandali v. UK* (28 May 1985) was incorporated into Dutch jurisprudence within a year (Vervaele 1992: 224).

Executive and legislative compliance with the ECHR

The Netherlands is no exception to the pattern we found of a mixed record with respect to policy reforms by the political branches. On the one hand, there is much evidence to support its reputation as exemplary in the degree of its cooperation with the ECHR regime. In one case, in anticipation of a decision of the ECtHR, the Dutch government (spurred merely by the lodging of a complaint) corrected a challenged statute (on confinement of the criminally mentally ill) in 1988, two years before the Strasbourg Court ruled it a violation. Yet even the Netherlands can take as long as five years after a negative ECtHR decision for the legislature to respond with appropriate reform: not until 1991 did the Dutch legislature change its labor statutory regulations to conform to the ECHR standards announced in *Feldbrugge v. the Netherlands* of 29 May 1986.

Spain

Constitution and judicial doctrine

In Spain, while the Constitution does not single out the ECHR, it clearly places treaty obligations above domestic law. It reads, "The norms relative to basic rights and liberties which are recognized by the Constitution shall be interpreted in conformity with the Universal Declaration of Human Rights and the international treaties and agreements on those matters ratified by Spain" (Articles 10–12). Since as early as 1981, the Spanish Constitutional Court, which holds an official monopoly over constitution-based judicial review, has been issuing ECHR-friendly rulings (Spanish Constitutional Court 2001: 22), and in 1984 it held specifically that all Spanish courts must follow ECtHR case-law. Thus, any individual under the jurisdiction of Spanish courts may challenge a statute on the grounds of conflict with ECtHR jurisprudence (Lembert 1999: 342, 354–5, 357; Goldstein and Ban 2003). Strasbourg case law thereby very quickly became an effective source of Spanish law (Cavagna and Monteiro 1992: 177).

The 1981 initiative by the Spanish Constitutional Court occurred well in advance of the late 1980s moves in the same direction by the constitutional courts of France and Germany, putting the Spanish judiciary at the forefront (along with the Netherlands) of our seven countries on the matter of ECHR compliance.

Executive and legislative cooperation with the ECHR

Spain's legislative and executive officials, no less than its judge, turn out to be model citizens of the ECHR regime. Spain actually overhauled statutory codes on three separate occasions in mere anticipation of an adverse ECtHR ruling on them. The Code of Criminal Procedure and the Criminal Code were amended (with respect to the actions of armed bands and terrorists) in May of 1988, in the early stages of the *Case of Barbera, Messegue and Jabardo*, judgment 6 December 1988. Similarly an act of 28 December 1988 re-organized the judicial system, in anticipation of the ECtHR decision in *Union Alimentaria Sanders SA v. Spain*, judgment of 7 July 1989. Spain also adopted a law on 9 June 1988 reforming its Constitutional Court procedures in anticipation of the ECtHR's *Ruiz-Mateos v. Spain*, judgment 23 June 1993.

Not only does Spain regularly correct its policies in response to mere complaints to, before actual negative decisions from, the ECtHR, but it was also the only country of the seven we examined where we could not find a single example of any foot-dragging.

Portugal

Constitutional and judicial doctrine

By contrast, in Portugal, the reception of the Convention was until the early 1990s much cooler. For one thing, the Portuguese Constitution specifies in its Article 16.2 only one international treaty in harmony with which domestic statutes and the Constitution must "be construed": the Universal Declaration of Human Rights. An attempted constitutional amendment to add the European Convention failed in 1982, on the purported grounds that it might have permitted derogation from the constitutional status of fundamental rights by introducing the "unforeseen restraints" of ECtHR jurisprudence (Cavagna and Monteiro 1992: 171–9).

In contrast to Spain, the Portuguese Constitutional Court for a long time did not actively promote the Convention as a normative framework for Portuguese domestic courts. Despite its constitutionally conferred monopoly on interpreting treaties, this court classified allegations of breaches of a treaty by a domestic statute as matters of "indirect constitutionality," which classification puts them into the jurisdiction of ordinary Portuguese courts, who do have constitution-interpreting, but not direct treaty-interpreting, authority (Cavagna and Monteiro 1992: 180). Thus, this court abandoned the opportunity to direct lower-court judges' interpretation of the Convention, even though the constitutional text constrained its powers no more than the German or Spanish constitutions restrained the Constitutional Court there.

Until the early 1990s Portuguese legal scholars and judges were maintaining that their country's Constitution surpassed the Convention in terms of the protection of individual rights (Leandro 2000), and therefore ignored ECtHR jurisprudence. The limitation of this viewpoint, as with that of their German counterparts, is that it construes the Convention as a textually fixed set of rules, when the reality is that of a continuous process of judicial interpretation and expansion of those rules. That is, even judges who heed the text of the Convention are ignoring rights under that Convention that have been developed by ECtHR jurisprudence. The clearest evidence of problems with their approach is the fact that both Germany and Portugal experience yearly condemnations in Strasbourg.

On the other hand, there are signs of change in Portugal, with respect to a recent turnabout by its Constitutional Court. In 2002 the Constitutional Court issued a lengthy report to a conference of constitutional courts in Brussels, in which it documented a decade of its own pro-active leadership in terms of revising Portuguese case-law to bring it into conformity with the ECHR. Moreover, this court specifically noted that while the text of the Portuguese Constitution offers more detailed protection of human rights than does the language of the Convention, nonetheless the interpretive case-law of the ECtHR ought to be used to flesh out the meaning of the correlative rights provisions in the Portuguese Constitution (Constitutional Court of Portugal 2002: 35).

Executive and legislative cooperation with the ECHR

As with all our cases except Spain, Portugal too shows a mixed picture: prompt cooperation in adopting reforms mandated by the ECtHR combines with occasional foot-dragging on specific policies. Portugal diligently redesigned its entire judicial system pursuant to three ECtHR decisions of 1994–1996 (COE Press Service 2000). By contrast, it let almost five years go by before rectifying a problem identified by the ECtHR on 19 September 1996 in the *Matos and Silva* case.

Greece

Constitution and judicial doctrine

The 1975 republican Constitution of Greece grants to international law and all international conventions entered by Greece both direct effect and primacy over "any contrary provision of the law" (Article 28.1). While Greece lacks a specialized "constitutional" court, the Greek Supreme Administrative Court ruled in 1976 and 1978 that the expression "any contrary provision of the law" is to be construed as placing the ECHR above all domestic law except the Constitution, and this interpretation is accepted in the other Greek courts (Perrakis 1996: 174).

Under Greek law all Greek judges are obliged to assure that domestic laws conform to the Constitution by refusing to apply any statute that violates the Constitution (Article 87.2). Also, all Greek courts are obliged to verify whether domestic laws comply with the ECHR (and other international law) and refuse to apply any domestic law that does not. The latter duty differs from constitution-based review because judges need explore this question only if a party to the case raises the issue. The way this dual system plays out in practice is that, unless a party has raised a question of Convention violation, Greek courts do not refuse to apply laws that are contrary to the ECHR so long as the court finds them in other respects constitutional (Bechlivanou 1992; Perrakis 1996). This approach has severely constrained the effectiveness of the Convention in Greece.

Apart from this limitation, a consensus for a long time prevailed among Greek courts and legal scholars that since the listing of human rights in the Greek Constitution matches that of the ECHR, their respect is assured by means of control over constitutionality, although one does find more recent scholarship now asserting the contrary (Bechlivanou 1992: 158; Perrakis 1996: 187). As in the case with Portugal, it becomes increasingly costly for Greek courts to ignore the law of ECtHR rulings: the right of individual petition to the ECtHR granted by Greece in 1985 is producing considerable pressure; in the year 2000, Greece figured sixth highest on the list of states condemned by the ECtHR for Convention violations.

Until Greece recognized the right to individual petition in 1985 and lost a long list of cases in Strasbourg, the Convention had little effect there (Bechlivanou 1992: 165–7; Perrakis 1996: 171). For years, many ordinary courts' decisions produced law later judged to be violations of the Convention, such as the interpretation of Article 6 of the Greek Constitution as not protecting the individual against civil imprisonment (Bechlivanou 1992: 164). In some cases, ordinary Greek courts issued judgments that directly violated explicit standards from an ECtHR case in which Greece itself had been a plaintiff (Committee of Ministers Resolution DH 97, 576 of 15 December 1997). Many Greek judges decide ECHR-relevant cases without providing adequate doctrinal foundations from ECtHR jurisprudence, and as recently as 2003, a Greek court defied a series of repeated ECtHR judgments that the Greek practice in question violated the Convention (Goldstein and Ban 2003). In sum, the Greek judiciary does relatively little to uphold the ECHR regime.

Executive and legislative cooperation with ECHR

By contrast, the Greek political branches have shown themselves to be notably cooperative; they implement reforms promptly in response to ECtHR criticism. In 1995, for instance, Greece reformed its pretrial detention system a few months in advance of the pending (negative) ECtHR decision. In other instances Greece implemented reforms, for instance, on the rights of monasteries, within a year or two of the ECtHR holding (Goldstein and Ban 2003).

While, Greece, too, sometimes engages in foot-dragging, we found no instance where it resisted reform for more than four years. In response to adverse ECtHR decisions, Greece took three years to fix its criminal military code (from 1992 to 1995) and four to amend the Constitution (Article 93.3) with respect to criminal procedures condemned in 1997 (Goldstein and Ban 2003).

Romania

Constitution and judicial doctrine

The Romanian Constitution of 1991 matches the Spanish as to international treaties: the protection of the human rights listed in the Constitution is to conform "with the Universal Declaration of Human Rights, with the covenants and other treaties" to which Romania has agreed; in case of conflict between treaty and domestic law (below the Constitution), the treaty prevails (Article 11; Article 20.1). The Romanian Constitutional Court (hereafter CC) has a monopoly over questions of constitutionality, including all human-rights issues. Ordinary courts are required to refer the conflict and comply with whatever the CC decides.

In 1998, four years before Strasbourg first decided a complaint from Romania, the CC ruled that the ECHR should guide the interpretation of the Constitution on human-rights questions. This independent and active court managed to shape the practice of ordinary domestic courts, and its decisions, after uneven levels of compliance by ordinary courts in the early 1990s, are now treated as binding by all of them (Goldstein and Ban 2003).[7]

Still, the CC's interpretive stance is marked by a tension. On the one hand, the CC treats silences in the Romanian Constitution as opportunities to enlarge the impact of the ECHR. Thus, in a 2000 landmark decision (CC judgment 146, 14 July 2000), the CC rejected the interpretation of the executive branch that a rule of criminal procedure is constitutional so long as the human right invoked to challenge it (here, reasonable length of criminal proceedings) is not explicitly forbidden in the Constitution. The CC ruled that if a right is protected by the ECHR, since the Convention must be effective in Romanian law, any domestic norm infringing the right is unconstitutional.

On the other hand, in matters where the Romanian Constitution itself addresses a particular right also covered by the ECHR, decisions of the CC have been inconsistent in addressing the relevance of the text of the ECHR and of ECtHR jurisprudence (interview with Romanian law professor Radu Chirita 7/4/03). Its application of the Convention varies: on many occasions it has declared unconstitutional a domestic norm on the grounds of violation of the ECHR and has even done so on its own initiative; but at other times it has (1) failed to offer any guidelines for applying concededly relevant ECtHR case law; (2) failed to cite and apply obviously relevant ECtHR case-law despite its obligation to do so; (3) dismissed a complainant's reference to specific articles of the Convention as unduly detailed; and/or (4) failed to address litigants' arguments based on the Convention and case-law (citations in Goldstein and Ban 2003). These inconsistencies weakened the European human-rights regime in Romania in that they exhibited patterns of reasoning that departed from those of the ECtHR and reflected the "old" understanding of sovereignty. Moreover, to the extent that the CC assumed the posture of the official promoter of the ECHR in Romanian law, its lack of consistency in upholding the ECHR regime has promoted a climate in which ordinary courts have not diligently been referring to it cases that pose a potential conflict between the Convention and Romanian law.

Aside from these caveats, one can conclude that the CC has considerably strengthened the ECHR regime in Romania, because it both reversed numerous longstanding practices that were out of line with ECtHR rulings and challenged a complacent attitude of the judiciary toward international legal norms. It did, however, face resistance in the lower courts.

Despite both ECHR ratification and the CC ruling on its impact in 1994, only after two ECtHR rulings against Romania in 1998, did Romanian courts start in noticeable numbers to address the ECHR. Then, from 1999 through 2002, the basic picture was that a minority of the judges increasingly honored the law of the ECHR, while most judges treated it as just another ineffectual international treaty (Goldstein and Ban 2003). The dominant pattern since 1999 has been that Romanian lawyers only sporadically deploy ECHR-based claims, due to their accurate perception of widespread unresponsiveness by low-level courts to such arguments. Indeed, despite several atypical examples one could cite, neither the Supreme Court nor the intermediate courts of appeals, as of the first half of 2003, had shown any intent to incorporate the body of ECHR law systematically into Romanian jurisprudence.

Mid-year 2003, however, seems to have ushered in a new era for the Romanian judiciary. In response to a 3 June 2003 decision of the ECtHR that declared the Romanian arrest-warrant system inconsistent with the ECHR requirement of separation between the executive and judicial branches, the Romanian Supreme Court (on 27 June 2003) released a judge arrested on corruption charges. In doing so, it declared that Romanian prosecutors must cease issuing arrest warrants (because they must come from a neutral magistrate), despite their statutory authorization to do so, and despite the fact that a parliamentary debate to amend this statute was in process at the time. In other words, for the first time, the Supreme Court (in effect) declared void a Romanian statute on the grounds of a conflict with the ECHR, despite the Constitution's reserving of constitution-based judicial review to the CC. Several lower courts immediately followed the lead of the Supreme Court, in ordering releases of persons held on (newly) improper warrants.

Executive and legislative cooperation with the ECHR

Within weeks of the June 2003 Supreme Court action, the Parliament completed its ECHR-stimulated overhaul of the Code of Criminal Procedure. This whole process received enormous media coverage and provoked nationwide public discussion. Then, in early July, the Ministry of Justice announced plans to send to Parliament a draft Law of the Magistracy that requires all judges and prosecutors to follow ECtHR jurisprudence in (respectively) their rulings and their pleadings. It was quickly enacted into law. This move appears to be a direct expression of the strong desire of the Romanian political leadership for EU membership, pending in 2007 and contingent on, among other things, reform of the judiciary. As of fall 2003 the top Romanian law schools began to require coverage of ECtHR law in the curriculum.

This turn in 2003 was not the first time Romanian political branches had moved to implement the ECHR. Earlier, the Romanian Code of Civil Procedure was amended to allow individuals in the future to re-open their original case pursuant to ECtHR decisions that such individuals had been wronged, in order to assure full implementation of ECtHR decisions.

Still as with other countries, one can also see instances of foot-dragging: after *Vasilescu v. Romania* (ECtHR 22 May 1998) Romania took more than five years to amend its Code of Criminal Procedure to allow for appeals against certain prosecuting acts, as was required by the Committee of Ministers. Also, while the prosecuting arm of the executive branch in cooperation with a committee of Parliament expeditiously produced drafts for amending the Criminal Code with reference to the standards for filing criminal libel in response to the ECtHR's *Dalban v. Romania*, September 1999, the related legislation took five years to become law.

Summary and conclusions

Our findings can be summarized as follows. Within the seven countries we examined, on the matter of executive and legislative branch activity to correct problems identified, or likely to be identified, by the Court at Strasbourg, we found little difference—despite decades of difference in timing of entry into the COE; differences in length of experience either with membership in another supranational body, the EEC/EC/EU, or with rule-of-law liberal democracies;[8] and differences in constitutional text as to the supremacy of international treaty norms over domestic law. The sole exception here was the exemplary performance of the Spanish legislative and executive branches, which corrected all those policies likely to produce negative ECtHR rulings before the rulings were even handed down. All the others generally made prompt corrections when pushed by the ECtHR, but occasionally took as long as four or five years to enact reform.

On judicial implementation of the ECHR and its case-law within our seven case studies, what we found did not match our expectations. Despite later entry into the COE (and EU), and a recent history of dictatorship, Spain, right along with the Netherlands, ranked at the very top, both in thoroughness of judicial cooperation with the ECHR regime and in earliness of the start of this cooperation (1980 for Netherlands, 1981 for Spain).

Lower down (both on thoroughness and timing) were France and Germany, both of whose constitutional courts began to give precedence to ECHR law over domestic law only in 1986–8, despite long-time COE membership. Interestingly, in France the leadership toward making domestic law give way to transnational law came not from the *Conseil Constitutionnel*, but from the Supreme Appellate Court (which under the text of the French Constitution did not even have authority to declare void domestic law).

Portugal, Greece, and Romania were the three laggards, and within each country we found noteworthy differences among the courts. In all three ECHR regime implementation appears to be a top-down process, pushed in Portugal and Romania by the Constitutional Court and in Greece by the Supreme Administrative Court, with less cooperation below. Interestingly, in both France and Romania, the Supreme Appellate Court, which on paper has no authority to engage in constitution-based judicial review, on its own began to strike down domestic laws that conflicted with the ECHR, and this move has been followed by the other ordinary courts.

We found that the wording of national constitutions seemed to prove not as important as the willingness of high courts to provide leadership toward ECHR implementation. It probably mattered at the opposite extremes that the Netherlands Constitution was exceptionally explicit in endorsing higher-law status for rulings of transnational bodies, and that the Portuguese legislature resisted amending the Constitution to include higher law status for the ECHR in 1982, well after acceding to the Convention. But judicial leadership appears to have been crucial: the Constitutional Courts of France and Germany, despite different treatments of international law by their Constitutions, both refrained from according higher-law status to treaties until 1986–1988. Both shifted at that time, apparently caught up in the same pro-Europe political mood that produced the Single European Act of 1987. The constitutional texts of Spain and Romania are virtually identical as to the status of international law, but in each country's first decade of COE membership, the commitment of the Spanish Constitutional Court to ECtHR jurisprudence was far more thoroughgoing than that of its Romanian counterpart. The constitutions of Greece and Portugal were not amended on the subject between 1990 and 2000, but the constitutional courts of both countries embarked on campaigns in both countries to bring their judiciaries into line with ECtHR law beginning in the early 1990s.

Apart from the importance of domestic leadership in all three political branches, the other important variables for pushing regime acceptance that we uncovered were transpolitical. What we have called the Euro-centric "political mood" of the late 1980s, which brought about the Single European Act, evidently penetrated more than one high judicial body in two of our countries, France and Germany. (What forces created this political mood is beyond the scope of this study.) The accession processes of EU institutions (described in the Introduction) are a second transnational force that proved important. Clearly, Romania has made dramatic changes in the past two years, now that EU membership appears in sight. Future research that compared ECHR implementation in a number of twenty-first-century entrants into the EU might prove helpful in uncovering other important forces that promote or retard the transnational regimes that play an increasing role in global governance. And the third set of transnational political forces are the enforcement measures of the COE described in the Introduction. At least in the countries we looked at, these appear to be remarkably effective, for in all seven countries prompt reform of policies ruled violations of the ECHR was more typical than not.

Notes

1 We do not address in this chapter the prior question *why* such trans-state judicial governance regimes get put into place at all; a large literature on this subject has already accumulated: see Moravscik 2000 and citations in Goldstein 2001: Ch. 6.

2 It is perhaps significant for understanding the spread of trans-state regimes as pieces of global governance to observe that the American Convention on Human Rights, for the Organization of American States, operates in much the same format as the earlier ECHR.

3 Greece, despite its siding with the Allies, had a National Socialist (i.e. fascist) dictatorship from 1936 until 1945, a civil war from 1946–1949, then a constitutional monarchy with parliamentary rule until 1967, at which time it underwent a military coup. The military junta exercised a dictatorship from 1967 until 1974. The Greek Third Republic reintroduced the Convention into Greece in 1974 (Law No. 53).

4 The bulk of extant ECtHR studies either focus narrowly on the Court's structure, processes and jurisprudence (Beddard 1993; Merrills 1993; Yourow 1996; Clements 1999); or offer a series of country-by-country non-analytic descriptive studies of the reception of ECtHR law (Gardner 1993; Barkhuysen 1999); or do both (Delmas-Marty 1992; Tavernier 1996; and Gearty 1997). We have found only two analytic accounts that attempt to explain patterns of cross-national variation within the ECHR regime (Drzemczewski 1983 and Lembert 1999), and neither of these does so with a systematic analysis of political variables.

5 Two of the participants to the drafting Conference, Italy and Germany (observer), could hardly claim to be members of this select club immediately after the war, given their former embrace of Fascism (Italy: 1922–1944) and Nazism (Germany: 1933–1945). However, the delegations of these two countries were among the strongest supporters there for enforceability of the human-rights system (Moravscik 2000).

6 We initially had also included in our study an example of a former Soviet Republic (as distinguished from Soviet bloc member), Moldova (Ban and Goldstein 2002). Its Soviet-style institutions have been largely preserved since independence (1991), even though it joined the COE in 1995 and ratified the Convention in 1997. Further reflection caused us to eliminate all of the former Soviet republics from the scope of our study, although it would be desirable to include a study of such countries at some future date. The reason we segregated the cases in this way is our perception that the ECtHR for a time was apparently applying a double standard with respect to former Soviet republics, most notoriously Russia: for a long time the Court accepted no cases that presented claims of violations of human rights in these countries, evidently attempting to give these fledgling rule-of-law regimes extra time to adapt to Western rule-of-law standards. Because the standard applied by the ECtHR to such countries is markedly easier to attain than the standard applied to the more Western member states, there is not yet a viable way to measure "integration" of the former into the ECtHR regime. In effect, the Court seems to have granted them some sort of de facto apprenticeship period. In 2000, for instance, the ECtHR registered 1,323 applications to hear cases (i.e., claims of human-rights abuses) against Russia. It accepted none that year. For comparison purposes, the year 2000 figures for Romania are 31 out of 639 cases accepted; France, 80 out of 870 (www.echr.coe.int).

7 Despite an appointment process geared to guaranteeing judicial independence, observers like Transparency International do note that Romania continues to face difficulties in eliminating corruption from the ranks of its judges, as well as other public officials.

8 Contrary to the claims in the IR literature noted above about the importance of a well-entrenched liberal, rule-of law culture.

References

Abbot, K.H. (1989) "Modern International Relations Theory: A Prospectus for International Lawyers," *Yale Journal of International Law* 14: 335–411.

Alston, P. and Weiler, J.H.H. (1999) "An Ever Closer Union in Need of a Human Rights Policy: The European Union and Human Rights," The Jean Monnet Working Papers: www.jeanmonnetprogram.org.

Alter, K.J. (1996) "The European Court's Political Power," *West European Politics* 19: 458–87.

—— (2001) *Establishing the Supremacy of European Law*, Oxford: Oxford University Press.

Ban, Cornel and Goldstein, Leslie F. (2002) "Comparing Rule-of-Law Regimes: The Transnational Regime of the European Court of Human Rights," paper presented at Annual Meeting of Law and Society Association, Vancouver, Canada, July.

Barkhuysen, T., van Emmerick, M.L., and van Kempen, P.H. (1999) *Execution of Strasbourg and Geneva Human Rights Decisions in the National Legal Order*, The Hague: Martinus Nijhoff Publishers.

Bechlivanou, G. (1992) "Greece," in Delmas-Marty, 151–70.

Beddard, R. (1993) *Human Rights and Europe*, Cambridge: Cambridge University Press.

Burkhard, J. (2000) "The Implementation of the Procedural Guarantees of Article 6.1. of the European Convention of Human Rights in German Civil and Criminal Procedure," at the colloquium: Principes communs d'une justice des Etats de l'Union Européènne, Paris. Siège de la Cour de Cassation, 4–5 December.

Byers, M. (ed.) (2000) *The Role of Law in International Politics*, Oxford: Oxford University Press.

Cavagna, E. and Monteiro, E. (1992) "Iberian Peninsula: Spain and Portugal," in Delmas-Marty, 171–92.

Clements, L.J., Mole, N. and Simmons, A. (1999) *European Human Rights*, London: Sweet and Maxwell.

Cocozza, F. (1996) "Les droits fondamentaux en Europe. Entre justice constitutionelle transfrontière de la CEDH et justice constitutionelle nationale: Les lignes incertaines d'une rélation structurée," *Revue française de Droit constitutionnel* 7: 707–24.

Corstens, G. (2001) "L'application de l'Article 6.1. de la Convention de sauvgarde des droits de l'Homme et des libertès fondamentales dans la procédure pénale néerlandaise," *Revue de science criminelle et de droit pènal comparè* 3: 495–508.

de Bruyn, D. *et al.* (1997) *Les exceptions preliminaires dans la Convention européenne des droits de l'Homme*, Bruxelles: Bruylant.

de Gouttes, R. (2002) "Vers un Modèle Européen de Procédure Pénale," *Colloque* (Intervention dans le cadre de la session de formation de l'Ecole Normale de la Magistrature Centre de Ressources). Available online at: www.enm.justice.fr/centre_de_ressources

Delmas-Marty, M. (ed.) (1992) *The European Convention for the Protection of Human Rights*, Dordrecht: Martinus Nijhoff Publishers.

Fabre, M. and Gouron-Mazel, A. (1998) *Convention Européène des droits de l'Homme*, Paris: Litec.

Finnemore, M. (1996) *National Interest in International Society*, Cornell: Cornell University Press.

Frowein, J. Abr. (1992) "Germany," in Delmas-Marty, 121–8.

Gardner, J.P. (ed.) (1993) *Aspects of Incorporation of the European Convention of Human Rights into Domestic Law*, London: British Institute of International and Comparative Law and British Institute of Human Rights.

Gearty, C.A. (ed.) (1997) *European Civil Liberties and the European Convention on Human Rights*, The Hague: Martinus Nijhoff/Kluwer Law International.

Génevois, B. (1988) "Le droit international et le droit communautaire," paper read at Conseil Constitutionnel and Conseil d'Etat, Palais du Luxembourg, Paris: Librairie Général de Droit et Jurisprudence: 213–14; cited in Alter 2001, 158.

Goldstein, L.F. (1996) "Centripetal Courts and Centrifugal States: Early State Resistance to the European Court of Justice (1958–1994) and the U.S. Supreme Court (1789–1860)," *European Legacy*, I(2): 703–709.

—— (1997) "State Resistance to Authority in Federal Unions: The Early United States (1790–1860) and the European Community (1958–1994)," *Studies in American Political Development* 11: 149–89.

—— (2001) *Constituting Federal Sovereignty*, Baltimore: Johns Hopkins University Press.

Goldstein, L.F. and Ban, C. (2003) "The Rule of Law and the European Human Rights Regime," available online at: http://repositories.cdlib.org/cgi/viewcontent.cgi?article s=1012

Harmsen, R. (2000) "National Responsibility for the European Community Acts Under the European Convention of Human Rights: Recasting the Accession Debate," *European Journal of Public Law* 4: 623–47.

Helfer, L.R., and Slaughter, A. (1997) "Toward a Theory of Effective Supranational Adjudication," *Yale Law Journal* 107: 282–337.

Keohane, R.O. (1997) "International Relations and International Law: Two Optics," *Harvard Journal of International Law* 38: 482–502.

——(2000) "Governance in a Partially Globalized World," Address to the APSA Annual Convention, 31 August, in Washington, D.C.

Klerk, Y. and de Jonge, E.J. (1997) "The Netherlands," in Gearty, 105–41.

Koh, H.H. (1997) "Why Do Nations Obey International Law?" *Yale Law Journal* 106: 2559–69.

Koskenniemi, M. (1990) "The Politics of International Law," *European Journal of International Law* 1: 367–97.

Leandro, A. (2001) "La position des juridictions portugaises face à l'article 6 de la Convention Européenne pour la protection des Droits de l'Homme et des Libertés Fondamentales," at conference of European supreme courts organized by the French C. de Cassation, in Paris, France. Available online at: http://www.courdecassation.fr/ manifestations/colloques/

Lembert, E. (1999) *Les effets de la Cour européène des droits de l'Homme*, Bruxelles: Bruylant.

Marguenaud, J. (2001). "L'effectivité des arrêts de la Cour européène des Droits de l'Homme en France," *Journal des Droits de l'Homme* 24: 1–12.

Merrills, J.G. (1993) *The Development of International Law by the European Court of Human Rights*, Manchester: Manchester University Press.

Moravcsik, A. (1995) "Explaining International Human Rights Regimes: Liberal Theory and Western Europe," *European Journal of International Relations* 1: 157–89.

—— (2000) "Origins of Human Rights Regimes: Democratic Delegation in Postwar Europe," *International Organization* 54: 232–3.

Perrakis, S. (1996) "Le juge grec et la Cour de Strasbourg," in Tavernier: 171–87.

Reus-Smit, Christian (1997) "The Constitutional Structure of International Society and the Nature of Fundamental Institutions," *International Organization* 51: 555–89.

Schlette, V. (1996) "Les interactions entre les jurisprudences de la Cour européène des droits de l'Homme et de la Cour constitutionelle fédérale allemande," *Revue française de droit constitutionnel* 1: 746–68.

Seurin, J.L. (1994) "Towards a European Constitution? Problems of Political Integration," *Public Law* 1: 625–36.

Shapiro, M. and Stone Sweet, A. (2002) *On Law, Politics and Judicialization*, Oxford: Oxford University Press.

Shaw, J. (1996) "European Union: Legal Studies in Crisis? Towards a New Dynamic," *Oxford Journal of Legal Studies* 16: 231–54.

Slaughter, A. (1993) "International Law and International Relations Theory: A Dual Agenda," *American Journal of International Law* 87: 205–20.

—— (1995) "International Law in a World of Liberal States," *European Journal of International Law* 6: 510–24.

Slaughter, A., Tulumello, A.S. and Wood, S. (1998) "International Law and International Relations Theory: A New Generation of Interdisciplinary Scholarship," *American Journal of International Law* 92: 367–97.

Spanish Constitutional Court (2001) "Les relations entre les Cours constitutionnelles et les autres juridictions nationales y compris l'interférence, en cette matiere, de l'action des juridictions européènes," Report to Conférence des Cours Constitutionnelles Européènes, XIIième Congrès.

Steiner, E. (1997) "France," in Gearty, 267–307.

Tavernier, P. (ed.) (1996) *Quelle Europe pour les droits de l'Homme: La Cour de Strasbourg et la réalisation d'une "Union plus étroite,"* Bruxelles: Bruylant.

Troper, M. (2003) "Judicial Review and International Law," *San Diego International Law Journal* 4: 39–56.

Vervaele, J. (1992) "The Netherlands," in Delmas-Marty, 209–21.

Voss, E. (1997) "Germany," in Gearty, 143–73.

Weiler, J.H.H. (1994) "A Quiet Revolution: The European Court of Justice and Its Interlocutors," *Comparative Political Studies* 26: 510–34.

Yourow, C.H. (1996) *The Margin of Appreciation Doctrine in the Dynamics of the European Court of Human Rights Jurisprudence*, New York: Martinus Nijhoff/Kluwer.

10 A private authority perspective on global governance[1]

Timothy J. Sinclair

Introduction

As the editors of this volume make clear, global governance is not a concept around which much agreement exists between academics. Or so it seems. In fact, from another view, what we find is a broad hegemony around a problem-solving utilitarian view of what global governance is or should be, and a much smaller, feral account that refuses to accept the prevailing managerial commitments of the global governance concept (Cox with Sinclair 1996). Contrary to the editors, then, I take it that global governance has already been colonized and politically subordinated, and that for the most part, critical voices have been marginalized.

The purpose of this work, like some others in this volume, is to attack the conceptual hegemony, and undermine its claims to authoritativeness, precisely to allow the diversity of perspectives to which the editors refer to become real. One approach to this task is exegesis. This would involve a careful unpicking of the intellectual sinews of the mainstream views of global governance. While there is a place for this sort of work, my approach is to offer an alternative account of global governance, one which I hope is more convincing than that offered by the problem-solving literature.

What is this alternative account? I do not think the answer can be found in international-relations theory. Whatever school of thought is invoked, international-relations theory assumes an inter-state system. That this is the object of inquiry is not questioned. Legitimate questions revolve around how these states came to be what they are, and how they relate to each other. Because I do not think global governance is an issue of inter-state politics it is unclear to me whether international-relations theory can say much that is interesting about it.

I have come to the view that a network of private institutions produces global governance. This global governance is not an understanding of global governance that the hegemonic discourse would recognize. The global governance that is public is not unimportant, but it does not come close to rivalling the fundamentally coordinative impact of the occult form of global governance I want to highlight and understand.

In what follows I will outline some of the main themes in a private-authority perspective on global governance, and argue for the ability of a private-authority view to offer an altogether more meaningful account of the world order than that provided by the problem-solving mainstream. After this discussion, I will examine the process through which private authority produces global governance. I argue this happens through discrete private-authority mechanisms. Drawing upon evidence from my research in the financial markets, I will subsequently consider how private mechanisms of authority, and the global-governance outputs they produce, are challenged and come under stress. A private-authority perspective on global governance does not see the scope or form of global governance as immutable.

A private-authority perspective on global governance

A private-authority view of global governance is concerned with the substance of rule, rather than administrative mechanisms considered in abstraction (Rosenau 1995: 13). In the orthodox view, transactions are understood to occur exclusively in the realm of the market, and legal authority is a feature of governments. However, this orthodoxy is less persuasive in the contemporary world. A more effective conception acknowledges that non-state forms of governance have always been important, but that these institutions and networks have become more central to capitalism given globalization.

Ferguson and Mansbach contend that states are less important as a result of "historical sea changes" which have displaced one form of political organization from the "pride of place" in our world (Ferguson and Mansbach 1991: 371). They insist that limitation of authority to the legally binding actions of governments is no longer persuasive, and suggest instead that the idea of "*effective governance*" be substituted as a useful operationalization of the situation today (Ferguson and Mansbach 1991: 376).

Miller and Rose endorse this concern (1990: 2). They add that "technologies of thought" such as writing, numbering, compiling, and computing render a realm knowable, calculable, and thus governable. These "procedures of inscription" make objects such as the economy, the firm, and so forth amenable to intervention and regulation (1990: 5). Such "humble and mundane mechanisms," combined with interventionary policy goals (what Miller and Rose call "programs of government"), have over time dissolved the distinction between state and civil society as far as the location of governance goes (Miller and Rose 1990: 8). What has been most vital, they contend, are the ways in which these indirect mechanisms of rule have enabled "*government at a distance*" to be maintained. This form of rule involves "intellectual mastery" by those at the center over persons and events distant from them, based on the possession of critical information (Miller and Rose 1990: 9). The objective of rule at a distance is to create a framework in which social forces will be self-regulating within the norms of the system.

Globalization has created an unprecedented degree of volatility in socio-economic circumstances. One response to these circumstances has been initiatives to separate central-bank monetary policy from legislative intervention, and to establish "fiscal responsibility acts," as in the case of New Zealand, which set out principles for "prudent" fiscal policy (*The Economist*, 1 April 1995: 60). Another response has been a shift in emphasis between what have come to be called "fire alarm" and "police patrol"-type surveillance forms (McCubbins 1987: 427). The fire-alarm metaphor refers to a problem-focused, episodic approach to governance. Like municipal fire departments, problems—like fires—only receive attention when they have been identified and called in by non-specialists. A framework is established—that fires will be reported by those who see them—which only requires occasional "enforcement." Inspections are infrequent (perhaps annually) and the emphasis is on self-regulation in self-interest. In the case of police patrols, a much more aggressive process of looking for law-breaking is characteristic. The idea is that many problems never mature into crises because of surveillance and early intervention. Although fire-alarm approaches may be cheaper in cost–benefit terms, police-patrol surveillance is attractive when the immediate costs of dis-governance are very high, and losses are "lumpy"—what Hubert calls low-probability high consequence risk—such as, for example, when a major bond issuer unexpectedly defaults and gives rise to a crisis of confidence in financial markets as a whole (Hubert 1995).

Paradoxically, while public institutions seem to be increasingly moving from the police-patrol to the fire-alarm approach, under fiscal and competitive pressures in a context of globalization, a tightening of governance is developing in the private realm, as institutions with the capacity for governance seek to compensate for the risks and opportunities created by change. Bond-rating agencies are an example of this private authority.

Private-authority mechanisms

Rating agencies adjust the "ground rules" inside international capital markets and thereby shape the organization and behavior of those institutions seeking funds. This anticipation effect is reflected in the minds of capital-market participants in terms of their understandings and expectations of the agencies. In turn, anticipation acts as a point of origin from which business and policy initiatives are developed. This coordination, or government-at-a-distance effect, narrows the expectations of creditors and debtors to a shared set of norms.

The private authority represented by bond-rating agencies is not premised on power in the simple sense. Authority, an altogether more hidden form of social control than power, resides in the agencies' authority. The concept of authority is often used in a narrow, legal context to describe the legitimate, lawful status of an entity. That is not the usage here.

Based on work by Friedman, Lincoln makes a key distinction in his discussion of authority, between the epistemic authority of technical experts, scholars, and professionals, who are "an authority," and the executive authority of political leaders, military officers and police forces, those "in authority" (1994: 3–4). What both have in common characterizes the *auctoritas* of Roman law, namely that they produce "consequential speech" which quells doubts, winning the trust of audiences (1994: 4). Lincoln argues that the consequentiality of authoritative speech actually has little to do with the form or content of what is said. Instead, these consequences are best understood in "relational terms as the effect of a posited, perceived, or institutionally ascribed asymmetry between speaker and audience" (ibid.) This hierarchy allows some speakers to command not just audience attention, but also their confidence, respect, and trust

Lincoln concludes that historical circumstances are crucial to identifying the existence of authority. Authority is best understood as an effect of these circumstances, rather than as an entity or a characteristic of an actor or institution. Its existence is therefore not functional, easily understood through a rationalist lens, but always contingent on time, place, and circumstance. Capacities for producing these effects are central to understanding authority, as are understandings of who—what actors—have the capacity for producing the effect at specific times in particular places (Lincoln 1994: 10).

Authority is not the same as persuasion. The major rating agencies do not seek to persuade others to agree with their views. Indeed, as Lincoln suggests, "the exercise of authority need not involve argumentation and may rest on the naked assertion that the identity of the speaker warrants acceptance of the speech" (1994: 5). Persuasive efforts (and coercion too) reveal a lack of authority. As Hannah Arendt observed, authority is defined "in contradistinction to both coercion by force and persuasion by argument" (in Miller 1991: 29). Persuasion and coercion are implicit within authority, but are only actualized when authority itself is in jeopardy. Although implicitly constituting authority, their explicit actualization gives a signal that—at least temporarily—authority is negated (Lincoln 1994: 6).

Rating agencies, especially Moody's and Standard and Poor's, have worked hard at creating their reputation for impartiality over the last century or so. In some situations where people surrender their own powers of judgment to an institution or to a group, the surrender may be quite fragile, as in the case of a fad or fashion (Bikchandani *et al.* 1992: 1016). The circumstances, including the longevity of the rating agencies, make their particular authoritative niche more resilient than that of most other non-state institutions. Their position within the capital markets provides them with considerable resources. Moreover, as noted, even if individuals do become skeptical about the rating agencies, as often happens, they cannot necessarily assume others in the markets have too. Because of this risk, these skeptical individuals have incentives to continue to act based on the assumption that others will use the rating agencies as benchmarks, unless they know this definitely not to be the case.

What is missing in Lincoln's argument about authority is an understanding of the criteria that determine when the elements he identifies as the "right ones" actually become right. While what generates authority is, as Lincoln suggests, a reflection of the circumstances encountered, and therefore highly individuated, a characterization of the basic relationship between those with authority and those who acknowledge authority can be developed. This relationship centers on the social efficacy of the ideas held by those claiming authority. Here the "ideas and foreign policy" literature is useful (Goldstein and Keohane 1993: 3). These authors suggest ideas "provide road maps that increase actors' clarity about goals or ends-means relationships" (Goldstein and Keohane 1993: 3). This road-map analogy establishes a concrete mechanism at the heart of the relationship between the authoritative and the non-authoritative, which might otherwise seem nebulous.

Within the rating nexus, the "road map" that provides the mechanism through which the authority relation is established between authority and non-authority is creditworthiness. Creditworthiness is both a causal belief—being creditworthy means an issuer is likely to repay their debts—and a principled belief, in that placing a priority on repaying debt is morally right and obligatory. As a belief, creditworthiness becomes embedded in rules and norms—institutionalized—which act as "invisible switchmen," and "constrain public policy," by "turning action onto certain tracks," obscuring other tracks from view (Goldstein and Keohane 1993: 12). Katzenstein suggests that institutionalized norms like creditworthiness do not merely influence behavior by prescribing ends, but also operate indirectly to organize action (1993: 267). How creditworthiness came to be institutionalized like this is a fascinating question requiring what Goldstein and Keohane call an "archaeology of ideas," a task beyond the scope of this chapter (1993: 21). In any case, the mechanism is not monolithic. As Katzenstein (1993) warns, norms remain contested and contingent.

Private-authority mechanisms under stress

The notion of authority (or epistemic authority), as I use it above, may suggest to some a system of relations in which no opposition is possible, in which the rating agencies have an effective lock on the views and actions of all who need their services. This is not my intention in using the concept. Global governance premised on private authority is not invariant. The authority of rating agencies is ambiguous and shifting, like other norms. In writing about the Italian-American community of East Harlem, Orsi discusses the role of the southern Italian notion of *rispetto*. Orsi suggests *rispetto* was "above all ... a posture of obedience to authority ..." (1985: 93). Respect and fear were bound up together in the notion. But *rispetto* was a "public posture," which often concealed disagreement, what Scott calls the "hidden transcript" (Orsi 1985: 94; Scott 1990: xii). The important thing is that disagreement was rarely aired publicly and *rispetto* was maintained as a mask. Rispetto is a good approximation of the fear–respect relations that exist between rating agencies and those dependent on their judgments in contemporary conditions. The maintenance of authority would seem to be a two-faced thing.

Rating agencies have moved from a more persuasive role to that of epistemic authority. Persuasion implies a range of levels of respect. Epistemic authority is bivariate: authority either exists or is absent. Once generated, it is by its very nature hard to budge, as market participants tend to discount the "mistakes" or epistemic failures of the agencies, given their position and stock of eminence. Of course, these resources could be overwhelmed by a persistent record of perceived failure or by a change in the relationship between raters and those who use ratings—a change in the structure of capitalism. But in the absence of a coherent counter-hegemony, in the form of alternative, endogenous means for the production of judgments in disintermediated conditions, or a decline of the sort of disintermediated markets I identify, a collapse is unlikely. The Internet and other information-technology resources do not comprise a viable alternative, as the dispersal of information evaluation in the Net ignores the crucial point that certain evaluations are more consequential—more authoritative—than others. Some judgments—like those of the bond-rating agencies—are socially valorized, and others are understood intersubjectively as mere conjecture.

While the disintermediation of finance is bolstering the role of capital markets and thus the context in which rating agencies operate, financial innovation, a feature of disintermediation, is proving a difficult thing for the agencies to come to grips with. Miscalls (or perceived miscalls) were frequent during the 1990s (Orange County, East Asia, and Enron come to mind) but do not seem to have been great enough to effectively destabilize rating authority, even if they have made the agencies' *rispetto* more fragile. Despite controversy about rating "mistakes" about East Asia and Enron, I argue that rating has actually become more important in these places (especially Asia) subsequently, as investors seek information about financial circumstances, and as regulatory reforms create— albeit incrementally—more of a role for credit rating in new, more transparent financial systems of the future.

Let us consider the case of Enron. Enron and the other corporate financial scandals are a product of the basic incentives underpinning modern American (and global) capitalism. Just a few years ago the Texas-based energy-trading corporation, which declared bankruptcy on December 2, 2001, was America's seventh-largest company (*The Economist*, January 19, 2002: 9). At the start of 2001, Enron's market capitalization was $62.5 billion. By spring 2002, Enron stock was worth just pennies (Salter *et al.* 2002). The "one big issue" raised by Enron's demise, according to *The Economist*, was the role played by auditors, who missed the exotic financial strategies pursued by the firm (McNulty *et al.* 2002: 6). The question of who regulates accounting, conflict of interest problems when auditors are also consultants, and the rigor of America's GAAP standards, are all up for debate and action (Mayer 2002). The big victim of the public panic about Enron is their auditor, Arthur Andersen (Kulish and Wilke 2002: C1). What is interesting about the attack on Andersen is that it demonstrates that a high-repute institution, whose only real asset is its reputation, can see that asset go up in a puff of smoke if circumstances are right. Enron was not the first time in recent years that Andersen had made significant errors. It survived these other problems. It is Enron that destroyed the company (O'Toole 2002: 12A). It seems that private mechanisms of global governance are fragile and vulnerable to collapse.

Enron was a major crisis for the rating agencies too. They had got emerging markets "wrong" with the Asia crisis, and now here they had got it "wrong" in

America itself by failing to warn investors of the Enron collapse. This was serious. No longer were the victims unknown citizens of foreign countries, but red-blooded American citizens, who had lost their pensions, jobs, futures. John Diaz, Managing Director at Moody's, defended the company's work in front of the Senate Committee hearing in March 2002. "Enron was an anomaly," he said. "Its responses to our specific requests for information were misleading and incomplete." Moody's rating process, he observed, "was undermined by the missing information" (Diaz 2002: 2–3). Ronald M. Barone, the S&P analyst on Enron for several years, used harsher language. He suggested Enron had made "what we later learned were direct and deliberate misrepresentations to us relating to matters of great substance" (Barone 2002: 2).

Former Securities and Exchange Commission (SEC) Chairman Arthur Levitt—who actually had shown little enthusiasm for codification of the rules about rating agencies during the 1990s—called for "greater accountability" of the agencies, the requirement for the agencies to "reveal more about how they operate," an assessment of their "impact on the markets," and "new authority" for the SEC to "oversee" their work (Diaz 2002: 29). Much of the talk from the agencies focused on "speeding up" the rating process in response to market calls for change (Wiggins and Spiegel 2002: 1).

The SEC's role in creating and maintaining the environment in which the agencies operate was noted by White, who suggested the SEC's Nationally Recognized Statistical Rating Organization (NRSRO) designation was anti-competitive, and had "lured these rating agencies into complacency" (2002: 13). NRSRO designation was introduced in 1975, as a way of reducing the regula-tory capital requirements for bond issuers with bond ratings. At the Senate committee hearings, Isaac C. Hunt Jr., SEC Commissioner, defended the NRSRO designation as intended "largely to reflect the view of the marketplace as to credibility of the ratings [of an agency] rather than representing a 'seal of approval' of a federal regulatory agency" (Hunt 2002: 2 and 4). He noted the 1997 proposal to codify NRSRO criteria had not yet been acted on by the Commission, that the Commission had not determined that the NRSRO desig-nation was a "substantial barrier to entry" into the rating business (Hunt 2002: 4), and observed that "Growth in the business of several credit rating agencies, not recognized as NRSROs suggests that there may be a growing appetite among market participants for advice about credit quality ... and that this makes it possible for new entrants to develop a national following for their credit judg-ments" (Hunt 2002: 4). Nevertheless, the Commission determined to examine the competitive impact of the NRSRO designation. If greater supervision of NRSROs is needed, "additional oversight" could become a condition of NRSRO recognition of an agency (Hunt 2002: 4).

A law professor called to give testimony at the Senate Committee hearings attacked the NRSRO designation vigorously. Macey argued that NRSROs, free of competitive forces as a result of their government designation, have incentives to "reduce costs as much as possible." They know that regulation creates a steady demand whatever they do (Macey 2002: 3). Fees paid to the raters, he suggested, are better viewed as a form of tax, rather than a fee for service. Another lawyer, Schwarcz, suggested the anti-competitive effect of NRSRO designation, if any, was mitigated by the need of rating agencies to maintain their reputations with or without regulation. Further regulation would not be likely to materially improve on the effects of this reputational incentive (Schwarcz 2002: 2–3).

Another witness at the hearings cautioned the "need to make sure that the cure is not worse than the disease" in considering alternatives to the NRSRO designation (Reynolds 2002: 1). What needs to change, suggested Reynolds, is the quality of analysis; and the fees rating agencies earn are lucrative enough to fund a material improvement in their output. NRSROs should, he suggested, be more activist, and quality standards should be imposed on them by regulation (2002: 2). All material risks not covered by public disclosure should be reported to SEC by NRSROs (2002: 3). Reynolds feared the agencies have not so much improved the quality of their work as become "trigger happy to overcompensate for Enron," effectively changing the rules of the game (2002: 6).

One of the distinctive things about the rating agency reaction to the Enron crisis is the effort to consult with interested parties about developing the rating process in order to avoid future Enrons. When Moody's announced their intentions, concerns were expressed about a "dramatic increase in the volatility of ratings" which could raise the price of debt, as investors started to perceive higher risk (Purtle in Zuckerman and Richard 2002: C1). Moody's subsequently said that while they will incorporate stock and bond prices in analysis, Moody's will not "let market volatility displace fundamental credit analysis" (Dooley 2002: C16). Nor will Moody's engage in "'unannounced multinotch ratings changes'" (Mahoney in Dooley 2002). According to Moody's, market analysts were concerned that changes to ratings should not disrupt the markets, although they did expect the agencies to pursue accounting issues and demand undisclosed data. Although Moody's still expect ratings to be valid through business cycles, they will in future be adjusted more frequently "in periods of heightened credit stress" (Dooley 2002).

Emphasis on going beyond the information formally provided by issuers was reinforced in the Senate Committee hearings chaired by Senator Lieberman (Schroder 2002: A3). Senator Thompson (R., Tenn.) questioned whether the agencies added value, and noted they did not "'really go beyond the documents'" (Thompson in Schroeder 2002). The SEC announced a re-examination of the role of the agencies and possible need for greater regulation in future. Little is likely to come of this. The process does illustrate, however, the degree of concern that private-governance mechanisms should be effective in the circumstances of the twenty-first century.

Conclusions

Although a new concept, global governance has already generated its own orthodoxy premised on the actions of an interstate elite, their meetings and determinations. In this chapter, I have explored a private-authority understanding of global governance, using the example of bond-rating agencies, those institutions that rate the creditworthiness of $30 trillion in debt.

Rating agencies do not replace states as agents of governance, even though they are representative of newly emerging private authority. This authority interacts with pre-existing powers. At times, rating agencies wield power against states, corporations, and municipalities. At other times, the power of rating agencies is anticipated by these issuers. Political actors will use the rating agencies to show how effective they are at management, or to justify changes in public policy. National states, especially in emerging markets, enlist rating agencies in encouraging the development of their own capital markets, in order to increase transparency and cheapen the cost of lending.

A key feature of the new role of the agencies is its dependence on reputation. Rating agencies sell the understanding that their judgments are important and accurate, or at the least, that others think so and act accordingly. Through a combination of providing a rationalist solution to the "information problem" in disintermediated capital markets, and a long history of perceived accuracy, rating agencies have constructed the eminence of an epistemic authority like a judge, to the extent that what they say is not so much persuasive as widely perceived to be authoritative. The agencies are held to be eminent and worthy of being listened to, and in this context it takes a brave individual to go against their judgment. Once established, this is a very considerable resource at the disposal of the rating agencies. It seems to be resistant to strong assault, much like the stone walls of a castle. But, paradoxically, just like walls, rating agencies have to be careful they do not allow the basis of their power to be undermined, so precipitating a sudden collapse of their epistemic authority. After all, thousands of once mighty castles stand idle or in ruins throughout Europe. For this reason, rating agencies are attentive to what is said about them, and to presenting themselves in a strong self-confident way. They never know when the eminence they have established may be fatally weakened. As the executives at Arthur Andersen know, globalization throws up more risks of this happening today than in the sedate world of the 1940s and 1950s, when bond rating was institutionalized.

Rating agencies face many challenges. Newspapers often carry outraged headlines after a rating downgrade. The Japanese government has sought to undermine the system publicly as their creditworthiness has deteriorated since the early 1990s. Rarely does this lead anywhere more threatening to the agencies. The downgraded, it seems, will always need to vent their anger. But what is it that actually corrodes the authority of the rating agencies? What is it that can destroy their franchise? In recent years, the rise of numerous providers of market intelligence and the much greater availability of all manner of economic and financial data has raised the question of whether institutions can wield authority at all. People who possess heightened analytic skills cannot be fooled, we are told. But "fooling people" is not central to rating. The rules of thumb provided by the rating agencies become social facts of the market even the most highly skilled must take account. Are others using the rating judgments? If they are, then these ratings have a status in the markets, even if the analysis of the individual is divergent. They are part of the environment even the most skilled need to acknowledge, because they may be affecting the behavior of others, which in turn can change the market in which all bonds are priced. In other words, even if smart people do not "believe" in bond ratings, they must incorporate them to the extent others do. An authority, even if wrong, will still give rise to all manner of social action because what it does (and how it relates to others) is a "social fact."

What about rating "mistakes" or crises? Can these shatter the rating franchise? For a brief moment in 1997/98, and again in 2002, this was the question about rating agencies. Had the agencies destroyed their credibility by not providing sufficient or clear enough signals about Thailand, Korea, Indonesia, and Enron? Were they behind the game, and would they lose business because of this failure? Some of the weaknesses of the rating process—the focus on past performance, the application of western expectations to the East—plus the euphoria that surrounded the East Asian economies, contributed to a hesitant signaling of risk. Subsequently, the agencies downgraded everything in sight, which was similarly criticized. What has come of all this? Curiously, very little. What are needed in these markets are institutions able to solve the information problems they present. Hence the result of the crisis has been a greater not a lesser role for the agencies, and therefore the opportunity to grow and present themselves as having truly learnt from the Asian crisis experience. Although Asia showed the rating agencies are not omniscient, it also provided a long-run opportunity for the agencies to increase their authority rather than any meaningful deterioration. So much for the apparent rating meltdown.

There is no doubt that bond rating is—despite its bean counter image—something that stirs great passions. Perhaps this is because it reminds us all of the feelings of rejection generated by getting a bad grade in school. At a deeper level, some may have an inkling that it is precisely in the seemingly technical, the supposedly objective infrastructural phenomena such as rating that the big questions of today and tomorrow are increasingly being decided. If so, this represents a major challenge to the commonsense understandings we have of the things that shape global governance.

Note

1 This essay draws upon some ideas in Timothy J. Sinclair, "Global Monitor: Bond Rating Agencies," *New Political Economy*, Volume 8, Number 1, March 2003, pp. 147–161.

References

Barone, Ronald M., Managing Director, Standard & Poor's (2002). Testimony before the Committee on Governmental Affairs, United States Senate, March 20.
Bikchandani, S., Hirshleifer, D. and Welch, I. (1992) "A Theory of Fads, Fashion, Custom, and Cultural Change as Informational Cascades," *Journal of Political Economy*, 100: 1016.
Cox, R. W. and Sinclair, T. J. (1996) *Approaches to World Order*, Cambridge: Cambridge University Press.

Diaz, John, Managing Director, Moody's Investors Service (2002). Testimony before the Committee on Governmental Affairs, United States Senate, March 20.

Dooley, J. (2002) "Moody's Planned Overhaul of its Ratings Process Includes Effort to Limit Volatility, Shorten Reviews," *Wall Street Journal*, February 13, p. C16.

The Economist (1995) "The Great Escape?" April 1, p. 60.

The Economist (2002) "The Real Scandal," January 19, p. 9.

Ferguson, Y. H. and Mansbach, R. W. (1991) "Between Celebration and Despair: Constructive Suggestions for Future International Theory," *International Studies Quarterly*, 35(4): 363–386.

Goldstein, J. and Keohane, R. (1993) "Ideas and Foreign Policy: An Analytical Framework," in J. Goldstein and R. O. Keohane (eds) *Ideas and Foreign Policy: Beliefs, Institutions, and Political Change*, Ithaca, NY: Cornell University Press.

Hubert, D. (1995) "Popular Responses to Global Insecurity: Public Encounters with Low-probability High-consequence Risk," paper presented to the annual meeting of the International Studies Association, Chicago, February.

Hunt, Jr., Isaac C., Commissioner, U.S. Securities and Exchange Commission (2002). Testimony before the Committee on Governmental Affairs, United States Senate, March 20.

Katzenstein, P. J. (1993) "Coping with Terrorism: Norms and Internal Security in Germany and Japan," in J. Goldstein and R. O. Keohane (eds) (1993) *Ideas and Foreign Policy: Beliefs, Institutions, and Political Change*, Ithaca, NY: Cornell University Press.

Kulish, N. and Wilke, J.R. (2002) "Indictment Puts Andersen's Fate on Line," *Wall Street Journal*, March 15, p. C1.

Levitt, A. (2002) "Who Audits the Auditors?" *New York Times*, January 17, Section A, p. 29.

Lincoln, B. (1994) *Authority: Construction and Corrosion*, Chicago: University of Chicago Press.

Macey, Jonathan R., Cornell Law School (2002) Testimony before the Committee on Governmental Affairs, United States Senate, March 20.

Mayer, Jane (2002) "The Accountants' War," *New Yorker*, April 22 and 29, pp. 64–71.

McCubbins, M. D. and Schwartz, T. (1987) "Congressional Oversight Overlooked: Police Patrols versus Fire Alarms," in M. D. McCubbins and T. Sullivan (eds) *Congress: Structure and Policy*, Cambridge: Cambridge University Press.

McNulty, S., Martin, P., Michaels, A. and Peel, M. (2002) "Called to Account," *Financial Times*, January 12/13, p. 6.

Miller, D. (1991) "Authority," in David Miller (ed.) *The Blackwell Encyclopedia of Political Thought*, Oxford: Blackwell, p. 29.

Miller, P. and Rose, N. (1990) "Governing Economic Life," *Economy and Society*, 19: 1.

Orsi, R. A. (1985) *The Madonna of 115th Street: Faith and Community in Italian Harlem, 1880–1950*, New Haven, CT: Yale University Press.

O'Toole, D. (2002) "Where is Justice for Andersen Workers?" letter to the editor, *USA Today*, March 27, p. 12A.

Reynolds, Glenn, CEO of CreditSights, Inc. (2002) Testimony before the Committee on Governmental Affairs, United States Senate, March 20.

Rosenau, J. N. (1995) "Governance in the Twenty-first Century," *Global Governance*, 1: 13.

Salter, M. S., Levesque, L. C. and Ciampa, M. (2002) "The Rise and Fall of Enron," paper prepared for the Faculty Symposium on Enron Corp., Harvard Business School, April 10 (revised April 23).

Schroeder, M. (2002) "SEC Weighs Curbs on Credit-rating Firms," *Wall Street Journal*, March 21, p. A3.

Schwarcz, Steven L., Duke Law School (2002). Testimony before the Committee on Governmental Affairs, United States Senate, March 20.

Scott, J. C. (1990) *Domination and the Arts of Resistance*, New Haven, CT: Yale University Press.

White, L. (2002) "Credit and Credibility," *New York Times*, February 24, p. 13.

Wiggins, J. and Spiegel, P. (2002) "Enron's Fall May Spark Credit Rating Rethink," *Financial Times*, January 19/20, p. 1.

Zuckerman, G. and Richard, C. (2002) "Moody's and S&P Singed by Enron, May Speed Up Credit Downgrades," *Wall Street Journal*, January 22, p. C1.

11 Contested spaces

The politics of regional and global governance

Alice D. Ba

Introduction

This chapter explores the relationship between regional and global governance and responds mainly to the literature identified as "global governance" (GG). Despite an important diversity of views within the literature, different perspectives tend to share a number of assumptions and conclusions about the relationship between regional and global processes. Mostly, "regional governance" (RG) is characterized as an example, or subset, of GG. Regional developments suggest, however, that this characterization may be problematic. In particular, this characterization may obscure important tensions in the relationship between RG and GG, especially as viewed by those in non-core regions. In Southeast Asia, Latin America, and Africa views of GG often diverge from those of more advanced economies, which may result in different understandings of how RG relates to global processes and architectures. At very least, developments suggest a need for further inquiry into the relationship and nexus between GG and RG.

This chapter draws on developments taking place in one part of the world—Southeast Asia—to illustrate questions being raised about GG in different parts of the globe, as well as the particular constraints and dilemmas faced by non-core regions. While the particularities of regional developments in other regions are each in their own way unique, it is also evident that there are important similarities and parallels in how each region conceives its relationship to the larger global architecture and notions of GG.

In particular, this chapter takes as its point of focus the ongoing dialogue on GG and RG that is taking place in Southeast Asia, especially since the 1997–9 Asian financial crisis. While the full significance of that crisis remains to be seen, there is certainly an argument to be made that events of 1997–9 represented a "crisis" in all senses of the word. This was a crisis that destabilized individual economies, but even more important, especially as regards this discussion, it undermined the credibility of governance arrangements at all levels of politics. Much attention has been paid to how the crisis and associated developments forced re-evaluation of national development strategies, but what happened in 1997–8 was as much a crisis of RG and GG, as national. At the same time that some arrangements suffered, however, the crisis was also responsible for catalyzing activities that suggest a "new" or different regionalism along broader East Asian (Northeast plus Southeast Asia) lines. The crisis thus provides an excellent opportunity to explore how actors in Southeast Asia are conceiving regional governance in relation to global governance.

I divide this chapter into two sections. In the first section, I offer two views of the structure and process of GG as regards the relationship between the regional and the global. Beginning first with a more conventional view drawn from the GG literature, I discuss how that literature tends to characterize the relationship between RG and GG as mutually supporting processes in which RG is mostly a subset of GG. That discussion is then followed by an alternative view of RG and GG as being interdependent but also distinct and varied; that is, RG and GG are not necessarily all of one piece. The second section then brings together the discussion of structure and process by focusing on the significance of the 1997–9 financial crisis and how that crisis shifted the center of debates about regionalism, especially East Asian regionalism, in Southeast Asia. Finally, I offer some conclusions about the relationship between RG and GG processes. I argue that regionalism in Southeast Asia, like most regionalisms in the Global South, has an uneasy relationship with the structures and processes of GG and that despite strong structural pressures to conform, regional arrangements like those in Southeast Asia are also sources of dynamism when it comes to systemic change.

The structure and process of GG

The GG view

As discussed in the introduction to this volume, GG has different meanings and different usages in the GG literature. Despite those differences, however, there emerge some common assumptions and themes in how various perspectives conceive regionalism's relationship to GG. Specifically, there is a notable tendency—whether GG is a phenomenon (that is, the outgrowth of new needs and problems that demand management), a project (that is, the spread of liberal norms and rules), or world view (that is, new thinking for a new world)—to characterize RG as more or less the same as GG in form, function, and purpose. In particular, both RG and GG are often understood as responding to similar functional needs and as providing order to a characteristically disordered world. Indeed, if there is a common thread that runs through these discussions of RG and GG, it is that individual states are increasingly challenged and unable by themselves to provide their people adequate security—whether of the physical, economic, or human variety. States therefore must work with others and with different kinds of actors if they are to respond adequately to the challenges of a rapidly changing world. Both GG and RG are understood to be the product of these growing needs.

Thus, RG and GG are not only compatible and mutually supporting processes, but also a function of similar needs and logic. There is no real distinction between

RG and GG, except that the former operates on a smaller scale and with fewer actors (and as a consequence, may be more easily achieved). By this under-standing, regional arrangements are the building blocks of world order—the "halfway house between the nation state and a world not ready to become one" (Wilcox quoted by Fawcett 1995: 19). Joseph Nye's "peace in parts" characteriza-tion of the regional–global relationship offers a similar example of how RG arrangements are often conceived as pieces in a larger puzzle that is GG: "the most interesting linkage that regionalists have hypothesized between regional organization and peace relates to the capacity of micro-regional economic orga-nizations to foster integration that changes the character of relations between states and creates islands of peace in the international system" (1971: 11).

While less prominent in the neo-neo debates of the 1980s, the characteriza-tion of regionalism as "a principle of international order" is once again a theme of recent literature on the "new regionalism" (Fawcett and Hurrell 1995: 4). In contrasting the new regionalism[1] with the old, some scholars have contrasted a market-driven, open-inclusive, and integrationist logic with the politically driven, closed-exclusive, and protectionist logic of the regionalisms of the 1960s and 1970s (Bowles 1997: 225). In particular, this view sees regional arrangements as a stepping stone and way to integrate smaller, developing economies into the global trading system—that is, in Robert Lawrence's words, "to facilitate their participation in the world economy rather than their withdrawal from it" (Afrasiabi and Jalali 2001: 62). The new regionalism assigns particular impor-tance to economic and functional drivers and the necessity of adapting and conforming to a neoliberal trading regime, where regionalism "has been framed almost invariably as a means to the achievement of competitiveness in the glob-alizing world economy, and as a platform from which to participate in the international trading system and attract capital flows" (Phillips 2001: 565–6). By this view, regionalism is both product and facilitator of converging values. This neoliberal interpretation thus sees regional arrangements as integrative, not disintegrative, forces in terms of world order. Regionalism, by this view, is "part and parcel of the neoliberal globalization project" (Phillips 2001: 565).

Practitioners of GG, where GG refers to formal organizations like the United Nations, also tend to share this view of complementary regional and global processes. The World Trade Organization, in its 2002 Annual Report, affirmed this characterization of the regional as being complementary components and steps towards GG: "[Regional trade arrangements] can offer intermediate steps to the broader process of integration into the world economy and in some cases, achieve faster and deeper liberalization than is possible at the multilateral level" (p. 41). Former United Nations Secretary General Boutros Boutros-Ghali has similarly described the relationship between regional and GG arrangements as mutually supporting. Drawing on Chapter VIII of the UN Charter, which iden-tifies a "division of labour between the UN system and regional agencies and arrangements," Boutros-Ghali has argued for a more decentralized GG system involving greater "task sharing" between different organizations and in which regional organizations may "act as surrogates of the UN" (Boutros-Ghali 1996;

see also Knight 1996: 45; Smith and Weiss 1997). For Boutros-Ghali and other proponents of UN reform, regional organizations and regional responsibility offer an answer to an "over-stretched, uncoordinated and underfinanced" United Nations. In their view, the UN might "devolve responsibilities towards institutional units that are 'lower' (or more accurately, 'less universal') on a hierarchy of institutions" (Smith and Weiss 1997: 595). Importantly by this "subsidiarity" principle, global and regional processes and arrangements remain mutually supporting processes. Also important in this reformed global system is a very clear hierarchy between GG and RG, in which regional agencies, though they may play primary roles, are nevertheless subordinate to the "central authority" of the UN (Knight 1996). The main point is that "Regional organizations ... tend to be regarded as a natural outgrowth of international cooperation, compatible with the UN and indeed an indispensable element in its successful growth and functioning" (Fawcett 1995: 19).

Building blocks or sites of resistance?

The conventional view of GG—whether the subject is international organizations or neoliberal world order—therefore sees RG as a subset of GG. However, there is also an alternative view that the structure and process of GG are, in reality, not all of one piece, but rather a mix of multiple and overlapping rule systems and arrangements that exist at different levels of governance—local and national, as well as regional and global. Though a set of hegemonic ideas or ordering principles may emerge, we should not assume that all these different systems exist in harmony with one another. The presence of diversity practically assures, in fact, that we will find tensions and contradictions between different arrangements. Vis-à-vis so-called global or hegemonic ideologies and rule systems, the region especially has emerged as a particular site of contestation about governance rules and norms. In this sense, this chapter shares with O'Brien's view in this volume that the structure of GG is *both* a coherent, single system of rule (here, the set of globe-spanning dominant ideas and arrangements) *and* multiple-rule systems (here, the diverse, often competing, governance arrangements at regional and other levels of politics).

In this alternative view of RG's relationship to the global, contestation as a driver of change forms an important component in the process of GG. Recently, for example, a number of scholars have given particular attention to regionalism as a form of *resistance* to global processes and arrangements (Higgott and Phillips 2000; Phillips 2001; Nesadurai 2002). However, there is also an argument to be made that in the developing world at least, the notion of regionalism as resistance is not a new idea but instead a historical theme since the end of World War II when most developing states gained independence and control over their foreign policies. Indeed, their conceptualizations of themselves as part of a larger region and regional identity largely "grew out of the process of decolonization" (Väyrynen 2003: 27) and in reaction to existing global structures (Western imperialism, the Cold War and otherwise).[2] The 1950s and

1960s especially were characterized by great interest in pan-regional movements and regionalism around the globe. While many of those regional conferences and arrangements often proved overly ambitious and consequently were short-lived, what is notable and common to almost all of them were ideas of anti-colonialism, autonomy, and self-determination—that is, resistance vis-à-vis dominant interests, ideas, and power structures in the global system at that particular time.

Others too have observed that tensions between regional and global arrangements are a historical theme. As Smith and Weiss note in their discussion of the United Nations, for example, the relationship between the regional and global has historically been a problematic one. Not only is it problematic to assume a congruence of objectives but regional organizations have also been reluctant to accept the UN's authority over them (Smith and Weiss 1997). Meanwhile, the original debates over the UN charter reveal that those advocating a universal collective security system viewed regional arrangements as potential obstacles to GG (Acharya 2001: fn. 48). A similar observation might be made of GG as neoliberal project or as a set of neoliberal ideas and rules. Here, development debates, especially, have revealed tensions, even deep divisions, between the regional and the global. Of these debates, the ones over structural-adjustment programs as advocated by the IMF and World Bank have especially stood out. At heart, this has been a debate about the right and appropriateness of so-called global regimes to impose a certain set of rules and solutions on states that played minor, even nonexistent, roles in formulating them. By one account of the African case, core economies are engaged in no less than a "transnational neoliberal economic offensive to open African markets" (Nkiwane 2001: 283). It is testimony to both the global reach of certain hegemonic ideas and the widespread resentment about that imposition, that this debate has provided a common point of identification *across* developing regions in Africa, Latin America, and Asia.

This structure and pattern of interaction between core and non-core regions can be found across different issues. Expectations about appropriate international behavior have more often than not been generated by the dominant powers and dominant economies in the system. Rules are too often imposed on the Global South, rather than the product of equal and mutual exchange. Moreover, this pattern of interaction has over time helped to create a sense among non-European, non-North American states that they are unessential outsiders with respect to both the global economy and GG regimes. This is not to say that actors in the Global South do not have a role to play in the production of GG; rather, important relations of power structure relations between core and non-core economies. Such underlying "patterns of hegemony and domination" of the global system (Mittelman 1996: 205) are absolutely critical to understanding and explaining the complex relationship between the regional and global. As much as regional actors may resent being forced to conform to a certain set of rules and ideas, they also fear being left completely out of that hegemonic system.

In this context, regional efforts in the Global South reflect a dual concern. Specifically, they have concerns about both marginalization and domination: not to engage and participate in global economic and governance processes risks marginalization; however, participation practically guarantees vulnerability to external forces and an almost certain loss of political and economic autonomy. Recent regional integration efforts do indeed, as many argue, reflect a certain neoliberal impulse—but that impulse is importantly driven by a perceived necessity. One participates in the neoliberal system (however problematic it may be) *or* one is left behind and even worse, shut out all together. If states (and they are mostly states) and state elites adopt the language and discourse of neoliberalism in defining regional integration efforts, it is at least in part because they see that as a precondition of their entrée into the global marketplace and access to the opportunities that may be had there. For many of these elites "there is simply 'no alternative' to neoliberalism" (Taylor 2003: 320).

For these states and actors in non-core regions, GG therefore often represents, as Overbeek and Arrighi argue in this volume, a system of control and domination. At very least, GG is to these actors a set of hegemonic ideas and structures that constrain in important ways. But again, this is not to say that non-core actors see themselves without agency to contest what they see to be problematic. In such cases, regionalism has offered these states a platform and means to assert different ideas, different solutions, and different visions. Here, it is important to underscore that regionalism is to these actors more than an instrumental, tactical tool with which to manage actors' relationships with the global actors and interests; it is also importantly an assertion of a *right* to speak for a certain set of actors towards influencing both material and normative structures of GG, a call for political recognition, as well as a claim to a prerogative voice vis-à-vis non-regional actors for a particular political space. Regionalism is not simply a response to functional and economic needs. Regionalism is a fundamentally political exercise that takes place in a political context.

In summary, regional arrangements may not fit neatly (if at all) into existing global arrangements, but neither are they "islands" separated off from a larger global context and global power relations. Put another way, the regional and global are engaged in a process of constant interaction with interactive effects; they are interdependent and co-evolving systems. Whether that interaction will lead to "convergence" or "divergence", however, depends in large part on the nature of the interaction. In this sense, the popular dichotomy of regionalism being "building blocks" versus "stumbling blocks" in terms of world order is overly simplistic. Instead, as Boas and others observe, given the unevenness of globalization processes, as well as different levels at which actors engage and enter the global system, we should expect such interactions to have "created a whole range of diversified patterns of interactions and responses at the interrelated local, national, and regional levels" (Boas 1999: 1064; Taylor 2003: 314). Not only that, but even within particular arrangements we are likely to find tensions and contradictions. The multiplicity of interactions and responses means that globalizing processes will produce diversity and contradictions, as well as uniformity in the world (Taylor 2003: 314). If GG is the totality of governance structures and processes in the world, then it is characterized by neither complete unity nor fragmentation; rather it is, as Boas (1999) argues, "a weave-world" of intersecting and interacting systems and processes.

Crisis and contestation: the politics of East Asian regionalism

The 1997–9 Asian financial crisis offers a particularly good subject for this chapter and volume in that the crisis involved many of the dynamics associated with GG: transnational processes (financial markets), world organizations (the IMF, World Bank), non-state actors (international ratings agencies, investment funds, individual investors), economic interdependence (the "contagion" effect), to name just a few. For some the crisis also has special significance for representing the "first post-Cold War 'crisis of globalization' " (Higgott and Phillips 2000: 360) and more specifically of neoliberalism (Berger 1999). For those taking this view, the crisis illustrated all too well how the "expansion of global markets, institutions, and certain norms … progressively reduce[ed] the purely domestic aspects of politics everywhere" (Solingen 2001: 518). As such, the crisis brought into "sharp relief the tensions between domestic and external dynamics that governments must increasingly contend with in a globalizing world" (Nesadurai 2000: 75).

As a crisis, developments of, and since, 1997–9 are also especially useful in that they draw attention to the dynamism of world politics. In particular, they draw attention to how the ideological foundations for GG may be negotiated and renegotiated to produce reconfigurations of political authority. Crises by definition are moments of high stress and difficulty. And in that they are often unexpected and associated with failed strategies, they are also times of reflection and re-evaluation, if not arguments for change, new strategies, and new thinking (Kowert and Legro 1996; Legro 2000). Crises thus frequently mark critical turning points in political life. In all these different ways, developments experienced in Southeast Asia between 1997 and 1999 was a crisis. Not only were developments debilitating in economic, political, and human terms, but they also forced regional actors to rethink national development strategies, the nature of the global economy, and the problems of global processes and institutions. In short, what happened in 1997–9 had consequences for more than economics, but also the ideational foundations of national, regional, and global order and governance.

As in the globalization literature, discussions on the Asian financial crisis have tended to focus on the interaction between national and global level actors and processes. This is no surprise given the characterization of the Asian financial crisis as a crisis of globalization and the preoccupation of the globalization literature with the sovereign state, especially its eroding capacities to manage or mitigate external forces. This preoccupation was especially evident in two related debates that quickly took center stage at the height of the Asian financial crisis.

The first debate focused on the appropriateness of Western neoliberal models of development (represented by the "Washington Consensus") versus developmental statist models of development. That debate crystallized around (East and) Southeast Asia's developmental states and "the general capacity of the state to pursue the common good" in a globalized economy (Cerny 1995: 597). In that debate, Malaysia, in particular, received much attention for its ability to resist IMF involvement and for the capital controls it adopted during the height of the crisis (Beeson 2000; Nesadurai 2000). The second debate focused on the appropriateness of the IMF response, the deficiencies of existing global arrangements, as well as the lack of transparency in global decision-making processes.

Most relevant to both debates was a growing divergence of views between, on the one hand, advanced economies, especially the United States, and on the other, economies of Southeast Asia, Latin America, as well as Africa. Indeed, for some like Higgott and Phillips, the crises of 1997–9 (not just in East and Southeast Asia but also South America) do not merely suggest but instead "emphatically" demonstrate that "the dominant trend in the global political economy is...one of divergence rather than convergence" (2000: 361). Furthermore, in their view, divergence is fast redefining the relationship between regionalist and global governance (Phillips 2001). True, debates led to an important modification of the original Washington consensus—that is, a more "humanized" "post-Washington consensus" that also considered issues of human security and of limited regulatory capacities of the state—but there has nevertheless remained "a fundamental discrepancy between the rethinking process associated with the 'globalization backlash' in non-core regions like Southeast Asia and the dominant Anglo-American rhetoric of these [global governance] institutions and US policymakers" (Higgott and Phillips 2000: 361; see also Robison 2002).

Such discrepancies are transforming the shape and content of regional processes in Southeast Asia. While much has been discussed about how post-crisis reassessments (and resentments) have manifested themselves with respect to national and global arrangements, the discussion below highlights the regional level as another important level of contestation. In particular, disagreements between global and regional actors about the causes of Asia's 1997–9 financial crisis and, in turn, the appropriateness of global responses directly contributed to the post-crisis interest and activity in a broader East Asian regionalism. "East Asian" developments are especially interesting because they signaled an important shift in thinking about regional governance since the early 1990s when Southeast Asian states debated an earlier East Asian proposal, which took the form of Malaysia's East Asian Economic Group (EAEG). The next section offers a brief sketch of that debate and the specific ways that the crisis affected the discourse on regional and global governance.[3]

GG, RG, and the EAEG

As discussed, regionalist efforts in Southeast Asia and other non-core regions tend to reflect a dual concern about marginalization and domination. In the

Southeast Asian case, such concerns are made especially salient by the region's external orientation and its disproportionate (in relation to total GNP) reliance on extraregional trade and markets. That external orientation and dependence is why Southeast Asian regionalism has tended to be so sensitive to global fluctuations and uncertainties. It was in just such a context of global economic uncertainty, for example, that Southeast Asia's first[4] major debate about "East Asia" took place in the early 1990s. Against the backdrop of post-Cold War uncertainties (especially the ending of pro-Asia US trade policies), the failure of global governance negotiations on the General Agreement on Tariffs and Trade (GATT) combined with heightened regionalist activity in Europe (the Maastricht Treaty) and North America (NAFTA) to raise the specter of Western protectionism vis-à-vis a region highly dependent on Western markets. All this served to heighten Southeast Asian interest in economic regionalism.

However, considerable debate took place about what kind of regionalism it should be and along what lines. In particular, the early 1990s saw a vigorous debate between proponents of "open," neoliberal regionalism, represented mostly by the Australian-initiated and US-backed Asia-Pacific Economic Cooperation (APEC), and proponents of an exclusivist, racially defined regionalism, represented by Malaysian Prime Minister Mahathir's proposed East Asian Economic Group (EAEG). As discussed by Nesadurai, the EAEG expressed Mahathir's "long-held ideas on the dangers of unbridled market forces, his fears of potentially damaging challenges and obstacles for developing countries issuing from the global environment, and his deep resentment against perceived Western manipulations" (2000: 88). In the post-Cold War context where Western trading partners had become less tolerant of the needs of developing countries and more interventionist on human-rights and other related issues, Mahathir saw an East Asian group to be a way to give memebrs of the Association of Southeast Asian Nations (ASEAN) better ability to negotiate the "forces of globalisation and economic integration" and to shape emerging developments (Camroux 1994: 9). Regarding this goal, the EAEG proposal reflected Mahathir's underlying belief that ASEAN's coalition of weak-to-middle powers was ill-equipped to negotiate the world's political economy; ASEAN needed the larger economies of Japan, China, and South Korea to have a voice in shaping matters of concern to them. The fact that they were Asian states added to the appeal of widened regional cooperation. For Mahathir (1999), the three Northeast Asian economies were thus doubly attractive for being both larger economies and Asian (see also Camroux 1994).

Much has been made of Mahathir's racially based, exclusivist understanding of regionalism as a contrast to the supposedly race-neutral, non-exclusivist dynamic of open regionalism; however, it is important to note that from the standpoint of Mahathir and other critics of the neoliberal economy, open regionalism is just differently exclusivist (and, in the end, just as racist). Specifically, it privileges advanced economies that dominate both the economics and politics of global processes and arrangements. In Mahathir's view, East and Southeast Asian states were perfectly justified in their search for alternative arrangements. Just as power and development (or the guise of power and development) had denied smaller economies like Malaysia from participating in global rule-making, the EAEG, defined as it was along ethnic-cultural lines, would deny Western interests and powers (especially the United States) any special privilege or right with respect to East Asia. As Narramore argues, the political significance of this regionalist discourse is clear in that the debate over the EAEG was at its core a debate about who gets to participate and who does not. As Narramore puts it, "For the political significance of recognizing the existence of an essentially Asian way of regionalism is that non-Asian 'liberal' states must either work with this 'way' or accept that they have no basis for inclusion in an Asia-Pacific region beyond that as 'rational' self interested citizens" (Narramore 1998: 78). For Mahathir, who tended to view neoliberalism as a cover for an underlying, hidden racism, at least the EAEG was honest.

During these early pre-crisis debates, however, APEC and "open regionalism" claimed early victory, successfully pre-empting (for the time being at least) the creation of an East Asian group. In ASEAN, views of both APEC and the EAEG at the time tended to be mixed. ASEAN states did agree to a modified proposal, an East Asian economic caucus (EAEC) within APEC, a mostly token gesture to allow Mahathir to save face, but it was also clear that though many leaders may have shared Mahathir's sentiments about the global economy and governance arrangements, other concerns proved more compelling. In particular, fears that important Western trading partners would interpret the EAEG as a confrontational (protectionist) move led ASEAN decision makers to conclude that Mahathir's proposed EAEG was, in the end, too risky. At the very least, fears that Western trading partners would retaliate by restricting or denying Southeast Asian states access to North American and European markets provided strong incentives for elites to characterize regional arrangements as "building blocks" not "stumbling blocks" on the way to global free trade and thus fully consistent with first GATT and later WTO rules. Though there were also other reasons for APEC's early victory over the EAEG,[5] there is little doubt that strong and unambiguous opposition from the United States played a critical role in undermining the EAEG idea. The rejection of the proposal, however, was importantly framed in terms of its being contrary to principles of "open regionalism."

"Open regionalism" thus quickly emerged as the dominant frame in the pre-crisis regionalist discourse. "Open regionalism" signaled to major trading partners one's commitment to an open trading regime and thus ensured continued access to foreign markets. While mostly associated with APEC, great care was also taken to portray the ASEAN Free Trade Area (AFTA) in similar nondiscriminatory, non-exclusionary terms. For example, regional analysts like Hadi Soesastro and Dewi Fortuna Anwar, among others, took to describing AFTA as "an intermediate step between a protected domestic economy and a liberalized multilateral system" (Anwar 1996: 30) or "training ground," a way to ease less industrialized economies into becoming full participants in the global trading system. As such, regional arrangements were also frequently considered temporary measures, made redundant once global arrangements were achieved.

As Soesastro put it, "the objective measure of success [for a regional trading arrangement] …is if it is no longer needed" (1997: 85). This understanding of the relationship between regional and global processes tended to dominate pre-crisis discussions and debates about regionalism in Southeast Asia.

The financial crisis, however, dramatically revealed problems with the premises of open regionalism, especially neoliberal characterizations of the global economy as good, progressive, and at least benign. The crisis made especially clear the problematic interdependence between Southeast Asian economies and external actors and forces, as well as the biases of GG institutions like the IMF that were dominated by actors whose interests and world views were now proven to diverge greatly from those of Southeast Asia. In particular, Southeast Asian states found themselves at odds with the US and other representatives of GG arrangements over the causes of the crisis, which in turn led to different conclusions about the kinds of responses necessary to prevent and mitigate future crises.

The view of the United States and other representatives of the IMF and World Bank ("the Washington Consensus") was that the Asian financial crisis was home grown and an indictment of interventionist developmental strategies, government–business relations, and domestic systems of patronage. Consequently, IMF packages came with conditions aimed at "sweep[ing] away crony capitalism and free[ing] up markets along 'Western' lines" (Higgott and Phillips 2000: 360). In line with this view that "bad" governance had caused the crisis in Asia, Michel Camdessus, representing the IMF and Washington Consensus, saw the crisis as an opportunity to expand the IMF's "traditional mandate of promoting economic stability" to include "good governance" questions, in addition to promoting a neoliberal agenda that involved privatization, deregulation, and trade liberalization (Jayasuriya 2002: 100).

In Southeast Asia, however, the crisis was not so clear cut. While the crisis did call into question the developmental state model, it also raised important concerns about the neoliberal model of development and world order. Most significantly, for many in Southeast Asia, the crisis stemmed at very least as much, if not more, from the problems of an unfettered, unregulated global economy. While most academic and policymaking elites in East and Southeast Asia acknowledge that there were also important domestic sources to the crisis, most also believe that the crisis they experienced was extreme and that their macroeconomic fundamentals, in the words of Higgott and Phillips, "were not so distorted as to warrant the scale of financial and economic chaos which dominated 1997 and 1998" (2000: 363). Indeed, even among those who have argued for domestic reforms, there is the view that the magnitude of the crisis, at least, was caused by external forces (including collective investor panic) beyond their control and facilitated by the rapidity of modern technology. More than one observer has also made note of the indiscriminate nature of the crisis, hitting various economies "with little regard to the real differences in their economic fundamentals" (Tay *et al.* 2001: 208).

Thus, it was premature to conclude, as many Western commentators did, that the crisis marked the triumph of neoliberalism and the demise of the developmental state. Quite the contrary, in fact. Far from heralding the triumph of neoliberal development, the crisis instead "sorely tested" the commitment of more than one government to an open economy. After all, these economies were relatively open, even "very open," by international standards (Beeson 2000: 342). As Beeson observes, "two of the most unambiguous features of the crisis in Southeast Asia were that the meltdown 'followed close on the heels of programmes of far reaching financial liberalization,' and that the crisis 'without exception, spared those countries that had retained strong state directions of domestic and international financial institutions and flows'" (2002: 11). Similarly, write Tay *et al.*, "The crisis had made more economies in the region doubt aspects of the outward-oriented, export-led NIE model" (2001: 7).

Not surprisingly, then, Southeast Asian actors found themselves also questioning the appropriateness of the responses being pushed by the US and other GG representatives. Beginning with a list of "questionable judgments" blamed for exacerbating the crisis in affected economies (Sachs 1998), regional actors faulted the IMF for trying to apply universal prescriptions to particular situations and for imposing conditions that many believed exacerbated and prolonged the crisis. IMF prescriptions were also widely seen to be disadvantageous to developing economies and hardest on the very poor in those societies. Even more frustrating for affected economies in Southeast Asia was the fact that they had so little voice in influencing the decisions that directly affected them, a sentiment that was compounded by the general lack of transparency in terms of the IMF's decision-making process. As Stiglitz (2002: A16) observed, the problems with the IMF response extended beyond "bad economics"; they were also about "bad politics." Indeed, "Criticisms were so strong that the Fund itself, notoriously oblivious to them under normal conditions, seemed to feel shaken" (Cardim de Carvalho 2000/1: 236).

Rethinking the RG-GG relationship: ASEAN and APEC

In the end, the crisis above all showed that openness to market forces, without proper regulation, came with important vulnerability. As one observer put it, "The lesson from the 1997–98 crisis is that globalization needs strong governance and institutions" (Yue 2001: 136). However, neither national nor global level arrangements were able to provide the necessary regulation. The state— once the principle political institution regulating exchanges between external and domestic forces—proved inadequate at performing its historical role. Meanwhile, world governance bodies like the IMF offered assistance but with considerable and problematic strings attached. In short, for affected economies in Southeast Asia, the crisis indicted global arrangements as much as it did national ones for their failure to prevent, mitigate, or address the effects of the crisis.

Faced with the limitations of governance arrangements at national and global levels, states looked also to regional-level arrangements for help. However, existing regional governance arrangements like the Association of Southeast

Asian Nations (ASEAN) and Asia-Pacific Economic Forum (APEC) also proved woefully inadequate. Particular attention has been given those organizations' largely ad hoc, ineffectual responses to the crisis, which many observers have attributed to APEC's and ASEAN's characteristically informal, consensual style decision-making processes, long a source of contention between Asian and non-Asian states. However, as Webber argues, if actors considered this the primary failing of APEC and ASEAN, then one would expect the effects of the crisis on various regional arrangements to be similar, and newer arrangements to reflect a more formal institutionalism (Webber 2001). Instead, there continue to be both older and newer arrangements characterized by informal institutionalism. Even more significant, the crisis had notably different effects despite the fact that Southeast Asian (ASEAN), Asian Pacific (APEC), and emerging East Asian (ASEAN Plus Three or APT) arrangements all shared a similar informalism. While ASEAN and APEC clearly suffered some loss of credibility, the ASEAN-Plus-Three process was clearly strengthened by the crisis. The APT process also continues to be informal in its institutionalism.

The crisis also had different effects on APEC and ASEAN. Despite disappointment with both arrangements, ASEAN has generally recovered better than APEC among most Southeast Asian actors. Where there has been important new interest in strengthening and rejuvenating ASEAN, there has been no similar interest among Southeast Asian actors with respect to APEC.[6] These contrasting post-crisis developments point to important differences in how Southeast Asian actors view various arrangements. Of all the East and Southeast Asian regional arrangements, APEC, reflecting the strong influence of US and Australian viewpoints, most represents neoliberal characterizations of regionalism and world order. Despite being original members, however, ASEAN states have had since the beginning particular concerns about APEC, especially about whether APEC would respect the interests and views of its developing-state members and, relatedly, about APEC's larger powers pushing their own agendas (on trade and human rights) on smaller Southeast Asian powers—concerns that nearly prevented APEC from being formed at all (Crone 1993; Blass 1996: A5). Thus, well before the crisis in 1997, APEC as an expression of neoliberal, hegemonic interests had already been contentious, even if the open regionalist rhetoric of the early 1990s mostly obscured underlying tensions. In this sense, the crisis did not create new issues so much as it brought out pre-existing differences, tensions, and grievances. For Southeast Asian economies affected by the crisis, the problem with APEC was not its decision-making process, but rather the fact that members' interests, levels of development, and perspectives were too divergent—a fact confirmed when APEC, under considerable US pressure, supported the IMF and its prescriptions (Webber 2001: 355).

As for ASEAN, the crisis drew attention to important structural and institutional weaknesses. However, ASEAN's poor performance during the crisis has stimulated deep reflection on how to strengthen the organization in ways that the crisis did not do in APEC's case. The main reason for this is that ASEAN is on firmer ideological foundations than APEC. Unlike APEC, ASEAN is a multi-issue, multi-purpose organization. Its raison d'être is not the promotion of a neoliberal regional order, but rather the creation and maintenance of peaceful regional relations in Southeast Asia towards the goals of national and regional self-determination. Moreover, on such questions of intra-regional relations, members have generally felt that ASEAN has a proven track record in ways that APEC does not. Consequently, while ASEAN, like APEC, has lost important credibility due to its perceived ineffectual response to 1997–9 developments, the crisis has not delegitimated ASEAN—at least among ASEAN states—the same way that it has APEC. Facilitating trade and economic liberalization is only one function of ASEAN and, until the early 1990s, not even a main one.

These contrasting reactions suggest that the larger issue as regards Southeast Asia's post-crisis regionalism is not their informal institutionalism and instead how closely each is aligned with global interests. Consequently, while East and Southeast Asian actors reached important conclusions about the limitations of APEC and ASEAN, their criticisms of the two regional bodies were not the same. In ASEAN's case, the crisis highlighted well the divergence of interests, priorities, and world views between the United States and the ASEAN states, while the problematic international response demonstrated all too clearly that ASEAN was simply too small and too unimportant to have much impact on the policies made by GG institutions like the IMF. At the same time, despite this general consensus as to ASEAN's structural limitations, the organization also remains politically relevant and important to members as evidenced by new interest and efforts to rejuvenate and strengthen the organization.

By contrast, in APEC's case, Southeast Asian members tended to see the crisis as confirmation of the deep tensions in APEC, especially between APEC's more advanced and less advanced members. As a result, there has not been a similar kind of effort to strengthen APEC on the part of Southeast Asian members. Put another way, as problems associated with the global and US response to the crisis grew, it became ever more clear that Southeast Asia needed something more than ASEAN, but that APEC was too dominated by advanced economies like the United States and consequently offered neither assistance in managing the global integration process nor protection from problematic global forces.

In short, the 1997–9 Asian financial crisis revealed the clear inadequacies of existing governance arrangements at all major levels of governance—national, regional, and global—to avert or minimize the economic and human costs of globalization. Thus, it should also be no surprise, given such assessments, that the crisis should heighten interest in alternative governance arrangements. It is in this context that interest in East Asian cooperation was renewed and strengthened as a regional platform that would allow states to better negotiate the global economy and external pressures to conform.

East Asia redux and the APT process

In the final analysis, the crisis shifted the center of the debate on regionalism in Southeast Asia. Consequently, in contrast to the early 1990s when Southeast

Asian states found an EAEG-type regionalism too contentious and too confrontational, interest in an EAEG-type arrangement has grown since the 1997–9 financial crisis, and there now appears to be growing consensus about the necessity, even inevitability, of East Asia—or at least, some forms of regional cooperation along East Asian lines (East Asia Vision Group 2001; East Asia Study Group 2002).

In large part, the heightened interest is correspondent with heightened concerns about the global economy, many of which Mahathir had identified five years earlier. But also, as discussed, Mahathir's criticisms of the global financial architecture have resonated in Southeast Asia far more than has been given credit by some Western policymakers. By calling attention to the problems of neoliberalism—how vulnerable individual economies and particular populations were to global economic forces, as well as how powerless or, at the very least, ill-equipped and extremely constrained Southeast Asia states were in trying to respond to them—the financial crisis simply brought those concerns out from the cover of ASEAN's "open regionalism" rhetoric.

Evidence that "East Asia" was emerging as an important response to problems of existing global arrangements appeared as early as 1997. That year, Japan—a mostly ambivalent player in the drama of East Asian regionalism—proposed the creation of an Asian Monetary Fund (AMF), "a regional facility that would be prepared to disburse pre-committed emergency funds more promptly than the resource-strapped IMF" (Rapkin 2001: 375). As an attempt at "regional self help," the AMF was a regional response to the widespread "regional dissatisfaction both with global multilateral solutions and with the US reaction" (Rapkin 2001: 375; Chang and Rajan 1999: 273). Significantly, the AMF proposal received wide support from regional economies, receiving as much as $100 billion in contributions (Chang and Rajan 1999: 273). Though successfully "blocked" by the hegemonic interests and power of the United States, the basic idea of East Asian monetary cooperation remains and persists as an important feature of the emergent East Asian regionalism as evidenced by regional swap agreements through the Chiangmai Initiative (Rapkin 2001; Chirathivat 2001: 12; Narine 2002).

Most illustrative of the East Asian trend is the ASEAN Plus Three (ASEAN Plus China, Japan, Korea—APT) framework. Though it may trace its institutional origins to the Asia-Europe meetings (ASEM), which first met in 1996, its ideational background is more accurately traced to the EAEG. Both were conceived as a response to the problems of hegemonic global arrangements. Both the EAEG and the APT framework also reflect a similar activist vision—that is, a vision of East Asia as a "third pillar" of the post-Cold War economy alongside North America and Europe. The APT process did precede the 1997–9 financial crisis (the first "informal" meeting of APT leaders took place in 1997 but plans had been under way before the depth of the crisis was known); however, what the crisis did was to make the APT process now of vital interest.

Thus, *East Asian* regionalism has emerged as an important site of contestation about the rules and ordering principles of neoliberal GG. Though this was far from a new idea—"East Asia," as discussed, had been debated once before in the early 1990s— "East Asia" significantly did not become a *persuasive* idea until after the 1997–9 crisis. The crisis thus marked an important juncture in an ongoing debate about "East Asia." In particular, the 1997–9 crisis had an important effect on how elites conceived regional arrangements in relation to global ones. While open regionalism remains relevant, it is relevant mostly in terms of necessity, the desire not to cut off trade lifelines to North America and Western Europe. Steps towards liberalization, as Nesadurai argues in the Malaysian case, "do not [necessarily] signify any ideological or policy shift towards full acceptance of neoliberal norms and practices" (2000: 106; see also Beeson 2000: 341).

Most of all, what the crisis made "painfully obvious" was that even after two decades of tremendous growth, Southeast Asia's economies remained "highly vulnerable to the actions of powerful external political and economic forces" (Beeson 2002: 549). The Asian financial crisis was indeed most dramatic in illustrating Mittelman's point that neoliberalism is "structurally blind to" and "silent about structural inequalities" (Mittelman 205). In such a globalized world where individual states were limited, global institutions inadequate, and the neoliberal foundations of world order and world arrangements increasingly questioned, regionalism today is consequently being rethought. In contrast to the dominant pre-crisis view of regionalism as a complementary, integrationist process, the post-crisis view also sees regional institutions and arrangements as important buffers between individual economies and market forces, and as needed supplements, even potential alternatives, to GG. Philippine President Gloria Macapagal-Arroyo, for example, explained: "Regional and bilateral trade areas … [remain] hubs of open regionalism," but in that the financial crisis demonstrated that the globalized economy was "littered with quicksand," it was "imperative that Southeast Asia expand its cooperation to other areas" (in Lucas 2002).

As one final point, it is worth reflecting on the particular role played by the United States as both primary architect of global arrangements and primary opponent of "East Asia," and how those roles have contributed to Southeast Asia's search for alternative arrangements and interest in forging new regional relations (with Europe, as well as Northeast Asia) independently of US involvement and influence. Both ASEM[7] and the APT process were created at least partly in reaction to US dominance in APEC and the world economy in general. In addition, US opposition to the EAEG and AMF has been typical of a larger pattern in terms of US Asian policy since the late 1980s. The US has desired to reduce its economic and political-security obligations to the East and Southeast Asian region, but has been consistently unwilling to support regionalist arrangements. US opposition to the AMF seemed especially unreasonable to many, especially given its own unwillingness to contribute to the IMF package to Thailand (the first country affected) and the inadequacies of the IMF response. In that the US was also widely perceived to have benefited from Southeast Asia's misfortunes, the financial crisis thus added to the growing feeling that the US was more than willing to sacrifice its old Cold War allies for economic gain if necessary. This sense of being "let down," even "betrayed," by the US especially provides the driving impetus behind current East Asia regionalist efforts. It is largely this failure of US hegemony to live up to its promises (as Arrighi in this volume might also argue) that has catalyzed the search in Southeast Asia for new and different solutions. The 1997–9 Asian financial crisis may not have created "East Asia" or its driving concerns but, in revealing the problems with old relationships and old arrangements, it did make East Asia more necessary and arguments for a different kind of regionalism more compelling.

Conclusion

The significance of 'East Asia' for GG

With the 1997–9 financial crisis as its focus, this chapter has offered a discussion of how one part of the world—Southeast Asia—has viewed regionalism in relation to GG. As discussed above, the financial crisis involved more than economics; it also involved important ideational dynamics—changing ideas about world organizations, the conflict between neoliberal and developmental state ideologies, competing conceptualizations of both regional and global governance—each of which have relevance for GG. The crisis has forced Southeast Asian actors to rethink how national economies will relate to the larger global economy, and "how the region will deal with questions of global integration, global governance and developmental destinies" (Kelly and Olds 1999: 10). In this vein, the crisis's disparate consequences for regional arrangements and organizations in East and Southeast Asia are telling.

Most significant has been a heightened post-crisis interest in regional activities along *East Asian* lines. It is too early to tell yet what long-term significance these arrangements will have or how effective they will be. Nevertheless, the heightened activity in this area since 1997 points to an important dissatisfaction with the way the crisis was managed at the global level. ASEM, ASEAN Plus Three, the AMF proposal, the emergence of a network of overlapping currency "swap" arrangements—were all formed partly to compensate for the inadequacies of global arrangements, and partly as counterpoints to US influence over both bilateral and multilateral arrangements.

To be clear, integrationist interests and themes remain relevant. ASEAN states, in fact, remain very much committed to trade and export-led growth strategies. As Wesley argues, just as international trade and foreign investment had factored large in ASEAN's economic growth, international trade and foreign investment will also factor large in ASEAN's economic recovery (Wesley 1999). At the same time, "What was not accepted," as noted by Milner, "was the proposition that there is incompatibility between deep integration into the international economy and the survival of a considerable range of political institutions" (2003: 289). Equally unacceptable was integration without a safety net. Chirathivat and Murshed describe the post-crisis shift in thinking especially well: "The debate in the region is no longer focused on whether countries should seek to integrate into the global economy. But rather the question now relates to the appropriate terms on which that integration should take place" (2001: 2; see also Katzenstein 1996: 126). Again, we need to move away from the old dichotomy of building blocks versus stumbling blocks, a dichotomy that *assumes* the underlying normative foundations of the existing global order to be both good and universal, as well as static.

Southeast Asian states' different conclusions about different regional arrangement also speak to an important fact that is all too often unacknowledged and ignored by the "new regionalism" literature, and that is that regionalisms come in a variety of forms and they can have different purposes. In this case, APEC, ASEAN, and APT represent not only different geographic conceptualizations, but also different ideological conceptualizations of region that are not always compatible. Each also has a different relationship with the global neoliberal regime, which has affected post-crisis assessments and directions of each. Again regionalisms are not all of one kind; it should therefore be no surprise that "the impact of the Asian financial crisis on regional integration has been extremely contradictory" (Webber 2001: 345).

In short, if East Asian regionalism is emerging as an important site of contestation to certain hegemonic ideas and arrangements, it is because states and actors in that region find problematic certain patterns of their relations with the world. Even *despite* strong integrationist trends—or at least strong interests compelling and forcing integration—the emergence of East Asia points to underlying tensions and significant faultlines in the global system. While East Asian regionalist activity is a response to the perceived limitations of individual states and is thus consistent with much of the GG literature, it is also importantly a reaction to growing dissatisfactions with GG processes and, in this respect, it draws attention to notable tensions in the regional–global relationship. It should also be clear from the above discussion that themes of regional resistance and contestation are not new but rather part of a long and ongoing debate about GG. The 1997–9 financial crisis did not create East Asia so much as it made more relevant and necessary the idea of regionalism as buffer, supplement, even potential alternative, to GG arrangements. Post-crisis East Asian RG has gained ground in the ongoing Southeast Asian dialogue on regionalism largely *in reaction* to both the inadequacies of the global response and the perceived biases of existing arrangements. It is also a form of insurance should regional and global (read US) interests diverge even more.

What RG tells us about structure, process, and change in GG

Though the details above regard a specific case, the themes it raises are not unique. Latin America offers what may be the closest parallel in the sense that the US has had an especially strong economic and political presence in both regions. The debates between NAFTA and Mercosur ongoing in Latin America, for example, mirror many of the debates on the merits of APEC versus various East Asia proposals. Active US opposition to more autonomous regional initiatives has also influenced how each region has attempted to navigate the national–regional–global nexus (Tulchin *et al.* 1998; Bulmer-Thomas and Dunkerley 1999; Patomeki and Teivainen 2002).

Nevertheless, regionalist activities in periphery regions all must confront the underlying patterns of hegemony and domination that define interactions between the Global South and Global North. At the very least, many in both Latin America and Africa share Southeast Asia's general predicament and concerns about GG. Unlike GG proponents, these regions all have important questions about GG's interests and agenda, and are frustrated by what they see to be their marginalized voice. Writes Nkiwame on the subject of neoliberalism's appropriateness for African development, for example: "There is no firm consensus on the effects of liberal market reforms in Africa, but a powerful and growing African perspective argues that these reforms have not only failed to improve the African condition, they have actually worsened it" (2001: 283).

At the same time, what may make this particular case especially notable is that even for a relatively successful region like Southeast Asia, its future, like its past, remain constrained in important ways by the structural inequalities and hegemonic interests that underlie so-called global norms and global institutions. Thus, it seems equally important to acknowledge that deeper, transformative change can be a very constrained process. This is not to say that changes in the periphery cannot have ripple effects that will have consequences for the larger GG system, but it is nevertheless true that resistance is often hard, especially in a world defined by entrenched interests and ideas. As O'Brien (see next chapter) argues in a related vein, structural realities mean that some groups are better able to change their world (and GG) than others. Similarly, Sterling-Folker's point that change will be structurally bounded is a good one that needs to be considered seriously.

But if change at times seems elusive, it is also because with the collapse of the socialist bloc there has not yet emerged a clear set of ideas or practices that can compete with, or offer a persuasive alternative to, the current system based on the ideology of neoliberalism. Herein lies yet another layer of significance in terms of the 1997–9 financial crisis for GG: prior to 1997, economic success made East and Southeast Asia better positioned than most to offer some alternative to dominant ideas and practices. Vocal, confident statesmen like Malaysia's Mahathir and Singapore's Lee Kuan Yew, who could speak the hegemonic language of English and capitalism well, were also instrumental in presenting "Asia" as an alternative. Some will, no doubt, argue that the ideas being propounded by such elites were quite conservative (and at least, state-biased), but the point here is that East and Southeast Asia in the 1990s forced dominant actors to at least engage in some discussion about the priorities and interests of neoliberal global governance. The financial crisis, however, did much to set that dialogue back.

On the other hand, as this chapter's discussion illustrates, the fact that the current system of neoliberal GG is unchallenged may also in the end facilitate its demise. Adaptation is key to survival—but adaptation requires that actors recognize their potential shortcomings. In a situation where competition has been minimal, however, there has been no pressing reason for self-reflection and no driving imperative to change on the parts of actors representing dominant, neoliberal interests. The ensuing rigidity and inability to respond well to new forces and ideas are in part what create opportunity for contestation and challenge today.

As others in this volume also argue, the current system of neoliberal GG contains important contradictions especially with respect to its promises of equality, inclusion, and development. Those contradictions introduce important instabilities into GG foundations, in addition to opening up opportunities for creative agents to press forward alternative ideas and solutions. In this particular case, the 1997–9 Asian financial crisis may have pulled short East Asia's challenge in the early and mid-1990s, but it also compelled those in East and Southeast Asia to seriously rethink the character (and, ultimately, failings) of GG and to regroup based on lessons learned, thus setting the stage for another potential challenge from East Asia in future.

In sum, more attention needs to be paid to regional–global interactions and the ways that RG and GG are co-evolving systems. Southeast Asia's various debates about the form and content of regional activities illustrate especially well that, though neoliberal norms and institutions are certainly global in their reach, they are far from global in the views or interests it represents and reproduces. At the same time, processes of contestation have not left GG unchanged, especially as illustrated by the post-crisis rethinking about the priorities of the International Monetary Fund and World Bank, that is, the so-called Washington Consensus. True, the "post-Washington consensus" has not called for a particularly extensive overhauling of the rules and practices that guide global institutions on questions of development, and many will argue that there is still not enough critical thinking about the normative foundations and assumptions that underlie this system of neoliberal GG. But change is often gradual, and changes—even small changes—can have larger consequences, for example by destabilizing old ideas and practices and by providing new starting points for discussion and debate. In the current hegemonic context, resistance may be particularly hard, but regions will also remain important sites for contestation, resistance, and creative adaptation, as much as integration, making regional systems important sources of change and dynamism in a constantly evolving system of GG.

Notes

1 A distinction should be made between those that characterize recent regional integration efforts as "new regionalism" versus those who identify with a "New Regionalism approach." The first tends to emphasize a homogenizing economic process and market-driven convergence, whereas the latter emphasizes a multidimensional and heterogeneous process involving different kinds of actors. On the first, see, for example, Mansfield and Milner (1999) and on the second, see Hettne, *et al.* 2000. It is the first understanding of new regionalism that has been most prominent in theoretical debates.

2 Though not usually thought of as a "region," the Non-Aligned Movement (NAM) can also be seen as an example of regional resistance and as a product of similar tensions and processes.

3 To be clear, it is not my intent here to assess the viability or effectiveness of particular regional arrangements; rather, my purpose is to explore what the post-crisis dialogue on regionalism says about changing views of GG.
4 First since the pan-Asia movements of the 1950s and 1960s.
5 See Chapters 7 and 8 in Ba (n.d.).
6 APEC has also become less important to Northeast Asian economies like Korea and China.
7 European participants of the ASEM process were similarly motivated.

References

Afrasiabi, K.L. and Pour Jalali, Y. (2001) "The Economic Cooperation Organization: Regionalization in a Competitive Context," *Mediterranean Quarterly*, 12 (4): 62–79.

Anwar, D. (1996) "Regionalism versus Globalism: A Southeast Asian Perspective," *Korean Journal of Defense Analysis*, 18(2): 29–52.

"ASEAN Called on to Widen Zone of Peace Community" (1995) *Jakarta Post*, October 18.

Ba, A. (n.d.) *(Re)Negotiating East and Southeast Asia: Region, Regionalism and the Association of Southeast Asian Nations* (manuscript under review).

Beeson, M. (2000) "Mahathir and the Markets: Globalisation and the Pursuit of Economic Autonomy in Malaysia," *Pacific Affairs*, 73(3): 335–51.

—— (2002) "East Asia and the International Financial Institutions: The Politics of Regional Regulatory Reform," Working Papers Series 32, City University of Hong Kong.

Blass, A. (1996) "Bad Omen for America?" *Nation* (Thailand), March 2, A5.

Boas, M., Marchand, M. and Shaw, T. (1999) "The Weave-world: Regionalisms in the South in the New Millennium," *Third World Quarterly*, 20(5): 1061–70

Bulmer-Thomas, V. and Dunkerley, J. (eds) (1999) *The United States and Latin America: The New Agenda*, Cambridge: Harvard University Press.

Camroux, D. (1994) " 'Looking East' … and Inwards: Internal Factors in Malaysian Foreign Relations During the Mahathir Era, 1981–1994," Griffith University Australia–Asia Working Paper no. 72.

Cardim de Carvalho, F. (2000/1) "The IMF as Crisis Manager: An Assessment of the Strategy in Asia and of its Criticisms," *Journal of Post-Keynesian Economics*, 23(2): 235–66.

Chang L. and Rajan, R. (1999) "Regional Responses to the Southeast Asian Financial Crisis: A Case of Self Help or No Help?" *Australian Journal of International Affairs*, 53(3): 261–81.

Chirathivat, S. (2001) "Globalization and Openness," United Nations University/World Institute for Development Economics Research Discussion Paper 2001/35.

Crone, D. (1993) "Does Hegemony Matter?" *World Politics* 45 (July): 501–25.

Dent, C. (2002) "Reconciling Multiple Economic Multilateralisms: The Case of Singapore," *Contemporary Southeast Asia*, 24: 146–66.

Fawcett, L. (1995) "Regionalism in Historical Perspective" in *Regionalism in World Politics*, Oxford: Oxford University Press.

Fawcett, L. and Hurrell, A. (1995) "Introduction," in *Regionalism in World Politics*, Oxford: Oxford University Press.

Hettne, B., Inotai, A. and Sunkel, O. (2000) *National Perspectives on the New Regionalism in the South*, New York: St. Martin's Press.

Higgott, R. and Phillips, N. (2000) "Challenging Triumphalism and Convergence: The Limits of Global Liberalization in Asia and Latin America," *Review of International Studies*, 26: 359–79.

Jayasuriya, K. (1994) "Singapore: the Politics of Regional Definition," *Pacific Review*, 7:4.

—— (2001) "Governance, Post-Washington Consensus, and the New Anti-Politics," Working Paper Series No. 2, City University Hong Kong.

—— (2002) "The Rule of Law and Governance in East Asia," in Mark Beeson (ed.), *Reconfiguring East Asia*, London: RoutledgeCurzon.

Katzenstein, P. (1996) "Regionalism in Comparative Perspective," *Cooperation and Conflict*, 31(2): 123–59.

Lardy, N. (1998) *China's Unfinished Revolution*, Washington, DC: Brookings Institution.

Legro, J. (2000) "The Transformation of Policy Ideas," *American Journal of Political Science*, July, 419–32.

Lucas, D. (2002) "GMA Bats for East Asia Free Trade Area," *Business World (Philippines)*, May 22.

Mahathir bin Mohamed (1999) *A New Deal for Asia*, Subang Janya: Pelanduk Publications.

Mansfield, E. and Milner, H. (1999) "The New Wave of Regionalism," *International Organization*, 53: 589–627.

Mittelman, J. (1996) "Rethinking the 'New Regionalism' in the Context of Globalization," *Global Governance*, 2: 189–213.

Narine, S. (2002) "ASEAN in the Aftermath: The Consequences of the East Asian Economic Crisis," *Global Governance*, 8: 179–94.

Narramore, T. (1998) "Communities and Citizens: Identity and Difference," *Citizenship Studies*, 2: 69–88.

Nesadurai, H. (2000) "Malaysia's Response to the Financial Crisis," *Pacific Review*, 13: 73–113.

Nkiwane, T. (2001) "Africa and International Relations: Regional Lessons for a Global Discourse," *International Political Science Review*, 22: 279–90.

Kelly, P. and Olds, K. (1999) "Questions in a Crisis," in K. Olds, P. Dicken, P. Kelly, L. Kong and H. Yeung (eds) *Globalisation and the Asia-Pacific*, London: Routledge.

Nye, J. (1971) *Peace in Parts*, Boston: Little, Brown, and Company.

Patomaki, H. and Teivainen, T. (2002) "Critical Responses to Neoliberal Globalization in the Mercosur Region: Roads Towards Cosmopolitan Democracy?" *Review of International Political Economy*, 9: 37–71.

Phillips, N. (2001) "Regionalist Governance in the New Political Economy of Development: 'Relaunching' the Mercosur," *Third World Quarterly*, 22: 565–83.

Rapkin, D. (2001) "The United States, Japan, and the Power to Block: The APEC and AMF Cases," *Pacific Review*, 14: 373–410.

Rhodes, M. and Higgott, R. (2000) "Introduction: Asian Crises and the Myth of Capitalist 'Convergence,'" *Pacific Review*, 13; 1–19.

Robison, R., Rodan, G. and Hewison, K. (2002) "Transplanting the Regulatory State in Southeast Asia: A Pathology of Rejection," Working Paper No. 33, Southeast Asian Research Centre, City University Hong Kong.

Sachs, J. (1998) "The IMF and the Asian Flu," *American Prospect* (March/April), 16–22.

Sanchez Bajo, C. (1999) "The European Union and Mercosur: A Case of Inter-regionalism," *Third World Quarterly*, 20: 927–41.

Siazon, D. (1995) "The Emergence of Geoeconomics and Its Impact on Regional Security," *Kasarinian (Philippines)*, 10: 3 (First Quarter).

Smith, E. and Weiss, T. (1997) "UN Task-sharing: Towards or Away from Global Governance?" *Third World Quarterly*, 18: 595–619.

Soesastro, H. (1997) "Challenges to AFTA in the 21st Century," in H. Soesastro (ed.), *One Southeast Asia*, Jakarta: CSIS.

Solingen, S. (1999) "ASEAN: Quo Vadis? Domestic Coalitions and Regional Coopera-tion," *Contemporary Southeast Asia*, 21: 30–53.

Stiglitz, J. (2002) "Globalism's Discontents," *American Prospect*, 13: 16–22.

Tay, S., Estanislao, J. and Soesastro, H. (eds) (2001) *Reinventing ASEAN*, Singapore: ISEAS.

Taylor, I. (2003) "Globalization and Regionalization in Africa: Reactions to Attempts at Neo-liberal Regionalism," *Review of International Political Economy*, 10: 310–30.

Tulchin, J., Aravena, F.R. and Espach, R.H. (eds) (1998) *Strategic Balance and Confidence-building Measures in the Americas*, Washington, DC: Woodrow Wilson Press.

Väyrynen, R. (2003) "Regionalism: Old and New", *International Studies Review*, 5: 25–51.

Webber, D. (2001) "Two Funerals and a Wedding? The Ups and Downs of Regionalism in East Asia and the Asia-Pacific after the Asian Crisis," *Pacific Review*, 14: 339–72.

World Trade Organization (2002) *Annual Report*, Geneva: WTO.

Zoellick, R. (2002) "Unleashing the Trade Winds: A Building Block Approach," *Economist* (7–13 December).

12 Global civil society and global governance

Robert O'Brien

Introduction

Over recent years there has been a diverse and growing literature examining the activity of non-state actors in international relations. Academics have used a variety of approaches and terms to capture and label this activity. Prominent usages include: international society (Peterson 1992), international civil society (Colás 2002), transnational relations (Keohane and Nye 1972; Risse-Kappen 1995), transnational social movements (Smith *et al.* 1997; Khagram *et al.* 2002), NGOs (Nelson 1995; Charnovitz 1997), global civil society (Lipschutz 1992; Scholte 2000; Keane 2003), global social-change organizations (Gale 1998), global society (Shaw 1994), global social movements (O'Brien *et al.*, 2000), transnational-advocacy networks (Keck and Sikkink 1998), and world civic politics (Wapner 1995). Each of these terms signifies a different set of assumptions about the object under study and the relationship of that object to the international system. The question is whether this wide-ranging body of scholarship has anything significant to tell us about the concept of global governance (GG).

This chapter combines elements from some of the above-mentioned academic studies with recent civic-association activity and groups them under the title of "global civil society" (GCS). It argues that insights from this field can contribute to a distinctive understanding of GG. Although there is no single GCS perspective, work in this field is likely to highlight particular aspects of the structure and process of GG. In terms of structure one sees a single coherent system of rule that is composed of multiple disaggregated rule systems. It is a world order of uneven regulation with varying levels of intervention and enforcement depending upon the issue area or geographic location. It is characterized by hierarchy and inequality. In terms of process one sees a series of institutions created, sustained, and transformed by ongoing and contested interaction between state, corporate, and civic actors. Indeed, a proper discussion of *global* governance requires sustained attention to each of these three types of actors. While most international-relations approaches to GG highlight the state, fewer give adequate attention to the corporation or civic associations.

The argument begins by justifying the particular choice of GCS as a conceptual umbrella for a number of different approaches. This is accomplished by offering an overview of the GCS concept including some of the objections to its use. A definition is put forward and the relationship between GCS and globalization/GG is highlighted. The second part of the chapter argues that GCS is significant for GG by providing some empirical examples. The third section develops the implications GCS work has for key terms/concepts used in theorizing GG. These terms are GG, the state, the corporation, agency, power, and community. The conclusion of the chapter identifies the consistencies and contradictions between the position outlined here and other contributions to this volume and different theoretical approaches to GG.

What is global civil society?

As the list of terminology in the first paragraph indicates, there is no ideal term to capture the importance of citizen activity on issues of global scale. Some authors prefer the adjective "transnational" (Florini 2000) or "international" (Colás 2002) to global while others are more comfortable referring to networks than civil society (Johnston and Laxer 2003). The terms "global" and "civil society" excite considerable debate not least because they mean different things to different people. For example, Khilnani points out that the meaning of civil society ranges from an economic sphere free of state intervention to a social sphere which balances state and market to a cultural sphere which is defined by particular modes of behavior (i.e. civility) (Khilnani 2001). Because of its multiple uses and understandings the following section clarifies how and why the chapter is organized around the concept of GCS.

GCS is an arena or space where civic actors attempt to influence the way in which people live their lives around the world. For Scholte, GCS "encompasses civic activity that: (a) addresses transworld issues; (b) involves transborder communication; (c) has a global organization; (d) works on a premise of supraterritorial solidarity" (2000: 180). Groups need only fulfill one of these conditions to be part of GCS. Key to understanding this approach is his view that globalization and the adjective "global" refer to an environment marked by relative deterritorialization. Deterritorialization is a process where social space and territorial coordinates need no longer be synonymous. The compression of time and space fosters social relations that were previously extremely difficult.

GCS is primarily composed of voluntary, non-profit associations. To differentiate GCS actors from profit-seeking non-governmental organizations such as corporations this chapter uses the term "civic associations." The most visible and explicitly political civic associations tend to be those working in high-profile areas such as the environment (Greenpeace, Friends of the Earth) or human rights (Amnesty International). However, there are many other forms of organization. For example, international trade-union bodies such as the International Confederation of Free Trade Unions claim a representative (127 million members), as well as advocacy, role. Religious organizations are also very active. In terms of numbers of formal organizations the bulk of activity takes place in relatively uncontroversial and often apolitical forms such as industry associations and scientific-knowledge organizations (medicine, sciences, communications) (Boli and Thomas 1999: 41). Aggregating visible NGOs with less visible local activity one can point to the emergence of fluid social movements around issues such as development, human rights, labor, peace, and women's issues.

Although there are many groups and specific agendas, most politically active civic associations would describe themselves as pursuing the objectives of equity or social justice. Equity and justice could be sought in respect to gender relations (women's groups), distribution of resources (development groups) quality of life (environmental groups), human security (human rights). There are, of course, differences between members of civil society, just as there are conflicts between states or corporations. Organized labor is challenged by NGOs claiming to speak on behalf of the informal sector. Women's groups in the developing world have an ambivalent and sometimes conflictual relationship with northern feminist groups. Environmentalists seeking thorough changes to the doctrine of economic growth are in conflict with more conservative conservationist groups. Various NGOs claim to speak on behalf of social movements or constituencies, but the plethora of groups and lack of transparency makes it difficult to determine the legitimacy of their claims.

There is little question that at the empirical level something which bears resemblance to the GCS concept exists. Evidence can be gathered by joining 100,000 other people at the World Social Forums in Porto Alegre or monitoring media coverage of the simultaneous world-spanning demonstrations against the US and British plans for war in Iraq in February and March 2003. Yet, on the theoretical level there is considerable skepticism of whether such activity should be characterized under the phrase "global civil society." One could argue that transnational non-state, non-corporate activity is not truly global, often not civil and does not form part of a society. If a person thinks that global implies universal and equal, then transnational civic activity is clearly not global since many people do not or cannot participate in its activities. GCS is dominated by groups from wealthier countries with greater access to resources. However, the notion of deterritorialization outlined above does not contain assumptions either of equality or universality. GCS is constantly in a state of flux and need not have utopian standards of equality applied to it before it can be said to exist.

It is true that the space identified as GCS contains actors that are not very civil. This is a reflection of the fact that the global arena is not identical to its domestic counterpart. Global space has more limited political authority and a relative lack of policing institutions. Although it goes against the grain of our understanding of domestic civil society, there are groups in GCS that lack civility. Civility, or the agreement to manage interaction according to a common set of rules and without recourse to violence, is a hallmark of domestic notions of civil society. Those who choose not to be bound by such rules are considered to be outside the bounds of civil society. In the global system there is less agreement about common rules and much less enforcement than in most national societies. As a result, there is a greater space for uncivil groups to operate in the GCS space. Examples include organized crime, violent ethnic nationalists, and terror organizations. They are shunned by the majority of civic associations, but they exist in a similar space.

The GCS arena is also occupied by several actors which do not share the characteristics of being non-profit voluntary equity-seeking civic associations. One prominent group is composed of business associations. These associations seek to create an environment where corporations can maximize profits. A prominent example is the International Chamber of Commerce. In addition to lobbying state and civil-society actors it attempts to foster an environment which encourages self-regulation (Schneider 2000).

Another objection to the concept is that it is misleading because civil society and social movements are formed in relation to particular states. From this perspective civil-society groups can only exist in relationship to their states. Since there is no global state, there can hardly be a GCS or global social movements (Germain and Kenney 1998).

The general point that there is no global state is, of course, correct. However, there certainly are GG structures which regulate state, corporate, and social activity on a world-wide basis (Hewson and Sinclair 1999). Tarrow, who is skeptical of GCS, does acknowledge that transnational social movements are most likely to grow in those areas governed by international institutions (Tarrow 2000). Institutions such as the IMF, World Bank and WTO are indeed increasingly the target of mobilization that has significant deterritorialized attributes (O'Brien *et al.* 2000). The absence of a global state does not preclude the presence of a GCS or global social movements.

To a great extent this debate about transnational or global, as well as the boundaries of community and identity, arises from differences in analytic focus. One set of scholars, critical of the GCS begins from the state and domestic politics and moves out into the international system. For them, domestic politics is the norm against which other forms should be evaluated. Thus, a GCS must have the same characteristics as a national civil society. A global social movement must have the same characteristics as a national social movement. A second set of scholars begins with a systemic view and adds the adjective "global" to new phenomena that resemble (but are not identical to) national concepts. The increasing role of non-corporate, non-state activity in the international system is thus labeled GCS. The state-out view risks making the criteria for GCS so rigid that it is defined out of existence. The system-in view risks conflating so many forms of activity that probing analysis of the phenomenon becomes difficult and significant differences are ignored.

The differences in view between those starting from a unit or state analysis incorporating transnational relations and those beginning from a systemic analysis and utilizing global relations are captured in Figure 12.1. The dark squares represent the state and smaller shaded squares represent civil society within the state. In the transnational model, groups from one society make connections with a group from another society. This is represented by dark arrows. In the

Transnational Relations

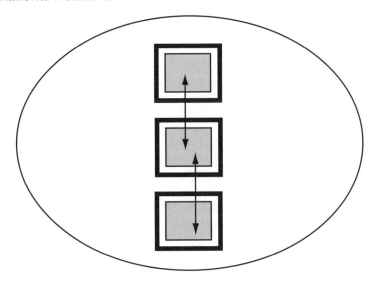

Global Relations

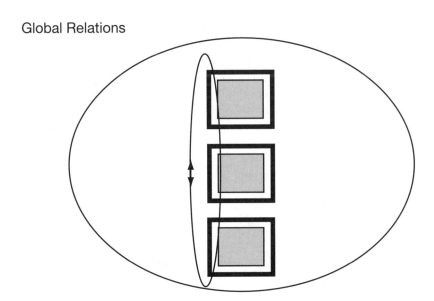

Figure 12.1 Transnational vs. Global Relations

global society model, relations cut across states and intersect in deterritorialized space. This is represented by the stretched oval and small two-way arrows. In the global model, sections of domestic society form a new grouping while remaining tied into the national groupings.

Despite these differences in terminology and definition it is possible to identify a common concern among analysts with the transnational continental-spanning activity of civic actors and their impact upon the global or international system.

The importance of GCS

A growing body of empirical and theoretical literature argues that GCS makes a difference to the process and content of GG. GCS groups contribute to GG by proposing alternative norms and mobilizing political support and opposition to existing governance structures. Civic associations' efforts to propagate alternative norms to those of state power and economic liberalism have probably received the most attention in academic literature (Khagram *et al.* 2002). In the 1980s and 1990s prominent civic actors played the role of unofficial opposition to GG agencies and interstate agreements. They stressed an agenda that put citizen autonomy and security at the center of governance questions. Peace groups have opposed particular weapons systems and military strategies. The campaign to ban the production and use of landmines is the most recent example (Cameron *et al.* 1998). Development, women's, environmental, and labor groups have opposed the dominance of liberal policies emanating from international economic institutions (O'Brien *et al.* 2000). Street protests against the WTO, IMF and World Bank have been the most visible aspect of this activity, but there is considerable effort expended upon policy and implementation work as well. Citizen action across state borders to overcome the anti-democratic actions of their own states has been described as "democratic internationalism" (Gilbert 1999).

Although the precise nature of GCS is debatable, it is less contentious that global civic actors are having an influence on world politics and interstate relations. International NGOs seeking social transformation operate on a number of levels to influence GG—they create and activate global networks, participate in multilateral arenas, facilitate interstate cooperation, act within states to influence policy and enhance public participation (Alger 1997). Even in areas often considered to be the sole domain of states such as international security, civil society groups can play a role in shaping the agenda and contributing to policy change (Price 1998).

At the minimum we can say that civic actors increasingly serve a role as disseminators of information, mobilizers of public opinion, articulators of dissent and protest. Ignoring their role, as the architects of the Multilateral Agreement on Investment (MAI) did, is likely to lead to governance breakdown (Mayne and Picciotto 1999). Civic associations can be instrumental in undermining the legitimacy of international organizations, even as states continue to support them. Civic associations are not the final decision-makers in GG, but they can have a significant role in influencing its content.

The implications of GCS

This section of the chapter outlines the implications of GCS studies for an understanding of key concepts and terms used in international relations discussions about GG. These terms are: GG, continuity and change, the state, the corporation, agency, power, and community. Attention to GCS results in complicating basic concepts and stressing elements that other perspectives treat lightly.

GG

An orthodox realist view of international relations would view the term "global governance" as an oxymoron (Gilpin 2002). However, GG in the sense of the creation and maintenance of rules and norms on a multicontinental scale (Nye and Donahue 2000: 2) certainly exists in the world of transnational civic associations. Rule makers aspire to create arrangements that will influence behavior around the world and civic associations do their utmost to shape the content of those rules. One can think of trade law at the WTO, conditions for IMF lending, creditworthiness criteria used by private bond-rating agencies, corporate codes of conduct, and social labeling as mechanisms designed to simultaneously shape behavior in many different countries.

The form and content of the governance varies considerably across issue and geographic areas. For example, global economic regulation benefits from elaborate and relatively powerful international institutions while social regulation is serviced by much more modest arrangements (O'Brien 2002). Thus, the intellectual-property rights of corporations are protected by the dispute-settlement mechanism of the WTO, but core labor standards are governed by the International Labour Organization (ILO) which must rely on the power of exhortation. Within the same broad issue area governance can vary widely depending upon the specific geographic location of the activity under question. For example, force was used to halt Serbian violations of human rights in Kosovo, but no such action took place to prevent genocide in Rwanda.

Some might be tempted to see such variance in governance as an indication of non-governance, but this is a mistake. As was argued in debates over the nature of power and democracy in the 1960s, non-decision making and the ability to keep items off the political agenda is an exercise of power (Bachrach and Baratz 1962). Non-action is a choice and a form of governance. The decision not to intervene militarily in a particular part of the world or not to create institutions with enforcement powers in particular issue areas is as much a form of governing as more interventionist initiatives. Uneven regulation may be a source of concern and injustice, but it is still a form of governance. It is only if one makes the normative connection between governance and goodness that poor outcomes are interpreted as a lack of governing or exercise of power.

What are the elements that make the present form of world order unique enough to deserve a term such as GG? Similar to other historical eras there are attempts to order international relations on a world-spanning scale, but the form and methods are quite distinct. One key element is the existence of over a hundred nominally sovereign states which contrasts with the nineteenth-century pattern of Western imperialism. The first stop for groups wishing to influence GG is with their own state which possesses legal sovereignty even if it lacks autonomy from outside forces. A second key element is the expansion in the number and influence of inter-state organizations. International organizations act as forums for debate and cooperation as well as sites of regulation of GG. In some cases, such as the international financial institutions (IFIs), the decisions and operation of these organizations have a significant impact upon living conditions. A third element is the rise of the transnational corporation (TNC) and the significance of foreign direct investment in economic growth. TNCs are significant actors in world politics and are actively engaged by states and the public. A final element is the subject of this chapter: the growth and mobilization of civic associations. All of these four elements have historical antecedents, but their maturation and combination are unprecedented. This unique constellation of actors leads to discussion of GG rather than international relations, world order or world society (Hewson and Sinclair 1999).

Continuity and change

The term "global civil society" raises the issue of continuity and change. One objection to the use of the term "global" whether it be in the context of globalization, GG or global economy is that the phenomenon is not particularly new or distinctive. Those working with the terms often reply that the quality of relations has changed to such an extent that the adjective "global" accurately reflects new or intensified relationships sufficiently different from their predecessors to warrant the use of a new term.

GCS connotes a qualitatively different set of social relations that coincided with the advent of information technology, mass communication, and relatively cheap rapid intercontinental travel. A *global* civil society requires awareness of the condition of people far removed from oneself. The development of a global awareness which diffused through mass societies was impossible before mass communication and its broadcast through television and the internet. As opposed to more limited transnational activity, GCS awaited technical innovation which brought large numbers of non-elite people in contact with each other.

In the same way that modern transnational corporations have predecessors in the British East India Company, GCS has predecessors in the activity of citizens groups dating back over two hundred years. Charnovitz traces the evolution of modern NGOs to the late eighteenth-century campaign against the slave trade and nineteenth-century peace societies (Charnovitz 1997: 191–3). Worker internationalism was first actively promoted in the 1860s by Karl Marx and the First International (Nimitz 2002). It is the extent rather than the existence that is new.

The GCS concept points to an intensification of deterritorialized social relations in the same way that globalization captures the unprecedented rapid compression of space and time characteristic of the late twentieth and early twenty-first centuries. Indeed one of the explanations for the need for a new GG vocabulary is this extension of transnational civic activity in the global realm (Hewson and Sinclair 1999).

The state

The state that civic associations encounter is not the rational-actor model deployed in a great deal of international-relations theory. The state is fragmented, bureaucratic, elitist and firmly caught in a broad web of state–society relations. Different parts of the state act as allies and opponents to various civic associations over a variety of issues. The national interest is not given, but is the subject of intense debate and conflict. National interest may be defined differently by various state agencies and contradictory policies may be followed by various branches of government. Once the national interest is defined, it is subject to revision and remains contested whether it is indeed the "national" interest. Two examples may illustrate the point.

The General Agreement on Trade in Services (GATS) is an arrangement for negotiating and promoting liberalization of trade in services. It has sparked considerable concern amongst some civic associations that the agreement will undermine government provision of public services by entrenching corporate rights (Jackson and Sanger 2003). While finance and trade ministries are unlikely to be sympathetic to civic concern about GATS, health, environment, education, and development ministries are more fruitful targets for lobbying and cooperation. Civic mobilization and engagement with "opposition" ministries may restrict the negotiating room of the dominant ministries and curtail the ambition of reregulation the services sector.

The events surrounding the Anglo-American war in Iraq in 2003 are another example of bureaucratic division and infighting that can be of advantage to civic associations. The apparent split between the intelligence community and the Prime Minister's office in the UK and between the CIA, State Department, Pentagon, and Oval Office in the United States allowed anti-war campaigners to strengthen their case and accuse government leaders of deception.

Rather than viewing the state as a neutral arbitrator of domestic society or a preference aggregator, civil-society experiences suggested states are very much shaped and influenced by the societies with which they interact. This implies both that elements of the state may be used against each other and that there will be tremendous policy and process variation between states. In comparative politics Migdal calls this a "state-in-society" approach and it is a more useful starting point than state-centric rational-actor models of GG (Migdal 2001).

The corporation

Civil-society studies often draw attention to the significant role of corporate activity for two reasons. First, associations of corporations are active and successful participants in GCS influencing other associations and state policy.

Second, many corporations and corporate associations exercise forms of governance, or private authority, which become the target of civic actors.

Corporations are active participants in the public civic debate over global
commercial regulation. One method of communicating with the public is through
advertising. For example, automobile company advertising uses pristine natural
environments to showcase polluting SUVs and mini-vans, encouraging consumers
to believe that buying such vehicles actually demonstrates their love of nature.
Pharmaceutical companies trumpet their contribution to public health in an effort
to defend patent rights. Corporations engaged in making genetically modified food
pledge to feed the world in an attempt to avoid regulation and turn the tide of
public option in their favor. The oil and gas industry buys advertisements in newspapers warning of the cost to consumers of ratifying the Kyoto Protocol.

In addition to participating in public discourse business groups take advantage of privileged access to decision makers at the national and global level.
Their efforts at lobbying for change have, in some cases, been extremely
successful. A striking example is provided by the success of several large US
corporations in inserting protection of intellectual property rights (IPRs) into the
remit of the World Trade Organization (WTO) (Sell 1999). This initiative
arguably runs counter to the interest of most developing countries and has little
to do with free trade. Yet, a corporate association was able to convince the US
government that IPR protection was in the national interest and it eventually
became global regulation. The success of this protection of corporate property
rights has been in stark contrast with the lack of enforceable labor rights protection in international trade agreements.

Corporations have moved beyond advocacy and lobbying to actually create
their own governance mechanisms through the provision of private authority.
Private authority exists where firms exercise decision-making power over a
particular issue area and this activity is viewed as legitimate. Cutler *et al.* have
identified six mechanisms for the exercise of private authority: industry norms;
coordination service firms (e.g. bond rating); production alliances; cartels; business associations; and private regimes (Cutler *et al.* 1999). They argue that private
firms are increasingly exercising authority in particular issue areas in the global
economy. Studies of the telecommunications industry, insurance business,
accountancy, and cartels supports the notion of private authority (Strange 1996).

Some civic associations have responded to the rise of private authority by
taking their campaigns directly to individual corporations. Decisions about
production locations and processes contribute to GG by reinforcing, challenging
or creating norms and rules. For example, divestment in apartheid-era South
Africa bolstered the norm of racial equality before the law. Investing in countries
which suppress labor unions challenges ILO norms and puts competitive pressure on other corporations to organize their production to take advantage of
artificially lower wages. The explosive growth in corporate codes of conduct as a
form of GG is a response to this civic–corporate conflict (Pearson and Seyfang
2001). In areas where state regulation lags or is absent governance will be
achieved by other means.

Civil-society work suggests that corporations are key actors for understanding GG. Whether it is individual corporate investment decisions, the lobbying of states, international organizations and citizens or the exercise of private authority, corporations are a significant part of the GG puzzle.

Agency

As indicated above, the state and the corporation are key actors in the civil-society world. However, civil-society studies also locate agency in social groups outside of and behind these entities. By definition, civil-society studies see civic actors as playing a noteworthy role in influencing GG. They also view social groups as being influential in setting the policy agenda of states and influencing corporate behavior.

This approach of identifying particular social groups as drivers of corporate, state, and civic behavior has two advantages. It allows increased attention to the distributional consequences of GG and it can serve as a better guide to political faultlines and conflicts. To use an example mentioned in other parts of this chapter, one can look at the entrenching of IPRs in the WTO. Conventionally this might be analyzed as a matter of inter-state bargaining where the US was able to exploit power advantages over other states or was able to convince other states it was in their mutual interest. Paying attention to the social forces supporting and later opposing the initiative as it plays out in drug-patent laws, one sees a conflict of interest between relatively wealthy shareholders and managers of a particular group of multinationals and poor people suffering from diseases such as HIV/AIDS. The stark contrast of power, wealth, and health between the groups has allowed civic mobilization to make some progress in challenging and undermining this particular inter-state agreement (Hoen 2001).

The extension of agency to social groups also allows for a reconsideration of how power is exercised in GG.

Power

GCS expands the understanding of power by adding a third dimension to international relations analysis. The first and most common approach to power has been to focus upon the ability of one state to force another state to bend to its will. For example, during the summer of 2003 the United States used its economic might to convince several small Latin American states that it is in their interest to send troops to assist with the occupation of Iraq even though this goes against their support of the United Nations (Sanchez 2003).

A second approach has been to consider notions of structural power where key actors are able to exercise influence by the virtue of operating in a system where the rules are biased towards those actors. The possessor of structural power "is able to change the range of choices open to others, without apparently putting pressure directly on them to take one decision or to make one choice rather than another" (Strange 1988: 31). This form of power is perhaps most evident in the impact of the globalization of finance on the balance of power between capital and labor. Increased capital mobility raises the costs of particular policies and provides incentives for other forms of action (Gill and Law 1993).

GCS studies do not deny these forms of power, but suggest that there are other forms as well. As nationally based social-movement studies have indicated, there is also power in movement (Tarrow 1998). Civic associations can mobilize members to either contest ideas about how the world should operate or directly disrupt the functioning of institutions and policy programs. For example, a citizen movement against the MAI succeeded in raising the profile of this formerly obscure negotiation to such a level that it became a prominent issue in several states, greatly complicating its negotiation. More direct social movement protests have been used against meetings of the WTO and IFIs. In other cases spontaneous protests against structural adjustment programs, or "IMF riots," can result in program changes.

In the short term, civic protest has the power to block, frustrate, and delay GG initiatives such as particular forms of trade regulations or financial restructuring. In the longer term, civic activity in shaping ideas of common sense and the structure of what is considered acceptable practice is likely to be more decisive. For example, while protest against the WTO and IFIs continues, the intellectual counter-attack against neoliberal policies is being institutionalized in the creation of the World Social Forum (www.forumsocialmundial.org). The annual WSF meetings and a proliferation of regional social forums are designed to support an alternative set of ordering principles to guide GG.

Community

GCS studies indicate that the national community is not the only significant grouping of people in the global system. National identities and nationalism persist, but there are times when people can work together across borders in internationalist or globalist projects.

One prominent example in international-relations literature is that of epistemic communities. Haas defined an epistemic community as "a network of professionals with recognized expertise and competence in a particular domain and an authoritative claim to policy-relevant knowledge within that domain or issue-area" (Haas 1992: 3). Epistemic or knowledge communities can form across borders and provide expert policy advice to state leaders in various countries. Although the environmental field has been the most prominent example of epistemic communities influencing policy, the term can also be applied to other areas such as the work of liberal economists (O'Brien 1995).

A more critical approach to GG notes the presence of globalizing elites (Gill 2003) which agree on a broad common project of globalizing the economies of their respective states. It is not unusual for liberal economists to suggest that the goal of trade liberalization is to raise the welfare of the global community rather than simply improve the position of any particular state or economy. Americans should phase out cotton subsidies not just because it is an inefficient practice, but because it will improve the welfare of people engaged in the cotton industry in developing countries.

Global communities have formed across a wide range of issues such as human rights, human security, development, environmental protection, gender equality, labor conditions, and economic deregulation. These identities sometimes challenge and sometimes reinforce national and regional identities and communities. The extent and significance of each community is the subject of investigation.

GCS and other approaches to GG

This conclusion highlights the similarities and differences between the vast and varied literature on what has been called here "global civil society" and the other contributions and perspectives in this collection of essays. The discussion is organized around the book's theme of structure and process in GG.

On the subject of the structure of GG there are two significant issues that highlight the similarities and differences between civil society work and other studies. The first issue is the question of the particularity of GG and the second is composition of the actors that need to be studied to understand GG.

On the issue of the particularity of existing GG, several of the approaches in this book take a long historical view and tend to regard the existing era as a slight modification of earlier systems of international relations. This is certainly true of the English school (Dunne), historical materialist (Overbeek), and world system (Arrighi) contributions. On the other hand, Rosenau's fragmegration analysis suggests that the world has changed so considerably in the past number of decades that few of the earlier certainties hold true. GCS studies suggest that the conservatism of the first group is too limited while the almost postmodern radicalism of the second ignores important continuities of power and inequality. As suggested above, the body of civil society literature suggests there are multiple conflicts, interests, and centers of authority in GG. However, there is also more order and hierarchy than an approach which treats all inputs equally would imply.

Work on GCS highlights the ability of subordinate groups in different parts of the world to interact and communicate. This opens up the possibility, for the first time, of moving towards a form of world order based on principles that would benefit the majority of the world's population (Kitching 2001). Just as the nature of modern states was transformed by national publics mobilized by print media, GG is being implicated by civic mobilization on a global scale facilitated by advances in communications technologies (Deibert 1997). The creation of a more just global order is a difficult and lengthy task, but it can now be seriously contemplated and pursued in a way that was impossible in the era of formal imperialism in the nineteenth century or the nationally focussed era of post-1945 embedded liberalism. Such a perspective has an element of utopianism in that there is a vision and a desire for another world, but it is also informed by a realist assessment of the changing dynamics and locations of power (Cox 1997).

This possibility of deterritorialized communication and solidarity helps to distinguish the present era of GG from other historical modes of world order. Analysis which minimizes the uniqueness of our present era should continue to use more traditional concepts such as international society, hegemonic or world orders which are congruent with their basic assumptions. If GG is to be useful, it must refer to a particular form of world order.

A second issue on the structure of GG is the composition of the range of actors that make up the entity in question. The possibilities extend from those that focus almost exclusively on the state (English school, realist) to those that include class (historical materialist), and capitalism (world system) to a very diverse list of characters including individuals and local governments ("frag-megration"). Civil-society studies sit most comfortably with those theoretical approaches that share a similar ontology. Approaches which view agency as lying with the social forces or groups which drive the policy choices of states, international organizations and corporations, share a similar world view. In this book, Overbeek's chapter on historical materialism is such a perspective. Although not represented in this collection, feminist approaches to GG (Steans 2002) would also view GG in a similar manner. However, reviewing the collection of actors in the civic association world one would need to go beyond single categories of identity and interest such as class, gender, race or species to build up an accurate picture of the contest underway. Post-structuralist contributions might be able to assist in this task.

Moving beyond the importance of social forces and states, civic actors confront another key entity—the corporation. In this volume, Sinclair's study of reputational authority of firms goes some way to moving the activity of corporate actors central to our understanding of governance. This suggests that one approach to the ontology of GG would be to view it as an interaction of inter-state, world economy, and GCS spheres and the dominant actors in those spheres (state, corporation, and civic association). The interaction between states, corporations, and civic associations has variously been labeled as "global corporatism" (Ottaway 2001) and "complex multilateralism' (O'Brien *et al.* 2000). Most of the contributions in this book fail to adequately weigh the significance of corporations in GG.

On the subject of the process of GG one issue that highlights the similarities and differences between civil-society work and other studies is the role of norms and ideas in GG. Several of the perspectives in this collection raise the issue of the significance of norms and ideas in the process of GG. The constructivst turn in international relations is the most fervent advocate of the position that people's ideas about the world help to shape reality. To the vast body of constructivist theory there are two messages from civil-society studies. For the state-centric constructivists such as Wendt (1999), the critique is similar to that aimed at the neoliberals and neorealists. States need to be disaggregated and located in a state–society complex. For the approach represented by Hoffman in this volume there would be agreement that social relations are constructed, but that this construction is grounded in material realities. Not all groups are equally capable of constructing their own reality and power relations must be confronted and dealt with in any attempt to build different socio-political arrangements. Many civil-society studies would thus be more realistic than constructivism by acknowledging the importance of material capabilities and power in the struggle over ideas and norms.

The vast regime literature, represented by Oran Young in this volume, stresses the importance of norms and principles in governing the international system. The study of regimes examines a subset of GG activities, but it is unable to reflect upon the larger governance undertaking. Civic actors often raise questions about the whole package of regimes rather than treating them as separate phenomena. For example, does the totality of regimes favor particular states and social groups? Alternatively, how is a hierarchy established between regimes such as trade and the environment or trade and health? Is there one set of values that dominates across different regimes? The focus upon rules, norms, and principles in one issue area obscures wider patterns of governance and domination.

Civic actors struggle to build cooperation and achieve agreement between parties from very different cultural and material conditions. The challenge of inter-cultural relations and building coalitions between dispersed groups is significant. While Goldstein and Ban's contribution on legal rule systems raises interesting issues of compliance and implementation, the disagreement about basic principles and norms on the global level is considerably greater. Given the different context it becomes interesting to consider what parts of the European (or American) experience may or may not be applicable to questions of GG. Some caution about exporting national or regional models of politics to the global level is warranted.

The conflict between different understandings of Regional Governance and GG is highlighted in Ba's chapter on Southeast Asia. It underlines the degree to which basic terms and meaning are contested. A civil-society study would add that these are not just conflicts between regions or states, but between social forces which cut across borders. Groups of Southeast Asians will be found on various sides of particular issues. Although the desire for greater regional autonomy may be shared, government leaders attending ASEAN meetings have a substantially different agenda from people participating in the Asian Social Forum. The politics can be very complicated and result in the creation of surprising alliances. For example, developmental state elites in Asia seeking to curb speculative capital flows may have their case supported by Western social activists advocating a Tobin Tax to prevent the undermining of state-welfare programs.

There is no single "global civil society" perspective. Indeed, there is considerable theoretical debate about the use of the term. Nevertheless, this chapter has argued that research in the area of GCS or transnational relations does have significant contributions to make to understanding GG. The literature paints a picture of a continent-spanning system of rule which privileges particular social forces, corporate activities, and states. It also documents the considerable activity and some successes of civic associations struggling to influence the composition and content of GG. GCS studies suggest that some of the perspectives on GG outlined in this collection would benefit from re-examining their core assumptions in light of this research.

References

Alger, C.F. (1997) "Transnational Social Movements, World Politics and Global Governance," in Smith, Chatfield and Pagnucco, 260–75.

Bachrach, P. and Baratz, M.S. (1962) "Two Faces of Power," *American Political Science Review* 56: 947–52.

Charnovitz, S. (1997) "Two Centuries of Participation: NGOs and International Governance," *Michigan Journal of International Law* 18, 2: 183–286.

Colás, A. (2002) *International Civil Society*, Cambridge: Polity.

Cox, R.W. (ed.) (1997) *The New Realism: Perspectives on Multilateralism and World Order*, New York: St. Martin's Press.

Diebert, R. (1997) *Parchment, Printing, and Hypermedia: Communication in World Order Transformation*, New York: Columbia University Press.

Florini, A.M. (ed.) (2000) *The Third Force: the Rise of Transnational Civil Society*, Washington: Carnegie Endowment for International Peace.

Gale, F. (1998) "Cave 'Cave! Hic dragones': a Neo-Gramscian Deconstruction and Reconstruction of International Regime Theory," *Review of International Political Economy* 5, 2: 252–83.

Germain, R. and Kenny, M. (1998) "Engaging Gramsci: International Relations Theory and the New Gramscians," *Review of International Studies* 24, 1: 2–21.

Gilbert, A. (1999) *Must Global Politics Constrain Democracy? Great Power Realism, Democratic Peace, and Democratic Internationalism*, Princeton: Princeton University Press.

Gill, S. (2003) "Globalizing Elites and the Emerging World Order," in *Power and Resistance in the New World Order*, New York: Palgrave.

Gill, S. and Law, D. (1993) "Global Hegemony and the Structural Power of Capital," in Gill, S. (ed.) *Gramsci, Historical Materialism and International Relations*, Cambridge: Cambridge University Press, 93–124.

Gilpin, R. (2002) "A Realist Perspective on International Governance," in Held, D. and McGrew, A. (eds) *Governing Globalization: Power, Authority and Global Governance*, Cambridge: Polity, 237–48.

Hass, P. (1992) "Introduction: Epistemic Communities and International Policy Coordination," *International Organization* 47 (Winter), 3.

Hewson, M. and Sinclair, T.J. (1999) "The Emergence of Global Governance Theory," in *Approaches to Global Governance Theory*, Albany: State University of New York, 3–22.

Hoen, E. (2001) "The Declaration on TRIPs and Public Health: A Step in the Right Direction," *BRIDGES* 5, 9: 11.

Keane, J. (2003) *Global Civil Society?* Cambridge: Cambridge University Press.

Keck, M. and Sikkink, K. (1998) *Activists Beyond Borders: Advocacy Networks in International Politics*, Ithaca: Cornell University Press

Keohane, R. and Nye, R. (1972) *Transnational Relations and World Politics*, Cambridge, Mass.: Harvard University Press.

Khagram, S., Riker, J. and Sikkink, K. (eds) (2002) *Restructuring World Politics: Transnational Movements, Networks and Norms*, Minneapolis: University of Minnesota Press.

Khilnani, S. (2001) "The Development of Civil Society", in Kaviraj, S. and Khilnani, S. (eds) *Civil Society: History and Possibilities*, Cambridge: Cambridge University Press.

Kitching, G. (2001) *Seeking Social Justice Through Globalization*, University Park, PA: Pennsylvania State University Press.

Jackson, A. and Sanger, M. (2003). *When Worlds Collide: Implications of International Trade and Investment Agreements for Non-profit Social Services*, Ottawa: Canadian Centre for Policy Alternatives.

Johnston, J. and Laxer, G. (2003) "Solidarity in the Age of Globalization: Lessons from the Anti-MAI and Zapatista Struggles," *Theory and Society* 32: 39–91.

Lipschutz, R.D. (1992) "Reconstructing World Politics: The Emergence of Global Civil Society," *Millennium* 21, 3: 389–420.

Mayne, R. and Picciotto, S. (eds) (1999) *Regulating International Business: Beyond Liberalization*, Basingstoke: Macmillan.

Migdal, J.S. (2001) *State in Society: Studying How States and Societies Transform and Constitute One Another*, Cambridge: Cambridge University Press.

Nelson, P. (1995) *The World Bank and Non-Governmental Organisations*, London: Macmillan.

Nye, J.S. and Donahue, J.D. (eds) (2000) "Introduction", *Governance in a Globalizing World*, Washington: Brookings, 1–44.

O'Brien, R. (1995) "North American Integration and International Relations Theory," *Canadian Journal of Political Science* (December): 693–724.

—— (2002) "Organizational Politics, Multilateral Economic Organizations and Social Policy," *Global Social Policy* 2, 2: 141–62.

O'Brien, R., Goetz, A.M., Scholte, J.A., and Williams, M. (2000) *Contesting Global Governance: Multilateral Economic Institutions and Global Social Movements*, Cambridge: Cambridge University Press.

Ottaway, M. (2001) "Corporatism goes Global: International Organizations, Nongovernmental Organization Networks, and Transnational Business," *Global Governance* 7: 265–92.

Pearson, R. and Seyfang, G. (2001) "New Hope or False Dawn? Voluntary Codes of Conduct, Labour Regulation and Social Policy in a Globalizing World," *Global Social Policy* 1, 1: 49–78.

Peterson, M.J. (1992) "Transnational Activity, International Society and World Politics," *Millennium* 21, 3: 371–89.

Price, R. (1998) "Reversing the Gun Sights: Transnational Civil Society Targets Land Mines," *International Organization* 52, 3: 613–44

Risse-Kappen, T. (ed.) (1995) *Bringing Transnational Relations Back In*, Cambridge: Cambridge University Press.

Sanchez, M. (2003) "Answering Uncle Sam's Call With Soldiers for Iraq," *Washington Post*, 10 July.

Scholte, J.A. (2000) "Global Civil Society," in Woods, N. (ed.) *The Political Economy of Globalization*, Macmillan: London.

Sell, S. (1999) "Multinational Corporations as Agents of Change: The Globalization of Intellectual Property Rights," in Cutler, C.A., Haufler, V., and Porter, T. (eds) *Private Authority and International Affairs*, Albany: State University of New York Press.

Shaw, M. (1994) *Global Society and International Relations: Sociological Concepts and Political Perspectives*, Cambridge: Polity.

Smith, J., Chatfield, C. and Pagnucco, R. (1997) *Transnational Social Movements and Global Politics: Solidarity Beyond the State*, Syracuse: Syracuse University Press.

Steans, J. (2002) "Global Governance: A Feminist Perspective," in Held, D. and McGrew, A. (eds) *Governing Globalization: Power, Authority and Global Governance*, Cambridge: Polity, 87–108.

Strange, S. (1988) *States and Markets*, London: Pinter.

—— (1996) *The Retreat of the State: The Diffusion of Power in the World Economy*, Cambridge: Cambridge University Press.

Tarrow, S. (1998) *Power in Movement*, Cambridge: Cambridge University Press.

—— (2000) "Beyond Globalization: Why Creating Transnational Social Movements is so Hard and When is it Most Likely to Happen," online posting, available at Global Solidarity Dialogue: www.anennna.nl/waterman/tarrow.html

Wapner, P. (1995) "Politics Beyond the State: Environmental Activism and World Civic Politics," *World Politics* 47 (April): 311–40.

Wendt, A. (1999) *Social Theory of International Politics*, Cambridge: Cambridge University Press.

13 Liberal imperialism as global-governance perspective

Daniel Green

This chapter examines "liberal imperialism" as a perspective on global governance (GG). Though perhaps an unorthodox choice, this perspective is—if not a formal analytic perspective common in academe—certainly a familiar critical theme and diagnosis of contemporary order. Closer inspection, however, suggests that the story of a domineering liberal "imperialism" enforced upon others—of the Reagan administration and/or the World Bank and the IMF since the early 1980s, of the US and close allies after 1990—actually represents a subset of patterns and events from a larger phenomenon of "liberal order," and seems best illuminated and dissected via developments in liberal international-relations (IR) theory. As such, this chapter first examines current popular thinking about liberal empire, and then looks for the enabling conditions for such an empire in the liberal IR and democratic-peace literatures, examining regularities in the behavior of liberal actors and their effects in the long run. The next section briefly outlines the historical unfolding of the liberal order. Policies and processes that smack of liberal "empire" can be seen as quite logical and predictable in the world after the end of the Cold War. Finally, I conclude with comparative arguments about the value and contribution of the liberal perspective against other "coherent," structural approaches to GG.

While the "liberal imperialism perspective" is a somewhat obscure approach to global order and governance when compared to realism, world-systems, or the English School, I hope to show that a liberal/liberal imperial approach is actually the best at explaining the patterns and outcomes of GG in the world today and in future. In fact, it provides the intellectual framework and historical context in which several of the others—regime theory, global civil society, notions of private authority, international/public law—exist. These perspectives are made analytically relevant because of the stability and special variety of order created by liberal processes in the past 200–300 years. Thus, the liberal perspective deserves more attention and respect from the scholarly community than it has heretofore received (Moravcsik 1997).

Why liberal? Why imperial?

While notions of liberal and/or American empire have been with us for some time, there is no doubt that liberal imperialism is suddenly a *cause célèbre*, with an explosion of writing about it since September 11 and American-led adventures in Afghanistan and Iraq. It has become the topic of the day, and by late 2003 literally dozens of articles had been published around the notion, American and otherwise (Bacevich 2002; Cooper 2002; Walker 2002; Kurtz 2003). The common theme of all is some sort of active, assertive maintenance of order in the world, along liberal lines, to control terrorism and WMDs, to end rogue states and help failed, chaotic states, to intervene in humanitarian crises, to prevent ethnic cleansings. All done via a forced expansion of classic liberal values—"peace, democracy and free markets" (Mandelbaum 2002)—across all spheres of social life.

The term "liberal empire" intuitively seems to contradict itself—liberal *and* imperial? Imperial implies dominium—extensive territory under control, a forced submission to outside rule, an imperial center and pledges of fealty to it, with discipline for the disobedient. What does it imply for GG? A liberal account of contemporary GG would both find and commend the triumph of the valued goals and principles of liberal thought about IR over the last couple of centuries: democracy over dictatorship, free trade over mercantilism, collective security over balance of power. Since the end of World War II the value of exporting democracy to nonliberal states has become a crucial new component. All are designed to achieve international peace (a systemic goal), especially so that personal freedom and autonomy (domestic goals) are safeguarded. Contra realism, this perspective does not find war and systemic anarchy to be inevitable, nor does it necessarily respect sovereign rights to non-intervention. Unlike GG approaches which find governance to be composed of "multiple, disaggregated rule systems," it does not find order to be accidental or loosely grouped around systems of rules.

Liberal empire as **American** *empire*

Much of the writing on liberal imperialism today is really about a particular *American* liberal imperialism and an imperial temptation America should or should not succumb to. However, this theme can easily be traced back further than 2001–2002 and the wars in Afghanistan or Iraq. The end of the Cold War was a key catalyst for writing about varieties of liberal hegemony and America's new preferred role (Krauthammer 1990/91). American experiences in the 1990–91 Gulf War also sparked discussions of American imperial potential (Tucker and Hendrickson 1992). By the mid-1990s—with Bosnia, Somalia and Haiti in view—observers teamed arguments about a new global "unipolarity" and America's preponderance of power with a sober appreciation for the chaos of the post-Cold War world and the need for someone to take charge (Kristol and Kagan 1996). The string of humanitarian interventions and the rise of human-rights discourse to hegemonic status in rationales for such interventions seemed to indicate that a new liberal order had emerged in which human rights were regularly enforced in trouble spots around the world, by outside forces. For some, instead of an ambitious push for liberal empire by imperially-minded opportunists, there was actually an anarchic vacuum pulling America and other liberal powers/institutions to provide a new liberal imperial order (Rieff 1999; Bacevich 2002; Mallaby 2002). For example, wars begun after 1980 are found to last three times as long as those before, because no one is "in charge" any more (Mallaby 2002). Some describe a pull for a new liberal imperialism without emphasizing America—the agents of order might be NATO instead, or a revised system of League of Nations-like mandates to do multilateral nation-building in failed states (Rieff 1999). More benign representations of America's new primacy and role, as in the title of Richard Haass' book *The Reluctant Sheriff* (1997), argue that America is the key power which must work multilaterally to periodically lead "posses" of like-minded nations to fix global crises.

A second strain in this literature moves beyond any "accidental" liberal empire and is more fervently ambitious and unilateralist, beginning from the premise of truly massive American power (Kristol and Kagan 1996; Brooks and Wohlforth 2002; Krauthammer 2002/03). These authors have little interest in working through international institutions and "posses" of allies unless absolutely necessary. Instead, America is now uniquely called to a role in the international system that only she can fulfill, of global ordering and policing. Kristol and Kagan called for a "neo-Reaganite foreign policy" in 1996, encouraging the US to reassert itself, and Tucker and Hendrickson nicely describe this desire for assertive liberal hegemony in the foreign-policy shift marked by the Reagan Doctrine in the early 1980s:

> For the authors of the Reagan Doctrine, America was the crusader for freedom, not the guarantor of international law and order. The Reagan Doctrine, certainly in its more expansive version, subordinated the traditional bases of international order to a particular version of legitimacy by proclaiming a right of intervention against nondemocratic governments and particularly against Marxist-Leninist governments. In doing so, it went well beyond the grounds for intervention sanctioned by the traditions and practice of states. It declared that even when a state's security interests, conventionally defined, were not in jeopardy and when its support of rebel movements was not a form of counter-intervention, intervention might nevertheless be justified to overturn illegitimate governments. The latter presumably had no rights, legitimacy being defined in terms of conformity to the democratic process. The Reagan Doctrine cast the nation in the role of extending freedom and not only of defending it, as earlier the Truman Doctrine had done. The essence of the Reagan Doctrine ... was the promotion of freedom at the risk of greater disorder.
>
> (1992: 53)

Kristol and Kagan have largely gotten their wish, in the Bush administration's return to Reaganite policy after September 11. And the pushy, unilateralist nature of this approach, disrespectful of international law and institutions, is precisely what feels like imperialism to the rest of the world. Finally, it should be noted that none of these writers proposes a true American empire in the traditional sense of the term, with conquest and lasting authoritarian domination of occupied territories, as one would a colony. Instead, it is understood by its advocates that American empire would be a very limited and benevolent arrangement, for the purposes of securing the world against post-Cold War threats (WMDs, terrorism, rogue states) and expanding freedom and peace.

America-ness or liberal-ness?

The underlying assumption of these authors, both proponents and critics, is that the crusading imperial tendency America displays is hers alone, built into American political culture and self-identity from the Founding. It is as if America has an age-old "empire complex" that drives her to such excesses. Yet there is good reason to try and step back from the particularities of the American case, for some perspective. After all, America has had British and other companions since 9/11 and Tony Blair was actually far more aggressive about liberal interventions in the 1990s than American President Bill Clinton. One of Blair's chief advisers is also a well-known advocate of liberal "neo-imperialism" (Cooper 2002). Going back further in history, Briton Rudyard Kipling's poetic characterization of the "White Man's Burden" was actually a plea addressed to the United States, in 1898, regarding looming action in the Philippines and urging the US to join the fight for civilization in difficult places. Unfortunately, few if any of the current imperial-America authors make reference to the general tenets of liberalism, or to liberal IR theory. Instead, their work is informed by knowledge of the history of American foreign policy and by varieties of realism, neo-realism and hegemonic stability theory. The exception is mention of American values as restraints against truly imperial behavior. Lundestad, for example, notes how American "empire" in Europe after World War II hasn't really been very imperial or at all typical of Great Powers, because of the values—"federalism, democracy, and open markets"—America holds (1998: 154–155). Of course, these are not just American values, but liberal values generally.

It is an unfortunate blind spot, since greater familiarity with liberal IR theory would reveal how the practices of liberal imperialism are well-explicated by theories other than realism and American particularism. Liberal IR theory provides strong evidence that these are simply the logical actions that any country with such values might undertake, provided that it has the power to pursue them. Liberal theory departs from the famous neo-realist premise that states are essentially "like units" and black boxes (Waltz 1979: 93–97), to take into account ideology, values, domestic institutional structure, and identity issues in explaining state behavior. Closer examination of the influence of liberal values reveals how they act both as restraint and as impetus for sometimes wild actions. In general, remedying the excessive fixation on American particularism is a key step to better analyses of power and change in the international system today.

The reader should now have a sense of how liberal "empire" differs from a liberal order in general. But a mere claim that liberal order exists tells us little about how such an order came to be. This chapter argues that what looks like liberal imperialism today is just an overbearing, aggressive "agentic" phase of a liberal international order that has been unfolding for some time. Assertive, liberal hubris today is somewhat different because it has large numbers of adherents and advocates—among the political elites of the US and UK, for example—enabled by liberal international structural advantages and now making their way into political power. Overwhelming military and economic power creates these possibilities: "Great power may or may not corrupt, but it certainly tempts" (Walt 2002: 153). Liberal crusading brings the acceleration of a liberal order that has spread gradually over the past several hundred years. These accelerations have happened before, and are part of the broader historical process of the accretion of a liberal order (Latham 1997; Green 1999). All has been constructed from the general behavioral inclinations of liberal actors over time, now increasingly well-understood by liberal IR theory. These sets of general conclusions about liberal behavior are the subject I turn to next.

The mechanisms of liberal order (and imperialism)

Many argue that we basically live in a liberal world order (Ikenberry 1996; Ruggie 1996; Latham 1997; Mandelbaum 2002), and have for some years now. But how did we get to this point? Where did a liberal order come from? Was it an accident? A fortuitous result of a couple of modern hegemons? Or are there elements of intentionality, planning, and identifiable, recurring causal mechanisms which made this outcome possible, even predictable? The answer appears to be that liberal countries, values, and practices have key advantages over other sets of values and practices, which have helped them to prevail. Classical liberal IR (or idealism) did not undertake detailed analytic dissection of liberal behavioral patterns (Moravcsik 1997: 513–514). Instead, its approach was more ideological and bluntly normative: because anarchy is not inevitable and world peace is possible, states should do X, Y, and Z to promote peace—create an international organization, increase their economic interdependence, sign arms-limitation treaties, pursue international law. Today, liberal IR theory is more developed and analytically powerful (Huntley 1996; Moravcsik 1997), building in particular from the findings and arguments of democratic-peace theory since the early 1980s. Its self-confidence has undoubtedly made liberal imperialism itself more possible, as the democratic-peace argument has entered American foreign-policy doctrine.

The postulates of liberal IR theory

The liberal approach has been called an "inside-out" perspective on IR because, problematizing state identity, it emphasizes domestic political order of a certain kind (democratic) and then dreams that this can be spread throughout the international system (Burchill 2001; see also Moravcsik 1997). Conversely, Immanuel Kant's writings on IR have recently been revisited to show how they offer a rival systemic theory of IR in which anarchy gradually produces liberal states and a liberal peace (Huntley 1996; Harrison 2002). These suggest that it is important to look at both the advantages of liberal "domestic" practices and patterns (explaining the advent and persistence of liberal states in their internal contexts), and liberal international practices (which allow them to prevail in international competition and expand their numbers).

There are several well-known arguments for why liberal states appear in history in the first place. Most revolve around human-nature arguments about a compulsion for freedom or a natural desire to be free (Doyle 1995: 89). The human development of separate languages and religions may guarantee a world that eschews empire and instead fosters autonomous units. Subsequently, free populations fear losing their freedom a great deal, and act in all kinds of ways to preserve it. For Kant, of course, there is a fundamental "categorical impera-tive" in human nature, regarding our urge to "ought"—to live moral lives and act morally—which requires freedom. More germane are the many ways in which liberal domestic and international practices are advantageous, and liberal characteristics select positively. Liberal IR theory gives us important generaliza-tions about how liberal states behave internationally, how they will tend to treat liberal and nonliberal states, and how they are able to prevail in international conflict.

Several studies reveal how liberal states have discernible—sometimes marginal, sometimes highly significant—advantages over nonliberal states. This literature began with the empirical finding that "democracies don't fight each other," a claim that has been picked at from many sides (Russett 1993: 25–30; Layne 1994; Jervis 2002), but remains generally accepted. Liberal domestic institutions put limits on bellicosity—Kant's notion of democratic "caution"—which in European history allowed a crucial advance over "monarchical caprice" (Doyle 1983a: 230). Liberal principles also help to create a separate peace among liberal states. Indeed, liberal entities have uniformly peaceful rela-tions going back to ancient Greece, through medieval Europe, to today (Weart 1998).

Similarly, whenever there are liberal states in proximity, they almost always form alliances with each other, and these tend to be more durable than alliances between non-liberals (Weart 1998). Liberal, open states allow numerous channels of interaction across borders, increasing interdependence and familiarity over levels possible amongst authoritarian regimes (Gaubatz 1996: 119–120). Based in pluralistic and free societies, liberal alliances tend to be more flexible and stable, not vulnerable to leadership changes or international fits of pique (Huntley 1996: 58; Owen 2001/02: 126). Trust and accurate communication are crucial, and their absence is likewise an impediment for nonliberal powers. "Publicity"—international free speech and accurate communication—"is essential to establish and preserve the understanding on which the guarantee of respect depends" (Doyle 1983a: 230). "The experience of cooperation helps engender further cooperative behavior."

Of course, as is now well known in this literature, this does not rule out war and aggressive behavior by democratic countries, since "liberal states are peaceful only in relations with other liberal states" (Doyle 1983a: 225). This is because liberal tendencies simultaneously tend to generate liberal aggression against nonliberal states. Relations with autocracies are more likely to be tense and less likely to be resolved peacefully, and if a war is undertaken it is often waged as a crusade to spread liberal values. Indeed, the ways in which democracies are likely to treat nonliberal states are quite worrying:

> In relation with powerful states of a nonliberal character, liberal policy has been characterized by repeated failures of diplomacy. It has often raised conflicts of interest into crusades; it has delayed in taking full advantage of rivalries within nonliberal alliances; it has failed to negotiate stable mutual accommodations of interests. In relations with weak states of nonliberal character, liberal policy has succumbed to imperial interventions that it has been unable to sustain or to profit from. Its interventions, designed to create liberal societies by promoting the economic development and political stability of nonliberal societies, have frequently failed to achieve their objects. Confusion, drift, costly crusades, spasmodic imperialism are the contrasting record of liberal foreign policy *outside* the liberal world.
>
> (Doyle 1983b: 324; emphasis in original)

British philosopher David Hume pointed out flaws such as these as early as 1741, commenting on Britain's "imprudent vehemence" and "careless complaisance" in its foreign relations of the time (Doyle 1983b: 322). The former refers to the liberal tendency to pursue wars with nonliberal powers (France in this instance) with crusader-like zeal, long beyond good sensibility. The problem of complacency refers to tendencies to isolationism and exhaustion. Both reflect, even in mid-eighteenth-century Britain, the influence of popular opinion and representative government. A kind of bellicosity makes perfect sense to liberal states. Frequent foreign interventions are permissible since, because nonliberal states "do not authentically represent the rights of individuals, [they] have no rights to noninterference" (Doyle 1986: 1162). Democratic leaders will find it relatively easy to mobilize hostility towards a foreign state if it is governed autocratically (Russett 1993: 30).

What appears significant in these relations is the strong influence of the social identities and perceptions of the actors (Weart 1998; Owen 2001/02). Liberal leaders have a strong tendency to treat their fellow liberals well, as they would their own domestic colleagues, whereas illiberal foreign leaders get very different treatment, of distrust and hostility.

Other studies discuss at length the unusual and crucial advantages that liberal states have in actual warfare (Lake 1992; Reiter and Stam 1998).

Democratic leaders tend to select their wars carefully, choosing the ones they can win since defeat is rarely popular with electorates. Democracies are also highly likely to win wars that they enter or initiate, for a variety of reasons: better leaders, better soldiers and generals, as well as more open and accurate information systems (Lake 1992). Official transparency and open societies also mean less debilitating rent-seeking opportunities, consequently greater material capabilities, with societal support more easily and durably mobilized. And in major multi-country wars, liberal states end up on the same side, most likely victorious.

Commercial and material factors are significant as well in giving liberal states competitive advantages. All liberal theorists have noted that liberal states are best able to tap internal resources in case of conflict. Other kinds of states fail to do so and therefore lose in key global competition, especially over the long haul (Schutz and Weingast 2003). Further, liberal states are more trusted and thus better able to raise funds internationally. There are the gains from regularized trade, of course, and evidence that liberal states have lower tariff barriers between each other. But also the free operation of domestic market forces (and internationally) "removes difficult decisions of production and distribution from the direct sphere of state policy" (Doyle 1983a: 231). Liberal states thus enjoy relatively de-politicized economic competition that nurtures productivity and innovation rather than violence.

If we look in greater detail at how liberal states further propagate liberalism and liberal order, even very forcefully, we see a number of familiar mechanisms used through history: constitutionalism itself, forced democratizations of defeated enemies, political conditionalities attached to economic assistance, the forming of liberal international organizations, regional economic associations, and collective-security groupings that require members to be democracies. In the very big picture, Ikenberry (2001, 2002) describes how democracies are particularly well suited to engage in international order-building after conflict, since the transparency of their political institutions makes them particularly trustworthy bargaining partners in the eyes of weaker states.

In sum, liberal states and practices enjoy major and decisive advantages that, especially over time, have constructed the liberal world we see today. Interestingly, by this account these outcomes have not necessarily hinged upon the unique features and drives of one country; they instead inhere in liberal states generally. In this sense, the United States need never have existed, but it is not surprising that it does, nor that a country like it rose to global prominence.

Caveats: the diversity of liberal identity and strategy

By way of qualification, however, there do appear to be liberal limits to cooperation and integration, and definitely different paths to liberal aims. We can, for example, expect that some liberal states will be cautious about significant international institution-building, the ceding of international sovereignty, and any moves towards a supranational state (as has America been globally, Britain in the EU). The liberal state should not be subject to "the external authority of other states" since it has granted full authority to its people only. This may be another instance of Kant's prescience, in his prediction not of a future world government, but of a looser pacific union of republics. It is a portent of inclinations to isolationism and unilateralism as well.

Sharing a basic liberal identity does not imply total agreement on what to do thereafter, since how one should best behave liberally is debatable. We can therefore expect real differences of opinion about proper liberal strategy in international affairs (Doyle 1983a; 1999): low roads and high roads, cosmopolitan caution and universalist crusading. Doyle notes the basic division between "conservative" and "liberal" paths within liberalism (laissez-faire liberalism vs. social-welfare liberalism) (1983a: 208, fn. 4). Sources of these differences are many. Deepening of liberal international order does not imply that liberal states have entirely escaped from the realist security dilemma, only that they have "tamed anarchy" a bit (Doyle 1983a: 232). Some are more likely to be subject to international violence than others, and therefore will behave differently (Cooper 2002; Kagan 2002). There can also still be conflicts of interest between democracies—and dozens are evident in the news every day. Small liberal states may also not behave entirely according to script because they have different incentives and foreign-policy preferences because of their size. Nor will all liberal states ally. They also have regional security concerns or other ambitions, as in India's antagonisms with the US over the years (Owen 2001/02: 127)

"Liberal" character is therefore somewhat variable. Important historical experiences can change a country's orientations, nurturing an aggressive liberalism in America's case, or German pacifism. Certainly many have come to make arguments about the peculiarities of American national character to explain its behavior (e.g., Cox 2003). Of course, the key point is that it is highly unlikely that these differences will ever lead to intra-democracy war (Jervis 2002: 5), or even result in the breaking of alliances, for all the reasons noted above.

The historical liberalization of GG

If these are the behavioral tendencies of liberal states, what is the world order they have produced over the last century? In broad strokes, we can imagine that a realist world of self-seeking states is born at Westphalia and persists for decades. But what may have been "like units" begin to differentiate and states that take on liberal identities come to behave differently—liberal identity comes to affect international relations, order, and ultimately GG.

Liberal IR theorists have begun to construct the history of this "liberalism effect," liberal advantages, and the separate peace. Liberal advantages in alliance-making and war-fighting go back centuries, and helped to create the predominant Dutch and then British empires, as well as a phenomenon such as the United States of America (Doyle 1983a; Weart 1998). Subsequently, "conventions of mutual respect" between liberal powers became important by the late eighteenth century (Doyle 1983a: 213). After 1832 and Britain's democratizing Reform Act of that year, Anglo-American tensions were reduced and conflicts resolved by negotiation (Doyle 1986: 1156). Then the modern liberal zone of peace started in the 1890s, with the alliance between the US and Britain born after the British Guiana–Venezuela crises. France was next incorporated, after the Fashoda issue was resolved in 1898 (Russett 1993). For World War I, liberal France and Britain formed an alliance against illiberal Germany and liberal Italy switched sides in 1915 to join this Entente.

Liberal values were clearly a guide to Woodrow Wilson and his efforts to make World War I a war for democracy, a new diplomacy, and peace through international law. Liberal victory in World War I ensured that the post-war settlement was relatively liberal, at least on paper: the break-up of several empires (Austro-Hungarian, German, Ottoman and Russian) along national self-determination principles, a collective security pact to adjudicate disputes and protect small states, an anti-colonial "mandate" system to prepare colonies for independence. But the forces of liberalism were insufficiently vigilant after World War I, as almost everything they had worked for collapsed, and Italy and Germany were allowed to fall into fascism (see Green 1999).

Shared liberality greatly eased the transition in world leadership from Britain to the US in this period (Jervis 2002: 5). Liberal advantages then proved pivotal in helping the liberal side win World War II against fascism, and American institution-building at the end of that war had liberalism going for it (Ikenberry 2002: 298). America dictated that institutions for governing the global economy would be liberal, and to the extent that they were not (e.g., embedded liberalism), they subsequently evolved in that direction (the closing of the gold window, the neoliberalization of World Bank development strategies, the creation of the WTO). America's liberal hegemony was thereafter relatively inoffensive and therefore durable (Owen 2001/02; Ikenberry 2002). America helped create institutions in the post-war world that actually restrained its own power, making it appear as less of a domineering hegemon. America's core identity is also "cosmopolitan" and not exclusionary nationalist (Ikenberry 2002: 298–299). American hegemony, and the UN and Bretton Woods economic order, was thus much less threatening and more easily accepted by other powers.

The Cold War then appeared and paralyzed the UN, though not the Bretton Woods order of embedded liberalism and ultimately neoliberal economic principles. This was supervised by the IMF and the World Bank, an institutional team which came into its own after the debt crises of the 1970s and began to remake the world along strictly liberal lines. Democracy was seen as a "binding principle" for many countries on one side of the Cold War, but that coalition obviously included many distasteful non-democracies, and liberal powers acted very illiberally during it (Russett 1993: 10). By the late 1970s there were more democracies around, and by the early 1980s the democratic peace was increasingly recognized by both academics and policy-makers.

Liberal values and the precepts of liberal IR theory also greatly contributed to ending the Cold War itself. Ronald Reagan used democratic peace arguments in a famous speech in 1982—not about the natural restraint of liberal states, but about the need for a new "crusade for freedom"—and to guide his foreign policy against the Soviet bloc (Doyle 1995: 86). The timing and nature of the Cold War's end, often held to be a miraculous surprise, was quite predictable from a liberal perspective, the logical product of accumulating liberal advantage as totalitarian weaknesses combined to deadly effect: an internal legitimation crisis, worsening economic performance, growing costs of maintaining the Eastern bloc alliance (Deudney and Ikenberry 1990/01; Doyle 1995; Huntley 1996: 67–69). The first Bush administration also let liberal peace arguments guide their foreign policy in the 1989–92 period, in effect waiting for the Soviet Union to change enough to be trusted (Russett 1993: 128–129). The "democratic expansion" theme of the Clinton Doctrine and the more assertive regime-change ideas of Tony Blair and the George W. Bush administration continue the trend today.

Gradual liberal expansion and liberal behavioral regularities have produced the world as we see it today. It is a world without precedent in that war is largely unthinkable within the major-power security community (Jervis 2002). As Kant predicted 200 years ago, a liberal zone of peace has fully emerged and now includes over 100 countries whose members need not worry about armed conflict with each other. Instead, the post-Cold War era features a new kind of security environment and warfare, shaped by the prevailing liberal consensus (McInnes 2003). Wars now tend to be limited and aimed at leaders rather than populations; national populations are more likely to be viewed as victims of bad government and repression. Interventions tend to be quick and clean, to prevent damage and restore just government. Liberal IR theory further explains nicely such outcomes as the persistence and even the expansion of NATO, and the relative lack of interest in balancing against American hegemony (Owen 2001/02).

Finally, at the end of this record we come to the issue of liberal *imperialism*. Given the above, a more strident liberal "imperialism" that we can see in Clinton/Blair/Bush foreign policy after 1997 or so should not come as a surprise. It may be arrogant and culturally imperialist, but liberal states, having wandered on to a winning formula, could be expected to have such tendencies within them. Liberal powers, safe in their zone of peace, might be expected to at times foist their values on to other nonliberal states, particularly if illiberal states and ideologies attacked them. Kant himself would have likely recommended against a forced expansion of liberalism, preferring a tolerant, gradual approach and teaching by example (Huntley 1996: 70–72), but liberal strategies are multiple and will vary depending upon who occupies leadership positions.

Once major powers are conscious of powerful liberal tendencies, or at least believe in their existence, the liberal world order becomes more self-fulfilling, and political rhetoric can become very self-assured:

> The great struggles of the twentieth century between liberty and totalitarianism ended with a decisive victory for the forces of freedom—and a single

sustainable model for national success: freedom, democracy, and free enterprise. In the twenty-first century, only nations that share a commitment to
protecting basic human rights and guaranteeing political and economic
freedom will be able to unleash the potential of their people and assure their
future prosperity. ... [V]alues of freedom are right and true for every
person, in every society—and the duty of protecting these values against
their enemies is the common calling of freedom-loving people across the
globe and across the ages.

(Bush 2002)

A liberal approach in comparative perspective

Having laid out the basic elements of the liberal/liberal imperial GG perspective, I now turn to a comparative analysis of this perspective against others, using
the language of "coherence and contestation," along with structure and process,
that are organizing themes of this volume. Structure and process in analysis of
GG can relate to whether GG is a "verb or a noun." Does a given GG perspective posit open-ended, multi-dimensional systems of rule (haphazard and
non-teleological), or a coherent order? By these terms, the liberal/liberal imperial perspective would be classed as coherent and very structural, since it seems
determinate and has an increasingly elaborate account of history. In this, the
liberal approach is most similar to other structural-historical GG perspectives,
such as those of the English School, world-systems, Gramscian and transnational
class perspectives, and perhaps a realist approach as well.

A handy caricature of differing coherent/structural perspectives might go as
follows. Realists think the international system is anarchic and not governed by
norms. The English School knows it is somewhat norm-governed but has not
decided upon their common theme. Liberals know the system is very much
norm-governed, know what kind of norms predominate, and are happy about
them. More critical approaches such as the Gramscian, world-systems and
transnational-class approaches also see considerable order but dislike its unjust,
exploitative character intensely. Put another way, in its basics the liberal school is
very similar to a cosmopolitan, "solidarist" English School perspective, which
emphasizes the possibilities for major global social cooperation and agreement
on human-rights universalism (Buzan 1993; Linklater 2001). The solidarists
believe in the possibility of a just global order, and that would be a liberal one.

We can see further lines of distinction between these perspectives by looking
at two other issues: (1) their varying understandings of history; and (2) their
micro-foundational suppositions about human nature.

Explaining history and the direction of change

Liberal IR theorists have taken note of the profound implications of their
perspective for understanding the history of IR. Bruce Russett (1993) argues that
liberal insights mean there could be an "end of history," if history is seen as one

of war and conflict. Findings about liberal alliance durability alone suggest that eventually the world will be one entirely of liberal states. Indeed, based on a tracking of the regular expansion of the number of liberal regimes since 1800 (roughly a doubling every fifty years), we can expect complete global democratization by 2100 (Doyle 1995: 98). This also means that the international history of the past couple of centuries or so has had a *direction*, just as Kantian philosophical tenets would insist (Huntley 1996: 61–62). Such conclusions are horribly controversial but liberal IR theory today, in some ways simply picking up where Kant left off 200 years ago, now gives them a much more rigorous grounding (see Huntley 1996; Harrison 2002). From this vantage, cyclical and ahistorical perspectives in IR (history repeats/history is always the same) are hamstrung and blinded by their basic suppositions. Neither tunes into differences and historical discontinuities very well, nor is capable of seeing history as having secular directionality. Such approaches could not see a liberal order's development or its possibilities. Liberals are much less hesitant to talk of directionality and the future, however (Doyle 1995; Huntley 1996; Harrison 2002). Indeed, a "systemic" liberal IR theory illustrates precisely how competition and selection in anarchy will eventually transform anarchy (Huntley 1996; Harrison 2002).

Liberalism attacks realism for ignoring change and history in favor of cycles and atemporalism (Moravscik 1997: 535). Liberalism does not suffer from these, though admittedly its accounts of history are not yet as detailed and elaborate as other "coherent" GG perspectives. Liberal IR can rise above the utopian ideology of idealism by building a theory of historical change on specific, actor-level behaviors. Behavioral inclinations slowly beget structural features, accumulate over time and give history directionality. Liberal actors treat each other deferentially in ways that are more functional, their regimes and alliances are hardier. Liberal states can then be expected to become among the most powerful major powers, and inherently committed to preventing nonliberal hegemonies. Eventually a zone of peace breaks out as the number of democracies increases.

Liberal processes and mechanisms today produce liberal structures and institutions of considerable weight and influence, which then expand via all the mechanisms that create liberal advantage in the first place, plus new more intentional and agentic behaviors (consciously seeking to promote democracies and touting democratic peace arguments, for example). Liberal structure is ideational and discursive, it includes institutionalized norms, political institutions themselves, liberal constitutions which establish democratic countries, liberal laws both national and international, liberal alliances and regional groupings, such as NATO and the EU.

Secularity and cyclicality also figure into the rival accounts of power in these perspectives. The liberal perspective on global order as described here draws heavily from the democratic-peace literature and its generic conclusions about liberal actor-level behavior. Its accounts of historical processes of liberal accumulation do not center on hegemony and cycles of leadership, as a world-systems approach would for example. The Americans, the British, and the

Dutch, have certainly had important roles in history, but by the liberal account these have been as servants of liberal and universal goals. Liberal-advantage mechanisms, after all, go back to long before these countries existed (Weart 1998). Because it de-privileges hegemony, a liberal approach does not require the cyclicality of hegemonic rise and fall.

Is this line of argument basically a power-cleansing device designed to hide class/capitalist dominance? This would certainly be the counter-argument of more critical approaches. They would accuse liberal IR of promoting "false consciousness" to obfuscate genuine imperialism. The liberal approach, for example, certainly does not find that the dominance of liberal values is due to their ability to give the "appearance" of serving the needs of many—it accepts that this is real, not trickery.

First-image micro-foundations of governance patterns

Liberal processes are many and extensive. We can think of them, in ideal-typical ways only, as varying in intentionality and agency as well as scale. Processes of "liberal internationalism" as discussed by Doyle (1995: 96–101), from Kant, include liberal rebellion against tyranny and liberal processes of modernization and social mobilization. Finally, "transnationalism," in the guise of trade, societal exchanges, tourism, and transgovernmental meetings, is another key part of the processes by which liberalism spreads to nonliberal places (like the former Soviet bloc).

We can also think of "process" as micro- and individual-level features that every perspective has, whether consciously or not; micro-level motives and causal mechanisms that explain why actors behave as they do, as in Sterling-Folker's arguments about the hostile gregariousness of human nature. The processes of liberal imperialism would be the more agentic mechanisms by which liberalism has propagated itself down through the centuries, and built up the structures that shape liberal agency today. Why do liberal states act the way they do? What are the reasons for such behavior? What are the sources of the processes of liberal expansion and imperialism?

The micro-processes and driving motives of other GG perspectives are revealing. In Sterling-Folker's version of realism, this is basically at the human nature level ("first image" of Waltz) in gregarious group-forming combined with a genetic human disposition for conflict. For more Marxian and class-focused approaches, such as those of Arrighi and Overbeek in this volume, micro-level elements are greed and the desire to exploit for selfish gain, the profit motive, etc. These drive the creation of structures of exploitative control both domestically and internationally, and put the focus of such analyses on the economic.

Core processes, values, and mechanisms in the critical approaches are greed and exploitation, but for a Kantian approach it is freedom and learning. This difference removes the persistent negativeness and the cyclicality from liberal theory, giving it a panglossian feel. The core micro-foundation of greed makes some structural perspectives basically vulnerable to the charge of economism, while the liberal micro-foundation of political freedom in turn de-emphasizes the economic and tends to "politicism." As to the English School, their central element is the existence of international society, which functions as a problem-solving mechanism for the construction of systemic social norms. It also provides order and predictability for the society of states.

Explanatory scale is also an issue, particularly when contrasting the coherent/structural approaches with the process/contestation ones. From a liberal perspective, there are certainly likely to be strong elements of contestation, but these exist within a framework of liberal *grundnorms*.

Finally, it is notable that liberal IR's tenets are not well known, or not considered worthy of the status of a full-blown analytic perspective (Moravcsik 1997). This is unfortunate, because it means that the most appropriate and timely perspective to understanding and predicting the actions of liberal powers and global outcomes is relatively neglected by academics, perhaps more likely used by journalists and popularizers, yet clearly lingers in the backs (and fronts) of the heads of many important policy-makers.

Liberal imperialism today

At present, two key conditions prevail: (1) liberal values and practices have achieved ideological dominance and legitimacy; and (2) international actors are increasingly aware of this and phenomena like democratic peace theory. Together, this has meant that many more consciously liberal expansionist ("imperial") processes are evident, from the Bush administration's idea of pre-emptive intervention for regime change to the EU's extensive Copenhagen criteria for EU membership. September 11 activated a strong liberal imperialist thread in American foreign policy, this time taken on by the neoconservatives. A common theme in liberal imperialism today is the notion of imperial means to liberal ends. This is found on both sides of the Atlantic. Robert Cooper's arguments about neo-colonialism to restore failed states are classically liberal in ends, but imperial in means.

Currently, the Bush administration contains and is influenced by both nationalists and neo-conservatives. Nationalists are not liberal in means and ends. Neoconservatives are liberal imperialist in ends, but not means. They seek to establish liberalism because it prevents threats from rising. This is a clever marriage of liberal ideals with national security interests, an old trick "process," but one which satisfies many different groups.

Conclusions

To return to some of the opening questions inspiring this volume. Is there GG? The answer is yes, most definitely. We live in a world of ordered GG, not anarchy or tenuous cooperation, and this order is liberal. It is both old and new, and liberal IR theory offers the best means of understanding the accumulation of liberal order and its future direction. It problematizes the character of states, breaking the "like units" assumption and examining the domestic sources of state behavior, strategies, ascents, and descents in power over time. This is a substantial leap forward from approaches that ignore or explain away such issues. From this, an elaborated yet theoretically grounded perspective on GG can be built, one that has the advantage of predictive and prescriptive abilities. However, the "paradigm" of liberal IR remains young and underdeveloped. It has begun constructing a description of international history and, more importantly, it is developing a sophisticated theory of that history. In this endeavor it can learn from the English School and world-systems approaches and their willingness to periodize and speak of historical phases of international life. The secularity of the liberal account, however, and its highlighting of liberal progress and predictions of a liberal-world endpoint, are both controversial and unique among perspectives on GG, against ahistorical and cyclical approaches.

If liberal-advantage mechanisms persist at the process level, liberal-order structures and dominance will as well. If the special treatment liberal states accord each other changes dramatically, however, all bets are off. This would require a true and deep schism amongst major liberal states, such that they are willing to attack each other in warfare. Will the spread of democracy to ubiquity mean new factionalizations and hatreds? Interestingly, we are only now at the point in history at which such hypotheses can be tested.

References

Bacevich, A. J. (2002) "New Rome, New Jerusalem," *The Wilson Quarterly* 26: 50–58.

Brooks, S. and Wohlforth, W. (2002) "American Primacy in Perspective," *Foreign Affairs* 81: 20–33.

Burchill, S. (2001) "Liberalism," in Scott Burchill, Richard Devetak, *et al.*, *Theories of International Relations*, Basingstoke, UK: Palgrave, 2nd edition, 29–69.

Bush, G.W. (2002) Introduction to "The National Security Strategy of the United States," Washington, DC: US Government.

Buzan, B. (1993) "From International System to International Society: Structural Realism and Regime Theory Meet the English School," *International Organization* 47: 327–352.

Cooper, R. (2002) "The Post-modern State," in M. Leonard, (ed.) *Re-ordering the World*, London: The Foreign Policy Centre, 119–124.

Cox, M. (2003) "The Empire's Back in Town: or America's Imperial Temptation—Again," *Millennium* 32: 1–27.

Deudney, D. and Ikenberry, G.J. (1990/91) "The International Sources of Soviet Change," *International Security* 16: 74–118.

—— (1993/94) "The Logic of the West," *World Policy Journal* 10: 17–26.

Doyle, M. (1983a) "Kant, Liberal Legacies, and Foreign Affairs: Part I," *Philosophy and Public Affairs* 12: 205–235.

—— (1983b) "Kant, Liberal Legacies, and Foreign Affairs: Part II," *Philosophy and Public Affairs* 12: 323–353.

—— (1986) "Liberalism and World Politics," *American Political Science Review* 80: 1151–1169.

—— (1995) "Liberalism and the End of the Cold War," in Richard Ned Lebow and Thomas Risse-Kappen (eds) *International Relations Theory and the End of the Cold War*, New York: Columbia University Press, 85–102.

—— (1999) "A Liberal View: Preserving and Expanding the Liberal Pacific Union," in T.V. Paul and John A. Hall (eds) *International Order and the Future of World Politics*, Cambridge UK: Cambridge University Press, 41–66.

Gaubatz, K.T. (1996) "Democratic States and Commitment in International Relations," *International Organization*, 50: 109–139.

Green, D. (1999) "The Lingering Liberal Moment: An Historical Perspective on the Global Durability of Democracy after 1989," *Democratization* 6: 1–41.

Haass, R. (1997) *The Reluctant Sheriff: The United States after the Cold War*, New York: Council on Foreign Relations Press.

Harrison, E. (2002) "Waltz, Kant and Systemic Approaches to International Relations," *Review of International Studies* 28: 143–162.

Huntley, W. L. (1996) "Kant's Third Image: Systemic Sources of the Liberal Peace," *International Studies Quarterly* 40: 45–76.

Ikenberry, G.J. (1996) "The Future of International Leadership," *Political Science Quarterly* 111: 385–403.

—— (2001) *After Victory: Institutions, Strategic Restraint, and the Rebuilding of Order after Major War*, Princeton: Princeton University Press.

—— (2002) "American Unipolarity: The Sources of Persistence and Decline," in G.J. Ikenberry (ed.) *America Unrivaled: The Future of the Balance of Power*, Ithaca: Cornell University Press, 284–310.

Jervis, R. (2002) "Theories of War in an Era of Leading-power Peace," *American Political Science Review* 96: 1–14.

Kagan, R. (2002) "Power and Weakness," *Policy Review* 113: 3–28.

Krauthammer, C. (1990/91) "The Unipolar Moment," *Foreign Affairs: America and the World* 70: 10–25.

—— (2002/03) "The Unipolar Moment Revisited," *The National Interest* 70: 5–17.

Kristol, W. and Kagan, R. (1996) "Towards a Neo-Reaganite Foreign Policy," *Foreign Affairs* 75: 36–53.

Kurtz, S. (2003) "Democratic Imperialism: A Blueprint," *Policy Review* 118: 3–20.

Lake, D. (1992) "Powerful Pacifists: Democratic States and War," *American Political Science Review* 86: 24–37.

Latham, R. (1997) *The Liberal Moment: Modernity, Security, and the Making of the Postwar International Order*, New York: Columbia University Press.

Layne, C. (1994) "Kant or Cant: The Myth of the Democratic Peace," *International Security* 19: 5–49.

Linklater, A. (2001) "Rationalism," in Scott Burchill, Richard Devetak, *et al.*, *Theories of International Relations*, Basingstoke, UK: Palgrave, 2nd edition, 103–128.

Lundestad, G. (1998) *"Empire" By Integration: The United States and European Integration, 1945–1997*, Oxford: Oxford University Press.

Mallaby, S. (2002) "The Reluctant Imperialist," *Foreign Affairs* 98: 2–7.

Mandelbaum, M. (2002) *The Ideas That Conquered the World*, New York: Public Affairs.

McInnes, C. (2003) "A Different Kind of War? September 11 and the United States' Afghan War," *Review of International Studies* 29: 165–184.

Moravcsik, A. (1997) "Taking Preferences Seriously: A Liberal Theory of International Politics," *International Organization* 51: 513–553.

Owen, J. M. (1994) "How Liberalism Produces Democratic Peace," *International Security* 19: 87–125.

—— (2001/02) "Transnational Liberalism and US Primacy," *International Security* 26: 117–152.

Reiter, D. and Stam III, Allan (1998) "Democracy, War Initiation, and Victory," *American Political Science Review* 92: 377–389.

Rieff, D. (1999) "A New Age of Liberal Imperialism?" *World Policy Journal* 16: 1–10.

Ruggie, J. (1996) *Winning the Peace: America and World Order in the New Era*, New York: Columbia University Press.

Russett, B.M. (1993) *Grasping the Democratic Peace: Principles for a Post-Cold War World*, Princeton: Princeton University Press.

Schultz, K.A., and Barry, K.W. (2003) "The Democratic Advantage: Institutional Foundations of Financial Power in International Competition," *International Organization* 57: 3–42.

Tucker, R.C. and Hendrickson, D. (1992) *The Imperial Temptation: The New World Order and America's Purpose*, New York: Council on Foreign Relations Press.

Walker, M. (2002) "What Kind of Empire?" *The Wilson Quarterly* 26: 36–49.

Walt, S. (2002) "Keeping the World 'Off Balance': Self Restraint and US Foreign Policy," in G.J. Ikenberry (ed.) *America Unrivaled: The Future of the Balance of Power*, Ithaca, NY: Cornell University Press, 121–154.

Waltz, K.N. (1979) *Theory of International Politics*, Boston: McGraw-Hill.

Weart, S.R. (1998) *Never At War: Why Democracies Will Not Fight One Another*, New Haven, CN: Yale University Press.

14 Contending perspectives on global governance

Dialogue and debate

Matthew J. Hoffmann and Alice D. Ba

The preceding chapters map broad outlines of global-governance (GG) knowledge and research. The map is not straightforward but neither was it meant to be. The goal of this volume was never to produce the definitive description or statement of GG. Rather, from the beginning, the volume's primary aim was to make some sense from the cacophony of voices speaking on GG, to identify the ideas and dynamics commonly associated with its emergence, and to shed light on key points of contestation in ongoing debates about the significance of GG—whether as a set of new phenomena to be studied, as liberal project, or as a new analytic approach to the study of world politics. As the running thread of this volume, the structure and process of GG has provided authors with a common focus and common vocabulary. We hope that it has helped better identify focal points for debate across the 12 different perspectives and between older and newer approaches to the study of international relations without privileging any one perspective or sacrificing the diversity of thought on the subject. Together, these chapters provide what we think is a step towards answering Craig Murphy's challenge that we make GG better done and better understood.

In this concluding chapter, we return to the underlying, though not always explicit, question that has framed this entire volume: is there anything to the hype surrounding the concept of GG? To an author, all of the contributors to the volume agree that GG exists, which in and of itself is an interesting phenomenon. While authors disagree about a great many of the details of what GG is and what significance it has for the study of world politics, it also seems paradoxically clear that the notion of GG is also not entirely up for grabs. At very least there seems to be a common recognition that *something* about our world or our perceptions of the world must be different, or GG would not have gained the currency it has.

Thus, in this concluding chapter we explore what has and has not changed (and what can and cannot change) according to the perspectives represented in this volume. Rather than listing all the changes author by author, we instead organize our final discussion around four dialogues that have emerged from the preceding chapters. These dialogues each speak to the question of change and transition—be it in our world, our politics, or our thinking about world politics. The first dialogue concerns the foundations of GG with an eye towards identifying the material and ideational changes that distinguish this era from previous ones. The second explores notions of agency and agents, uncovering where and by whom governance is taking place. The third dialogue looks to the significance of those changes for world politics in practice and theory. Finally, the last dialogue delves into governance in the current, post-Cold War, post-9/11 era, ruminating on the role of the US, the liberal content of contemporary GG, and the prospects for governance in the near future. Together, these dialogues lead us to the conclusion that there is something to GG—the world and our perceptions of it have changed—even if there remains a lack of consensus as to what that something is.

Dialogue 1: material and ideational foundations of GG

Discussing and debating the role of material conditions/power versus the power of ideas is familiar terrain for international relations theory—familiar and mostly arid because the debate too often involves polemics and forceful stating of one's own positions. At the same time, no theory is wholly ideational or material. Even the most ardent materialists—take your pick between realists or Marxists—rely at least implicitly on ideational factors in their explanations. Similarly, those who claim that politics is ideas all the way down still must contend with how ideational factors influence and are influenced by material power. Thus rather than pursue a useless dichotomy, we are interested in what different perspectives seem to be the key material/ideational changes (if any) in the unfolding of world politics or in the theories we use to understand it.

Let us begin where the perspectives for the most part fail to see change—the interaction of ideational and material forces. This is not surprising as such inter-actions are at the core of any theory. For example Overbeek, Arrighi, and Sterling-Folker predictably call upon material conditions and material power to explain the rules and patterns of GG. Material conditions shape the ideational rules of GG through the logic of capital accumulation, the logic of hegemony, and inherent competitive sociability respectively. Hoffmann, on the other hand, claims that GG is ideas all the way down. He captures well the view of a number of authors that the ideational foundations of GG cannot be ignored because in the end ideas provide the most basic foundations of governance: who partici-pates, how actors interrelate with one another, what issues are considered important, and even how actors get what they want. The struggle to define (if not, claim) GG, as noted by Sinclair, Ba, as well as Hoffmann, is important precisely because ideas have real consequences for the actors that take part in that system.

The causal relationship between material and ideational forces is thus a fundamental assumption of any perspective. Perspectives may differ on how the material and ideational interact but they each see that interaction as more or less unchanged. Yet, our contributors do see changes in the material and/or ideational conditions that differentiate this current era from previous ones. To a chapter, no one claims that the world is entirely unchanged materially or ideationally. Thus cross-perspective dialogue in this instance surrounds the question of whether the changes can be incorporated into an existing perspective. In other words, can a perspective's identified causal connection between material and ideational forces accommodate the changes in world politics? Or is it the case that changes call for new thinking and new conceptions about how the material and ideational come together? From the preceding chapters, we see an implicit dialogue emerge about the changes associated with this era that spawned GG, as well as debate about whether those changes are sufficiently fundamental so as to generate new politics and new thinking about those politics.

Material changes

So what has changed in the world? Regarding material conditions and power, this era of GG has been shaped by the dynamics of globalization in important ways according to many of our contributors. Rosenau describes four changing material conditions that are driving the fragmegrative process of GG: microelectronic technologies, the skill revolution, increased mobility, and economic globalization. Similarly, O'Brien claims that the "possibility of deterritorialized communication and solidarity helps to distinguish the present era of GG from other historical modes of world order." Further, while many authors focus on communication and the speed of information, financial and population flows, Overbeek calls our attention to an accompanying change in the material condition that is part and parcel of globalization: increasing commodification. He argues that "The decades since the late 1970s have shown a sudden and unprecedented process of deepening commodification …"

Related questions on the bases of material power are also important to understandings of the world. All perspectives on GG must reconcile themselves to questions of power and our contributors see important continuities and changes. While Arrighi sees age-old conditions still prevalent today regarding patterns of "interstate competition for mobile capital," he nonetheless is sensitive to today's novel characteristics as well. Specifically, he sees the "bifurcation of military and financial capabilities that has no precedent in earlier hegemonic transitions." In contrast, Ba, Dunne, and Green all point to the enormous concentration of US/Western power as the novelty of the present era and the change that must be incorporated into our analyses.

But observations of the changing bases of power are not restricted to questions of where power is located (i.e. which state or group of states is in power or has more power than the rest). Other contributors, notably Rosenau, Young, O'Brien, and Sinclair question this state-centric reasoning and point out that power (and authority) is diffusing beyond states in terms of both the actors that have power and the bases of power itself. Regimes, NGOs, private companies, and even loosely organized publics are increasingly considered powerful. Perhaps more importantly, what makes an actor or group of actors powerful is also being transformed in the current era. O'Brien, for example, considers the "power in movement" of global civil society actors, while Sinclair describes how expertise and reputation have become sources of power in the global economy. The power/authority of Sinclair's bond-rating agencies "is not premised on power in the simple sense. Authority, an altogether more hidden form of social control than power resides in the agencies' authority [to provide a mostly unquestioned, though not unchanging, expertise]."

Taken together we see a picture of material conditions vastly different than in previous eras. There is a concentration of material, military power in the United States/West, while some observe an accompanying diffusion of economic power. Such traditional power dynamics are counterbalanced by the increasing number of powerful actors as well as a transformation in the bases of power. In addition, this era that spawned the concept of GG finds the world smaller both temporally and geographically and characterized by the increasing commodification of all aspects of life. This new and changing set of material conditions is the reality that actors in world politics face and observers of world politics must take into account.

Ideational changes

Material conditions are not the only things that have changed, however. Other contributors call attention to how understandings of the world have changed— ideas about how world politics works, social rules and interactions, and even understandings of what the world looks like. A common theme across chapters (discussed further in the fourth dialogue) is the increasingly liberal character of world politics. Whether viewed critically or welcomed, the ideas associated with liberalism are seen to pervade world politics in this era, shaping the global economy as well as the "moral purpose" of the powerful actors.

Green is the most explicit in describing the growing—indeed, the progressively—liberal character of world politics, which he claims stems at least in part from the "liberal advantage." In essence, the recent "triumph" of the West can be traced to the inherent advantages and persuasiveness of liberal ideas over other sets of values. Overbeek and Arrighi concur about the spread of liberalism, but do not necessarily see this as a departure—rather it is a product of the historical dynamics of global capitalism. Perhaps the intensity of liberal domination is new, but this is not a change in the ideational conditions of the world.

Similarly ambivalent about whether the growth of liberal ideas is new or not, Goldstein and Ban discuss how this ideational condition has influenced the governance of human rights. The change comes in a deepening of commitment to liberal tenets and in the relationship between national and supranational legal jurisdictions. The growth and spread of liberalism is seen to spawn a different set of ideational conditions by Ba and O'Brien. They see the growth of liberal ideas as accompanied by actual or potential contestation—providing a potentially shaky foundation for governance.

While liberalism is a pervasive concern, it is not the only change in ideational conditions that our contributors observe. The authors also collectively highlight changing notions of the target of governance—ideas about what is to be governed. Hoffmann discusses the evolution of what is understood to be "global" in environmental politics. Far from being obvious, the definition of global is highly political and contested—the global in global environmental governance can mean worldwide or it can mean a subset of the globe. Rosenau observes that this current era is operating on different ideational foundations precisely because this is the first era that can even consider the globe as a space of governance. Similarly, O'Brien and Goldstein and Ban point to new forms of transnational political space that either did not exist in previous eras, or were not considered to be crucial—global civil society and the space of the European Union.

There has thus been a sea change in not only the material conditions of the world, but also in the ideational shape of world politics and in how we think about the world. According to our contributors this GG era is characterized by liberal ideas for good or ill. Further, ideas about political space have changed radically, making it possible to conceive of *global* governance and to conceive of it in multiple ways.

As with each of the dialogues discussed in this concluding chapter, there is no resolution; no single way to conceive of the interaction between material and ideational factors; no single viewpoint on the transformation of material and ideational conditions; and certainly no single notion of the ramifications of the changes. However, it is clear that *something* (or more accurately a number of somethings) is different in this era. The material and ideational changes that our contributors observe more than justify the emergence of the term GG, at very least as a signal that something new is happening in world politics.

Dialogue 2: agency, agents, and the capacity to change the world

If there are new conditions in this GG era, are there also new politics? The implications of changing material/ideational conditions are profound for how the different perspectives see the politics of GG. Whether or not a contributor feels that the changes are fundamental or easily accommodated, all of our contributors see the politics of GG as having changed in important ways because of the altered conditions. We see this clearly in their collective discussions of agency and agents. As with the previous dialogue we concentrate on what has been (can be) changed and what remains unchanged.

Agentic opportunities and structural constraints

In this era that gave rise to GG, have actors gained a different ability to alter/control the shape and direction of world politics individually or collectively? Again we begin with what has not changed according to the perspectives. Those theories that see agency as effective or possible in the face of structural constraints continue to do so in this era of GG. Those that find it unlikely for actors to be able to break free from conditions not of their making find nothing new in this era of GG, except perhaps a deepening of the bonds of global capitalism. However, though our contributors see little change in the dynamics of agency, they do present an interesting range of ideas on the ability of agents to produce fundamental change in this GG era.

Some see agency as possible in principle—i.e. actors have always had the ability and wherewithal to affect their own conditions. Hoffmann's constructivism and Young's regime theory are examples of this type of thinking. Agency is half of the mutual constitution dynamic and Hoffmann considers that states, in his case, are even able to reconceptualize what global means. For his part, Young describes a GG system predicated on individual regimes that are conscious efforts to address collective action problems.

Others look upon the current era as having produced opportunities for agency. Rosenau considers that the growing complexity of world politics along with the dynamics of "fragmegration" have changed the opportunities for agency, leading to the authority crises, bifurcation of world politics, and organizational explosion that he observes. Ba sees the opportunity for agency somewhat differently. In her discussion of regional/global interactions, it is the emergence of what some call GG systems (primarily economic, but political as well) that have produced a space for agency in the cracks between regional and global systems. She argues that

> "global governance" therefore often represents ... a set of hegemonic ideas and structures that constrain in important ways. However, this is not to say that those ideas and structures are not constantly undergoing contestation; nor is it to say that non-core actors see themselves without agency. In particular, regionalism has offered these states a platform and means to assert different ideas, different solutions, and different visions.

Still others are skeptical about agency. They see world politics as caught up in large-scale historical patterns or tied to our biological make-up as human beings. Overbeek and Arrighi both find the forces of global capitalism to be very powerful, but both also hold out the hope of a break in historical cycles or a counter-hegemonic movement. Overbeek refers to GG's original potential as a counter-hegemonic discourse, while Arrighi calls for an enlightened hegemony on the part of the US that accommodates the changes evident in this GG era. Nevertheless, neither author sees much hope for an emancipatory GG brought about through active agency. Overbeek is especially skeptical. Though he acknowledges that the strategic agency of social forces can affect the historical mode of GG, he nevertheless argues that the structural constraints and historical process that is world capitalism has a tendency to overwhelm any forces working against it. He concludes,

> the concept of GG thus has suffered the same fate of other initially progressive normative concepts such as "new international economic order" or "sustainable development": it has been hijacked by social forces that have

emptied it of its counter-hegemonic content and redefined it in such a way that the concept in fact supports the further consolidation of the world-wide rule of capital.

In the end, our contributors appear to heed O'Brien's call for recognition of both historical continuities and the possibility of change. Even those who see world dynamics as firmly entrenched acknowledge that change is possible. For example, in Sterling-Folker's version of neoclassical realism, anarchy and biology provide a bedrock of structural conditions that is beyond agency, but the particular governance conditions of any particular era are still open to the influence of agents (even if extremely constrained): "The creation of social practice and intersubjective meanings is an imaginative act and our imaginations are vast and amazing indeed, but it is not imagination without limits. It is bounded by why we needed to be social in the first place."

What has changed? Not a great deal when it comes to the potential for actors to influence the politics in which they are embedded. This GG era has not fundamentally changed the nature of agency in politics according to the perspectives represented in this volume. However, that is not to say that the perspectives have nothing interesting to say about agency in GG. While the enduring dichotomy between those who focus on structural constraints and those who focus on agentic opportunity remains, the current era does seem to have presented interesting and novel opportunities for agency. The question becomes which actors truly have agency—which actors are agents of GG?

New actors, new politics?

None of the perspectives are blind to the emergence of new actors in world politics. Some, like Sinclair, do object to the popular characterization of non-state actors as being "new." As he puts it, "A more effective conception [of GG] acknowledges that non-state forms of governance have always been important." Nevertheless, he, like most authors in this volume, acknowledges that intensified globalization has given private authority and non-state actors expanded, even more central, roles to play.

Even traditional approaches such as Young's regime theory and Overbeek's transhistorical materialism acknowledge this crucial characteristic of the current GG era. Young acknowledges that "there are significant regimes in which some—or even all—of the members are non-state actors." Similarly, Overbeek readily admits that "Governance in the contemporary global political economy is increasingly characterized by ... the creation of additional formal and informal structures of authority and sovereignty besides and beyond the state." Indeed, he sounds a bit like Rosenau when he observes, "What is also striking is the multiplicity of governance sites and modes involving any combination of intergovernmental and trans-governmental regulation, 'public–private' regimes, and forms of private authority and self-regulation."

However, being aware of new actors does not necessarily translate into seeing an increased role for them in the governing of world affairs. This part of the dialogue presents perhaps the sharpest contrast between perspectives, with some proclaiming the efficacy of new actors and others relying on traditional actors such as states and classes as the main players of world politics. Yet it is not as simple as merely splitting the contributors into two camps—those that see new actors as efficacious and those that do not. What is interesting is how the perspectives incorporate the undeniable growth of other actors in world politics. One set of perspectives make the new actors the central players in world politics in this new era of GG. Sinclair's take on the emergence of private authority in the global political economy, for example, explicitly calls into question the predominant place of states. But other perspectives are not willing to move beyond the state too quickly. Some, as in Hoffmann's discussion of environmental governance, are willing to focus on states when states appear to be the most important actor—preferring to make the importance of actors an empirical question. Similarly, Dunne makes it clear that the study of GG from an English School perspective has been inextricably tied to the state because of its role in international society.

This dialogue on the importance and *potentially* transformative role of new actors is made most clear by examining the positions of Rosenau, O'Brien, Young, and Sterling-Folker. They represent a good portion of the spectrum of thought on this issue and, by examining their positions, we get a good sense of the contours of GG politics and what this GG era (potentially) looks like.

Rosenau stakes out the most radical claims when it comes to new actors. He is ready, not to dismiss the state, but to remove it from its accustomed pedestal. He decries what he sees as methodological territorialism and the fact that "Lip service is paid to the role of NGOs and publics and their modes of interaction, but in the end allowance for such dynamics is essentially limited. The state continues to be posited as the prime, if not the only, wielder of effective authority." Instead, Rosenau envisions an entirely different world order where spheres of authority, composed of a multitude of actors, are main units of governance. We are, he argues, witnessing an organizational explosion, involving the emergence of new actors at all levels of politics that is revolutionizing world politics.

Taking a step back from this radical position, O'Brien gives priority to non-state actors in his exposition on global civil society, but he also admits that often times, global civil society actors are reactive—reacting to the actions and systemic rules set up by the state. He does find that NGOs and other global civil society actors have the potential to transform GG, but not in the unfettered fashion that Rosenau conceives of: "Global civil society groups contribute to global governance by proposing alternative norms and mobilizing political support and opposition to existing governance structures." Put another way, global civil society actors are often outsiders looking in, constantly struggling to carve out a space in what remains a state-dominated system of GG.

Young's regime theory, which remains dominated by states, takes an even greater step back from Rosenau's view of GG in terms of shared authority amongst multiple actors, though this is not to say that it is not open to new actors and the possibility that their inclusion might generate different kinds of politics or structures. In observing that state-centric regimes are having to accommodate new actors and their perspectives, Young sees these accommodations as having played an important part in the creation of global civil society and its expanded, if not institutionalized, role in world politics. In this sense, even innovations introduced in narrowly defined, issue-specific settings can have broader consequences for international society and world politics.

Finally Sterling-Folker takes the most conservative approach to new actors in GG. She concedes that they have recently exploded in numbers and activities, and that "NGOs have done much to raise awareness within nation-states about a myriad of problems." They may even have "saved real lives and people in the process." Nevertheless, she argues that it is important to understand that pluralism is not, in fact, "the essence of things." More radical notions of governance are deceiving because they suggest that "regulation, restraint, and control do not depend on or require the existence of sovereign political units." In that NGOs "obtain legal and economic status only through a system of governance which promotes ordering principles determined by the powerful nation-states," NGOs are unlikely to "emancipate us from the evils of particularism embodied by the nation-state" or transform existing governance structures and processes in any fundamental way. Simply put, for Sterling-Folker, the universalism and transnationalism associated with NGOs and global civil society are unattainable in a GG of nation states.

In sum, these dialogues on agents and agency point to a world in which new (and not so new), non-state actors have assumed new and expanded roles for themselves. Changed material conditions, as well as heightened socioeconomic volatility, have created new needs and new opportunities. They have also exposed new fault lines and new tensions that, for some authors, mean openings for contestation. However, whether these changes mean a more fundamental change in our politics continues to be debated.

Dialogue 3: is GG well understood?

Where do the dialogues on material/ideational foundations as well as that of agency and agents leave us? What do the changes evident in the world imply for the emergence of GG and our understanding of it? We turn to this question in the final two dialogues. In this dialogue we consider how well GG is understood. The final dialogue then takes up the accompanying normative question of how well GG is performed in the world today.

The first step in assessing how well GG is understood is parsing out the spectrum of thought evident on GG in the scholarly literature. This volume represents an attempt to do so and the previous two dialogues give a sense of the discussions to be found in the literature. Essentially we have found both agreement and debate in conceptions of GG. Further, the dialogue breaks down along the same line that divides the volume into two parts: some authors feel that understanding GG requires breaking new theoretical ground, while others feel comfortable examining GG with traditional, though expanded, theoretical perspectives.

Agreement and debate in conceiving of GG

We still have no single answer to the question of what is GG. The perspectives are just too varied for a unified answer, beyond the simple notion that GG is rules, to make sense. As noted in the previous dialogues, there is a great deal of cross-perspective debate as to the nature of this GG era and the nature of politics within it. Such debate, of course, extends to how the perspectives understand GG itself. We see diverse thought on the scope of GG (both geographically and by issue), on the novelty of GG, the coherence of GG, and the malleability of GG, to name but a few.

However, as noted in the introduction, there is not so much variation that we cannot discern patterns in the literature. There is enough intersubjective understanding of GG to provide starting points for discussion. At very least, there is common recognition that there has emerged something called GG that is calling into question the adequacy of "international relations" for understanding world politics. Perhaps, then, Murphy's challenge to better understand GG can only be met by looking at the totality of perspectives on GG. While one theoretical perspective on GG may not capture all important dynamics, the collected wisdom of multiple perspectives might. At very least, it might shed light on different aspects of GG—for instance, Overbeek's transhistorical materialism captures aspects of GG that Young's issue-based regimes will not and vice versa. In addition, treating GG from different perspectives ensures that critical and peripheral voices (too often marginalized) are also included in the discussion.

Yet this is not a call for taking the (perhaps dangerous) path towards theoretical eclecticism. Rather it is a plea for understanding that GG is an enormous, complex topic that different perspectives approach differently, describe differently, and analyze differently. Quite simply put, GG is not a singular endeavor or phenomenon. Thus, authors may offer contending perspectives; however, they are also analyzing different GGs, and dialogues amongst the perspectives have the potential to shed light on a number of these GGs and their different politics.

Consider that Dunne, Overbeek, Arrighi, Green, and Ba observe a global capitalist/liberal GG. This GG consists of (liberal) rules of planetary scope, a (more or less) coherent organizing principle for the entire world. This set of world-wide rules pervades all levels of political life, and one interesting aspect of today's world is how these global rules collide with the explosion of new actors and transnational ties, facilitated by the technological changes that global capitalism itself has spawned. Within this subset, the authors see more GGs. Just because these authors observe governance at the planetary scale does not mean they agree on the content or nature of this governance. The planetary GG looks different in politics than it does in the global economy. There is also debate about contestation regionally and across issues.

On the other hand there are those authors who conceive of governance at less grand scales. Rosenau, Young, Hoffmann, Goldstein, and Sinclair all focus in on the active governance of particular problems. There is a vast set of transnational issues that are actively being governed with rules that are time, space, and issue specific. In fact, Rosenau even goes so far as to claim that world politics has become so complex that a coherent set of rules (like those posited by Overbeek, Arrighi, and Green) are a chimera. Additionally, Young laments that it is unlikely that we will see a coherent GG system based on an amalgamation of issue-specific regimes.

Of course, these two GGs are far from mutually exclusive—both O'Brien and Sterling-Folker consider GG to be somewhere between these two gross characterizations of GG as global or less than global. In addition, it is clear when reading Goldstein and Ban and Sinclair that the circumscribed rules they analyze— human-rights regimes in Europe and bond-rating companies respectively—are set on a foundation of deeper and broader rules, and liberal ones at that. The GGs that the authors observe interact in fascinating (and not yet well-understood) ways.

But this discussion of strength through diversity should not naively overlook the very real differences among perspectives. Claiming that there are different GGs to analyze does not settle the question of understanding GG. An overview of the multiple perspectives presents a fine picture of GG, but it is in the debates between them—not in attempts to synthesize them—that knowledge moves forward. Indeed, at the most fundamental level our contending perspectives on GG speak directly to the question of whether traditional approaches to IR theory are sufficient for this GG era or whether a fundamental change in our theorizing is necessary.

From IR to GG?

For both scholars and practitioners, the concept GG is becoming more ensconced in the lexicon of IR. Clearly, when faced with the emergence of a new phenomenon, IR scholars have responded with a diversity of thought about what GG is, how it unfolds, and its utility as a concept or approach. The diversity in thought extends to the question of the adequacy of IR theory itself.

Although GG is often seen as novel and is often used to signal a break from traditional understandings of world politics, many international theorists from across the theoretical spectrum consider GG to be explicable using existing theoretical tools. The chapters that comprise Part I of this volume serve as a warning not to ignore the insights of traditional IR theory when approaching GG.

Sterling-Folker sounds the biggest alarm at the rising tide of GG literature, reminding us of the realist insight that powerful actors always hold sway over not just the rules in any system, but also the ways in which different actors can even participate in the system. Any notion of GG must work within these fundamental constraints, and any theoretical revolution must at least account for these dynamics. Young's analysis demonstrates that regime theory is constantly evolving, but reminds us that bargaining among states (and other actors) is likely to play a role in GG for the foreseeable future. Similarly, Dunne's English School perspective views GG in traditional ways—an extension of international society. However, Dunne does not rule out the possibility of breakpoint change in the functioning of world politics in the aftermath of the Cold War, given the challenges that the international society of states now faces.

From a different side of IR theory, Arrighi and Overbeek stress the historical roots and dynamics of what we now call GG. In their views, we do not need radically new tools to understand GG; rather it is a manifestation of hegemonic cycles or the workings of the global capitalist system. While today's details may be novel, the underlying dynamics are familiar. Finally, Hoffmann sees no need to move beyond or modify the constructivist approach to world politics for the sake of studying GG. The process of social construction through mutual constitution is taken to be a constant. While the nature of the politics that it is applied to may be changing, the analytic approach remains useful.

Taken together, the authors in Part I believe that IR theory already has a great deal to say about GG. Though much (or some) of the world is in flux, traditional approaches still capture important aspects of the world. Thus, we are cautioned against a radical departure from our current understandings.

Nevertheless, the recent nature of the response from traditional approaches to the emergence of the term GG is interesting in and of itself. Even more established international relation approaches have adjusted their vocabulary to accommodate the dynamics of GG and find their attention drawn to the change and dynamism that has become a hallmark of the GG "literature." At the very least, there seems to be an implicit acknowledgment that GG as empirical phenomenon and as theoretical concept is both a reflection of, and response to, the increasing size and complexity of the system. As Rosenau explains, this is not necessarily surprising. It is only in the last two to three decades that a "global" consciousness—the idea of the globe as a single unit—has arisen, and with it has come a concern with the governing of the globe.

Moreover, though some may doubt how significant recent changes are for the essential structure and process of GG, they are already producing new thinking within established theoretical perspectives. The discussions in Part I illustrate how even more established theories are undergoing modification and refinement, if not moving in significantly new directions.

Yet, modifying and tinkering with traditional IR perspectives to accommodate GG is not enough according to the authors in Part II of this volume. They are even more inclined to believe that as structures and processes become more truly global new lines of inquiry and new perspectives are necessary. In contrast to the authors in Part I who see the emerging politics as new only at the margins, newer approaches recognize that even changes in the margins can have destabilizing effects, and that the emergence of new actors and new issues can indeed produce new politics. For authors in the second half of this volume, changes have generated new areas for further investigation, areas that can expand, if not revolutionize, our knowledge of the structure and process of GG.

Rosenau may be the most radical in his claim that we may be witnessing breakpoint change in how world politics works. For Rosenau, who describes a post-international world characterized by multiple spheres of authority, the tools used to understand a world of inter-state relations may no longer be as appropriate or useful. In a world where diverse non-state actors can have an effect on the global discourse and the global agenda, where processes of globalization are forcing state and sub-state entities to adapt and change, and where the decisions of certain organizations and actors can touch even those in the remotest parts of the globe and provoke resistance, scholars will need to expand not only what they study but also how they study politics.

Not all of the authors in Part II are willing to go as far as Rosenau in his rejection of traditional approaches, but all, to some degree, call for a revolution in thinking. Sinclair and O'Brien base their call for new thinking on the explosion in numbers and importance of non-state actors. Sinclair puts it bluntly:

> Whatever school of thought is invoked, IR theory assumes an interstate system. That this is the object of inquiry is not questioned. Legitimate questions revolve around how these states came to be what they are, and how they relate to each other. Because I do not think GG is an issue of interstate politics it is unclear to me whether IR theory can say much that is interesting about it.

Conversely, while Goldstein and Ban do not deny that GG is a matter of interstate politics, they point to the ways in which politics between states is being transcended by the very actions of states. The emergence of supranational authority structures calls into question the very efficacy of a system of inquiry (IR theory) that is based, as Sinclair puts it on the existence and importance of the interstate system.

Green and Ba provide additional arguments for rethinking IR theory. Green's discussion of liberal empire is reminiscent of Hart and Negri's (2000) account of world politics of a different kind. Green does not go so far as to claim that a global empire is evident or imminent, but the liberal imperialism he describes, while based on liberal theory, goes beyond how liberals have typically analyzed world politics. Similarly, Ba's discussion of the contest between regional and global governance reminds a generally Euro-centric IR theory that the system that has been the subject of its theorizing may not be so singular. For Ba, a discussion of GG provides the opportunity to move beyond traditional accounts of Western domination to new theorizing on North–South contestation.

The contrast between Parts I and II of the volume are thus striking on the question of the adequacy of IR theory. But even in this dialogue, we see hope for making GG better understood. The very notion of GG has certainly inspired new thinking—either modification or revolution—and it appears to be a focal point for the dialogues and debates that IR theory and practitioners of world politics must have. While GG may not be well understood yet, the emergence of the term GG and the phenomena GG (however conceived) may be catalyzing efforts to rethink old concepts and theories so that we can understand it better.

Dialogue 4: Is GG well done? Will it be in the future?

The preceding dialogues have centered on analytic concerns—how the different perspectives perceive, describe, and understand GG. These concerns cannot be divorced from normative questions that address how well GG is performed in the world.[1] In this final dialogue, we take up some of the normative questions raised by authors, especially as regards GG in the current era. Almost all of our authors find that contemporary GG is an expression of liberal values and neoliberal interests and, further, that this particular era of GG is distinguished from past eras by the primacy of US power. However, there is also a rich dialogue across perspectives about what contemporary GG signifies for questions of equity and justice. In this final dialogue we thus echo Craig Murphy and Rorden Wilkinson's question from the 2001 GG workshop at the University of Delaware: "In whose interests is global governance being pursued?"

For many of this volume's authors, the answer to that question is large corporations, large states, and global capitalism. Murphy's and Wilkinson's question is also implicit in other questions our authors take up in their dialogue on contemporary GG. These questions include whether GG (liberal or not) is something to aspire to, the implications of a liberal order (whether fragmented or coherent) dominated by the US, and the possibilities of systemic transition to a post-US/post-liberal GG that may or may not be more just and equitable. Perhaps most striking are our contributors' sober reflections on what the world can and might be. For a good number of authors, their reflections derive from an acute awareness that the early twenty-first century continues to find persistent inequalities, great power politics, as well as the re-emergence of old, and emergence of new, political fault lines.

Is GG a good thing?

A consistent theme across self-labeled GG studies is that GG is an improvement over the status quo of IR. Reminiscent of the cooperation and regime debates of the 1980s and 1990s, governance has a positive connotation and is considered something to which the world should aspire. Governance is order instead of chaos, cooperation instead of conflict. It tends to imply institutional, rational (in the reasoning sense, not in the rational choice sense) solutions to problems. Overbeek, for example, points to the definition provided by the Commission on GG as one telling illustration where GG is equated with accommodation and cooperation—presumably good things—and is reflective of "a desire for a more equitable and just world order." Governance, according to conventional wisdom, is good. However, among those taking umbrage with this conventional understanding are Dunne, Sterling-Folker, Overbeek, O'Brien, Sinclair, and Ba, who are explicitly critical of the tendency of some treatments to portray GG as necessarily good or as universally aspired to.

Our authors find such notions of GG problematic on different levels. Following Susan Strange's (1983) polemic against regime theory, Sterling-Folker is especially critical of such conceptions of GG because they obfuscate underlying power structures and suggest a world politics that is more orderly and progressive than it is. We would be wise, she argues, to remember that the normative complexes and meta-value ensembles of GG that end up ordering collective interactions will always be those of the most powerful states. The problem with contemporary GG is that it encourages the "erroneous belief" in global progress and transnationalism, as well as the false hope in humankind's ability to overcome its biological need to see difference and to act on it.

More than Sterling-Folker's neoclassical realism, Overbeek's transhistorical materialism finds itself in want of a more equitable and just order, though Overbeek also agrees that contemporary GG has come to mask important structures of domination, force, and control. Nor is Overbeek alone in his concerns, as evidenced by O'Brien's identification with Overbeek's "instinct to ask how the system of GG would be transformed to operate in a more just and egalitarian method." However, where Sterling-Folker focuses on states and powerful actors, Overbeek directs our attention to the "class character of governance practices in a capitalist economy." He argues that contemporary GG's overemphasis on the cooperative (normative) side of GG "depoliticizes" the term, robbing it of "any possible connotation of domination and force, which … is also part of 'governance.' " Not only does this misrepresent what the global order is and how it works, but also it may ultimately work against the desired objective of justice. Consequently, GG, which may have started out as a counter-hegemonic concept, has become instead a concept that entrenches existing structures of domination and keeps "potentially rebellious social forces and states" at bay.

Of course, Dunne points out, "vast inequalities of power" have always pervaded international society—not just contemporary GG. At the same time, English School arguments do not see all inequalities in the system as necessarily bad. Major powers can play a stabilizing role in defining and maintaining systems of GG for the common good. They act in the service of their own interests, to be sure, but they also can provide needed leadership in an anarchic world. Green, whose argument on liberal empire contains echoes of the English School, agrees and is explicit on this point. Writing about the United States and its early twenty-first-century adventures into Afghanistan and Iraq, Green argues that the US has in the last 15 years assumed a more activist/interventionist role because of a "sober appreciation for the chaos of the post-Cold War world and the need for someone to take charge." Thus, the US has assumed the role it has not because of imperial opportunity but because of an "anarchic vacuum pulling America" to provide leadership and order.

Those authors that view GG at a smaller scale—disaggregated rule systems—also tend to be slightly more optimistic. In the very least, governance does not have to imply inequity and injustice. Goldstein and Ban detail the spread of human rights, and Hoffmann details the rules developing to address (more or less effectively) global environmental problems. If GG is conceived to consist of series of functional regimes or overlapping spheres of authority (SOAs) then there is the possibility that GG can be both good and bad in different times, spaces, and issue areas.

Implications of a liberal world order and US dominance

However, the question of whether GG is good or bad must be addressed within a context of broad agreement that (neo)liberal values and interests are at the foundation of contemporary GG. In whatever guise, our authors implicitly or explicitly tend to see a liberal world order. The implications of this liberal world order form the basis for perhaps the most spirited dialogue.

We return to Green's notion of imperial leadership as the basis for GG—the anarchic vacuum is pulling not just any leadership, but specifically *liberal* leadership "to provide a new liberal imperial order." In Green's discussion, especially, there is an underlying assumption—a contested one by the accounts of Overbeek, Arrighi, Hoffmann, Ba, and O'Brien—about the progressive character and normative good-ness of liberal leadership and "liberal power actions." Compared to others, Green's liberal view of global governance draws a different conclusion about what others see to be the contradictions of a liberalism that uses force to spread "classic liberal values" around the globe. According to Green, there are contradictions only if one sees liberalism solely in terms of equality and pluralism, but in fact liberalism views those values as more circumscribed. Equality and pluralism may be organizing principles in the domestic context, but the international context is a different situa-tion. More to the point, liberalism distinguishes between states. States that deny their populations self-determination cannot very well expect self-determination themselves in the international context. In short, there is no contradiction in liberal America or liberal Britain intervening to establish or force democracy because liber-alism values the rights of the individual over the rights of illiberal states. Thus, liberal tenets might lead liberal states to actively pursue and justify an activist, even interventionist, liberal agenda; it also helps to explain why so many self-identified liberals in the United States and the United Kingdom supported what many in the world (as well as in their own countries) considered an illegitimate war in Iraq.

Where does this leave us in terms of contemporary GG? Green makes clear that it does not leave us with liberal internationalism. As he puts it, liberal states will be cautious about ceding international sovereignty to international institu-tions. Popular sovereignty means that full authority rests only with its own people; "the liberal state should not be subject to 'the external authority of other states.' " So if not liberal internationalism, then what? For Green, the future sees contemporary GG eventually taking the form of a Kantian union of republics.

While Sterling-Folker agrees that liberal internationalism is unlikely, she might, however, also argue that the distinctions Green draws between liberal and illiberal states are overdrawn. Her chapter suggests that it is not just liberal states, but in fact all nation-states that are unwilling to cede authority to another body because each nation-state (liberal and illiberal) exists "to help its *own* individual members achieve equal rights and personal fulfillment" (emphasis original). In short, "its moral obligation is to its citizens alone." Of course, liberal theorists like Green would dispute the argument that all nation-states are so committed to individual expression. On the other hand, it is also possible to see the two arguments as more similar than what the surface suggests if one considers Sterling-Folker's focus on the largest, most powerful states. The "process of actualization, augmen-tation, and possibly self-perfection" may not be a priority of all nation-states, but it is a priority of liberal ones, which happen to be the most powerful actors today and are thus responsible for giving contemporary GG its liberal content.

At the very least, Sterling-Folker might argue that the inclination to see one's own values as superior and to forcibly spread those values abroad is hardly unique to liberal states. Given the tendency of all groups to draw on an ethical universalism to justify their existence and their own particularism, it is hardly a surprise to find this proselytizing/universalizing element in liberalism too. She adds that it is precisely this internationalization of domestic norms that is the source of the tensions in contemporary GG. While suffrage and equality are fine in the domestic context where the system exists to protect and enable the individual, it is not in the international context where "a structure of authority does not exist (and will not given the human imperative to form groups that will compete)." As she puts it, "It is an ironic twist of history that the nation-state, as the dominant political unit of the moment, produces a particularly parochial licensing mentality, yet the shared desire for universal suffrage and equality is a direct result of it."

In the end, most authors, compared to Green, are not so sanguine about the recent turn in US foreign policy and what it may signify for contemporary GG. At the very least, they question how central liberalism is to "the global good life." Unlike Green who sees no contradiction in liberal imperialism and Sterling-Folker who recognizes the contradiction but minimizes its significance, Dunne and others take issue with what they see to be double standards, as well as the problems of what Arrighi calls "unfulfilled promises." Especially problematic are US efforts to circumvent established processes and procedural justice norms. Dunne, whose English School perspective calls attention to "the power of critique" in producing world change, adds that the world is especially troubled by the US practice of upholding only those rules convenient to its interpretation of national interest and only when it suits its interests to do so. For Dunne and Arrighi, such contradictions erode the legitimacy, moral authority, and thus the power of the US to define GG as it wishes.

In short, Dunne's English School perspective may see possibilities in a responsible great power leadership, but the possibilities are also contingent on their ability to act for the greater good and within the bounds of societal (international) norms. Unfortunately, argues Dunne, recent commentaries point to an important concern that leading powers today are acting more like "great irresponsibles," raising the possibility that "the main threat [to international society] today would appear to be a revolt against the institutions of international society by the United States and its allies."

Hope for the future?

The question that Dunne raises is an interesting one. Specifically, do recent developments signal an upcoming systemic transition? For most authors,[2] in fact, there is an acknowledgment that there are instabilities in today's system of GG (even if authors may disagree on the specifics of that system or how those instabilities will manifest themselves). These instabilities stem from core–periphery tensions (Arrighi, Ba, Hoffmann), the entrance of different actors (Rosenau, Arrighi, O'Brien, Hoffmann, Young), as well as the particular situation of unrivaled US dominance and a world that has become less accepting of that dominance (Dunne, Arrighi, Ba).

For Dunne specifically, US actions have stretched societal (international) norms to near breaking point and "what is potentially different today is that international society does *not* appear to accept the special privileges that the United States now demands." Nor is he alone in considering the possibility that contemporary GG may be at a crossroads. Arrighi, especially, considers the gap between liberal rhetoric and reality, as well as the legacies of unfulfilled promises, and how these contradictions are contributing to a "crisis of US hegemony." Arrighi's discussion which identifies the conditions and dynamics of hegemonic transitions notes that this is a unique historical period. While it is possible that the material and social novelties associated with the US position in the world will allow the system to survive, it is just as possible that the contradictions will grow and eventually become unsustainable. Moreover, if the current hegemonic power (the US) fails to recognize and adapt to the transition, the world may have to prepare itself for "severe and seemingly irremediable systemic disorganization, that is, of systemic chaos."

At the same time, even if growing numbers find the US today as one of the largest threats to the international rule of law, authors also acknowledge the difficulty involved in producing real change since the United States also remains one of the primary (if not *the* primary) disseminators of power and ideas. Consequently, change (both the possibility of change and the extent of change) will be extremely constrained. Ba's chapter on East Asia provides one empirical example of a region that increasingly views US actions as less than legitimate, and yet still finds itself compelled to follow the United States in key ways. As Ba argues, opting out of contemporary GG processes can be almost-certain suicide, while resistance is hard in a world where there are established rules and institutions, all designed to reflect and serve the interests of its creators (in this case, the United States and other Western advanced economies). Of course, such conclusions come as no surprise to Sterling-Folker, who is most blunt on this point:

> Such outcomes and processes can only occur because the contemporary system of GG steers potential challenges to it into avenues that are both acceptable to and controllable by the creators of that system. Thus to challenge the United States with its own rules when one is essentially playing by those same rules is not much of a challenge to history and is certainly none to structure.

Of course those that see less of a coherent world order are more likely to see the possibility of GG being well done in the future. Hoffmann's chapter describes the limits of the hegemon's ability to get its way in climate change governance, but leaves unanswered the question of whether this is positive or negative in the long term. Similarly Rosenau finds hope in the crazy-quilt of multiple SOAs. He finds that "The world is simply too interdependent, and authority is too dispersed, for any one country to command the global scene as fully as earlier empires did."

Evident optimism notwithstanding, it is clear from the totality of this volume that there is a good deal of work to do before GG can be well done. Structural inequalities remain and powerful actors retain a good deal of control. Hope is found in the changes the world is undergoing and the possibility that these changes will provide opportunities to shape GG for justice and peace.

Conclusion—where does GG go from here?

We end this volume by noting that the preceding chapters represent only a bare beginning in the quest for understanding GG. Numerous areas of further inquiry remain. First, this volume does not exhaust the existing perspectives of GG. Feminism, world polity, and post-structuralism are only three of potentially numerous uncovered perspectives. In fact, we realize that we have unintentionally, but de facto, reified the marginalization of some perspectives by not including them. However, we are not in search of a single orthodoxy for GG and we encourage further dialogues with the perspectives represented and those not present in this volume.

Second, it was obvious from our workshop discussions that disaggregated rule systems and coherent world orders are connected, while it was less obvious how they are connected. Is it a top-down relationship whereby the liberal world order structures the disaggregated rule systems that some of our authors see? Or alternatively, do disaggregated rule systems have the potential to shape/determine the larger world order? These questions remain unanswered yet are crucial for the continuing GG dialogue.

Finally, and perhaps most importantly, further empirical analysis of GG from all perspectives is necessary. This volume, while not designed to be an empirical exploration, provides a number of intriguing areas of research, outlining a burgeoning empirical research agenda across perspectives. We hope that by clarifying how different perspectives approach GG, this volume facilitates further empirical study as well as further critical thought with an eye towards improving the human condition on the globe.

Notes

1 This is not the forum for discussing the separation (or lack thereof) between analytic and normative inquiry.
2 The exceptions may be Sterling-Folker, Overbeek, and Green. Sterling-Folker argues that the current GG system is pretty well entrenched and that challengers will find themselves having to adapt. Overbeek does not see instability so much as a strengthening of capitalist forces and interests, which are today even more insulated from democratic accountability than they were previously. Green sees the steady, progressive march to liberal republicanism.

References

Hardt, M. and Negri, A. (2000) *Empire*, Cambridge, MA: Harvard University Press.
Strange, S. (1983) "*Cave! hic dragones*: A Critique of Regime Analysis," in S. D. Krasner (ed.) *International Regimes*, Ithaca: Cornell University Press.

Index